HIPAA

Certification

D1279081

HIPAA
Certification

Uday O. Ali Pabrai

Premier
p
Press™

©2003 by Premier Press, a division of Course Technology. All rights reserved. No part of this book may be reproduced or transmitted in any form or by any means, electronic or mechanical, including photocopying, recording, or by any information storage or retrieval system without written permission from Premier Press, except for the inclusion of brief quotations in a review.

The Premier Press logo and related trade dress are trademarks of Premier Press and may not be used without written permission.

Microsoft and Windows are either registered trademarks or trademarks of Microsoft Corporation in the United States and/or other countries. Sybase is a registered trademark of Sybase in the U.S. and other countries. Washington Publishing Company is a registered trademark of Washington Publishing Company in the U.S. and other countries.

All other trademarks are the property of their respective owners.

Important: Premier Press cannot provide software support. Please contact the appropriate software manufacturer's technical support line or Web site for assistance.

Premier Press and the author have attempted throughout this book to distinguish proprietary trademarks from descriptive terms by following the capitalization style used by the manufacturer.

Information contained in this book has been obtained by Premier Press from sources believed to be reliable. However, because of the possibility of human or mechanical error by our sources, Premier Press, or others, the Publisher does not guarantee the accuracy, adequacy, or completeness of any information and is not responsible for any errors or omissions or the results obtained from use of such information. Readers should be particularly aware of the fact that the Internet is an ever-changing entity. Some facts may have changed since this book went to press.

ISBN: 1-59200-054-1
Library of Congress Catalog Card Number: 2003101203
Printed in the United States of America

03 04 05 06 BH 10 9 8 7 6 5 4 3 2

Premier Press, a division of Course Technology
25 Thomson Place
Boston, MA 02210

Publisher
Stacy L. Hiquet

Senior Marketing Manager
Martine Edwards

Marketing Manager
Heather Hurley

Associate Marketing Manager
Kristin Eisenzopf

Manager of Editorial Services
Heather Talbot

Acquisitions Editor
Stacy L. Hiquet

Project Editor
Howard A. Jones

Technical Reviewer
Linda Long

Retail Market Coordinator
Sarah Dubois

Copy Editor
Howard A. Jones

Interior Layout
Marian Hartsough

Cover Designer
Mike Tanamachi or
Phil Velikan

Indexer
Sharon Shock

Proofreader
Linda Quigley

Dedication

To Jaanu, my wife,
and my dearest friend, Nazeela.
I have found my peace and thank God
for bringing us together to share and care.
To our future.
—Arshiyaan

Acknowledgments

First, I would like to thank all the students of the HIPAA Academy. Their industry, insight, review, and experiences have had a terrific impact in furthering my understanding of the HIPAA regulations and development of practical solution alternatives.

Matt McCright, a good friend and a security expert, worked closely with me in reviewing and enhancing the content in several areas, especially security. Matt—thank you.

Gary Bard and Jasvinder Kakar—thank you for your disciplined approach in reviewing solutions in the transactions area, especially products such as Microsoft's BizTalk Accelerator and Sybase's HIPAA Studio. Mark Glowacki, Tom Eilers, and Lorna L. Waggoner—thank you for reviewing and assisting to further improve the quality of the material.

Allen Nguyen, my partner and good friend: there is an incredible strength in peace, patience, and perseverance. I have always placed trust and faith in our relationship.

This work has involved terrific and relentless coordination efforts from Michael T. Curry. Mike—thanks. I love your attitude and humor. Allen, Mike, and I are very appreciative of the efforts of several individuals including Bhavan Mehta, Jerome Schuster, Lisa Barton, Tad Anhalt, Hemant Birari, Sunny Chng, Suhas Sankolli, and Scott and Amita Mehta. Sunny—I have to say that you have delivered an exceptional Web site in building HIPAAacademy.Net—awesome work!

To all my friends at the State of Oregon, Prometric, New Horizons, NCPDP, NetG, MeasureUp/Dice, CESC and Course Technology—thank you.

To organizations that were a part of my roots and learning—Maneckji Cooper in Mumbai, Air Force Central School in New Delhi, and the Indian High School in Dubai, UAE—thank you, I am grateful. To organizations that extended my thinking forever—Clemson University, Illinois Institute of Technology, Wells Fargo, Fermi National Accelerator Laboratory, and the U.S. Department of Energy—I am sincerely appreciative.

Tashi and Nathan—no need to "control your excitement!" Have fun and thank you for your passionate support Mummy, Ammee, Baba, Ashkan and most of all Ammajaan—thank you for your prayers and faith.

Nazeela—your prayers, patience, and unquestioned support cannot be appreciated enough. You have an amazing peace about yourself. I am truly blessed to have you as my companion for life. Most of all, thank you—aapka ali.

And finally, to all my readers, as you get started, a word of caution,

Control Your Excitement!!!!

—Uday O. Ali Pabrai

America Is One

September 11, 2001, changed all of us, especially Americans, forever. I pray for the men, women, and children we lost on that day. I hope that we as Americans always remain fierce in safeguarding our values of freedom and peace.

To all my Muslim brothers and sisters—too often we blame others and do not take responsibility for our actions. We can never justify the killing of innocent women, children, and men by cowards in the name of Islam. We must practice Islam, with peace and perseverance, from within. We must truly understand and deliver the rich values of patience, truth, and tolerance emphasized throughout the Holy Quran.

Words from the Holy Quran

◆ For God is with those who patiently persevere (10:46).

◆ For God is with those who restrain themselves, and those who do good (14:128).

◆ The reward of God (in the Hereafter) is best for those who believe and work righteousness: but this none shall attain, save those who steadfastly persevere (in good) (20:80).

About the Author

UDAY O. ALI PABRAI is a highly sought after HIPAA consultant and speaker. Ali has delivered keynote and other sessions at numerous events including the National Council for Prescription Drug Programs (NCPDP), State of Oregon's Department of Human Services (DHS), COMDEX, COMNET, Internet World, and DCI's Internet Expo. Ali is an accomplished expert in the areas of HIPAA, e-business, and enterprise security policy and architecture.

Ali has delivered HIPAA Executive Briefs, Awareness training, the Certified HIPAA Professional (CHP), and Certified HIPAA Security Specialist (CHSS) programs nationally. His attendees have included hospital professionals, pharmacies, legal professionals, physicians, office administrators, clinicians, HIPAA compliance officers, as well as IT professionals such as CISSPs, transactions experts, and security experts. Ali's clients have included Blue Cross Blue Shield affiliates, Wells Fargo, Seabury and Smith/Marsh and many others.

Ali created the industry-leading CIW program and is the co-creator of the highly successful Security Certified Program (SecurityCertified.Net). Ali is the author of numerous books and articles on HIPAA, privacy, e-business, security and business threats. At ecfirst.com, Ali developed E-Accelerator, a HIPAA security-related implementation methodology.

Contents at a Glance

Introduction xxii

1   What Is HIPAA? 1
2   Transactions, Code Sets, and Identifiers Rule 39
3   HIPAA Privacy Rule. 107
4   Understanding the HIPAA Security Rule 195
5   Getting Started with HIPAA Transactions 267
6   Getting Started with HIPAA Privacy 323
7   Getting Started with HIPAA Security. 473

A   HIPAA Glossary. 501
B   HIPAA Frequently Asked Questions (FAQs)
C   HIPAA Privacy FAQ 525
D   Case Study: P3P, A Privacy Standard. 533
E   Bibliography 537
F   HHS Fact Sheet, modifications to Final Privacy Rule 539
G   HIPAA Academy 545

Index 563

Contents

Introduction xxii

Chapter 1 **What Is HIPAA?** **1**

Introduction 3

HIPAA, An Act of Congress 4

Conflict with State Law 9

HIPAA's Administrative Simplification Title 9

HIPAA Titles 10

The IT Component of the HIPAA Legislation 10

HIPAA EDI: Transactions and Code Sets 13

HIPAA Transaction Implementation Guides 14

HIPAA Privacy and Security 15

Secure Information Delivery 16

What Will the Impact of HIPAA Be? 17

HIPAA Timeline 18

HIPAA's Teeth: Penalties 19

Who Can File a Complaint? 21

Window for Filing Complaint 21

Who Is Impacted? 21

HHS Secretary Authorization 22

Effective Date of Penalties 22

HIPAA-Related Organizations 22

Centers for Medicare and Medicaid Services (CMS) 23

Designated Standards Maintenance Organization (DSMO) 24

Workgroup for Electronic Data Interchange (WEDI) 24

Health Level Seven (HL7) 25

Washington Publishing Company (WPC) 25

National Council for Prescription Drug Programs (NCPDP) 26

National Committee on Vital and Health Statistics (NCVHS) 26

HIPAA: Key Concepts 27

Covered Entities 27

Health Plans 27

Health Care Clearinghouse 29

Health Care Provider 31

Health Information 31

Individually Identifiable Health Information (IIHI) 31

Patient Identifiable Information (PH) 32

Protected Health Information 32

Treatment, Payment, or Health care operation (TPO) 33

Business Associate 34

Small Health Plan 35

Participant 35

Medical Care 35

Secretary 35

Compliance Date 35

Transaction 36

Data Content 36

Transaction Standard 36

Code Set 37

Long-Term Care 37

Patient Event 37

Requester 37

Service Provider 38

Summary 38

References 38

Lesson 2   **Transactions, Code Sets, and Identifiers Rule. . . 39**

Impacted Health Care Transactions 41

    Target Audience 42

    Scope 42

    Compliance Dates. 43

HIPAA Administrative Simplification Compliance Act (ASCA) 50

ANSI ASC X12 Standard 65

    Health Insurance Claim Form (HCFA-1500) 67

    "Standard" Claim Form (UB-92). 67

    Loop Iterations and File Sizes. 67

    270—Health Care Eligibility Request 68

    271—Eligibility, Coverage, or Benefit Information 71

    276—Health Care Claim Status Request. 72

    277—Health Care Claim Status Response 74

    287—Health Care Services Review: Request for Review 76

    820—Payment Order/Remittance Advice 77

    834—Benefit Enrollment and Maintenance 79

    835—Health Care Claim Payment/Advice 81

    837—Health Care Claim: Professional, Institutional
        and Dental 83

Code Sets 88

    Timeline. 89

    ICD-9-CM Volumes 1 and 2 89

    CPT-4 89

    CDT 90

    ICD-9-CM, Volume 3 90

    NDC 90

    HCPCS 90

    Health Plans. 92

    Local Codes 92

    Date of Service 93

Codes and Data Values 93

National Health Care Identifiers 93

    Motivation 94

    National Provider Identifiers (NPI) 94

    National Employer Identifier for Health Care 103

    National Health Plan Identifier (PlanID) 104

Summary 105

References 106

Lesson 3   **HIPAA Privacy Rule** **107**

Introduction to Privacy 108

    Defining Privacy 109

Key Terminology 120

    Individually Identifiable Health Information 120

    Patient Identifiable Information 120

    Protected Health Information 121

    Deidentifiable Information (DII) 121

Use and Disclosure 126

    Routine Disclosures 126

    Non-Routine Disclosures 127

    Payment 127

Notice Requirement: Notice of Privacy Practices 133

    Core Elements of a Notice 134

    Consent (Optional) 137

    Authorization 138

Key Parties Impacted 143

    Individuals 143

    Health Care Providers and Payers 147

    Indirect Treatment Relationships 149

    Parent and Minors 150

    Business Associates 152

Hybrid Covered Entities 156

Employers. 157

Organized Health Care Arrangements (OCHA) 157

Minimum Necessary 158

PHI Uses, Disclosures, and Requests. 159

Impact of Final Privacy Rule 169

Oral Communications 169

Research 178

Using and Disclosing PHI for Research 179

IRBs and Privacy Boards. 183

Privacy Rule and Common Rule 183

Patients Right to Inspect. 183

Clinical Laboratory Improvements Amendments
of 1998 (CLIA) 184

Privacy Rule's Authorization and Common Rule's
Informed Consent 184

Final Privacy Rule Impact 185

Government Access to Health Information 185

Medical Records to Government. 186

Government Enforcement Process. 186

Law Enforcement Agencies. 187

Public Health 188

Federal Privacy Act of 1974. 188

Example Scenarios. 188

Use and Disclosure Scenarios 189

Business Associate Scenarios 192

Summary. 193

Lesson 4   Understanding the HIPAA Security Rule 195

Security Standards 196

The Threat 198

Types of Threats 202

Types of Attacks and Attackers 202
Definition and Terminology. 204
    Defining Security 205
    Security Services 208
    Security Mechanisms 210
Key HIPAA Security Terminology. 212
HIPAA Security Requirements 216
    Security Rule Implementation Specifications 217
    Approach and Philosophy 218
    Security Principals. 219
    Security Rule Selection Criteria. 220
HIPAA Security 221
    Administrative Safeguards (164.308) 221
    Security Management Process (standard). 223
    Assigned Security Responsibility (Standard) 225
    Workforce Security (Standard) 226
    Information Access Management (Standard). 227
    Security Awareness and Training (Standard) 229
    Security Incident Procedures (Standard) 230
    Response and Reporting (Required) 231
    Contingency Plan (Standard) 231
    Evaluation (Required). 233
    Business Associate Contract or Other Arrangements
        (Standard) 234
Physical Safeguards (164.310) 235
    Facility Access Controls (Standard). 236
    Workstation Use (Standard) 237
    Workstation Security (Standard) 237
    Device and Media Controls (Standard) 237
    Technical Safeguards (164.312). 238
    Organizational Requirements (164.314) 241

Policies, Procedures, and Documentation Requirements
(164.316) 243

Electronic Signatures (proposed Rule Only) 245

Scenario: Enterprise TCP/IP Security Policy 248

Questions to Address to Create TCP/IP Security
Policy Document 248

Security Perimeter. 249

Template: For Your Enterprise TCP/IP Security Policy 250

Recommendations for Enterprise TCP/IP Security Policy 252

Summary. 265

Footnotes. 266

Lesson 5   Getting Started with HIPAA Transactions. 267

HIPAA Transactions 268

EDI Issues 270

Healthy Health Insurance (HEALS) 270

Problem Statement . . . . 271`

E-Accelerator Methodology 271

Microsoft's BizTalk Accelerator Components. 275

Key Components 276

Advantages 276

Microsoft's SQL Server. 279

Microsoft's BizTalk Server 2002 279

BizTalk Accelerator for HIPAA 282

Microsoft Visio 2002 282

Microsoft's Application Center 2000. 282

HIPAA Data and Schemas 283

Transaction Set Identifiers. 283

Data Segments 285

HIPAA Transaction Sets (Schemas) 285

Representing Data and Documents 288

Document Mapping 297

Orchestration 298

BizTalk Accelerator for HIPAA—Execution and Tracking 307

Document Tracking 310

Sybase HIPAA Studio 312

ECMap 314

Document Processing Path 320

Summary 321

References 322

Lesson 6   Getting Started with HIPAA Privacy 323

Administrative Requirements 324

Assigned Responsibility 326

Development of Policies and Procedures 326

Safeguards 327

Documentation 327

Training 327

Complaints 328

Sanctions 329

Mitigation 328

No Intimidation Acts 329

No Waiver of Rights 329

HIPAA Privacy Officer Responsibilities 330

Privacy Policy Development and Implementation 330

Key Responsibilities 331

Flow of PHI 332

Scenario: Releasing PHI to Third Parties 335

Step 1: Receiving the Request 335

Step 2: Patient's Permission 335

Step 3: Review of Information Requested 336

Step 4: Preparing Information Requested 336

Step 5: Sending the Information Requested. 336

Assessment and Gap Analysis 336

Assessment 337

Gap Analysis. 338

Business Associates 340

Physician's/Dentist's Office Scenario 358

Site Assessment 358

Gap Analysis. 359

Remediation 359

Policies and Procedures 359

Certification 360

Computer Requirements 360

Fax Requirements 361

Privacy Compliance Documents. 362

Sample: Notice of Privacy Practices 362

Sample: Notice of Privacy Practice. 372

Model Authorization 377

Sample Form: Request for Access to Patient's Health
Information 381

Sample: Request for Amendment of Health Information 386

Sample Privacy Policies 389

General Privacy Policy. 390

Client Rights Policy 390

Uses and Disclosures of Clients or Participants
Information Policy 391

Minimum Necessary Policy. 391

Administrative, Technical, and Physical Safeguards Policy 391

Use and Disclosures for research Purposes and Waivers Policy 392

Deidentification of Client Information and Use of
Limited Data Sets Policy 392

Business Associates Policy. 392

Enforcement, Sanctions, and Penalties for Violation
of Individual Privacy Policy. 393

Summary. 472

Lesson 7 Getting Started with HIPAA Security 473

Privacy Requirements: Starting Point for Security
Implementation 474

Secure Information Delivery 475

Security Implementation Considerations 476

Framework for Security Requirements. 476

HIPAA Security Project Phases. 477

HIPAA Security Phases for Initiatives. 478

Getting Started: Security Assessment. 480

Objective 480

Scope 481

Assessment Deliverables 483

Case Study: Securing an Operating System: Windows XP 483

Core Capabilities 484

Policies and Templates. 486

XP Security Parameters. 488

Software Policies. 488

Internet Connection Firewall (ICF) 490

A Scenario: Securing a Small Physician's Office 491

Security Policy. 495

Security Standard. 496

Example: Enterprise TCP/IP Security Policy. 498

Summary. 500

References 500

Appendix A   HIPAA Glossary **501**

Appendix B   HIPAA Frequently Asked Questions (FAQs) **519**

General Overview 520

Compliance and Planning 521

Privacy Standards. 523

Technology and security Solutions 523

Appendix C   HIPAA Privacy FAQ. **525**

Appendix D   Case Study: P3P, A Privacy Standard **533**

About P3P. 534

P3P and Cookies 534

What P3P Is Not 535

P3P and Other Languages 535

How P3P Works 535

Getting Started with P3P 536

Appendix E   Bibliography **537**

**Appendix F   HHS Fact Sheet, Modifications
to Final Privacy Rule** **539**

Modifications to the Standards for Privacy of Individually
Identifiable Health Information—Final Rule 540

Final Modifications. 540

Appendix G   HIPAA Academy. **545**

Certification Exams 546

Exam Fees 547

Pricing 547

AAPC CEU Credits for HIPAA Academy Program 549

ACHE Grants Continuing Education Credits
     to HIPAA Academy Programs 550

National Accreditations and CE Credits 550

Testimonials 551

Pabrai Addresses the National Council for Prescription
     Drug Programs (NCPDP) 559

Index. 563

Introduction

The Health Insurance Portability and Accountability Act (HIPAA) is about insurance portability, fraud, and administrative simplification. I hope you are excited about HIPAA and take advantage of the legislation to transform skills and core business practices. It all starts with Protected Health Information (PHI), but will end with several e-business initiatives.

At the HIPAA Academy (www.HIPAAAcademy.Net) we are very passionate about the legislation and associated solutions. In the long term, the positive impacts of HIPAA will not be insignificant. HIPAA will result in a transformation of your business for the better. HIPAA initiatives will lead to more transparency between the organization and patients. HIPAA is about transformation, transparency, and the application of technology.

Leverage the legislation to introduce change to enable your organization to be more efficient. Remember, your competitors and partners are moving ahead with changes. As you get started implementing HIPAA, view it as the floor and not the ceiling.

—Uday O. **Ali** Pabrai, CHSS, SCNA

Lesson 1

What Is HIPAA?

HIPAA

After reading this chapter, you will be able to

- Understand motivation and drivers for HIPAA legislation
- Examine the specifics of HIPAA's Administrative Simplification requirement
- Understand penalties for not being in compliance with HIPAA requirements
- Identify HIPAA-related organizations
- Describe key HIPAA concepts and terminology

The *Health Insurance Portability and Accountability Act* (HIPAA) is about information efficiency, privacy, and security in the U.S. health care industry. The issues that relate to HIPAA deal with the transaction efficiency, as well as the security and privacy, of patient and medical records and information. This is very similar to the needs all businesses have to secure information related to employees, customers, and suppliers.

HIPAA's goal is to bring about national standards for consistent data formats for health care transactions. Besides data format consistency, another key benefit from HIPAA compliance is the substantial reduction in paper-handling costs for health care claims. These costs are likely to be reduced from $6 to $8 per claim to less than $1.

Far more than just another government regulation, HIPAA is a defining standard for how the health care industry will securely handle patient data. In addition, HIPAA provisions will result in e-business initiatives that will substantially reduce the costs of processing medical claims and transactions.

Any patient-identifiable information is now *Protected Health Information* (PHI) regardless of the media form it is or was in. PHI is protected under HIPAA during data at rest or in transit. *At rest* refers to data that is accessed, stored, processed, or maintained. *In transit* means data that is transmitted in any form.

HIPAA is about e-business initiatives inside organizations. It is about protecting health care information. HIPAA not only provides more timely availability of information, enabling faster decision-making, but also enables substantial cost savings and increased opportunities for revenue as a direct result of efficiencies created. HIPAA initiatives will result in the development of applications as well as the deployment of technology. It is important to note that HIPAA is a challenge from a technology perspective as much as it is a business process challenge. Careful attention needs to be paid to the business processes that would guide the application of the appropriate technology for HIPAA compliance.

Organizations need to take advantage of the guidelines laid out by HIPAA and use them to accelerate the pace for the development of e-business applications and a secure, trusted infrastructure. Use the guidelines to build a resilient enterprise that is agile and increasingly virtual. Again, rather than just another government regulation with which to comply, HIPPA represents an enormous, unprecedented opportunity that will result in new efficiencies and enhanced profitability for the health care industry.

HIPAA must be viewed as the starting point and not the end point of changes that organizations need to make to the workplace as well as policies, procedures, systems, and applications.

Introduction

Health care is a trillion dollar industry, employing over 12 million individuals in numerous fields; the United States Department of Labor recognizes 400 different job titles in the health care industry. The health care delivery industry is highly fragmented and very complex, and is in the process of rapid transformation. It is beginning to change the way it electronically processes information. The Health Insurance Portability and Accountability Act (HIPAA) is largely responsible for serving as a business driver, accelerating the digitization of the health care industry.

In this lesson we review the scope of the legislation with specific focus on the Administrative Simplification subtitle of the Act. We then review core requirements as well as timelines and associated penalties for violations. We close this lesson by reviewing some key organizations associated with the legislation as well as terminology that is used extensively in the standards documents.

HIPAA, An Act of Congress

HIPAA is about insurance portability, fraud, and administrative simplification. This book examines the basics of the Administrative Simplification title of the HIPAA legislation. This title is the watershed legislation for health care information systems, and results in substantial investment in e-business initiatives and deployment of security technology specifically in the health care and insurance industries.

The U.S. Congress passed HIPAA legislation, Public Law 104–191 [H.R. 3103], "to improve portability and continuity of health insurance coverage in the group and individual markets, to combat waste, fraud, and abuse in health insurance and health care delivery, to promote the use of medical savings accounts, to improve access to long-term care services and coverage, to simplify the administration of health insurance, and for other purposes."

HIPAA is an act of Congress and became law on August 21, 1996. HIPAA, also known as the *Kennedy-Kassebaum bill*, is not only about ensuring the continuation of health insurance for individuals changing employment, but it is about protecting the privacy of patient records and any other patient identifiable information in any media form.

To enable these sweeping goals, the original HIPAA legislation included a number of sections (called *titles* in the law), each addressing a different facet of the overall objective. The first title is about ensuring and enhancing insurance access, portability, and renewability.

The HIPAA access, portability, and renewability title provides the following new protections for millions of working Americans and their families:

- Increases their ability to get health coverage if they start a new job
- Reduces the probability of their losing existing health care coverage
- Helps them maintain continuous health coverage when changing jobs
- Helps them purchase health insurance coverage on their own if they lose coverage under an employer's group health plan and have no other health coverage available

Among its specific protections, HIPAA

- Limits the use of pre-existing condition exclusions
- Prohibits group health plans from discriminating by denying you coverage or charging you extra for coverage based on your or your family member's past or present poor health

◆ Guarantees certain small employers, and certain individuals who lose job-related coverage, the right to purchase health insurance

◆ Guarantees, in most cases, that employers or individuals who purchase health insurance can renew the coverage regardless of any health conditions of individuals covered under the insurance policy

In short, the first title of the HIPAA legislation is intended to lower the probability of an individual or family losing existing coverage, ease their ability to switch health plans, and help those who are without coverage to find it on their own if they lose their employer's plan and have no other coverage available. Regulations in support of the first title are relatively well integrated into the American health care infrastructure today.

In a similar manner, the last three titles of the HIPAA legislation have been generally addressed by Congress and the various regulatory agencies that play a role in the American health care delivery and financing infrastructure. These titles are: Tax-related Health Provisions, Application and Enforcement of Group Health Insurance Requirements, and Revenue Offsets.

This book covers the specific details of title 2 of HIPAA as it relates to administrative simplification that includes within its scope protecting the privacy and confidentiality of patient records and any other patient identifiable information in any media form.

Today, health plans, hospitals, pharmacies, laboratories, doctors, and other health care entities use a wide array of systems to process and track health care bills and other information. Hospitals and doctor's offices treat patients with many different types of health insurance and must spend time and money ensuring that each claim contains the format, codes, and other details required by each insurer. Similarly, health plans spend time and money to ensure their systems can handle transactions from various health care providers and clearinghouses. Congress has identified some portion of these transaction-related expenses as waste.

Congress included provisions in HIPAA to require the Department of Health and Human Services (HHS) to adopt national standards for certain electronic health care transactions, codes, identifiers, and security. HIPAA also set a three-year deadline for Congress to enact comprehensive privacy legislation to protect medical records and other personal health information. When Congress did not enact such legislation by August 1999, HIPAA required the HHS to issue health privacy regulations. These regulations did not appear quickly.

The development of the HHS draft Privacy regulations, initially released in November 1999, was an exercise in political maneuvering, influence, and consensus building. HHS worked through more than 52,000 formal comments concerning the initial draft Privacy regulations. The Final Privacy Rule was released August 14, 2002. In the Final Privacy Rule, requirements for consent were loosened, while notice requirements were tightened.

Why privacy? Security and privacy standards can promote higher quality care by assuring consumers that their personal health information will be protected from inappropriate uses and disclosures. A survey conducted by Princeton Survey Research Associates for the California Health Care Association in 1999 submits that Americans are increasingly concerned about the loss of privacy in everyday life, and especially about their health information.

In the last two decades, the lack of privacy has led people to withdraw from full participation in their own health care because they are afraid that their most sensitive health records will fall into the wrong hands, leading to discrimination, loss of benefits, stigma, and unwanted exposure.

The study found that one out of every six people engages in some form of privacy-protective behavior to shield herself from the misuse of health information, including withholding information, providing inaccurate information, doctor-hopping to avoid a consolidated medical record, paying out of pocket for care that is covered by insurance, and—in the worst cases—avoiding care altogether.

This is especially true when researchers investigate populations having cancer, AIDS, sexually transmitted diseases, substance abuse, and mental illness. These health service consumer behaviors cost our nation billions of dollars in lost productivity and in increased costs for dealing with diseases that have progressed needlessly.

Addressing these issues via HIPAA regulations will cost the American health care industry (and its customers) somewhere between $17 billion over the first decade and more than $22 billion over the first five years, depending on which experts you believe. That seems like a lot of money. Why bother?

The intent is that uniform national standards will save billions of dollars each year for health care businesses by lowering the costs of developing and maintaining software and reducing the time and expense needed to handle health care transactions. HHS estimates that compliance will generate cost savings associated with implementing HIPAA's transactions standards of approximately $29 billion over ten years.

If the transaction standards are implemented by providers and payers together, as contemplated by congress, consumers and health care organizations should benefit. Gartner Group researchers have suggested that many health care providers are depending on their vendors and clearinghouses for compliance. If this suggestion is accurate, then the health care industry will not reap savings to the extent intended in the legislation.

Health care organizations that focus their efforts on achieving full compliance in provider-payer transactions will be much better positioned than their peers waiting for vendor or clearinghouse solutions to appear. Similarly, those organizations that give security and privacy compliance the appropriate priority will be able to more quickly refocus on their core competencies. Security compliance will be difficult. Health care organizations that wait will have a hard time avoiding penalties.

The health care industry today is in a process of rapid transformation. It is changing the way it electronically processes information. The health care industry is facing a significant challenge coordinating information exchange across the enterprise—add to this the complexity of not just information exchange, but secure information exchange.

Currently, in the health care industry, providers, insurers, and plans use many different electronic formats. This results in transactions inefficiencies as patient and medical records and payment information need to be moved between providers, insurers, and plans. Further, there are minimal procedures, policies, and technologies in place to secure the movement or storage of all such medical and related payment information.

Ignoring HIPAA involves significant peril since an organization's competitors might be well on their way to compliance.

Far more than just another government regulation, HIPAA is a defining standard for how the health care industry will securely handle patient data. In addition, HIPAA provisions will result in e-business initiatives that substantially reduce the costs of processing medical claims and transactions.

HIPAA is about information efficiency, privacy, and security in the U.S. health care industry. The issues that relate to HIPAA deal with the transaction efficiency, as well as the security and privacy of patient and medical records and information. This is very similar to the needs all businesses have to secure information related to employees, customers, and suppliers.

One of HIPAA's goals is to bring about national standards for consistent data formats for health care transactions. Besides data format consistency, another key benefit from HIPAA compliance is the substantial reduction in paper-handling costs for health care claims. These costs are likely to be reduced significantly.

Health care applications that have been used to maintain, transform, transmit, and verify/audit are being seriously impacted as a direct consequence of HIPAA.

There are other challenges that many organizations must face when making relatively radical changes in any of their core line-of-business systems. Many larger physician's practices/clinics, hospitals, and other more complex health care organizations depend upon a intricate Web of internal, outsourced, and service-provider applications. Many of these applications use, display, or store protected health information. Some examples of these kinds of systems include (but are not limited to) the following:

- ◆ Call/contact center system
- ◆ Claims clearinghouse
- ◆ Customer relationship management system
- ◆ Document imaging management system
- ◆ Emergency department systems
- ◆ Enterprise resource planning systems
- ◆ General financial systems
- ◆ Materials management systems
- ◆ Nurse triage system
- ◆ Operating room systems
- ◆ Patient accounting/billing systems
- ◆ Practice management systems
- ◆ Technology-enabled marketing systems

Many organizations also attempt to drive out increasing efficiencies by tightly coupling systems and implementing automated workflow. In a Gartner Group research note, authors M. Davis, R. Dearborn, and T. Berg argue that a significant number of health related businesses are using HIPAA mandates to justify replacement of a number of key applications.[1] It is critical that you keep in mind that in an integrated infrastructure characterized by automated workflow and tight coupling of groups of systems, any significant change in any one system requires that you test (possibly even modify) many of your other systems. This kind of effort can be notoriously difficult and time-consuming. That said, HIPAA compliance still requires that most health related organizations need to make these kinds of relatively high-risk changes.

The health care industry is facing a significant challenge coordinating information exchange across the enterprise—add to this the complexity of secure information exchange.

Conflict with State Law

Section 1178 of the Act outlines the relationships between HIPAA's legal and regulatory framework and state law that may address analogous situations or interactions. The general rule is that HIPAA preempts contrary state law. There are three exceptions to this general rule:

- The Secretary of HHS determines that certain state laws are necessary for technical purposes outlined in the statute.
- State laws that the Secretary of HHS determines address controlled substances.
- State laws relating to the privacy of individually identifiable health information that are contrary to and more stringent than the federal requirements.

HIPAA's Administrative Simplification Title

HIPAA is about health information efficiency, privacy, and security. The industries directly impacted by the HIPAA legislation include health care and insurance organizations and businesses in the United States. The issues that relate to HIPAA deal with the transaction efficiency, as well as the security and privacy of patient and medical records and information. These needs are very similar to the needs for all businesses to secure information related to employees, customers, and suppliers.

It is the Administrative Simplification portion of the HIPAA legislation that is fueling initiatives within organizations to address health care priorities in the areas of transactions, privacy, and security.

HIPAA Titles

HIPAA has five top-level titles:

- **Title I.** Health Care Insurance Access, Portability, and Renewability
- **Title II.** Preventing Health Care Fraud and Abuse, Administrative Simplification, Medical Liability Reform
- **Title III.** Tax-related Health Provisions
- **Title IV.** Application and Enforcement of Group Health Insurance Requirements
- **Title V.** Revenue Offsets

The HIPAA Title II is further broken into seven subtitles. Subtitle F of HIPAA Title II, Administrative Simplification, is watershed legislation for health care information systems. The purpose of the Administrative Simplification subtitle is to improve the Medicare program under Title XVIII of the Social Security Act, the Medicaid program under Title XIX of such Act, and the efficiency and effectiveness of the health care system by encouraging the development of a health information system through the establishment of standards and requirements for the electronic transmission of certain health information

The IT Component of the HIPAA Legislation

Mandated by HIPAA, the HHS has established a set of rules under the Administrative Simplification title. It is the Administrative Simplification portion of the HIPAA legislation that is fueling initiatives within organizations to address health care priorities. These priorities are primarily focused in the areas of

- Electronic Data Interchange (EDI)
  - Transactions
  - Medical code sets
  - Identifiers
- Privacy
- Security

Health care business applications include patient scheduling, registration, clinical reporting, and billing. These business applications have to be secure and need to integrate with the health organization's security infrastructure. Specifically, it is the Administrative Simplification subtitle of HIPAA Title II that makes the storage and movement of medical records and transactions more efficient as well as secure. This subtitle is fueling initiatives within organizations to address health care:

- **Transactions.** As defined in the HIPAA Administrative Simplification regulation, "Standards for Electronic Transactions," also referred to as "Transactions and Code Sets"
- **Identifiers.** As defined in the HIPAA Administrative Simplification regulation as identifiers for health care providers, health plans, employers and individuals
- **Privacy.** As defined in the HIPAA Administrative Simplification regulation, "Standards for Privacy of Individually Identifiable Health Information"
- **Security.** As defined in the HIPAA Administrative Simplification regulation, "Security and Electronic Signature Standard"

 NOTE

Together, the first letters of each initiative spell TIPS, which is an excellent mnemonic for remembering what these items are.

The focus of this section is on the Administrative Simplification subtitle of HIPAA Title II. The Administrative Simplification subtitle is the launch pad for e-business initiatives for electronic and secure medical information.

The Administrative Simplification Act directly impacts IT initiatives in the health care and insurance industries. A key goal of HIPAA includes an objective of accountability to reduce fraud and abuse in the health care system on a national basis. The U.S. General Accounting Office (GAO) has estimated that 11 cents of every health care dollar is spent fraudulently. This is a significant figure when we consider that health care spending in the U.S. topped $1 trillion in 1998.

The Administrative Simplification subtitle is intended to reduce the costs and administrative burden of health care. Costs will be reduced through the implementation of Electronic Data Interchange (EDI) standards for the electronic transmission of many administrative and financial transactions that are predominantly performed on paper, and to provide the appropriate level of protection for the privacy and security of patient health information the transactions are based on.

So whom does the HIPAA Administrative Simplification subtitle affect? Specifically, health care providers, payers, clearinghouses, billing agents, third-party administrators, and other related entities are all affected by the requirements of administrative simplification and patient privacy. Health care transactions are quite varied and include

- ♦ Insurance eligibility verification
- ♦ Insurance plan enrollment
- ♦ Insurance pre-certification and adjudication
- ♦ Scheduling and ordering
- ♦ Disease management
- ♦ Insurance claims submissions
- ♦ Coordination of benefits
- ♦ Billing and claims acceptance
- ♦ Sharing of patient information between a doctor's office and a hospital

All of these transactions are impacted by HIPAA. Health care business applications include patient scheduling, registration, clinical reporting, and billing. These business applications have to be secure and need to integrate with the health organization's security infrastructure. HIPAA also mandates standardization in electronic health care administration. This means that (at least some of) your business applications need to integrate with other external business applications via HIPAA-standard transactions.

The U.S. GAO estimates that more than 20 cents of every health care dollar is spent on administrative overhead in our health care system. This overhead is largely driven by billing and administrative costs because of the complexity of transactions involving hundreds of insurers as shown in Figure 1.1.

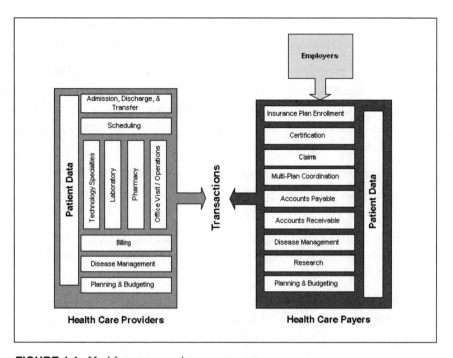

FIGURE 1.1 *Health care transactions.*

HIPAA EDI: Transactions and Code Sets

The U.S. GAO estimates that more than 20 cents of every health care dollar is spent on administrative overhead in our health care system. This overhead is largely driven by billing and administrative costs because of the complexity of transactions involving hundreds of insurers.

The efficiency of information exchange and processing of administrative and financial transactions between health organizations (payers and providers) can be greatly improved through the use of computer-to-computer interfaces using EDI transaction standards, which will eliminate human intervention and reduce errors and processing time. The HIPAA Administrative Simplification legislation requires the adoption of EDI transaction standards for certain administrative and financial health care transactions that are currently executed manually (on paper) or electronically without a consistently implemented national standard.

The adoption of transaction standards will also require the implementation of several supporting standards, which will make the implementation of these transaction standards more effective. Currently, payers use hundreds of formats to conduct transactions for claims and payments. The following supporting standards are required to get everyone on the "same page":

◆ **Transaction and Code Sets.** For diagnosis and procedure codes

◆ **Identifiers.** For plan sponsors (typically employers), health plans, health care providers, and individuals

◆ **Security and Privacy.** To protect the privacy and confidentiality of health information while being stored (data at rest) or transmitted (data in transmission)

The use of EDI combined with stronger security practices, also called for by AS, will improve the ability of health information systems to guard against fraud. Through implementation of strong authentication techniques, access to health information will be better protected. Information systems will be required to automatically log accesses to health information and administrative and financial transactions processed, thus making it much more difficult for fraud to occur. Together, EDI and stronger security practices will help to make significant reductions in health care costs.

HIPAA Transaction Implementation Guides

The HIPAA Transaction Implementation Guides are published by the Washington Publishing Company (WPC). You can download all of the HIPAA Implementation Guides for free from http://hipaa.wpc-edi.com/. The WPC site also lists prices for printed bound copies. You also can purchase the entire collection on a CD-ROM.

To download these HIPAA Transaction Standard Implementation Guides, you must have a Washington Publishing Company (WPC) username (login). You can create a login at the site in a few minutes by providing some basic contact information.

You can consult http://aspe.os.dhhs.gov/admnsimp/for additional information concerning the Transaction Standards and the HIPAA. The standards are

- Identifier Standards
- Privacy Standards
- Security Standards

You can consult http://www.ncpdp.org for information concerning the Transaction Standard for retail pharmacy claims.

The Final ASC X12N Implementation Guides adopted by HIPAA are available in these formats:

- **PDF download**. Free
- **PDF on CD-ROM**. $35.00 each
- Complete collection of **PDFs on CD-ROM**. $199.00
- **Bound**. $45.00 to $79.20 each

You can download the Draft ASC X12N Guides for free. The downloadable guides are self-extracting ZIP files. You can save the file on your system and then double-click its icon to install it. The Draft Addenda is available for all nine 004010 Implementation Guides.

HIPAA Privacy and Security

Privacy and security are addressed separately under HIPAA, and, therefore, two distinct rules were established. In the context of HIPAA, privacy defines who is authorized to access information and includes the right of individuals to keep information about themselves from being disclosed. Security, in this context, is the ability to control access and protect information from accidental or intentional disclosure to unauthorized persons and from alteration, destruction, or loss.

Achieving even a base level of this type of security can be harder that one might think. John Pescatore, a Gartner Research Vice President, argues "Software can be made to do whatever any clever programmer wants it do; however, it is more difficult to prevent software from doing what you don't want it to do. Even worse, even if you succeed at that, it is nearly impossible to keep someone else from changing the software to do what you don't want it do."

In a HIPAA-compliant environment where certainty, reliability, and carefully proscribed access to information is key, software's fluidity, relatively weak self-protection, and constant state of flux can make it an inappropriate foundation for protecting your highest-value information assets. Mr. Pescatore recently concluded that hardware provides "high levels of security by being more difficult to change than software." For systems that are relatively stable and must resist modification, he states, "hardware will be required to provide an appropriate level of security."

The HIPAA privacy regulations require that patients must sign consent forms allowing disclosures of their information for billing and treatment and be told how their information is being used and by whom. Health Care Organizations (HCOs) and their business associates will be held accountable for inappropriate disclosures of patient information and will be expected to implement administrative changes to protect information. The Privacy Rule covers the policies and procedures that must be in place to ensure that the patients' health information is protected and that their rights are upheld.

The Security Standard is a companion to the Privacy Rule—to protect the information, HCOs will be expected to put security safeguards in place. Complementing the Security Rule, the HIPAA Privacy Rule defines who is authorized to access patient-identifiable information. It also establishes the rights of individuals to keep information about them from being disclosed.

The provisions of the Privacy Rule likely will overlap with the Security Rule in some areas. For instance, the proposed Security Rule also requires that health care organizations maintain an audit trail of who accesses patient-identifiable information.

Businesses need the assistance of skilled security professionals and architects for a successful implementation of HIPAA-related security assessment, policies, and technologies.

Secure Information Delivery

One of the goals of the HIPAA Administrative Simplification subtitle is to secure information delivery between administrators, patients, and caregivers. The legislation deals with the electronic capture, transformation, and delivery across the health care industry entities because traditionally, the health care industry has been impeded by

- Limited technology budgets
- Multiple proprietary systems
- Multiple legacy systems
- Paper-based processes

The mandated HIPAA regulations are the catalyst to improve processes and information flow throughout the health care industry.

As a direct consequence of health care transactions, it is becoming much more important to protect patient and medical information. This requires a health care organization to build a secure infrastructure. The key components of a secure infrastructure for a health care organization may include the deployment of technologies such as

- Firewall systems
- Intrusion Detection Systems (IDS)
- Secure Virtual Private Networks (VPNs)
- Public Key Infrastructure (PKI)
- Biometrics
- Smart cards
- Authentication tokens

Thus, a HIPAA-compliant health care organization is one that would use EDI for transactions; protect patient's medical information with a combination of notices, consents, and authorization; and secure all electronic medical records and transactions.

What Will the Impact of HIPAA Be?

HIPAA will result in

- Standardization of efficient and electronic administrative and financial health care transactions
- Unique health identifiers for employers, health plans, health care providers, and eventually individuals
- Privacy of protected health information

   ◆ Security standards protecting the confidentiality and integrity of "individually identifiable health information," past, present, or future

   ◆ Standards for electronic medical records

HIPAA Timeline

The following are important dates related to HIPAA compliance:

   ◆ **October 16, 2002.** Transactions and code sets (extended to October 16, 2003)

   ◆ **April 16, 2003.** Schedule for testing to begin no later than April 16, 2003

   ◆ **April 14, 2003.** Privacy

On December 27, 2001, President Bush signed into law the Administrative Simplification Compliance Act (ASCA) (also known as H.R. 3323), delaying the date of compliance for the HIPAA Transaction and Code Set Regulations to October 16, 2003. This date only applies to health plans (except small health plans) and health care providers that submit compliance plans to the Secretary of the Department of Health and Human Services by October 15, 2002.

Under ASCA, health care plans and providers *must* submit information about their compliance activities, including budget, assessment of compliance concerns, whether a contractor or vendor might be used to help achieve compliance, and a schedule for testing to begin no later than April 16, 2003.

The HHS model compliance plan involves answering only 26 questions, yet Gartner Group research found that only 65 percent of providers said that they intended to file this document. Instead, Gartner reports, it appears that these health care organizations are anticipating that their software vendors will provide HIPAA-compliant upgrades that will make the solution simply routine.

For most organizations, this is a high-risk gamble involving a naïve perception that their infrastructure is less complex than it really is. Consider the portions of your organization and its IS infrastructure that are impacted by introducing the new HIPAA transaction and code sets. For many, the impact covers a vast array of interfaces, applications, and data bases, and, likely, some of the processes and procedures that support them. Then consider the time and expense required to perform effective testing and rollout of any of your core line of business systems. Given the numbers of components of your infrastructure that are likely to change, the testing effort will involve non-trivial time and resource.

Depending on your vendor may involve another risk. The vendor may not deliver what you need.

The compliance date for the HIPAA Privacy Rule is set for April 14, 2003. The compliance date for the HIPAA Security Rule has not yet been set as it is still in the proposal stage. The expected compliance date is 2005.

HIPAA's Teeth: Penalties

HIPAA sets severe penalties for noncompliance. The penalties can be both civil and criminal, and result in financial penalty or imprisonment.

For example, penalties for violation of patient confidentiality standards are substantial, with monetary fines and, in some cases imprisonment. Under the Administrative Simplification subtitle, section 1176 states that the Secretary of HHS may impose a civil monetary penalty (a fine) on any person or covered entity that violates any HIPAA requirement. The civil monetary penalty for violating transaction standards is up to $100 per person per violation and up to $25,000 per person per violation of a single standard per calendar year.

The Secretary of HHS may reduce the amount of a fine or waive it entirely if the violation was not due to willful neglect of the requirements, and if the entity corrects it within 30 days of becoming aware of it.

Federal criminal penalties can also be placed upon health plans, providers, and health care clearinghouses that knowingly and improperly disclose information or obtain information under false pretenses. Penalties would be higher for actions designed to generate monetary gain.

Section 1177 of HIPAA establishes penalties for a knowing misuse of unique health identifiers and individually identifiable health information:

◆ A fine of not more than $50,000 and/or imprisonment of not more than 1 year

◆ If misuse is "under false pretenses," a fine of not more than $100,000 and/or imprisonment of not more than 5 years

◆ If misuse is with intent to sell, transfer, or use individually identifiable health information for commercial advantage, personal gain, or malicious harm, a fine of not more than $250,000 and/or imprisonment of not more than 10 years

The specific offenses to which harsher penalties apply include

◆ Using a unique health identifier in violation of the HIPAA requirements. Unique health identifiers include

- Provider identifiers
- Employer identifiers
- Health plan identifiers
- Individual identifiers

◆ Obtaining or using individually identifiable health information in violation of the HIPAA privacy requirements.

◆ Disclosing individually identifiable health information in violation of the HIPAA privacy requirement.

Tables 1.1 and 1.2 summarize the possible penalties for non-compliance.

Table 1.1 Summary of HIPAA Civil Penalties

Monetary Penalty	Terms of Imprisonment	Offenses
$100	N/A	Single violation of a provision (*can be multiple violations with a penalty of $100 each as long as each violation is for a different provision*)
$25,000	N/A	Multiple violations of an identical requirement or prohibition made during a calendar year

Table 1.2 Summary of HIPAA Criminal Penalties

Monetary Penalty	Terms of Imprisonment	Offenses
Up to $50,000	Up to 1 year	Wrongful disclosure of individually identifiable health information
Up to $100,000	Up to 5 years	Wrongful disclosure of individually identifiable health information committed under false pretenses
Up to $250,000	Up to 10 years	Wrongful disclosure of individually identifiable health information committed under false pretenses with intent to sell, transfer, or use for commercial advantage, personal gain, or malicious harm

In addition to significant financial penalties, remaining transaction non-compliant involves additional consequences:

◆ Claims not honored

◆ Bad press

◆ Legislative auditors

Who Can File a Complaint?

Any person who believes that a provider, health plan, or clearinghouse has not complied with HIPAA's provision may file a complaint.

Window for Filing Complaint

The complaint must be filed within 180 days of the time the person filing the complaint became aware of a HIPAA violation.

Who Is Impacted?

The HIPAA penalties apply to covered entities. Senior individuals within covered entities may be punished for non-compliance. A senior manager who is aware of a violation cannot avoid responsibility by avoiding active participation.

A covered entity is liable for violations of HIPAA requirements by

◆ Employees

◆ Other members of its workforce

◆ Business associates

A covered entity must establish and apply sanctions to members of its workforce who fail to comply with HIPAA's privacy and security policies and requirements. It must also maintain records of any sanctions that are applied and is obligated to make those records available to the Secretary of HHS, when requested, during the investigation of any complaint.

At a minimum, HIPAA requires

◆ Compliance with standard transaction sets

◆ Providing information to patients about their privacy rights and how their information can be used

- Adopting clear privacy/security procedures
- Training employees so that they understand the privacy/security procedures
- Designating an individual to be responsible for seeing that the privacy/security procedures are adopted and followed
- Securing patient records containing individually identifiable health information so that they are not readily available to those who do not need them

HHS Secretary Authorization

The Secretary of HHS is authorized to launch a compliance review of a covered entity whether or not a complaint alleging a violation of HIPAA's provisions has been received.

Effective Date of Penalties

The earliest date of an infraction that will be subject to HIPAA's penalty provision is April 14, 2003.

HIPAA-Related Organizations

In this section we review some organizations closely associated with the HIPAA legislation.

One of the largest federal agencies, the Department of Health and Human Services (HHS) is the principal agency for protecting the health of all Americans. Comprising 12 operating divisions, HHS' responsibilities include public health, biomedical research, Medicare and Medicaid, welfare, social services, and more. An overview of the department is provided in the document "HHS: What We Do," which you can download from **www.hhs.gov/about/profile.html**.

HHS includes more than 300 programs, covering a wide spectrum of activities. Some programs include

- Medical and social science research
- Preventing outbreak of infectious disease, including immunization services

- Assuring food and drug safety
- Medicare (health insurance for elderly and disabled Americans) and Medicaid (health insurance for low-income people)
- Financial assistance and services for low-income families
- Improving maternal and infant health
- Head Start (pre-school education and services)
- Preventing child abuse and domestic violence
- Substance abuse treatment and prevention
- Services for older Americans, including home-delivered meals
- Comprehensive health services for Native Americans

HHS is the largest grant-making agency in the federal government, providing some 60,000 grants per year. HHS' Medicare program is the nation's largest health insurer, handling more than 900 million claims per year.

HHS includes several agencies especially one that is working closely on HIPAA initiatives: the Centers for Medicare and Medicaid Services (CMS).

Their Web site can be found at: www.hhs.gov.

Centers for Medicare and Medicaid Services (CMS)

The Centers for Medicare and Medicaid Services (CMS) provides health insurance for over 74 million Americans through Medicare, Medicaid, and State Children's Health Insurance Program (SCHIP). This Federal government agency was previously known as the *Health Care Financing Administration* (HCFA) until July 2001.

In addition to providing health insurance, CMS also performs a number of quality-focused activities, including regulation of laboratory testing, development of coverage policies, and quality-of-care improvement. CMS maintains oversight of the survey and certification of nursing homes and continuing care providers (including home health agencies, intermediate care facilities for the mentally retarded, and hospitals), and makes available to beneficiaries, providers, researchers, and state surveyors information about these activities and nursing home quality.

HIPAA is an initiative of the Department of Health and Human Services/CMS. CMS is responsible for implementing various unrelated provisions of HIPAA.

CMS's business activities with regard to HIPAA include

◆ HIPAA health insurance reform

◆ HIPAA administrative simplification

CMS will also be responsible for enforcing the Transactions Rule.

The Web site for CMS can be found at www.cms.hhs.gov

Designated Standards Maintenance Organization (DSMO)

The Secretary of HHS named six organizations to maintain the standards using criteria specified in the Privacy Rule and Security Rule. These organizations are referred to as Designated Standards Maintenance Organizations (DSMOs). They are

◆ ANSI Accredited Standards Committee (ASC) X12

◆ Dental Content Committee of the American Dental Association

◆ Health Level Seven (HL7)

◆ National Council for Prescription Drug Programs (NCPDP)

◆ National Uniform Billing Committee (NUBC)

◆ National Uniform Claim Committee (NUCC)

The Web site for DSMOs can be found at www.hipaa-dsmo.org.

Workgroup for Electronic Data Interchange (WEDI)

The Workgroup for Electronic Data Interchange (WEDI) was established in 1991 to address administrative costs in the nation's health care system. WEDI is a voluntary, public/private task force created to streamline health care administration by standardizing electronic communication across the industry. The mission of WEDI includes serving as the primary catalyst for the identification, communication, and resolution of obstacles that impede the growth of electronic commerce within health care.

WEDI members have included Blue Cross Blue Shield Association, Travelers Insurance, and many others.

The Web site for the WEDI can be found at www.wedi.org.

Health Level Seven (HL7)

Health Level Seven (HL7) standards are widely used to interface the with independent systems in health care institutions concerned with clinical information. HL7 became an ANSI-accredited Standards Developing Organization (SDO) in 1994. HL7's involvement with HIPAA has been with claims attachments.

There are several HL7 documents, including those that cover:

♦ Ambulance

♦ Clinical reports

♦ Emergency department

♦ Laboratory results

♦ Medications

♦ Rehabilitation services

The Web site for HL7 can be found at www.hl7.org.

Washington Publishing Company (WPC)

The Washington Publishing Company (WPC) specializes in managing and distributing Electronic Data Interchange (EDI) information, primarily in the form of documentation for organizations that develop, maintain, and implement EDI standards. The EDI subsets, called *implementation guides*, also address industry- or company-specific EDI implementation issues, and often include explanatory front matter, figures, examples, and cross-references.

WPC has published several EDI implementation guides for several industries, including

♦ Association of American Railroads (AAR)

♦ American Trucking Association (ATA)

♦ Information System Agreement

♦ Telecommunications Information Forum

♦ Petroleum Industry Data Exchange

♦ Book Industry Systems Advisory Committee (BISAC)

♦ Serials Industry Systems Advisory Committee (SISAC)

♦ Automotive Industry Action Group (AIAG)

- National Association of Purchasing Managers (NAPM)
- American Iron and Steel Institute (AISI)
- Aluminum Association

The Web site for the WPC can be found at www.wpc-edi.com.

National Council for Prescription Drug Programs (NCPDP)

The National Council for Prescription Drug Programs (NCPDP) first started developing standards in 1977 with the Universal Claim Form. Transactions between pharmacies and health plans are typically executed in the NCPDP standard, while the transactions between all other providers and plans are done with X12 standards.

For Health Care Eligibility Benefit Inquiry and Response as well as Health Care Payment and Remittance Advice, the standard transaction for retail pharmacy drugs is the NCPDP Telecommunication Standard for Eligibility Verification and Response and Enrollment. The NCPDP's Telecommunication Standard processes over one billion claims per year. NCPDP received ANSI accreditation status in 1996.

NCPDP is a not-for-profit organization. Its target audience includes the pharmacy services sector of the health care industry. This includes organizations such as:

- Pharmacy chains
- Database management organizations
- Pharmaceutical manufacturers
- Telecommunication and systems vendors
- Wholesale drug distributors

The Web site for the NCPDP can be found at www.ncpdp.org.

National Committee on Vital and Health Statistics (NCVHS)

The National Committee on Vital and Health Statistics (NCVHS) is an advisory committee to the Secretary of Health and Human Services.

The HIPAA Administrative Simplification Compliance Act (ASCA) requires that a sample of the plans be provided to NCVHS. The NCVHS will review the sample to identify common problems that are complicating compliance activities, and will periodically publish recommendations for solving the problems.

The Web site for the NCVHS can be found at www.ncvhs.hhs.gov.

HIPAA: Key Concepts

The HIPAA regulations provide a number of key concepts that need to be understood when considering the impact and breadth of the rules that have been defined.

Covered Entities

The regulations place specific obligations upon covered entities. *Covered entities* include payers and providers. *Payers* include health plans (including most employer-sponsored group health plans) and health care clearinghouses. *Providers* include any "health care provider who transmits any health information in electronic form in connection with (regulated health care claims administration and financial transactions with payers)."

Most health care providers use electronic transmission in some form or the other when processing claims or in their financial dealings with their payers, such as with Medicare or commercial plans. These regulations, thus, apply to most health care providers.

In today's health care system, however, most health care providers and payers do not independently carry out all their health care activities and functions. They require assistance from a variety of service providers and contractors. HIPAA describes these supporting entities *business associates*.

Health Plans

Health plans are considered covered entities. Health plans include employee welfare benefit plans under ERISA, including insured and self-insured plans, that have 50 or more participants or which are administered by an entity other than the employer who establishes and maintains the plan.

Health plans under the regulations also include a health insurance issuer, an HMO, the Medicare and Medicaid programs, as well as most all health care programs, issuers of long-term care policies, and any other individual or group plan (or combination of individual or group plans) that provides or pays for the cost of medical care.

Health plans include the following, singly or in combination:

◆ **Active Military Personnel Health Plan.** The health care program for active military personnel under title 10 of the United States Code.

◆ **CHAMPUS.** The Civilian Health and Medical Program of the Uniformed Services. CHAMPUS primarily covers services furnished by civilian medical providers to dependents of active duty members of the uniformed services and retirees and their dependents under age 65.

◆ **Employee Welfare Benefit Plan.** An employee welfare benefit plan or any other arrangement that is established or maintained for the purpose of offering or providing health benefits to the employees of two or more employers. This includes plans that are referred to as *Multiple Employer Welfare Arrangements* (MEWAs).

◆ **Federal Employees Health Benefits Program.** The Federal Employees Health Benefits Program consists of health insurance plans offered to active and retired Federal employees and their dependents. Depending on the health plan, the services may be furnished on a fee-for-service basis or through a health maintenance organization.

◆ **Group Health Plan.** A group health plan is a plan that has 50 or more participants or is administered by an entity other than the employer that established and maintains the plan. This definition includes both insured and self-insured plans.

◆ **Health Insurance Issuer.** A health insurance issuer is an insurance company, insurance service, or insurance organization that is licensed to engage in the business of insurance in a state and is subject to state law that regulates insurance.

◆ **HMO.** A *Health Maintenance Organization* (HMO) may include preferred provider organizations, provider sponsored organizations, independent practice associations, competitive medical plans, exclusive provider organizations, and foundations for medical care.

◆ **Indian Health Service.** The Indian Health Service program furnishes services, generally through its own health care providers, primarily to persons who are eligible to receive services because they are of American Indian or Alaskan Native descent.

- **Long Term Care Policy.** A long-term care policy including a nursing home fixed-indemnity policy. A long-term care policy is considered to be a health plan regardless of how comprehensive it is.

- **Medicaid.** The Medicaid program (title XIX of the Act).

- **Medicare.** Part A or Part B of the Medicare program (title XVIII of the Act).

- **Medicare + Choice.** The Medicare + Choice program under part C of Title XVIII of the Act, 42 U.S.C. 1395w-21 through 1395w-28.

- **Medicare Supplemental Policy.** A Medicare supplemental policy is a health insurance policy that a private entity offers a Medicare beneficiary to provide payment for expenses incurred for services and items that are not reimbursed by Medicare because of deductible, coinsurance, or other limitations under Medicare. The statutory definition of a Medicare supplemental policy excludes a number of plans that are generally considered to be Medicare supplemental plans, such as health plans for employees and former employees and for members and former members of trade associations and unions.

- **State Child Health Plan.** An approved state child health plan under Title XXI of the Act, providing benefits that meet the requirements of section 2103 of the Act, 42 U.S.C. 1397 et. Seq.

- **Veterans Health Care Program.** The veterans health care program under chapter 17 of title 38 of the United States Code. This health plan primarily furnishes medical care through hospitals and clinics administered by the Department of Veterans Affairs for veterans with a service-connected disability that is compensable. Veterans with non-service-connected disabilities (and no other health benefit plan) may receive health care under this health plan to the extent resources and facilities are available.

- **Other.** Any other individual or group health plan, or combination thereof, that provides or pays for the cost of medical care.

Health Care Clearinghouse

The term health care clearinghouse is any public or private entity that

- Processes or facilitates the processing of information received from another entity in a nonstandard format or containing nonstandard data content into standard data elements or a standard transaction

Or

> ◆ Receives a standard transaction from another entity and processes or facilitates the processing of information into nonstandard format or nonstandard data content for a receiving entity

A health care clearinghouse is an entity that performs the functions of format translation and data conversion. When they are engaged in these activities, a billing service company, re-pricing company, community health management information system or community health information system, or value-added networks and switches are considered a health care clearinghouse.

Health care industry businesses of a threshold size have used software data and transaction mapping tools to convert EDI transactions between their external exchange formats and the internal core system-specific formats. Over time, some of these systems matured into sophisticated transaction brokers, or were built upon one of the commercial transaction brokers. The new HIPAA transactions cause owners of these "older," often highly customized or proprietary gateways, to make a difficult decision: Should they "re-write" or otherwise extend existing transaction switches, or purchase one of the new commercial switches that are emerging in the health care support services market?

Another way to look at these EDI/transaction switches is to view them as high-level middleware. Gartner Group calls these systems *Integration Brokers* (IB). They describe the new family of transaction switches as facilitating "communication among different applications by negotiating a variety of native data formats and communication protocols, and help ensure the timely and reliable delivery of messages from one application to another."

A number of vendors are marketing specialized HIPAA supporting transaction switches. These systems include pre-configured mappings for the HIPAA transactions. Some of the leading vendors that support HIPAA-related transaction products and solutions include

◆ IBM	◆ SeeBeyond
◆ Mercator	◆ Sybase
◆ Microsoft	◆ TIBCO
◆ Optio	◆ Vitria

Health Care Provider

Regulations define a health care provider as limited to those entities that furnish, or bill and are paid for, health care services in the normal course of business. Examples of health care providers include

- ◆ Physicians
- ◆ Dentists
- ◆ Clinics
- ◆ Laboratories
- ◆ Hospitals

Health Information

Health information means any information, whether oral or recorded in any form or medium, that

- ◆ Is created or received by a health care provider, health plan, public health authority, employer, life insurer, school or university, or health care clearinghouse

- ◆ Relates to the past, present, or future physical or mental health or condition of an individual; the provision of health care to an individual; or the past, present, or future payment for the provision of health care to an individual

Individually Identifiable Health Information (IIHI)

The concept of what information constitutes "individually identifiable health information" and what information may be "protected health information" is important for understanding the obligations placed upon covered entities by the privacy regulations. Individually identifiable health information includes that health information, including demographic information collected from an individual, that

- ◆ Is created or received by a health care provider, health plan, employer, or health care clearinghouse

- Relates to the past, present, or future physical or mental health or condition of an individual; the provision of health care to an individual; or the past, present or future payment for the provision of health care to an individual
  - That identifies the individual or
  - With respect to which there is a reasonable basis to believe the information can be used to identify the individual

Patient Identifiable Information (PII)

Identifiers within health information, which could be used to identify an individual and which would constitute "patient identifiable information," may include any one of the following:

- The individual's name
- City or county where the individual lives
- Zip code
- Social security number
- Finger print
- Telephone number
- Medical record number or fax number

The regulations list a number of other identifiers. Thus, any health information maintained by a covered entity where the individual could, in any possible way, be identified, needs to be treated as individually identifiable health information.

Protected Health Information

Any patient identifiable information is now Protected Health Information (PHI) regardless of the media form it is or was in HIPAA data may be at rest or in transit. At rest can mean data that is

- Accessed
- Stored
- Processed
- Maintained

In transit can mean data that is transmitted in any form.

Treatment, Payment, or Health Care Operation (TPO)

The term Treatment, Payment, or Health Care Operation is used extensively in the HIPAA Privacy Rule. The term *TPO* is often used in reference to the use and disclosure of health care information.

Treatment implies the use and disclosure of protected health information to provide, coordinate, or manage health care and any related services. This includes the coordination or management of patient health care with a third party that has already obtained permission to have access to the patient's protected health information. For example, an entity would disclose your protected health information, as necessary, to a home health agency that provides care to you; or your protected health information may be provided to a physician to whom you have been referred to ensure that the physician has the necessary information to diagnose or treat you.

In addition, the entity may disclose your protected health information from time-to-time to another physician or health care provider (for example, a specialist or laboratory) who, at the request of your physician, becomes involved in your care by providing assistance with your health care diagnosis or treatment.

Your protected health information will be used, as needed, to obtain *payment* for your health care services. This may include certain activities that your health insurance plan may undertake before it approves or pays for the health care services that the entity recommends for you, such as making a determination of eligibility or coverage for insurance benefits, reviewing services provided to you for medical necessity, and undertaking utilization review activities. For example, obtaining approval for a hospital stay may require that your relevant protected health information be disclosed to the health plan to obtain approval for the hospital admission.

As for health care operations, the health care entity may use or disclose, as-needed, your protected health information in order to support the business activities of your physician's practice. These activities include, but are not limited to, quality assessment activities, employee review activities, training of medical students, licensing, marketing and fund-raising activities, and conducting or arranging for other business activities.

Business Associate

These regulations also place requirements on covered entities when they disclose protected health information to their business associates. A *business associate* of a covered entity is generally a person (other than a member of its workforce) who, on behalf of the covered entity, performs or assists in the performance of a function or activity involving the use or disclosure of individually identifiable health information, including claims processing or administration, data analysis, processing or administration, utilization review, quality assurance, billing, benefit management, practice management, and re-pricing.

It also includes a person (other than a member of the covered entity's work force) who provides legal, actuarial, accounting consulting, data aggregation, management, administrative, accreditation, or financial services to or for such covered entity, "where the provision of the service involves the disclosure of individually identifiable health information from such covered entity to the person."

Exceptions to the definition apply to the arrangements between participants in certain joint health care arrangements.

Providers and payers are able to give protected health information to business associates, but must

- ◆ Ensure that the business associates will use the information only for the purpose(s) for which they were engaged by the covered entity.
- ◆ Safeguard the information from misuse.
- ◆ Comply with the covered entity's obligation to provide individuals with access to their health information and history of certain disclosures.
- ◆ Never use protected health information for any purpose independent of their explicit responsibilities to the contracting covered provider or payer.

Given the broad definition of business associates, covered entities need to carefully consider how these regulations may apply to anyone with whom they contract when that arrangement may result in the disclosure of individually identifiable health information.

Four business associate exceptions involve treatment, financial transactions, disclosures between a group health plan and plan sponsor, and organized health care arrangements.

Small Health Plan

A *small health plan* is one with annual receipts of $5 million or less. A small health plan is typically an individual health plan or group health plan with fewer than 50 participants.

Participant

A *participant* is any employee, or former employee, of an employer or any member or former member of an employee organization who is or may be eligible to receive a benefit of any type from an employee benefit plan that covers employees of that employer or members of such an organization, or whose beneficiaries may be eligible to receive any of these benefits.

Medical Care

Medical care includes the diagnosis, cure, mitigation, treatment, or prevention of disease or amounts paid for the purpose of affecting any body structure or function of the body. It also includes the amount paid for transportation primarily for and essential to the items identified. Finally, it includes the amount paid for insurance to cover the items as well as the transportation of all such items.

Secretary

Secretary means the Secretary of the Department of Health and Human Services or any other officer or employee of the Department of Health and Human Services to whom the authority involved has been delegated.

Compliance Date

The *compliance date* is the latest date by which a health plan, health care clearinghouse, or health care provider must comply with a rule. The compliance date for HIPAA standards generally is 24 months after the effective date of a final rule. The compliance date for small health plans, however, is 36 months after the effective date of the final rule.

Transaction

Transaction means the exchange of information between two parties to carry out financial or administrative activities related to health care. It includes the following types of information exchanges:

- Health claims or equivalent encounter information
- Health care payment and remittance advice
- Coordination of benefits
- Health claims status
- Enrollment and disenrollment in a health plan
- Eligibility for a health plan
- Health plan premium payments
- Referral certification and authorization
- First report of injury
- Health claims attachments
- Other transactions that the Secretary may prescribe by regulation

In general, a health plan must conduct the above transaction electronically when requested by a provider or another entity.

A transaction consists of code sets and identifiers, as discussed in the following sections.

Data Content

Data content includes the data elements and code sets inherent to a transaction and not related to the format of the transaction. Data elements that are related to the format are not data content.

Data issues impact both payers and providers. HIPAA transactions introduce new data elements and revised lengths for other data elements. For example, HIPAA standards introduce a new system of identifiers for providers and health plans. When used to describe a transaction, *format* refers to those data elements that structure it or assist in identifying its data content.

Transaction Standard

Transaction standards are a set of rules, conditions, or requirements describing the classification and components of a transaction. Transaction standards define the data elements, code sets, and details of inter-system interactions that must be used in a transaction.

The transaction standard will likely require some insurance providers to invest in relatively complex application and/or interface development to support more intrusive requirements.

For example, even though it is common practice to "bundle" remittance advice, HIPAA compliance requires that remittance advice must be expressed using the same record of services that were submitted in the corresponding claim. Depending on the state of a given insurer's systems, this new business-to-business interaction logic will require more or less coding, testing, documentation, training, and project management.

Code Set

A *code set* is any set of codes used for encoding data elements, such as tables of terms, medical concepts, medical diagnostic codes, or medical procedure codes.

Long-Term Care

Long-term care refers to the range of services typically provided at skilled nursing, intermediate-care, personal care, or eldercare facilities.

Patient Event

A *patient event* refers to the service or group of services associated with a single episode of care. Examples include

- ◆ An admission to a facility for treatment related to a specific patient condition or diagnosis or related group of diagnoses.
- ◆ A referral to a specialty provider for a consult or testing to determine a specific diagnosis and appropriate treatment.
- ◆ Services to be administered at a patient visit such as chiropractic treatment delivered in a single patient visit. The same treatment can be approved for a series of visits. It is recommended by the ANSI ASC X12N standard to limit each request to a single patient event.

Requester

Requester refers to providers such as physicians, medical groups, independent physician associations, facilities, and others who request authorization or certification for a patient to receive health care services.

Service Provider

A *service provider* is the referred-to provider, specialist, specialty entity, group, or facility where the requested services are to be performed.

Summary

This chapter examined the motivation for the HIPAA legislation and its key titles. It then reviewed the types of health care and other entities that would be impacted by HIPAA. HIPAA's Administrative Simplification subtitle is the core component of the HIPAA legislation that impacts electronic transactions within health care organizations.

The Administrative Simplification rules include

- ◆ National standard for identifiers
- ◆ Security and electronic signature standards
- ◆ Standards for code sets
- ◆ Standards for electronic transactions
- ◆ Standards for privacy of individually identifiable health information

There are a number of organizations that have worked closely with the Department of Health and Human Services in coordinating and managing several aspects of the legislation—these entities were discussed in detail.

HIPAA has real penalties and timelines associated with it. More so than just a legislative requirement, it is a business driver, a catalyst for substantial changes that an entity is required to implement. All entities need to examine how the application of HIPAA requirements will improve business processes, communications, and systems. The bottom line is that the HIPAA legislation should be viewed as the starting point and not the end point for business-process and operational changes—that will lead to efficiencies that enable the business to compete effectively in an increasingly electronic health care industry.

References

1. Michael Davis, et al. "Care Delivery Organization Financial and Administrative Application Study: 2002 Results." Gartner Group Note Number: R-17-0375. June 12 2002.

Lesson 2

HIPAA

After reading this chapter you will be able to:

- ◆ Understand motivation and drivers for HIPAA transaction legislation
- ◆ Examine the ANSI ASC X12 transaction types
- ◆ Identify HIPAA code set requirements
- ◆ Describe types of HIPAA standardized identifiers

The HIPAA Administrative Simplification Standard for Electronic Transactions, also referred to as the *Transaction and Code Sets*, facilitates standardized information exchange between providers and payers. The Transaction Rule applies to all administrative and financial transactions covered by HIPAA.

Congress and the health care industry agreed that standards for the electronic exchange of administrative and financial health care transactions were needed to improve the efficiency and effectiveness of the health care system. The Health Insurance Portability and Accountability Act of 1996 (HIPAA) required the Secretary of the Department of Health and Human Services (HHS) to adopt such standards.

National standards for electronic health care transactions encourage electronic commerce in the health care industry and ultimately simplify the processes involved. This results in savings from the reduction in administrative burdens on health care providers and health plans. Today, health care providers and health plans that conduct business electronically must use many different formats for electronic transactions. The lack of standardization makes it difficult and expensive to develop and maintain software.

For example, there are over a hundred different formats that exist today for health care claims. And even in situations where different entities are using the same format, there are subtle differences. This requires companies to extensively test with each trading partner to ensure that they are both using the same variant of the file format. With a national standard for electronic claims and other transactions, health care providers will be able to submit the same transaction to any health plan in the United States, and the health plan must accept it. Health plans will be able to send standard electronic transactions, such as remittance advice and referral authorizations to health care providers.

These national standards will make electronic data interchange a viable and preferable alternative to paper processing for providers and health plans alike. At some point in the relatively near future, the added per-unit expense of relying on paper processing will become a competitive disadvantage.

Impacted Health Care Transactions

As required by HIPAA, the Secretary of HHS has adopted standards for the following administrative and financial health care transactions:

- **270**. Eligibility, Coverage, or Benefit Inquiry
- **271**. Eligibility, Coverage, or Benefit Information
- **276**. Health Care Claim Status Request
- **277**. Health Care Claim Status Notification
- **278**. Health Care Services Review—Request for Review
- **278**. Health Care Services Review—Response to Request for Review
- **820**. Payment Order/Remittance Advice
- **834**. Benefit Enrollment and Maintenance
- **835**. Health Care Claim Payment/Advice
- **837**. Health Care Claim—Professional
- **837**. Health Care Claim—Dental
- **837**. Health Care Claim—Institutional

Also, the NCPDP Telecommunication Guide Version 5.1 has been adopted as a standard in the final Transaction Rule. This standard allows the reporting of information necessary to process retail pharmacy drug claims. That standard and the NCPDP Batch Implementation Guide Version 1.1 have been adopted for retail pharmacy drug claims or equivalent encounter information eligibility for a health plan and coordination of benefits.

To ensure a given level of standardization is in use, HIPAA also requires use of a number of standard identifiers. For example, there are standard medical diagnosis, procedure, and clinical code sets within these transactions. There also are

National Provider Identifications (NPI), *National Employer Identifiers* (NEI), and *National Health Plan Identifiers* (NHPI).

Standards for the first report of injury and claims attachments (also required by HIPAA) will be adopted at a later date.

Target Audience

All private sector health plans (including managed care organizations and ERISA plans, but excluding certain small self-administered health plans) and government health plans (including Medicare, State Medicaid programs, the Military Health System for active duty and civilian personnel, the Veterans Health Administration, and Indian Health Service programs), all health care clearinghouses, and all health care providers that choose to submit or receive transactions electronically are required to use the transaction standards.

Covered entities must use the transaction standards when electronically conducting any of the defined transactions covered under the HIPAA.

A health care clearinghouse may accept nonstandard transactions for the sole purpose of translating them into standard transactions for sending customers and may accept standard transactions and translate them into nonstandard transactions for receiving customers.

If the health plan performs a business function, whether electronically, on paper, or via phone, it must be able to support the electronic standard for that transaction. It can do this directly or through a clearinghouse. It also can outsource the business function to a third party, but that party must then support the standards related to the outsourced function.

Scope

The transaction standards will apply only to electronic data interchange (EDI)— when data is transmitted electronically between health care providers and health plans as part of a standard transaction. Data can be stored in any format as long as it can be translated into the standard transaction when required. Security standards, on the other hand, will apply to all health care information.

To comply with the transaction standards, health care providers and health plans can exchange the standard transactions directly, or they can contract with a clearinghouse to perform this function. Clearinghouses can receive nonstandard transactions from a provider, but they must convert these into standard transactions for submission to the health plan. Similarly, if a health plan contracts with a clearinghouse, the health plan can submit nonstandard transactions to the clearinghouse, but the clearinghouse must convert these into standard transactions for submission to the provider.

Health plans are required to support all of the transactions that correspond to business that it conducts. For example, if a health plan has accepted electronic claims, but has used paper forms for enrollment, then the health plan must now accept standard electronic enrollment transactions to be compliant.

Providers are the only covered entity with an element of choice regarding the standards. Providers are allowed to stay with paper transactions and avoid electronic standards. Health plans and clearinghouses must support the standard transactions. Although some providers might opt for paper, most will likely move to the transactions to gain efficiencies. Under HIPAA the provider will have one electronic "claim form" that replaces a great many paper forms now in existence.

Even though HIPAA does not force providers to use the transactions, health plans can require it where they have the ability. For example, an HMO might require doctors to file electronic claims as a condition of being a participating provider. Medicare is also expected to require nearly all providers to file electronically using the standard transactions.

Employers are not a covered entity. Many large employers currently use electronic transactions to enroll and maintain benefits. These employers are not forced to use the standard transactions. It is anticipated that many will choose to convert to the standard over time because it will simplify the process of switching health plans. Health plans that currently support nonstandard enrollment transactions are free to continue to do so. However, they must also support the ANSI transaction specified by HIPAA.

Compliance Dates

All health plans, all health care clearinghouses, and any health care provider that chooses to transmit transactions in electronic form must comply within 24 months after the effective date of the final Transaction Rule (small health plans have 36 months). The effective date of the Transaction Rule is 2 months after publication. Therefore, compliance with the final Transaction Rule is required by

October 16, 2003 (if an extension was requested; otherwise, it is October 16, 2002). Entities can begin using these standards earlier than the compliance date. The final Transactions and Code Sets Rule published on February 20, 2003 did not result in any change for compliance dates for this Rule.

The final Transaction Rule did clarify information related to compliance dates, if one side of the transaction had requested the extension while the other had not. The final Rule specifically states that if both sides to a transaction are not required to conduct it in standard form (that is, if one side is required to conduct the transaction in standard form but the other side is not), then neither side is required to conduct it in standard form.

Thus, for example, even where a covered health care provider failed to submit a compliance plan, it would not be required to comply with the Transaction Rule with respect to the covered transactions that it actually conducts during the period of October 16, 2002 through October 15, 2003 insofar as the transactions are with a health plan that is not required to comply during this period because it (1) has obtained a one-year extension under ASCA, or (2) is a small health plan. Similarly, a health plan that is subject to the October 16, 2002 compliance date would not be required to conduct coordination of benefits in standard form with another health plan, if the latter plan was not conducting the transaction in standard form because it (1) has obtained a one-year extension under ASCA, or (2) is a small health plan.

Further, even where compliance is required (that is, the October 16, 2002 compliance date applies to both sides of the covered transaction and neither covered entity submitted a compliance plan), DHS recognizes that the modifications adopted are necessary to permit the transactions covered by these proposed rules to be conducted in standard form, and that such transactions could not feasibly be required before the compliance date for the modifications in this final rule, October 16, 2003. Covered entities that have a present compliance obligation have the opportunity to comply with either the unmodified transaction standards or the modified transaction standards in this interim one-year period.

DHS intends to take into account the numerous obstacles to compliance that exist and will be working with covered entities to bring them into compliance during this interim period, through among other things, corrective action plans. DHS may penalize noncompliance for those cases of noncompliance where such voluntary efforts fail or where covered entities fail to make reasonable efforts to come into compliance.

Trading partner agreements should determine the processing requirements for non-compliant claims submitted by covered entities that have requested a compliance extension until October 16, 2003.

There are no other provisions to extend the compliance date beyond October 16, 2003.

4050 Version of Implementation Guides

The 4050 Version of the Implementation Guides is a newer version of the 4010 Implementation Guides. The final Transaction Rule did not adopt the 4050 Version of the Implementation Guides as DHS felt that adopting a new version of the guides would unfairly burden those who are completing the testing and implementation of the 4010 Version.

Extent of Standard

The decision on when a standard must be used does not depend on whether the transaction is being sent inside or outside corporate boundaries. A simple two-part test, in question form, can be used to determine whether the standards are required.

- ◆ **Question 1.** Is the transaction initiated by a covered entity or its business associate? If no, the standard need not be used.

- ◆ **Question 2.** Is the transaction one for which the Secretary had adopted a standard? If yes, the standard must be used. If no, the standard need not be used.

For purposes of Question 1, a business associate acting on behalf of a covered entity can only perform those particular functions that the covered entity itself could perform in the transaction. The regulation requires health plans to accept standard transactions from any person.

For purposes of Question 2, the definitions of the transactions themselves, as stipulated in Subpart K through Subpart R of the regulation, must be used to determine if the function is a transaction for which the Secretary has adopted a standard. If the data exchange does not meet the definition of the transaction, then the answer to Question 2 is "no."

For example, a large employer with operations in many states has created its own health plan. The health plan has outsourced claim processing to several insurers who act as Third Party Administrators (TPAs). The employer's health plan also uses a data services company to hold and maintain eligibility information. Each of the insurance companies sends eligibility inquiries to the data services company to verify eligibility before processing a claim.

Are these eligibility inquiries required to use the standard transaction format? The insurance companies are not covered entities in this contractual relationship because they are functioning as TPAs, which are not covered entities. However, as TPAs they are business associates of a covered entity (the employer's health plan). Question 1 would be answered "yes."

The definition of the eligibility transaction is an inquiry from a provider to a health plan, or from one health plan to another health plan, to determine eligibility, coverage, or benefits. In the example, the TPAs are not acting as providers because they are trying to pay claims. The inquiry is from one business associate of the health plan to another business associate of the same health plan. Therefore the inquiry doesn't meet the definition of the eligibility transaction and it does not have to use the standard.

Impact of Internet

Internet transactions are being treated the same as other electronic transactions. However, it is recognized that there are certain transmission modes in which the format portion of the standard is inappropriate. In these cases, the transaction must conform to the data content portion of the standard.

In particular, a direct data entry process, where the data are directly keyed by a health care provider into a health plan's computer using dumb terminals or computer browser screens, would not have to use the format portion of the standard, but the data content must conform. If the data are directly entered into a system that is outside the health plan's system, to be transmitted later to the health plan, the transaction must be sent using the format and content of the standard.

Impact on State Medicaid Programs

Title XIX, Section 1171(5)(E) of the Social Security Act, as enacted by HIPAA, identifies the State Medicaid programs as health plans, which therefore must be capable of receiving, processing, and sending standard transactions electronically. There is no requirement that internal information systems maintain data in accordance with the standards. However, Medicaid programs need the capacity to process standard claim, encounter, enrollment, eligibility, remittance advice, and other transactions. In addition, as health plans, the state Medicaid programs will be required to comply with other HIPAA standards two years after adoption of the standards.[1]

The standards should benefit Medicaid programs in multiple areas. Here are a few examples:

- ◆ A national standard for encounter transactions will provide a much-needed method for collecting encounter data on Medicaid beneficiaries enrolled in managed care. Because of the standards, it will be possible to combine encounter data from managed care with similar claims data from fee-for-service, thus enhancing the ability to monitor utilization, costs, and quality of care in managed care and to compare managed care with fee-for-service.

- ◆ The standard transactions will include methods for electronic exchange of enrollment information between the Medicaid program and private managed care plans enrolling Medicaid beneficiaries. This will reduce administrative costs of exchanging such information and enhance the reliability of such information.

- ◆ The conversion to national standards provides an opportunity for Medicaid programs to shift to commercial software or clearinghouses and to stop the expensive maintenance of old, customized transaction systems.

Penalties

The law gives the Secretary of HHS the authority to impose monetary penalties for failure to comply with a standard. The Secretary of HHS is required by statute to impose penalties of not more than $100 per violation on any person or entity who fails to comply with a standard except that the total amount imposed on any one person in each calendar year may not exceed $25,000 for violations of one requirement.

Changes to Standard Claim

Currently, some insurers accept the de facto claim standard, the electronic version of the UB-92 claim form, but also require additional records (for instance, a proprietary cover sheet) for each claim submitted. Others have special requirements for data entered into the claim, which make it a standard that has many variations in content. There have been many other standard claim files promoted by claims clearinghouses as well. These file formats have had similar problems.

Under the law, any electronic claim transaction must conform to the published HIPAA standard transaction format. The electronic UB-92 will no longer be allowed for claim processing; neither will any of the other claim file formats. However, a clearinghouse that accepts a HIPAA-compliant transaction can translate it into any electronic format for transmission to a health plan. Therefore, many of these older formats are expected to continue to have a business purpose.

Health plans are required to accept the HIPAA standard claim submitted electronically. They may **not** require providers to make changes or additions to the standard claim. They must go through the private sector standards setting process to get their requirements added to the standard in order to effect desired changes. Health plans cannot refuse the standard transaction or delay payment of a proper standard transaction.

Paper versions of the UB-92 can be filed by providers who do not use electronic transactions. HIPAA does not force paper forms to use its standard code sets.

An additional standard has been adopted for electronic health claims attachments, which health plans will also be required to accept.

Enhancement to Standards

Electronic transactions must go through two levels of scrutiny:

- ◆ **Compliance with the HIPAA standard.** The requirements for compliance must be completely described in the HIPAA implementation guides and may not be modified by the health plans or by the health care providers using the particular transaction. Implementation guides are available from the Washington Publishing Company (WPC) at http://www.wpc-edi.com/hipaa/HIPAA_40.asp.

- ◆ **Specific processing or adjudication by the particular system reading or writing the standard transaction.** Specific processing systems vary from health plan to health plan, and additional information regarding the processing or adjudication policies of a particular health plan may be helpful to providers.

Additional information can be provided; however, such additional information cannot be used to modify the standard and **cannot** include

◆ Instructions to modify the definition, condition, or use of a data element or segment in the HIPAA standard implementation guide.

◆ Requests for data elements or segments that are not stipulated in the HIPAA standard implementation guide.

◆ Requests for codes or data values that are not valid based on the HIPAA standard implementation guide. Such codes or values could be invalid because they are marked not used in the implementation guide or because they are simply not mentioned in the guide.

◆ Changes to the meaning or intent of a HIPAA standard implementation guide.

Health Plan Documents

The health plan must read and write HIPAA standard transactions exactly as they are described in the standard implementation guides. The only exception would be if the guide explicitly gives discretion regarding a data element to a health plan. For claims and most other transactions, the receiver must accept and process any transaction that meets the national standard. This is necessary because multiple health plans may be scheduled to receive a given transaction (for instance, a single claim may be processed by multiple health plans).

◆ **Example 1.** Medicare currently instructs providers to bill for certain services only under certain circumstances. Once HIPAA standard transactions are implemented, Medicare will have to forego that policy and process all claims that meet HIPAA specifications. This does not mean that Medicare, or any other health plan, has to change payment policy. Today, Medicare would refuse to accept and process a bill for a face-lift for cosmetic purposes only. Once the HIPAA standards are implemented, Medicare will be required to accept and process the bill, but still will not pay for a face-lift that is purely for cosmetic purposes.

◆ **Example 2.** In the past, some large insurers had claim systems that could only accept the numeric disease codes from ICD-9-CM Volumes 1 and 2. Yet these volumes have codes for external causes that start with an E, vaccination codes that start with V, and morphology codes that start with an M. If one of these non-numeric codes was used, the claim would be rejected. The provider had to find a "best match" from the disease codes and recode the diagnosis if they wanted to be paid. Once the HIPAA standards are implemented these insurers have to accept all valid diagnostic codes.

HIPAA Administrative Simplification Compliance Act (ASCA)

The HIPAA Administrative Simplification Compliance Act (ASCA) is what enabled a number of covered entities to get a one year extension for compliance with the Transactions Rule. All entities that completed and submitted this form, automatically received a one year extension from October 16, 2002 to October 16, 2003.

In this section we review the information that covered entities reviewed to complete the extension form. If you are a covered entity and will not be compliant with the HIPAA Electronic Health Care Transactions and Code Sets standards by October 16, 2002, you must file a compliance plan.

If you are a member of a group practice, the extension will be granted to all physicians/practitioners who are members of that practice. It is not necessary to file separate compliance plans for each physician in the practice if the practice files all claims on your behalf. However, if you submit claims for payment outside of the group's claims processing system, you need to file your own compliance plan.

You do not have to file a compliance plan if you will be compliant by October 16, 2002, but one or more of your trading partners is not yet HIPAA compliant. But remember that you/your organization must be HIPAA compliant by this date (or by October 16, 2003 if you are filing a compliance plan) for all transactions that apply to you.

Compliance plans must be submitted electronically no later than October 15, 2002. Paper submissions should be postmarked no later than October 15, 2002. Providers who file electronic and paper submissions received electronically or postmarked after this date will not receive an extension.

The one year extension of the Final Electronic Transactions and Code Sets required by HIPAA to October 16, 2003 gives covered entities more time to build, test, and successfully implement the new Final Electronic Transactions and

Code Sets required by HIPAA. The compliance date for the privacy standards is still April 14, 2003 or, for small health plans, April 14, 2004. The compliance date for small plans does not change.

Covered entities must submit a compliance extension plan to the Department of Health and Human Services (HHS) before October 16, 2002 to get an extension. The requirement to submit a compliance extension plan provides assurance that covered entities have plans in place that will allow them to be compliant by the new deadline of October 16, 2003. Submission of a properly completed extension plan is sufficient to secure the one-year extension. The model compliance extension form is available on the Web site of the Centers for Medicare and Medicaid Services at http://cms.hhs.gov.

The compliance extension form developed is a model and is strongly recommended as the form to be used; covered entities may submit plans using other formats. The ASCA requires the plans to contain summary information regarding compliance activities, including:

◆ Budget, schedule, work plan, and implementation strategy for achieving compliance

◆ Planned use of contractors or vendors

◆ Assessment of compliance problems

◆ A time frame for testing to begin no later than April 16, 2003

The compliance extension form asks only for summary information from your detailed plan. You do not need to send other information. Covered entities must have submitted their compliance extension plans on or before October 15, 2002.

Each covered entity should communicate directly with its own trading partners to determine which ones have submitted plans. This information could be included in establishing schedules for the testing activities that are to begin by April 16, 2003, culminating in a migration to the new standards that meet the needs of all trading partners.

A covered entity is not required to conduct compliant transactions with covered entities who are not yet required to be in compliance and therefore would not need to submit a compliance extension plan. Neither HIPAA nor ASCA preclude plans from requiring that their providers use standard transactions in advance of the compliance deadline, but HIPAA non-compliance penalties do not apply to a provider that has submitted a plan until 2003.

ASCA requires that a sample of the plans be provided to the National Committee on Vital and Health Statistics (NCVHS), an advisory committee to the Secretary of Health and Human Services. The NCVHS will review the sample to identify common problems that are complicating compliance activities, and will periodically publish recommendations for solving the problems.

Under the Freedom of Information Act (FOIA), information held by the federal government is available to the public on request, unless it falls within one of several exemptions. The model form will be designed to avoid collection of any information that would be subject to exemption, such as confidential personal or proprietary information. If such information is submitted, both the FOIA and the ASCA require that it be redacted before the files are released either to the NCVHS or to the public.

Note that Medicare will continue to implement the HIPAA transaction standards on a sequenced basis, and that schedule is not expected to change significantly. It is expected that claims and several other transactions will be ready for testing by Spring 2002, but implementation of several transactions (such as the referral/authorization transaction) will be in early 2003. Once a provider has successfully tested a transaction with Medicare systems, it will be able to use the standard in their production environment.

Each Medicaid State Agency has its own project plan for achieving HIPAA compliance, and will decide whether to submit a compliance extension plan. If you are a trading partner, you will receive notice of testing directly from the Medicaid State Agency(s) with whom you do business.

Only covered entities—plans, clearinghouses, and providers—must file. In fact, vendors need to maintain their current delivery schedules for compliant software for covered entities to make use of the additional implementation time. ASCA requires that compliance plans include a testing phase that would begin no later than April 16, 2003. We strongly recommend that all covered entities begin to test as soon as they are ready to allow adequate time to address and correct problems.

ASCA prohibits HHS from paying Medicare claims that are not submitted electronically after October 16, 2003, unless the Secretary of HHS grants a waiver from this requirement. It further provides that the Secretary of HHS must grant such a waiver if there is no method available for the submission of claims in electronic form or if the entity submitting the claim is a small provider of services or supplies. Beneficiaries will also be able to continue to file paper claims if they need to file a claim on their own behalf. The Secretary of HHS also can grant such a waiver in other circumstances.

Electronic Health Care Transactions and Code Sets Model Compliance Plan

Information in this section is a copy of the Model Compliance Plan that was available from the Department of Health and Human Services.

In 1996, the Health Insurance Portability and Accountability Act (HIPAA) became law. It requires, among other things, that the Department of Health and Human Services establish national standards for electronic health care transactions and code sets. October 16, 2002 was the original deadline for covered entities to comply with these new national standards.

However, in December 2001, the Administrative Simplification Compliance Act (ASCA) extended the deadline for compliance with HIPAA Electronic Health Care Transactions and Code Sets standards (codified at 45 C.F.R. Parts 160, 162) one year—to October 16, 2003—for all *covered entities* other than *small health plans* (which have a compliance deadline of October 16, 2003). To qualify for this extension, *covered entities* must submit a compliance plan by October 15, 2002. Completion and timely submission of this model compliance plan will satisfy this federal requirement, and assist in identifying and addressing impediments to your timely and effective implementation of the HIPAA Electronic Health Care Transactions and Code Sets standards.

If you are a *covered entity* other than a *small health plan* and do not submit a compliance plan, you must be compliant with the HIPAA Electronic Health Care Transactions and Code Sets standards by October 16, 2002.

For general information about HIPAA and instructions on how to complete this compliance plan, refer to Centers for Medicare & Medicaid Services (hereafter CMS) Web site, www.cms.hhs.gov/hipaa. You can go to the Web site and submit this online compliance plan electronically, and CMS will provide an online confirmation number as acknowledgment of your extension. This online compliance plan is a model only and is provided for your information. *Covered entities* have the option of submitting their own version of a compliance plan that provides equivalent information. Refer to the instructions on the CMS Web site for information about how to file alternative submissions.

For those filing electronically, your electronic confirmation number will be the only notice that you have received an extension. No other notice will be provided for electronic or paper submissions. If your paper plan consists of the equivalent information required by the statute (covered entity and contact information; reasons for filing for the extension; implementation budget, and the three phases of the implementation strategy) your plan is complete and you may consider your extension granted.

For information on *defined terms* used in this document, refer to 45 C.F.R. 160.103 or 162.103.

Section A: Covered Entity and Contact Information

1. Name of Covered Entity
2. Tax Identification Number
3. Medicare Identification Number(s)
4. Type of *Covered Entity* (check all that apply from these drop-down menus)

    Health Care Clearinghouse

    Health Plan

    Health Care Provider

    > Dentist
    > DME Supplier
    > Home Health Agency
    > Hospice
    > Hospital
    > Nursing Home
    > Pharmacy
    > Physician/Group Practice
    > Other

5. Authorized Person
6. Title
7. Street
8. City State Zip
9. Telephone Number

Section B: Reason for Filing for This Extension

10. Please check the box next to the reason(s) that you do not expect to be compliant with the HIPAA Electronic Health Care Transactions and Code Sets standards (45 C.F.R. Parts 160,162) by October 16, 2002. Multiple boxes may be checked.

- ❏ Need more money
- ❏ Need more staff
- ❏ Need to buy hardware
- ❏ Need more information about the standards
- ❏ Waiting for vendor(s) to provide software
- ❏ Need more time to complete implementation
- ❏ Waiting for clearinghouse/billing service to update my system
- ❏ Need more time for testing
- ❏ Problems implementing code set changes
- ❏ Problems completing additional data requirements
- ❏ Need additional clarification on standards
- ❏ Other

Section C: Implementation Budget

This question relates to the general financial impact of the HIPAA Electronic Health Care Transactions and Code Sets standards (45 C.F.R. Parts 160,162) on your organization.

11. Select from the drop-down menu the range of your estimated cost of compliance with the HIPAA Electronic Health Care Transactions and Code Sets standards (45 C.F.R. Parts 160,162):

Less than $10,000

$10,000–$100,000

$100,000–$500,000

$500,000–$1 million

Over $1 million

Don't know

Section D: Implementation Strategy

This Implementation Strategy section encompasses HIPAA Awareness, Operational Assessment, and Development and Testing. For more details on completing each of these subsections, refer to the model compliance plan instructions at www.cms.hhs.gov/hipaa.

Implementation Strategy Phase One—HIPAA Awareness

These questions relate to your general understanding of the HIPAA Electronic Health Care Transactions and Code Sets standards (45 C.F.R. Parts 160,162).

12. Please indicate whether you have completed this Awareness phase of the Implementation Strategy.

     Yes   No

     If yes, skip to (14), and then to Phase Two—Operational Assessment. If no, please answer both (13) and (14). Have you determined a:

13. Projected/Actual Start Date: (select month/year from this drop-down menu)

14. Projected/Actual Completion Date: (select month/year from this drop-down menu)

Implementation Strategy Phase Two— Operational Assessment

These questions relate to HIPAA operational issues and your progress in this area.

15. Please indicate whether you have completed this Operational Assessment phase of the Implementation Strategy.

     Yes   No

     If yes, proceed to (20) and then Phase Three—Development and Testing. If no, please answer all the following questions. Have you:

16. Reviewed current processes against HIPAA Electronic Health Care Transactions and Code Sets standards (45 C.F.R. Parts 160,162) requirements?

     Yes   No   Initiated But Not Completed

17. Identified internal implementation issues and developed a work plan?

       Yes   No   Initiated But Not Completed

18. Do you plan to or might you use a contractor/vendor to help achieve compliance?

       Yes   No   Undecided

19. Projected/Actual Start Date: (select month/year from this drop-down menu)

20. Projected/Actual Completion Date: (select month/year from this drop-down menu)

Implementation Strategy Phase Three—Development and Testing

These questions relate to HIPAA development and testing issues. ASCA legislation requires that testing begin no later than April 16, 2003. For more details, refer to the model compliance plan instructions at www.cms.hhs.gov/hipaa.

21. Please indicate whether you have completed this Development and Testing phase of the Implementation Strategy.

       Yes   No

If yes, proceed to (26). If no, please answer all the following questions. Have you:

22. Completed software development/installation?

       Yes   No   Initiated But Not Completed

23. Completed staff training?

       Yes   No   Initiated But Not Completed

24. Projected/Actual Development Start Date: (select month/year from this drop-down menu)

25. Projected/Actual Initial Internal Software Testing Start Date: (select month/year from this drop-down menu)

26. Projected/Actual Testing Completion Date: (select month/year from this drop-down menu)

CLICK HERE TO SUBMIT ELECTRONICALLY
CLICK HERE TO CLEAR PLAN

For Paper Submissions

Please mail paper versions of this model compliance plan to:

Attention: Model Compliance Plans
Centers for Medicare & Medicaid Services
P.O. Box 8040
Baltimore, MD 21244-8040

CMS will not provide an acknowledgment of receipt of paper submissions of this model compliance plan. For proof of delivery, we suggest that you use the U.S. Postal Service.

Model Compliance Plan Instructions: Overview

In 1996, the Health Insurance Portability and Accountability Act (HIPAA) became law. It requires, among other things, that the Department of Health and Human Services establish national standards for electronic health care transactions and code sets. October 16, 2002 was the original deadline for *covered entities* to comply with these new national standards. However, in December 2001, the Administrative Simplification Compliance Act (ASCA) extended the deadline for compliance with HIPAA Electronic Health Care Transactions and Code Sets standards (codified at 45 C.F.R. Parts 160,162) one year—to October 16, 2003—for all *covered entities* other than *small health plans* (which already had a compliance deadline is of October 16, 2003).

To qualify for this extension, *covered entities* must submit a compliance plan by October 15, 2002. Completion and timely submission of this model compliance plan will satisfy this federal requirement, and assist us in identifying and addressing impediments to your timely and effective implementation of the HIPAA Electronic Health Care Transactions and Code Sets standards. If you are a *covered entity* other than a *small health plan* and do not submit a compliance plan, you must be compliant with the HIPAA Electronic Health Care Transactions and Code Sets standards by October 16, 2002.

You can submit this online model compliance plan electronically, and we will provide an online confirmation number as acknowledgment of your extension. This online compliance plan is a model only, and is provided for your information. *Covered entities* have the option of submitting their own version of a compliance plan that provides equivalent information. Refer to the "Alternative Submissions" section of these instructions for more information.

For those filing electronically, your electronic confirmation number will be the only notice that you have received an extension. No other notice will be provided for electronic or paper submissions. If your paper plan consists of the equivalent information required by the statute (*covered entity* and contact information; reasons for filing for the extension; implementation budget; and the three phases of the implementation strategy) your plan is complete and you may consider your extension granted.

Completing this model compliance plan takes about 15–20 minutes. Simply answer a few questions about compliance concerns you may have, and tell us where you are in the implementation process. The Centers for Medicare & Medicaid Services (CMS) will share information obtained from submitted compliance plans with the National Committee on Vital and Health Statistics (NCVHS) as required by the Administrative Simplification Compliance Act.

The NCVHS serves as the statutory public advisory body to the Secretary of Health and Human Services in the area of health data and statistics. The NCVHS will use this information to identify barriers to compliance. All information shared with the NCVHS will have identifying information deleted.

For information on *defined terms* used in this document, refer to 45 C.F.R. 160.103 or 162.103.

Who Should File

If you are a *covered entity* and will not be compliant with the HIPAA Electronic Health Care Transactions and Code Sets standards by October 16, 2002, you must file a compliance plan to obtain an extension.

A *covered entity* is a *health plan, a health care clearinghouse, or a health care provider* who transmits any health information in electronic form in connection with a transaction for which the Secretary has adopted standards at 45 C.F.R. Part 162. These terms are defined at 45 C.F.R. 160.103. The term *health care provider* includes individual physicians, physician group practices, dentists, other health care practitioners, hospitals, nursing facilities, and so on.

If you are a member of a group practice, the extension will be granted to all physicians/practitioners who are members of that practice. It is not necessary to file separate compliance plans for each physician in the practice if the practice files all claims on your behalf.

However, if you submit claims for payment outside of the group's claims processing system, you need to file your own compliance plan. You do not have to file a compliance plan if you will be compliant by October 16, 2002 but one or more of your trading partners is not yet HIPAA compliant. But remember that you/your organization must be HIPAA compliant by this date (or by October 16, 2003 if you are filing a compliance plan) for all transactions that apply to you.

When to File

Compliance plans must be submitted electronically no later than October 15, 2002. Paper submissions should be postmarked no later than October 15, 2002. Compliance plans filed electronically and paper submissions received or postmarked after this date will not qualify for the extension.

How to File

Electronic submission is the fastest, easiest way to file your compliance plan. Just complete the model compliance plan online, click "Submit" at the end, and it will be on its way to us electronically. For those filing electronically, your electronic confirmation number will be the only notice that you have received an extension. No other notice will be provided for electronic or paper submissions.

If your paper plan consists of the equivalent information required by the statute (*covered entity* and contact information; reasons for filing for the extension; implementation budget; and the three phases of the implementation strategy) your plan is complete and you may consider your extension granted.

Please do NOT electronically submit AND mail paper copies of this model compliance plan. One submission per *covered entity*, either electronically OR paper, will suffice.

Alternative Submissions

Covered entities that use the model compliance plan provided on our Web site, www.cms.hhs.gov/hipaa, can file electronically. If you cannot submit your compliance plan electronically via our Web site, or you want to submit your own version of a compliance plan that provides equivalent information, it must be printed and mailed to us. Please send paper submissions of your compliance plan postmarked no later than October 15, 2002 to:

> Attention: Model Compliance Plans
> Centers for Medicare & Medicaid Services
> P.O. Box 8040
> Baltimore, MD 21244-8040

CMS will not acknowledge receipt of paper submissions. For proof of delivery, we suggest you use the U.S. Postal Service.

Section A: Covered Entity and Contact Information

(1) Name of *Covered Entity*. Please enter the name of the *covered entity* for which you are filing this compliance plan. See "Who Must File " above for more information. If you are filing for multiple related *covered entities* that are operating under a single implementation plan, list their names, tax identification numbers, and Medicare identification numbers.

Compliance plans for unrelated multiple *covered entities* or for related *covered entities* that are not included under the same implementation plan must be filed separately. Are you filing for a health plan, health care clearinghouse, or other health care organization that has multiple components? If they are operating under the same implementation plan, then you can file one compliance plan on their behalf. If not, then you must file separate compliance plans for each entity. See also (5) "Authorized Person" for more information.

(2) Tax Identification Number. Enter each *covered entity's* IRS Employer Identification Number (EIN). If there is no EIN, enter the *covered entity's* Social Security Number. While an EIN or Social Security Number is not required, this information facilitates ensuring that the correct *covered entity* obtains the extension.

(3) Medicare Identification Number. Please enter the identification number that applies to each *covered entity* listed.

- If you are a Medicare physician or physician group, enter your UPIN number.

- If you are a supplier of durable medical equipment, enter your NSC number. If you have multiple locations under one EIN, just report the initial location's number (a 6-digit number followed by 0001).

- If you are an institution, enter your OSCAR number. This is your 6-digit Medicare billing number. If you are not a Medicare provider, you need not enter any identification number in (3).

(4) Type of *Covered Entity*. Tell us which *covered entity* category applies to your organization. Check all boxes that apply.

(5) Authorized Person. Provide the name of a person who is authorized to request the extension and provide the information. This might be the individual physician, business/practice manager, a corporate officer, chief information officer, or other individual who is responsible for certifying that the information provided is accurate and correct. (You may include a title, for example, Dr.) If filing for multiple *covered entities*, this person should be authorized to request the extension for all the listed *covered entities*.

Otherwise, a separate compliance plan must be filed to indicate the authorized person for each respective *covered entity*.

(6) Title. Provide the title for the person shown in (5).

(7) Street. Enter the street mailing address/post office box for the person shown in (5).

(8) City/State/Zip. Enter this information for the person 's address as shown in (5).

(9) Telephone Number: Enter the telephone number (including area code) for the person shown in (5).

Section B: Reason for Filing for This Extension

(10) Please let us know the reason(s) why you will not be in compliance with the HIPAA Electronic Health Care Transactions and Code Sets standards (45 C.F.R. Parts 160,162) by October 16, 2002. Check all boxes that apply. If the reason you will

not be compliant is not shown, check "Other" and briefly specify the reason for non-compliance.

Section C: Implementation Budget

This question asks about the estimated financial impact of HIPAA compliance on your organization. Please respond to (11) by indicating on the drop-down menu which category most closely reflects your estimate of your HIPAA compliance costs. If you're not sure, check "Don't Know."

Section D: Implementation Strategy

This section asks about overall awareness of the HIPAA Transactions and Code Set Standards, Operational Assessment, and Development and Testing. These are collectively referred to as the Implementation Strategy.

Implementation Strategy Phase One—HIPAA Awareness

If you have completed this Awareness phase of the Implementation Strategy, check YES (12) and skip to (14), indicating your completion date for this phase. Then proceed to Phase Two—Operational Assessment. If you answer (12) NO, answer (13) and (14).

To complete this Awareness phase you should

- Obtain information regarding HIPAA Electronic Transactions and Code Sets Standards
- Discuss this information with your vendors
- Conduct preliminary staff education

Tell us when you started or plan to start this activity (13), and when you completed or plan to complete activity for this Awareness phase of the Implementation Strategy (14).

Implementation Strategy Phase Two— Operational Assessment

If you have completed this Operational Assessment phase of the Implementation Strategy, check YES (15) and skip to (20), indicating your completion date for this phase. Then proceed to Phase Three—Development and Testing. If you answer (15) NO, answer all questions (16) through (20).

To complete this Operational Assessment phase you should

- Inventory the HIPAA gaps in your organization
- Identify internal implementation issues and develop a work plan to address them
- Consider and decide whether or not to use a vendor or other contractor to assist you in becoming compliant with the HIPAA Electronic Health Care Transactions and Code Sets standards

Indicate your progress for tasks (16) through (18), and projected/actual start and completion dates for this phase in the boxes provided (19) and (20).

Implementation Strategy Phase Three— Development and Testing

If you have completed this Development and Testing phase, check YES (21) and skip to (26), indicating your completion date. If you answer (21) NO, answer all questions (22) through (26).

To complete this Development and Testing phase, you should

- Finalize development of applicable software and install it
- Complete staff training on how to use the software
- Start and finish all software and systems testing

Show your progress for tasks (22) and (23) for resolving computer software conversion to a HIPAA compliant system and training your staff. Indicate your projected/actual development start dates (24), projected/actual initial internal software testing date (25), and final testing completion date (26).

The model compliance plan is now complete. You may click on "Clear Plan " to delete your entries and revise your information, or "Submit Electronically" to electronically submit this model compliance plan; or print it and follow the instructions for paper submissions in the "How to File " section of these instructions.

ANSI ASC X12 Standard

HIPAA required the Secretary to adopt standards, when possible, that have been developed by private sector standards development organizations (SDOs) accredited by the American National Standards Institute (ANSI). These are not government agencies. All of the transactions adopted by this rule are from such organizations. All are from the Accredited Standards Committee (ASC) X12N except the standards for retail pharmacy transactions, which are from the National Council for Prescription Drug Programs (NCPDP).

An ANSI ASC X12N standard, Version 4010, was chosen for all of the transactions except retail pharmacy transactions. The subcommittees in ANSI ASC X12 perform technical work. The choice for the retail pharmacy transactions was the standard maintained by the NCPDP because it is already in widespread use. The NCPDP Telecommunications Standard Format Version 5.1 and equivalent NCPDP Batch Standard Version 1.0 have been adopted in this rule (health plans will be required to support one of these two NCPDP formats).

X12 specifies an envelope structure for messages where the "envelope" is created by wrapping groups of data elements between a specified type of header and trailer. Figure 2.1 illustrates the concept. The information on the envelope is used in routing messages through electronic networks, as well as through applications.

Data transmission of data is structured according to very strict format rules to ensure the integrity and maintain the efficiency of each interchange. Each business-relevant grouping of data is called a *transaction set*. For instance, a group of benefit inquiries sent from a provider to a payer is considered a transaction set.

Individual transaction sets contain a group of logically related data in units called a *segment*. A transaction set is the smallest meaningful set of data exchanged between trading partners. Any given transaction set must include a transaction set header, one or more data segments in a given order, and a transaction set trailer.

The sequence of the elements within a segment is specified by the relevant ASC X12 standard(s). The sequence of segments in a given transaction set is generally also specified in the relevant ASC X12 standard(s).

Similar to data segment transaction sets, a *functional group* adds relevance to two or more data segments. A functional group is introduced by a group start segment, and a functional group is concluded by a group end segment.

Figure 2.1 establishes the relationship between concepts such as communications envelope, interchange envelope, functional groups, and detail segments.

The largest subcommittee in X12 is the Insurance subcommittee. This committee is referred to as X12N. Their membership is identified at

http://www.x12.org/x12org/subcommittees/

The X12N standard is a framework for structuring and defining various types of information. The X12N standard provides flexibility regarding how application data is represented. Application data can be mapped to one of several different EDI structures. To remove ambiguities with the X12N standard and to ensure successful exchange of information, trading partners adhere to Implementation Guides. The HHS has adopted the Implementation Guides as standards for HIPAA transactions.

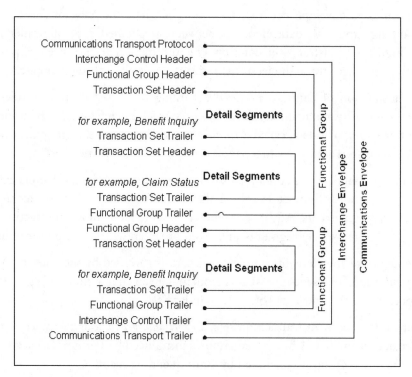

FIGURE 2.1 *Transmission envelope schematic.*

The X12N Implementation Guides specify how to use X12N standards. The Implementation Guides stipulate specific usage of the transaction set segments and data elements.

The implementation guides are available from the WPC at

http://www.wpc-edi.com/hipaa/HIPAA_40.asp

Health Insurance Claim Form (HCFA-1500)

The American Medical Association (AMA) approved the Universal Claim Form called Health Insurance Claim Form or HCFA-1500 in 1975. This claim form is widely used in the health care industry for professional services like doctor office visits. The 837 Health Claim Form—Professional can be used in place of this paper form.

"Standard" Claim Form (UB-92)

The National Uniform Billing Committee (NUBC) approved the UB-92 as a standard form for claims filed by facilities like hospitals. The 837 Health Claim Form—Institutional can be used in place of this paper form.

Loop Iterations and File Sizes

Anyone using the transactions must support any loop iterations as well as file sizes stipulated in the implementation guides. If the file sizes or loops cause difficulties for anyone using the transactions, that party can contact the ANSI committee that supports the transaction. It is the committee's decision as to what will and will not change.

Typical data files are of a fixed format. If the file was a paper with columns for each character, then each row on the paper is a "record." A data field is defined to exist in specific columns in this record.

ANSI transactions are free-form. There is a relative order that tells you which loops precede and follow other loops and segments. Labels are used to identify segments. Fields within the segments exist in a specific sequence, separated by a delimiter character like an asterisk. This organization makes retrieving information more complicated. Many companies use translating and mapping software to retrieve the data and ready it for their internal systems.

An advantage of the ANSI format is that it frequently results in a smaller file than a fixed format file with the same content. If a claim only needs to transmit information for a single doctor office visit, then only the required fields and situational fields pertaining to the visit will have values. With ANSI transactions the general rule is to send a field if a value exists for it.

270—Health Care Eligibility Request

Prior to HIPAA, providers of medical services submitted health care eligibility and benefit inquiries by a variety of methods, either on paper, by phone, or electronically. The information requirements varied depending on

- Type of insurance plan
- Specific insurer's requirements
- Type of service performed
- Where the service is performed
- Where the inquiry is initiated
- Where the inquiry is sent

A provider uses the benefit inquiry transaction to ask about the benefits, deductibles, and co-pays of the patient's health plan and if the patient is on file and currently covered by the plan. The inquiry can ask whether a specific benefit is covered by the plan. The transaction has the capability to inquire if a specific benefit will be covered for the patient on a given day, but the payer is not required to answer in this level of detail. The response is conditional. That is, it is not a guarantee of payment.

This transaction will be used by agents of all lines of insurance (Health, Life, and Property and Casualty) to inquire about the eligibility, coverage, and benefits accorded a prospective subscriber by a health benefit plan. The inquiry is designed so the submitter can determine if a subscriber or dependent is enrolled in a health benefit plan and whether projected services for the subscriber or dependent are covered by the plan.

The Health Care Eligibility Request is designed so that the inquiry submitter (information receiver) can determine

- Whether an information source organization (for example, a payer, employer, or HMO) has a particular subscriber or dependent on file

◆ The health care eligibility and/or benefit information about that subscriber and/or dependent(s)

This transaction is used to inquire about a number of different general and specific eligibility, coverage, and benefit attributes or conditions, for example:

◆ General Requests
  • Eligibility status (for instance, active or not active in the plan)
  • Maximum benefits (policy limits)
  • Exclusions
  • In-plan/out-of-plan benefits
  • C.O.B information
  • Deductible
  • Co-pays
◆ Specific Requests
  • Procedure coverage dates
  • Procedure coverage maximum amount(s) allowed
  • Deductible amount(s)
  • Remaining deductible amount(s)
  • Co-insurance amount(s)
  • Co-pay amount(s)
  • Coverage limitation percentage
  • Patient responsibility amount(s)
  • Non-covered amount(s)

The 270 is designed to be flexible enough to encompass all the information
requirements of various entities. These entities include, but are not limited to

◆ Insurance companies
◆ HMOs
◆ PPOs
◆ Health care purchasers (employers)
◆ Professional Review Organizations (PROs)
◆ Social worker organizations
◆ Health care providers (physicians, hospitals, laboratories)
◆ Third Party Administrators (TPAs)

- Health care vendors (practice management vendors, billing services)
- Service bureaus
- Government agencies such as Medicare, Medicaid, and Civilian Health and Medical Program of the Uniformed Services (CHAMPUS)

Some submitters do not have ready access to all the information needed to generate an inquiry to a payer. An outside lab or pharmacy that furnishes services to a health care provider might need to ask that provider which payer a health care eligibility inquiry or benefit inquiry should be routed to. In this scenario, a 270 might originate from a provider and be sent to another provider if the receiving provider supports the inquiry.

This transaction is more flexible than most X12 transactions, allowing a requestor to enter a very small amount of patient information to identify them to a payer. This approach is not without limitations, and the more information that you provide, the more likely the payer will find a match in their systems. If the patient is the subscriber, the minimum information includes

- Patient's member ID (or the HIPAA Unique Patient Identifier once mandated for use)
- Patient's first name
- Patient's last name
- Patient's date of birth

If the patient is a dependent of a subscriber, the minimum information includes

- Subscriber's member ID (or the HIPAA Unique Patient Identifier once mandated for use)
- Patient's first name
- Patient's last name
- Patient's date of birth

If a provider submits all four of the required elements, the payer source must generate a response if the patient is in their database.

In the absence of the required data elements, for example in an emergency situation or if the patient has forgotten to bring his insurance card, this transaction may be transmitted with as many of the required pieces of data that are available along with any of the other items identified in the transaction (for example a Social Security Number). The payer should attempt to look up the patient when a reasonable number of data elements are submitted.

271—Eligibility, Coverage, or Benefit Information

The eligibility or benefit reply information from the information source organization (payer or employer) is contained in the 271 in an Eligibility or Benefit Information (EB) data segment. The information source can also return other information about eligibility and benefits based on its business agreement with the inquiry submitter and available information that it might be able to provide.

The content of the Eligibility, Coverage, and Benefit Information transaction set varies depending on the level of data the information source organization makes available as well as the type of request (see the "general" and "specific" request types described earlier in this chapter).

To summarize, 271 is the reply vehicle for the 270. When an provider submits an eligibility, coverage, or benefit inquiry, the receiver will

- ◆ Initiate the Eligibility, Coverage, or Benefit Information transaction form explaining the conditions of the health coverage pertaining the principal (subscriber or dependent)
- ◆ Forward the request to the most appropriate next destination(s)

The transaction form is designed to respond to general and specific requests. General requests include information pertinent to eligibility status, policy limits, exclusions, benefits, deductibles, and co-pays. Specific requests relate to issues such as procedure coverage dates, procedure coverage limits, and deductibles for procedures. The details of these requests and replies will, in many cases, involve significant complexity, as intermediaries are used throughout the health care services industry. Review the three different types of transaction flows described in Figures 2.2, 2.3, and 2.4.

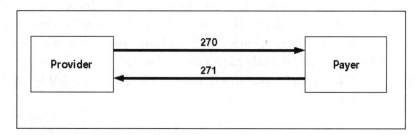

FIGURE 2.2 *270/271—Basic transaction flow.*

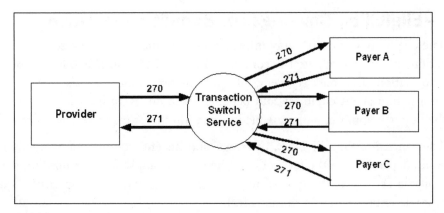

FIGURE 2.3 *270/271—Multiple-payer transaction flow.*

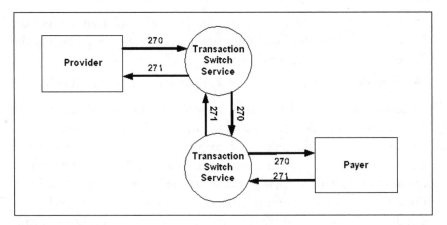

FIGURE 2.4 *270/271—Multiple intermediary transaction flow.*

276—Health Care Claim Status Request

Transaction 276 is used to inquire into the status of a claim. Its response tool is the 277 Health Care Claim Status Response. The form is usually submitted by health care service providing agencies such as hospitals, physicians, dentists, employers, billing agencies, and other agencies with vested interest in the progress of a claim. The 276 cannot be submitted unless it has been preceded by an 837 Health Care Claim.

Thus, the 276 is used to request the current status of a specified claim. The business partners affiliated with the 276 include

- Billing services
- Consulting services
- Vendors of systems
- EDI network intermediaries such as automated clearinghouses, value-added Networks, and telecommunications services

Payers or certain intermediaries involved with processing any given claim need to track the claim's current status through the adjudication process. The purpose of submitting this transaction is to obtain the current status of the claim within the adjudication process. An authorized entity can request status information at the claim and/or line level. A valid health care claim status request includes data necessary for the payer to identify the specific claim in question. The most efficient inquiry includes the "Claim Submitter Trace Number," which uniquely identifies a specific transaction to an application. The transaction trace number is an important key to match the response to a specific request transaction.

Supplying the primary, or unique, identifying element(s) should allow the requestor to obtain an exact match. Conditions, though, are not always ideal; and when the requester does not know the unique element(s), the claim should be located by supplying several parameters, including the provider number, patient identifier, date(s) of service, and submitted charge(s) from the original claim.

The following are sample primary elements:

- Information source (the decision maker in the business transaction; for example, the payer)
- Information receiver (who expects the response from the information source; for example, a provider (*group*), a clearinghouse, a service bureau, an employer, and so on)
- Service provider (who delivered the health care service)
- Subscriber (known by the insurance carrier)
- Requested claim(s) identification

277—Health Care Claim Status Response

The 277 is used in three ways:

- Reply to a 276 Health Care Claim Status Request
- Unsolicited notification of a health care claim status
- Request for additional information about a health care claim

Organizations sending the 277 Health Care Claim Status Response include payers such as

- Insurance companies
- Third Party Administrators (TPAs)
- Service corporations
- State and Federal agencies and their contractors
- Plan purchasers
- Any other entity that processes health care claims

Other business partners affiliated with the 277 include

- Billing services
- Consulting services
- Vendors of payments
- EDI network intermediaries such as automated clearinghouses, value-added networks, and telecommunications services.

A provider uses the claim status inquiry to ask about the status of processing for a particular claim or claims that remain outstanding within its accounts receivable system.

A transaction 277 response might include (but is not limited to)

- Accepted/rejected claim
- Claim pending, incorrect/incomplete claim(s), or suspended claim(s)
- Final: rejected claim(s)
- Final: denied claim(s)
- Final: approved claim(s) pre-payment
- Final: approved claim(s) post-payment

Insurance companies, intermediaries, government agencies and auditors, or billing agents and services usually submit the form. The form is not to be used in place of the 835 Health Care Claim Payment/Advice transaction set and should not be used for posting of account payments. Figure 2.5 illustrates the relationships between transactions 276 and 277 and other communications in a service payment scenario:

NOTE

The "Acknowledgement" is often performed by the ANSI 997 Functional Acknowledgement transaction. This transaction is not a HIPAA standard. However, if commerce and efficiency are best served by using it, trading partners are free to do so. The 997 may not be used for a function otherwise supported by a standard transaction like the 277.

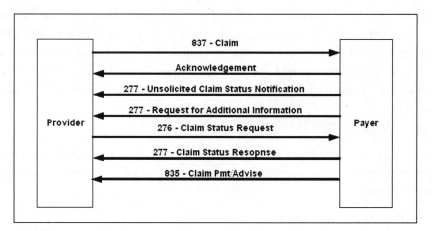

FIGURE 2.5 *276 and 277 within an example claim submission/payment scenario.*

278—Health Care Services Review: Request for Review

The Request for Review and the Response to that Request Transaction Sets cover the following business events:

- Admission certification review request and response
- Referral review request and response
- Health care services certification review request and response
- Extend certification review request and response

Terms used in the services review transactions include

- Long-term care
- Patient event
- Requester
- Service provider
- Utilization Management Organization (UMO)

Review requests are submitted using the 278 Health Care Services Review: "Request for Review." Issues addressed by the 278 differ from those for the 276 in that the Request for Review triggers an audit of a health care encounter and the forms, certifications, and adjudication arising from it. The requester is a provider who seeks authorization or certification for a patient to receive health care services.

Transaction 278 can be used to send unsolicited information to trading partners. This data can take the form of health service review copies, or notification of the beginning or end of treatment. This transaction should be routinely used in the following events:

- Patient arrival notice
- Patient discharge notice
- Certification change notice
- Notification of certification to primary provider(s), other provider(s), and UMOs

Figure 2.6 describes the basic transaction flow for the 278 Request and Response transaction types.

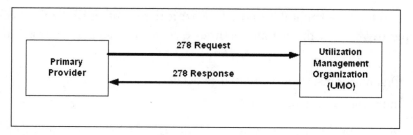

FIGURE 2.6 *278 basic transaction flow.*

The 278 is used to transmit information pertinent to subscriber or patient identification, demographics, treatment/diagnosis, or certification of provided or proposed services in response to a 278 Health Care Services Request for Review.

820—Payment Order/Remittance Advice

Transaction 820 is also known as the transaction supporting "Payroll Deducted and Other Group Premium Payment for Insurance Products." It is used to pay for insurance products (individual and group premiums), to forward remittance advice, or both. Payment is often in the form of a transaction order to a financial institution or directions to a payee's accounts receivable system. It is also used when sending premium payments to an insurance carrier. Electronic Funds Transfer (EFT) transactions are fully supported through submission of the 820.

Transaction 820 is applicable when sending premium payments to an insurance company, health care organization, or government agency. Business functions applicable under HIPAA compliance fall into two categories:

The first is the use of an Electronic Funds Transfer (EFT) with remittance information carried through the Automated Clearinghouse (ACH) system. The choice of which type of detail depends on the contract type. Detail may include

- ◆ Organization summary remittance detail
- ◆ Individual remittance detail

Individual remittance detail may only be sent for those contractors who require individual remittance information to properly apply the premium payments.

The second function applicable under HIPAA is the use of an EFT or a check to make the payment, with separate remittance advice containing information for either:

- Organization summary remittance detail
- Individual remittance detail

The movement of the remittance advice is through the 820 transaction communicated outside of the banking networks, where the choice of which type of detail again depends on contract type.

The 820 transaction can perform multiple functions:

- An 820 can be sent to a bank to move money only.
- An 820 can be sent to a bank to move money as well as detailed or summary remittance information.
- An 820 can be sent directly to a payee to move detailed or summary remittance information.

Each function changes the actual content of the transaction slightly. Figure 2.7 illustrates using transaction 820 to make an Automated Clearing House (ACH) payment and deliver the associated remittance information.

The X12N Payroll Deducted and Other Group Premium Payment for Insurance Products Implementation Guide provides standardized data requirements and content to all users of the ANSI ASC X12 Premium Payment Order/Remittance Advice (820) Transaction Set for the purpose of reporting payroll deducted and other group premiums. For HIPAA, only portions of the complete 820 Implementation Guide are applicable.

To summarize, the Payment and Remittance Advice transaction is frequently used in separate functions. In the payment role, it is a payment order directing a bank to effect payment to a health plan; in this role, the remittance advice is primarily payment reference information to enable the health plan's systems to match up the payment with coverage kept in force. Payments are frequently made in aggregate to cover several subscribers in a group policy. In the electronic remittance advice role, it explains payment and partial payment for each subscriber involved.

The remittance advice is intended to support automatic reconciliation of premiums in a health plan's accounts receivable systems and is one of the most attractive transactions from a health plan's viewpoint.

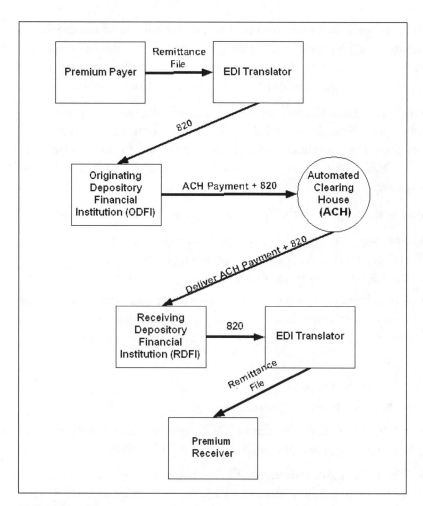

FIGURE 2.7 *820—ACH payment and associated remittance information.*

834—Benefit Enrollment and Maintenance

The 834 is used to transfer enrollment information from a sponsor to a health care insurance or benefit provider. The sponsor is the employer, association, or other agency that ultimately pays for the insurance coverage. The sponsor may also elect to designate a Third Party Administrator (TPA) to submit the information.

Thus, the 834 is to transfer enrollment information from the sponsor of the health care insurance coverage, benefits, or policy to a health plan.

This transaction is used to enroll, update, or dis-enroll employees and dependents in a health plan. The transaction is typically used in two modes: update and full replacement. In update mode, the employer, union, or other sponsor sends transactions to add, change, or terminate subscriber and dependent records.

In the full replacement mode, the sponsor periodically sends a complete file of all subscribers and dependents, and the payer does a comparison and reconciliation with its files. The enrollment transaction is expected to be popular with large accounts. Online screen services may be more popular with small and medium size accounts.

The parties that engage in the enrollment process include the following:

- **Sponsor.** A sponsor is a party that ultimately pays for the coverage, benefit, or product. A sponsor can be an employer, union, insurance agency, association, or government agency.

- **Payer/Insurer.** The payer is the party that claims and/or administers the insurance coverage, benefit, or product. A payer can be one of the following or another organization contracted by these groups.

  - HMO
  - Insurance company
  - Preferred Provider Organization (PPO)
  - Government agency such as Medicare or Civilian Health and Mental Program of the Uniformed Services (CHAMPUS)

- **Third Party Administrator (TPA).** A sponsor can elect to contract with a Third Party Administrator (TPA) or other vendor to handle collecting insured member data if the sponsor chooses not to perform this function.

- **Subscriber.** The subscriber is an individual eligible for coverage because of his or her association with a sponsor. Examples of subscribers include the following:

  - Employees
  - Union members
  - Individuals covered under government programs, such as Medicare and Medicaid

- **Dependent.** A dependent is an individual who is eligible for coverage because of his or her association with a subscriber. Typically, a dependent is a member of the subscriber's family.

◆ **Insured or Member.** An insured individual or member is a subscriber or dependent who has been enrolled for coverage under an insurance plan. Dependents of a subscriber who have not been individually enrolled for coverage are not included in Insured or Member.

These parties interact in a number of ways during the delivery of health care.

Figure 2.8 illustrates the location of transaction 834 in context with some of the other related transactions.

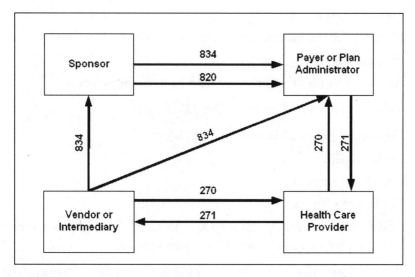

FIGURE 2.8 *834 in the context of health care eligibility and payment.*

835—Health Care Claim Payment/Advice

The 835 is used to send a payment and Explanation Of Benefits (EOB) remittance advice, or both only from a health care insurer to a health care provider. Payment can be issued directly or through a financial institution. As with the 820 transaction, the payment portion of this function may be done with a paper check.

The 835 is used to send and/or receive Electronic Remittance Advice (ERA) and/or payments. Health care providers receiving the 835 include but are not limited to

◆ Hospitals

◆ Nursing homes

- Laboratories
- Physicians
- Dentists
- Allied professional groups

Organizations sending the 835 include

- Insurance companies
- Third-party administrators
- Service corporations
- State and federal agencies and their contractors
- Plan purchasers
- Any other entities that process health care reimbursements

Other business partners affiliated with the 835 include

- Depository Financial Institutions (DFIs)
- Billing services
- Consulting services
- Vendors of systems
- EDI network intermediaries such as automated clearinghouses, value-added networks, and telecommunications services.

Figure 2.9 provides information on the Health Care Claim Payment/Advice Communication Flows.

Depending on the number of entities involved, health care claim payment and advice communications can become relatively complex. Use the following information to interpret Figure 2.9:

- **DFI.** Depository Financial Institution
- **EFT.** Electronic Funds Transfer
- **ERA.** Electronic Remittance Advice
- **FDN.** Funds Deposit Notification
- **Funds.** Actual dollars, check or other
- **Payee.** Actual providers and/or their agents
- **Payer.** Actual payer and any third-party agents

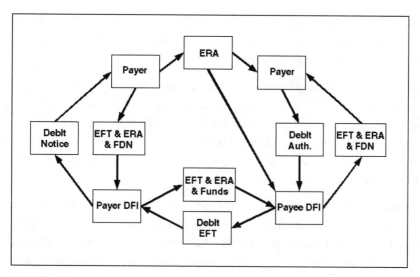

FIGURE 2.9 *835—Health care claim payment/advice communication flows.*

837—Health Care Claim: Professional, Institutional and Dental

The Health Care Claim Transaction (837) is intended to originate with the health care provider or the health care provider's designated agent. It also may originate with payers in an encounter-reporting situation. Transaction 837 provides all necessary information to allow the destination payer to at least begin to adjudicate the claim. All of the following transactions are generated by health care providers and transmitted to payers either directly or through intermediary billing services. Payers are such organizations as insurance companies, HMOs, and Medicare/Medicaid. All of these claims are intended to provide information that will allow the payer to begin to adjudicate the claim.

The *Health Care Claim: Professional* transaction set is used to submit health care encounter and billing information generated by health care providers, such as physicians, surgeons, radiologists, and mental health professionals.

The *Health Care Claim: Dental* originates with a dental health care service provider or designated agent. This transaction set is used to submit dental health care encounter and billing information.

The *Health Care Claim: Institutional* transaction set is used to submit health care encounter and billing information generated by health care facilities such as hospitals, acute care clinics, and so on.

Health care claims for pharmaceuticals use the NCPDP standard. All other claims use the X12 837 format. The 837 format replaces electronic versions of the uniform billing claim (UB-92) and the HCFA 1500. It can carry HMO medical encounter accounting information as well as billing claims. A key consideration for coordination with payer claim systems is a requirement for systems to retain all of the information received on the claim.

Payers must be able to electronically accept a transaction 837 with all the data for a given type of claim. The payer cannot summarily reject such a claim. That does not mean, however, that the payer is required to bring that data into their adjudication system. The payer, acting in accordance with his business partner policies and contractual agreements, can ignore information within the 837 transaction data set. Therefore, it is permissible for trading partners to specify a subset of the transaction 837 data they are able to process or act upon most efficiently.

See Figure 2.5 to see some of the relationship of transaction 837 and other claim-related transactions.

The following terms are relevant under 837 within the context of the X12N documents:

◆ **Dependent.** In the hierarchical loop coding, the dependent code indicates the use of the patient hierarchical loop.

◆ **Destination payer.** The destination payer is the payer who is specified in the subscriber/payer loop.

◆ **Patient.** The term patient is intended to convey the case where the patient loop is used. In that case, the patient is not the same person as the subscriber, and the patient is a person (for example, a spouse, child, or other) who is covered by the subscriber's insurance plan. However, it also happens that the patient is sometimes the same person as the subscriber. In that case, all information about the patient/subscriber is carried in the subscriber loop. Every effort has been made to ensure that the meaning of the word patient is clear in its specific context.

◆ **Provider.** In a generic sense, the provider is the entity that originally submitted the claim/encounter. A provider may also have provided or participated in some aspect of the health care service described in the transaction. Specific types of providers are identified in the transaction set.

- Billing provider
- Performing provider
- Referring provider

◆ **Secondary Payer.** The term secondary payer refers to any payer who is not the primary payer. The secondary payer might be the secondary, tertiary, or even quaternary payer.

◆ **Subscriber.** The subscriber is the person whose name is listed in the health insurance policy. Other synonymous terms include member and insured. In some cases the subscriber is the same person as the patient.

◆ **Transmission Intermediary.** A transmission intermediary is any entity that handles the transaction between the provider (originator of the claim/encounter transmission) and the destination payer. The term *intermediary* is not used to convey a specific Medicare contractor type.

The 837 format also can be used to convey other payer information and amounts paid by the primary payer to assist the coordination of benefits process.

Table 2.1 provides information about HIPAA Regulated Transactions and the corresponding X12 Transaction Set Identifier.

The following standard EDI transactions in this group are generally sent in batches for processing in daily batch processing systems.

First Report of Injury

The First Report of Injury transaction conveys information specific to accidents and other injuries that may or may not be covered under workers' compensation insurance.

Health Claims Attachment

The attachment transaction is a generally defined transaction that offers considerable flexibility for the transmission of information to support claims and other purposes. It is capable of carrying multiple formats, including binary and image data. At present, implementation guides have been written for several types of claims attachments, and additional ones will be added from time to time.

Table 2.1 HIPAA Transactions and Corresponding X12 Transaction Set Identifier

Regulated Transactions	X12 Transaction Set Identifier (X12N Identifier)
Health Care Claims or Equivalent Encounters	837 **Health Care Claim** Institutional (004010X096) Dental (004010X097) Professional (004010X098) **Pharmacy Claim** NCPDP Standard
Payment and Remittance Advice	835 **Health Care Claim** Payment/Advice (004010X091)
Coordination of Benefits	837 **Health Care Claim** Institutional (004010X096) Dental (004010X097) Professional (004010X098) 835 **Health Care Claim** Payment/Advice (004010X091)
Health Care Claim Status	276 & 277 Health Care Claim Status Request and Response (004010X093)
Enrollment or Dis-enrollment in a Health Plan	834 Benefit Enrollment and Maintenance (004010X095)
Health Plan Eligibility	270 & 271 Health Care Eligibility/Benefit Inquiry and Information Response (004010X092)
Health Plan Premium Payments	820 Payroll Deducted and Other Group Premium Payment for Insurance Products (004010X061)

Table 2.1 HIPAA Transactions and Corresponding X12 Transaction Set Identifier *(continued)*

Regulated Transactions	X12 Transaction Set Identifier (X12N Identifier)
Certification and Authorization of Referrals	278 Health Care Services Review—Request for Review and Response (004010X094)
First Report of Injuries	Standard not yet established.
Health Claims Attachments	Standard not yet established. The X12 transaction sets 277 and 275 will become the mandated standard for attachments. (004020X104 & 004020X107) 277 Health Care Claim Request for Additional Information (004010X104) 275 Health Care Claim Response to Request for Additional Information (004020X107)

In response mode, the provider returns attachment transaction in response to a 277 request for information. In unsolicited mode, the sender typically includes this transaction as an attachment to a claim.

Health Care Referral Certification and Authorization

This transaction is used to transmit referral information between providers and between provider and payer. It also is used for pre-certification, concurrent review, and other utilization management information. Note that referral from provider to provider is one of the most attractive transactions for providers.

Fast Response EDI Transactions

Fast response is the term used to include interactive, real-time, or batch-of-one EDI transactions to which the payer would respond quickly. The term refers to the speed of processing and response rather than the structure of the transaction.

HIPPA does not specify response times, and it is frequently inferred that all transactions could be processed in batch operations overnight, for example. However, fast response is necessary for some transactions to give good service to providers and for effective utilization management.

Initially, there are three fast response transactions that have been defined:

- ◆ Health Care Eligibility Inquiry and Response
- ◆ Health Care Claim Status Inquiry and Response
- ◆ Health Care Referral Certification and Authorization

Code Sets

Transactions contain both code sets and identifiers. Code sets are mandated by HIPAA to be standardized and certain fields in transactions must be completed only with values from code sets. Just as individuals within the United States have been assigned a unique Social Security Number, similarly every health care provider is assigned a unique national health care number, called an *identifier*, under HIPAA.

A code set is any set of codes used for encoding data elements. A number of different code sets have been adopted under HIPAA. The primary purpose of the code sets is to standardize the identification of those things for which health care providers submit claims for reimbursement. This includes

- ◆ Medical diagnosis codes
- ◆ Medical procedure codes
- ◆ Medical concepts
- ◆ Medical supplies

Code sets make it possible for people and organizations located throughout the world to identify or describe things in a standardized way. Their purpose is to eliminate subjectivity and ensure uniformity.

The code sets that have been adopted under HIPAA are

- ◆ International Classification of Diseases, Clinical Modification (ICD-9-CM) Volumes 1 and 2
- ◆ Current Procedural Terminology, fourth Revision (CPT-4)

◆ Code on Dental Procedures and Nomenclature (CDT)

◆ ICD-9-CM, Volume 3

◆ National Drug Code (NDC)

◆ Health Care Common Procedure Coding System (HCPCS)

The transaction standards specify the coding that must be used for a broad range of data elements.

Timeline

On August 17, 2000, HHS published the final rule on transaction standards and code sets. The effective date specified in the final Transaction Rule was October 16, 2001. On December 4, 2001 the House passed the bill, "Administrative Simplification Compliance Act" (HR 3323) delaying implementation until October 16, 2003.

ICD-9-CM Volumes 1 and 2

The International Classification of Diseases, ninth Revision, Clinical Modification, is the code set that must be used to describe or identify codes for the following conditions:

◆ Diseases

◆ Injuries

◆ Impairments

◆ Other health-related problems and their manifestations

The U.S. Department of Health and Human Services is responsible for updating the ICD-9-CM and ICD-10 code sets.

CPT-4

The Current Procedural Terminology, fourth Revision, is the code set that must be used to describe or identify physician services or procedures.

The American Medical Association (AMA) is responsible for updating the CPT code set. The AMA owns the CPT code set and makes printed manuals available, and offers licenses to organizations that need electronic access to the code set.

Codes include those services such as

♦ Physician services

♦ Physical and occupational therapy services

♦ Radiological procedures

♦ Clinical laboratory tests

♦ Medical diagnostic procedures

♦ Hearing and vision services

CDT

The Code on Dental Procedures and Nomenclature is the code set that must be used to describe or identify dentist services or procedures.

The American Dental Association (ADA) is responsible for updating the CDT code set. The ADA owns the CDT code set. It provides printed manuals describing the coding system and offers licenses to organizations that need electronic access to their code sets.

ICD-9-CM, Volume 3

The ICD-9-CM, Volume 3, is the code set that must be used to describe/identify inpatient hospital services and surgical procedures.

NDC

The National Drug Code (NDC) is the code set that must be used to identify drugs in HIPAA transactions.

The HHS Food and Drug Administration (FDA) is responsible for updating the NDC code set. HHS works with drug manufacturers for drugs and biologics.

HCPCS

The Health Care Common Procedure Coding System (Level II of HCPCS) is the code set that must be used to identify or describe health-related services that are not physician services, dentist services, or hospital surgical procedures.

NOTE

HCPCS was defined by HCFA to be a superset of codes. HCPCS Level I codes are defined to be CPT-4 codes to represent existing medical professional services. Level II codes were additional procedures and supplies not defined by Level I. HCPCS Level III codes are locally defined to allow for variations in health care practices. Level III codes are being eliminated by the standard (explanation follows in "Local Codes").

The Center for Medicare and Medicaid Services (CMS) is responsible for updating the HCPCS Level II code set. Codes include those services such as

◆ Medical and surgical supplies

◆ Certain drugs

◆ Certain durable medical equipment (DME)

◆ Orthotic and prosthetic devices

◆ Procedures and services performed by non-physicians

The combination of CPT-4 and HCPCS is considered the standard code set for physician services and other health care services.

The final Transactions Rule published on February 20, 2003 stated that both the NDC and HCPCS remain two of the most prevalent and useful code sets for reporting drugs and biologics in non-retail pharmacy transactions. The benefits of each code set complements the other's advantages very well. The final Rule repealed the adoption of the NDC for institutional and professional claims, while allowing the NDC to remain the standard medical data code set for reporting drugs and biologics for retail pharmacy claims. The choice of code sets must be governed by trading partner agreements. The intent of this decision was to give covered entities the full range of choices in determining which code set to use with respect to claims, including the HCPCS and NDC codes that have been adopted as standards for other uses. Covered entities that use HCPCS should utilize the established process for requesting new codes, rather than supplementing the code sets with locally developed codes.

The result of this repeal is that there is no identified standard medical data code set in place for reporting drugs and biologics on non-retail pharmacy transactions. The absence of a code set would not preclude the use of NDC for reporting drugs and biologics by covered entities on standard transactions. Covered entities could continue to report drugs and biologics as they prefer and agree upon with their trading partners.

The NCVHS believes that no drug coding system in existence today meets all the needs of the health care industry. A future coding system that could be used effectively and efficiently for drug inventory, pharmacy transactions, patient care, billing arenas, and ensuring patient safety would be the best answer to this problem.

Health Plans

HIPAA requires health plans to be able to accept every valid code contained in the approved medical code set.

Local Codes

The use of local codes is not allowed under the HIPAA code-set standard. Only those standards that are a part of the national standard code sets can be used in a HIPAA transaction.

HIPAA has established a centralized process that results in a single set of temporary codes that will be used until permanent codes are incorporated into the relevant code sets.

The elimination of local codes requires revisions to HCPCS, the coding system developed by CMS for coding Medicare claims. The process for revising HCPCS flows as follows:

- ◆ CMS will establish procedures for reviewing and approving—or disapproving—requests by public or private health plans for temporary codes to replace the local codes (HCPCS Level III).
- ◆ CMS will centrally administer the procedures for establishing temporary codes and will make additions to HCPCS electronically available to all health plans and providers.
- ◆ HHS anticipates that the loss of local codes will create some situations where no specific code applies. In these situations the Not Otherwise Specified (NOS) code should be used. The NOS code also should be used when new procedures occur until the code set has been updated.

All temporary codes will be reviewed on an annual basis to prevent duplication of established codes; for example, CPT codes for physician services.

Date of Service

The version of a clinical code set that must be used for a transaction is determined by the date the service was provided. It is not based on the date on which the claim is submitted or the transaction is initiated.

Codes and Data Values

The simplest implementation is the one that is identical to all others. If the standard adopted stipulates that Health Care Procedure Coding System (HCPCS) codes will be used to describe procedures, then the health plan must abide by the instructions for the use of HCPCS codes. A health plan could refuse a code that was not applied in accordance with the HIPAA national standard coding instructions, but could not refuse a code properly applied for reasons of policy unrelated to the standard.

For example, if the standard stipulates that the most specific code available must be used, then a health plan would be right to refuse a code that does not meet that criterion. The health plan would need to work with the committee(s) governing the particular coding scheme to have codes adopted that meet its needs.

National Health Care Identifiers

There are different types of national health care identifiers. The National Health Care Identifiers include

- ◆ National Provider Identifier (NPI)
- ◆ National Health Plan Identifier (PlanID)
- ◆ National Employer Identifier for Health Care
- ◆ National Health Identifier for Individuals

The identifiers can be alphanumeric—they are not just numbers, but a combination of letters and as well as numbers. It is possible that individuals and organizations might have several identifiers.

For example, a physician will have the following identifiers:

- ◆ A provider identifier
- ◆ An employer identifier

A Health Maintenance Organization (HMO) will have the following identifiers:

- A provider identifier
- An employer identifier
- A health plan identifier

Motivation

Identifiers are used extensively in all transactions between any combination of individuals, employers, health care providers, and health plans. For example, every billing transaction requires

- The identifier of the provider submitting the claim
- The individual who received the care
- The health plan to which the claim is sent for payment

Further, any other health plan that may have previously adjudicated any part of the claim must also be identified.

Similarly, transactions between health plans and employers that involve enrollment or premium payments must identify the health plan, the enrollee, and the employer.

Thus, when contacting health plans to request coverage or claims-submission information, providers will be required to obtain the patient's unique identifier. The provider will also identify itself to the health plan using its own unique identifier.

National Provider Identifier (NPI)

Typically, government and private health plans have assigned identification numbers to providers of health care services and suppliers. These health plans, independently of each other, assign identifiers to providers for program management and operations purposes. The identifiers are not standardized within a single health plan or across plans. This lack of uniformity results in health care providers having different numbers for the same program and often multiple billing numbers issued within the same program, significantly complicating provider's claims submission process.

Most health plans have coordination of benefits with other health plans to ensure appropriate payment. The lack of a single and unique identifier for each health care provider within and across health plans makes the exchanging of data expensive and difficult. The use of a standard, unique provider identifier would improve accuracy and assist in overcoming communication and coordination difficulties. All of these factors indicate the complexities of exchanging information among health care providers.

As organizations become more dependent on data automation and electronic commerce and proceed in planning for health care delivery, the need for a universal, standard health care provider identifier becomes more and more evident. Considerable effort and research has gone into developing the standard for the provider number. Participants in this effort came from the government and private sector. It is expected that the identifier is a 10-digit numeric identifier and is required on all standard electronic health care transactions that require provider identification.

The National Provider Identifier (NPI) will be assigned to

- ◆ Individual providers
- ◆ Organizational providers

Individual

An NPI for an individual is a personal identifier. An individual can obtain only one NPI and retains it for life. This specific identifier has received considerable attention because of the significance of the identifier. Areas of question include

- ◆ Confidentiality and privacy concerns
- ◆ Choice and implementation of an individual identifier
- ◆ Legal protection
- ◆ The model to be used for the identifier
- ◆ Costs associated with transition to a new identifier and who should pay for those costs
- ◆ Implementation issues

An individual is a human being who is licensed, certified, or otherwise authorized to perform medical services or provide medical care, equipment, and/or supplies in the normal course of business. Examples of individuals are physicians, nurses, dentists, pharmacists, and physical therapists.

Organization

Organizations, such as group practices, additional billing offices, hospitals, clinics, laboratories, and others can obtain sufficient NPIs for billing and payer-provider contractual purposes.

Each separate physical location of an organization, each member of an organization chain, and each subpart of an organization that needs to be identified would receive its own NPI. NPIs of organization providers would not be linked within the NPS to NPIs of other health care providers. Examples of organizations are hospitals, laboratories, ambulance companies, health maintenance organizations, and pharmacies.

Uses of NPI

The NPI must be used in connection with the electronic transactions identified in HIPAA. In addition, the NPI may be used in several other ways:

- By health care providers to identify themselves in health care transactions identified in HIPAA or on related correspondence
- By health care providers to identify other health care providers in health care transactions or on related correspondence
- By health care providers on prescriptions (however, the NPI could not replace requirements for the Drug Enforcement Administration number or State license number)
- By health plans in their internal provider files to process transactions and communicate with health care providers
- By health plans to coordinate benefits with other health plans
- By health care clearinghouses in their internal files to create and process standard transactions and to communicate with health care providers and health plans
- By electronic patient record systems to identify treating health care providers in patient medical records
- By the Department of Health and Human Services to cross-reference health care providers in fraud and abuse files and other program integrity files
- For any other lawful activity requiring individual identification of health care providers, including activities related to the Debt Collection Improvement Act of 1996 and the Balanced Budget Act of 1997

Size of NPI

The NPI is expected to be 10 numeric digits of which the right-most digit is a check digit. It does not carry intelligence within the number. There will be a national database, an online means for providers to ensure it is updated and accurate, and an electronic means for distribution of copies of the database so that payers and others can have an accurate and up-to-date copy on their own computers.

The National Provider System (NPS) has the capacity to assign unique identifiers to billions of providers.

Multiple Locations

Each individual practitioner or provider will receive a single unique identifier. Each practitioner may have several records in the National Provider File (NPF) that capture or describe the various locations at which he or she practices, or that explain the affiliation between an individual provider and any provider groups.

Enumerators

The organization that actually assigns the NPIs is referred to as an *enumerator*. The enumerator also is responsible for maintaining the NPS/NPF by entering the information sent by the providers who have completed the screening successfully and have been assigned an NPI.

There are two options being considered for selecting enumerators. The Notice of Proposed Rule Making (NPRM) welcomes feedback on these options, as well as other alternate solutions. Because the data needed to enumerate Medicare providers is already available in HCFA files, that information will be loaded into the National Provider System (NPS) and NPIs, and will be assigned automatically to Medicare providers under either of the following options. Medicare providers, therefore, would not have to apply for an NPI.

◆ **Option 1.** A Federally directed registry would be the enumerator of all health care providers. After the initial load of Medicare provider data and assignment of NPIs to Medicare providers, all the remaining health care providers would apply directly to the registry for an NPI. The registry could be operated by an agent or contractor. The registry would enter the provider's data into the National Provider System; the National Provider System would assign an NPI, and the registry would notify the provider of the NPI.

◆ **Option 2.** A combination of federal programs (health plans), Medicaid State agencies, and a registry would be enumerators.

Federal programs and Medicaid State agencies would enumerate their own health care providers by entering provider data into the National Provider System; the National Provider System would assign NPIs to the providers. Each health care provider participating in more than one federal or Medicaid health plan could choose the one by which it wishes to be enumerated. All other health care providers would apply directly to a federally directed registry for an NPI.

National Provider System (NPS)

HHS will implement the NPI through a central electronic enumerating system, the National Provider System (NPS). This system would be a comprehensive, uniform system for identifying and uniquely enumerating health care providers at the national level, not unlike the process now used to issue Social Security Numbers. HCFA would exercise overall responsibility for oversight and management of the system. Health care providers would not interact directly with the NPS.

The process of identifying and uniquely enumerating health care providers is separate from the process health plans follow for enrolling health care providers in their health programs. Even with the advent of assignment of NPIs by the NPS, health plans would still have to follow their own procedures for receiving and verifying information from health care providers that apply to them for enrollment in their health programs. Unique enumeration is less expensive than plan enrollment because it does not require as much information to be collected, edited, and verified.

NPIs would be issued by one or more organizations referred to as "enumerators." The NPS would edit the data, checking for consistency, formatting addresses, and validating the Social Security Number. It would then search the database to determine whether the health care provider already has an NPI. If so, that NPI would be displayed. If not, an NPI would be assigned. If the health care provider is similar (but not identical) to an already enumerated health care provider, the information would be passed back to the enumerator for further analysis.

Enumerators would also communicate NPIs back to the health care providers and maintain the NPS database. The number of enumerators would be limited in the interest of data quality and consistency.

Because the Medicare program maintains files on more health care providers than any other health care program in the country, data from these files will be used initially to populate the NPF that is being built by the NPS and would be accessed by the enumerator(s).

Applying for a NPI

The following steps will be involved in establishing and issuing an NPI:

1. A provider would submit an application to the designated enumerator.
2. The enumerator would validate the data entered on the application—check for accuracy and consistency.
3. After validation, the enumerator would submit data to or enter the data into the National Provider System (NPS) and update the NPF.
4. The NPS would either generate an NPI or return the application to the enumerator for further analysis. For example, the application may be returned for further analysis if the provider has already been assigned an NPI.
5. The enumerator would, after receiving an NPI from the NPS, transmit the NPI to the provider.

NPIs are expected to be assigned on the following basis:

◆ NPIs issued to all providers that have Medicare provider numbers
◆ NPIs issued to all Medicaid providers that do not have Medicare provider numbers
◆ NPIs issued to all providers that do not participate in Medicare or Medicaid
◆ NPIs issued to providers that are not required to comply with HIPAA's requirements because they do not perform any of the HIPAA transactions electronically

Information Required for an NPI

To obtain a NPI, providers have to provide detailed information in an application and submit them to the enumerator. Information required for an NPI is shown in Table 2.2.

Table 2.2   Information Required for NPI

NPI Information Required	Description
Provider's Current Name	First, middle, and last names required. Applies to individual providers only.
Provider's Other Name	Maiden or professional name. Includes first, middle, and last names. Applies to individual providers only.
Provider's Legal Business Name	Applies to groups and organizations only.
Provider's Name Suffix	Examples of suffixes are Jr., Sr., II, III, and IV. Applies to individual providers only.
Provider's Credential Designation	Examples include MD, DDS, CSW, CNA, AA, NP, RNA, PSY. Applies to individual providers only.
Provider's Social Security Number (SSN)	Applies to individual providers only.
Provider's Employer Identification Number (EIN)	EIN assigned to provider's business
Provider's Birth Date	Applies to individual providers only.
Provider's Birth State Code	Applies to individual providers only.
Provider's Birth Country	Applies to individual providers only.
Provider's Sex	Applies to individual providers only.
Provider's Race	Applies to individual providers only.
Provider's Date of Death	Applies to individual providers only.
Provider's Mailing Address	Includes two lines of street address, plus city, state, county, country, and five-or nine-position ZIP code.
Provider's Telephone Number	Phone number.
Provider's Fax Number	Fax number.
Provider's E-mail Address	E-mail address used.
Resident/Intern Code	Applies to individual providers only.
Provider Enumerate Date	Date provider was enumerated (the date an NPI was assigned by the NPS).

Table 2.2   Information Required for NPI *(continued)*

NPI Information Required	Description
Provider Update Date	The most recent date on which the provider data were updated; assigned by the NPS.
Establishing Enumerator/Agent Number	Identification number of the establishing enumerator.
Provider Practice Location Identifier (Location Code)	The location code is a two-position alphanumeric code assigned by the NPS.
Provider Practice Location Name	"Doing Business As" (DBA) name.
Provider Practice Location Address	Includes two lines of street address, plus city, state, county, country, and five-or nine-position ZIP code.
Provider's Practice Telephone Number	Practice phone number.
Provider's Practice Fax Number	Practice fax number.
Provider's Practice E-mail Address	Practice e-mail address used.
Provider Classification	Taken from the ASC X12N taxonomy and includes type(s), classification(s), and area(s) of specialization.
Provider Certification Code	Applies to individual providers only.
Provider Certification (Certificate) Number	Applies to individual providers only.
Provider License Number	Applies to individual providers only.
Provider License State	Applies to individual providers only.
School Code	Applies to individual providers only.
School Name	Applies to individual providers only.
School City, State, and Country	Applies to individual providers only.
School Graduation Year	Applies to individual providers only.
Other Provider Number Type	Type of provider identification number also or formerly used by the provider, including: UPIN, NSC, OSCAR, DEA, Medicaid State, PIN, and Payer ID.

(continued)

Table 2.2   Information Required for NPI *(continued)*

NPI Information Required	Description
Other Provider Number	Other provider identification number also or formerly used by the provider.
Group Member Name	Name of individual member group, including first, middle, and last names. Applies to groups only.
Group Member Name Suffix	Individual member's name suffix, e.g. Jr., Sr., II, III, and IV. Applies to groups only.
Organization Type Control Code	Optional and applies only to the following types of organizations: Government—Federal (Military) Government—Federal (Veterans) Government—Federal (Other) Government—State/County Government—Local Government—Combined Control Non-government—Non-profit Non-government—For-profit Non-government—Not-for-profit

Further, the NPF would include

◆ Effective date

◆ Termination date

These dates provide information on when an individual practitioner joined or terminated an affiliation with a provider group.

Implementation

To support the new identifiers for individuals, health plans have to update their computer systems. They can either replace the previous identifiers with the new identifier, or health plans can build crosswalks that translate proprietary identifiers to uniform national identifiers.

The NPI will eventually replace the Unique Physician Identification Number (UPIN) in the Medicare program. NPIs and UPINs will not be used concurrently on transactions specified by HIPAA. It is likely that a crosswalk will be created to match UPINs to NPIs.

National Employer Identifier for Health Care

The Transaction Rule also proposes a standard for a national employer identifier and requirements concerning its use by health plans, health care clearinghouses, and health care providers. The health plans, health care clearinghouses, and health care providers would use the identifier, among other uses, in connection with certain electronic transactions.

The use of this identifier would improve the Medicare and Medicaid programs and other Federal health programs and private health programs, and the effectiveness and efficiency of the health care industry in general, by simplifying the administration of the system and enabling the efficient electronic transmission of certain health information. It would implement some of the requirements of the Administrative Simplification subtitle of the HIPAA legislation.

Employer Identification Number (EIN)

Because of the widespread use of the Employer Identification Number (EIN) to identify employers in health transactions, the EIN is being proposed as the national standard for the employer identifier for electronic health transactions. The IRS issues EINs.

The EIN is an identifier that is already assigned to each employer for tax identification purposes and its adoption would not result in additional data collections or paperwork, thereby furthering the administrative simplification objectives. The EIN is defined as the taxpayer identifying number of an individual or other person (whether or not an employer).

The *EIN* would be 9 digits separated by a hyphen and would appear as 00-0000000.

This identifier is expected to require little if any change to payer or provider systems other than documentation.

The IRS has approved the type of EINs that are called for in HIPAA-associated transactions. Employers or providers would have to use EINs for the following purposes:

♦ By providers to identify the employer of a participant in a health plan

♦ By employers in transactions and correspondence with health plans concerning premium payments

♦ By employers or providers to identify the employer to a health plan in an eligibility inquiry

♦ By employers when enrolling or dis-enrolling employees or dependents of employees in a health plan

Health plans will most likely be allowed to add EINs to the information they make available to providers on health insurance identification cards and other materials.

National Health Plan Identifier (PlanID)

The National Health Plan Identifier (PlanID) is a standard and uniform identifier that would apply to health plans and payers referred to in the HIPAA legislation. *Health plan* is defined as an individual or group plan that provides for or pays the cost of medical care. This definition also includes a significant group of employee welfare benefit plans, state regulated insurance plans, managed care plans, and essentially all government health plans. The National Health Plan Identifier identifies three types of entities:

♦ Payers, such as insurance companies, HMOs, and government programs

♦ ERISA group health plans, Taft-Hartley trusts, and other plans

♦ PPOs and similar provider contract networks

The proposed rule for PlanID has not been published yet. The number will be numeric, probably 10 digits with no coincident values with NPI. There will be a national PlanID database, an online means for its maintenance, and an electronic means for distribution of accurate copies to payers and other users.

The PlanID will be printed on health insurance identification cards. PlanID will be the primary automatic identifier used to route transactions to the correct payer.

National Health Identifier for Individuals

The identifier for individuals was included in the HIPAA law; however, opposition to it and lack of specificity as to its purposes and uses has caused indefinite delay. It is largely being ignored in implementation planning for HIPAA because so little is known about what it might be and how it might be used. HHS officials have stated that it will not be the individual's Social Security Number.

Summary

The Electronic Data Interchange (EDI) standard ANSI ASC X12 is the standard for representation of health care claims, eligibility inquiries, enrollments, and other transactions.

The fields within these transactions must be completed with entries from specified code sets. In addition to code sets, the transactions also contain identifiers, such as a Provider Identifier. Under HIPAA, covered transactions are those that are created by *covered entities*, namely, health care providers (like physicians and hospitals), health care insurers, and clearinghouses (organizations that process health care transactions on behalf of providers and insurers).

In this lesson we also examined code sets and identifiers. Code sets and identifiers are a part of a health care transaction. As discussed, a code set is any set of codes for encoding data elements such as table of terms, medical concepts, or medical procedure codes. The use of standard transactions and code sets improves the effectiveness and efficiency of the health care industry.

Identifiers are used extensively in all transactions between any combination of individuals, employers, health care providers, and health plans. Standardized identifiers will help eliminate fraud and abuse in health care programs.

Footnote

1. Title XVIII of the Social Security Act makes HIPAA applicable to the Medicare program in a similar manner.

Lesson 3

HIPAA

After completing this chapter, you'll know how to

- Interpret the core requirements of the Privacy Rule
- Identify key Privacy Rule terms and definitions
- Explain the purpose and key sections of a privacy notice
- Analyze the requirements of a consent (optional) document
- Identify the need for authorization documents
- Examine key parties, such as individuals, clients, parents and minors, business associates, and others impacted by the Privacy Rule
- Describe minimum requirements
- Understand marketing requirements
- Identify requirements for oral communications
- Interpret requirements for research
- Examine requirements for government access to health information
- Step through scenarios as they relate to use, disclosures, and business associates

Introduction to Privacy

This chapter focuses on the privacy implications of the Administrative Simplification subtitle of HIPAA Title II. The HIPAA Privacy Rule is concerned with protecting the privacy of patients' health information. The Privacy Rule is about 860 pages longer than all the sections of HIPAA taken together. To many, the Privacy Rule *is* HIPAA.

On August 14, 2002, the Department of Health and Human Services (HHS) published the final modifications to the Privacy Rule. The HHS objective was to provide strong privacy protection without hindering access to quality health care. Based on the comments received on the Notice of Proposed Rule Making (NPRM), HHS issued a number of modifications to the Privacy Rule.

The Standards for Privacy of Individually Identifiable Health Information (the Privacy Rule) took effect on April 14, 2001. The Privacy Rule creates national standards to protect individuals' personal health information and gives patients increased access to their medical records. As required by HIPAA, the Privacy Rule covers health plans, health care clearinghouses, and those health care providers who conduct certain financial and administrative transactions electronically. Most covered entities must comply with the Privacy Rule by April 14, 2003. Small health plans have until April 14, 2004 to comply with the Rule. The key information that is covered by the Privacy Rule is Protected Health Information (PHI). The Privacy Rule protects health information that

◆ Identifies an individual and

◆ Is maintained or exchanged electronically

If the information has any components that could be used to identify a person, it is covered. The protection stays with the information as long as the information is in the hands of a covered entity or a business partner. HIPAA results in the deployment of security technology to protect the privacy of patient and medical information.

Defining Privacy

Privacy is an evolving legal, philosophical, technological, and compliance arena that is sometimes linked to competitive advantage in the marketplace. For the purposes of working through HIPAA mandates and guidelines, *privacy* is defined as having policies and procedures in place to control access to protected health information.

The privacy requirements of HIPAA outline specific rights for individuals regarding protected health information and obligations of health care providers, health plans, and health care clearinghouses. The privacy regulation grants health care consumers a greater level of control over the use and disclosure of personally identifiable health information.

In general, health care providers, health plans, and clearinghouses are prohibited from using or disclosing protected health information except as authorized by the patient or specifically permitted by the regulation. The final Privacy Rule's applicability is expanded to include all personally identifiable health information, regardless of media format.

Background

In April 2001, at the direction of President Bush and HHS Secretary Tommy G. Thompson, the first-ever federal privacy standards to protect patients' medical records and other health information provided to health plans, doctors, hospitals, and other health care providers, went into effect. These standards provide patients with access to their medical records and more control over how their personal health information is used and disclosed. Most covered entities must comply with the privacy standards by April 14, 2003.

Congress required HHS to issue patient privacy protections as part of HIPAA. The HIPAA law included provisions designed to encourage electronic transactions and also required new safeguards to protect the security and confidentiality of health information. In November 1999, HHS published proposed regulations to provide patients new rights and protections against the misuse or disclosure of their health records. HHS received more than 52,000 comments from the public. In December 2000 and then again on August 14, 2002, HHS issued the final modifications to the Privacy Rule that made significant changes from the proposed Privacy Rule in response to comments.

To ensure that the final privacy regulations protect patients' privacy without creating unanticipated consequences that might harm patients' access to care or quality of care, Secretary Thompson took public comments on the final Privacy Rule. In July 2001, HHS issued an initial set of guidance materials to address common misconceptions and answer other questions about the final Privacy Rule's provisions. On March 27, 2002, HHS published proposed changes to the Privacy Rule in the Federal Register to ensure that it protects privacy without interfering with access to care or quality of care. HHS considered public comments on the proposed changes before issuing a final set of modifications to the Privacy Rule on August 14, 2002.

Who Is Impacted?

As required by HIPAA, the final Privacy Rule covers health plans, health care clearinghouses, and those health care providers who conduct certain financial and administrative transactions (enrollment, billing, and eligibility verification) electronically.

Scope of Coverage

Medical records and other individually identifiable health information used or disclosed by a covered entity in any form, whether electronically, paper-based, or oral, are covered by the final Privacy Rule. Thus, the paper progeny of electronic information is covered (in other words, the information does not lose its protections simply because it is printed out of a computer).

Purpose

According to the National Research Council, individually identifiable health information frequently is shared with

- Consulting physicians
- Managed care organizations
- Health insurance companies and other third-party payers
- Life insurance companies
- Self-insured employers
- Pharmacies
- Pharmacy benefit managers
- Clinical laboratories
- Accrediting organizations
- State and Federal statistical agencies
- Medical information bureaus

In-house contractors are a fact across our front-line health care delivery institutions. Hospitals, ambulatory care centers, home health care providers, long-term care facilities, physician practices/clinics, and rehabilitation facilities are all HIPAA-regulated. At the same time, these institutions may use in-house contractors for case management/utilization review, dietary, laboratory, pharmacy, physical therapy, respiratory therapy, radiology, discharge planning, and social services. This relatively tight web of relationships requires constant patient health information sharing. Much of this sharing of information is done without the knowledge of the patient involved.

For example, a pharmacy benefit manager could receive information to determine whether an insurance plan or HMO should cover a prescription, but then use the information to market other products to the same patient.

Similarly, many of us obtain health insurance coverage though our employer and, in some instances, the employer itself acts as the insurer. In these cases, the employer will obtain identifiable health information about its employees as part of the legitimate health insurance functions, such as claims processing, quality improvement, and fraud detection activities. At the same time, there is no comprehensive protection prohibiting the employer from using that information to make decisions about promotions or job retention.

In the absence of a national legal framework of health privacy protections, consumers are increasingly vulnerable to the exposure of their personal health information. Disclosure of individually identifiable information can occur deliberately or accidentally and can occur within an organization or be the result of an external breach of security.

Examples of privacy breaches include

- A Michigan-based health system accidentally posted the medical records of thousands of patients on the Internet. (The *Ann Arbor News*, February 10, 1999).

- A Utah-based pharmaceutical benefits management firm used patient data to solicit business for its owner, a drug store. (*Kiplingers*, February 2000).

- An employee of the Tampa, Florida, health department took a computer disk containing the names of 4,000 people who had tested positive for HIV, the virus that causes AIDS. (*USA Today*, October 10, 1996).

- The health insurance claims forms of thousands of patients blew out of a truck on its way to a recycling center in East Hartford, Connecticut. (The *Hartford Courant*, May 14, 1999).

- A patient in a Boston-area hospital discovered that her medical record had been read by more than 200 of the hospital's employees. (The *Boston Globe*, August 1, 2000).

- A Nevada woman who purchased a used computer discovered that the computer still contained the prescription records of the customers of the pharmacy that had previously owned the computer. The pharmacy database included names, addresses, Social Security Numbers, and a list of all the medicines the customers had purchased. (The *New York Times*, April 4, 1997 and April 12, 1997).

◆ A speculator bid $4000 for the patient records of a family practice in South Carolina. Among the businessman's uses of the purchased records was selling them back to the former patients. (The *New York Times*, August 14, 1991).

◆ In 1993, the Boston Globe reported that Johnson and Johnson marketed a list of five million names and addresses of elderly incontinent women. (*ACLU Legislative Update*, April 1998).

◆ A few weeks after an Orlando woman had her doctor perform some routine tests, she received a letter from a drug company promoting a treatment for her high cholesterol. (*Orlando Sentinel*, November 30, 1997).

◆ In Maryland, a banker improperly accessed a medical database to determine which of his borrowers had been diagnosed with cancer. Once such individuals had been identified, the bank improperly attempted to terminate its lending relationship with them.

◆ The chain drugstore CVS and grocery chain Giant Food conceded that they had disclosed their customers' prescription records to a direct mail company that then tracked customers and solicited them to consider alternative treatments. After media reports sparked public concern, both companies discontinued this practice.

◆ A study by the University of Illinois found that 35 percent of Fortune 500 companies admitted to checking medical records prior to hiring or promoting employees.

The problem is very serious. In the face of industry evolution, the potential benefits of our changing health care system, and the real risks and occurrences of harm, protection of privacy must be built into the routine operations of our health care system.

The Privacy Rule for the first time creates national standards to protect individuals' medical records and other personal health information. The Privacy Rule is about

◆ Patient control of health information

◆ Boundaries on use and release of health information

◆ Establishment of appropriate safeguards to protect privacy

◆ Making violators accountable with civil and criminal penalties

◆ Guidelines for public responsibility regarding disclosure

The Privacy Rule addresses questions such as

- What information can an organization share or make use of without receiving an individual's permission?
- Under what circumstances can information be shared or used without an individual's permission?
- What types of information can be shared without authorization?
- For what types of information is an individual's permission required before it can be shared or used?
- What types of agreements must a provider or other entities establish to share information? Who must participate in these agreements?

Penalties

As discussed earlier, Congress provided penalties for covered entities that misuse personal health information. Penalties may be civil and/or criminal.

- **Civil penalties.** Health plans, providers, and clearinghouses that violate these standards are subject to civil liability. Civil money penalties are $100 per violation, up to $25,000 per year for each requirement or prohibition violated.
- **Criminal penalties.** Congress also established criminal penalties for certain actions, such as knowingly obtaining protected health information in violation of the law. Criminal penalties are up to $50,000 and 1 year in prison for certain offenses; up to $100,000 and up to 5 years in prison if the offenses are committed under "false pretenses"; and up to $250,000 and up to 10 years in prison if the offenses are committed with the intent to sell, transfer, or use protected health information for commercial advantage, personal gain, or malicious harm.

To summarize, the civil and criminal penalties for covered entities that misuse personal health information (PHI) are shown in Tables 3.1 and 3.2.

Table 3.1   Civil Penalties

Description	Minimum	Maximum
Offenses for each requirement or prohibition violated	$100 per violation	Up to $25,000 per year

Table 3.2   Criminal penalties

Description	Monetary	Prison
For certain offenses	Up to $50,000	Up to 1 year
False pretenses	Up to $100,000	Up to 5 years
Offenses committed with the intent to sell, transfer, or use protected health information for commercial advantage, personal gain, or malicious harm	Up to $250,000	Up to 10 years

Exceptions

In limited circumstances, the final Privacy Rule permits—but does not require—covered entities to continue certain existing disclosures of health information without individual authorization for specific public responsibilities.

Covered entities could use and disclose protected health information without authorization for their own treatment, payment, or health care operations. This would include purposes such as quality assurance, utilization review, credentialing, and other activities that are part of ensuring appropriate treatment and payment.

Limitations apply in regards to facilitating another party's activities. Exceptions are allowed to let a covered entity disclose PHI to

- Any other provider (even a non-covered entity) to facilitate that provider's treatment activities.
- Another covered entity or any provider (even a non-covered entity) to facilitate that party's payment activities.
- Another covered entity to facilitate some of that entity's health care operations. Examples of health care operations would include activities in the areas of
  - Fraud and abuse
  - Quality assessment and improvement
  - Improving health care for the population
  - Case management
  - Training
  - Accreditation and licensure
- Any other covered entity within the same organized health care relationship for any health care operations arrangement.

Covered entities could use and disclose protected health information without individual authorization for the following national priority activities:

♦ Oversight of the health care system, including quality assurance activities

♦ Public health, and in emergencies affecting life or safety

♦ Research

♦ Judicial and administrative proceedings

♦ Law enforcement

♦ To provide information to next of kin

♦ For government health data systems

♦ For identification of the body of a deceased person or the cause of death

♦ For facilities' (hospitals and so on) directories

♦ In other situations where the use of disclosure is mandated by other laws

The Privacy Rule generally establishes new safeguards and limits on these disclosures. If there is no other law requiring that information be disclosed, covered entities use their professional judgments to decide whether to disclose any information, reflecting their own policies and ethical principles.

Individuals can ask a covered entity to restrict further use and disclosure of protected health information for treatment, payment, or health care operations (with the exception of uses or disclosures required by law). The covered entity would not be required to agree to such a request, but if the covered entity and the individual agree to a restriction, the covered entity would be bound by the agreement.

Emergency Treatment Situation

The Privacy Rule provides an exception to the notice requirement for emergency treatment situations. In an emergency treatment situation, health care providers with a direct treatment relationship must make a good faith attempt to provide a Notice of Privacy Practices, as soon as reasonably practicable after the emergency treatment situation.

But emergency care providers are not expected to go to extremes to provide their notice. The nature of emergency medicine is that people seek care just for the emergency. HIPAA does not force an ambulance service to find the person they transported to deliver a Notice of Privacy Practices.

Special Protection for Psychotherapy Notes

Psychotherapy notes (used only by a mental health professional) are held to a higher standard of protection because they are not part of the medical record and are not intended to be shared with anyone else. All other personal health information is considered to be sensitive and protected consistently under the Privacy Rule.

One covered entity can't disclose psychotherapy notes to assist another covered entity's treatment, payment, or health care operations (TPO) activities. But it can disclose these notes for its own limited TPO:

◆ For its own treatment activities

◆ For training programs for its own mental health care professionals, trainees, and students

◆ To defend itself from a legal action brought by the individual

Government Entities

The provisions of the final Privacy Rule generally apply equally to private sector and public sector entities that are covered by the law. For example, both private hospitals and government medical units have to comply with the full range of requirements, such as providing notice, access rights, and designation of a privacy officer.

State Laws

State laws providing additional privacy protections continue to apply. The confidentiality protections are cumulative; the Privacy Rule will set a national floor of privacy standards that protect all Americans, and any state law providing additional protections would continue to apply. Where states have decided through law to require certain disclosures of health information, the final rule does not preempt these mandates.

Gramm-Leach-Bliley Act, Pub. L. 106-102

The Federal Trade Commission (FTC) published a final Privacy Rule as required by Section 504(a) of the Gramm-Leach-Bliley (GLB) Act, Pub. L. 106-102 (referred to in the rest of this book as the GLB Act), with respect to financial institutions and other persons under the Commission's jurisdiction, as set forth in

Section 505(a)(7) of the GLB Act. Section 504 of the GLB Act required the FTC to issue regulations as necessary to implement notice requirements and restrictions on a financial institution's ability to disclose nonpublic personal information about consumers to nonaffiliated third parties. The GLB Act clearly covers insurance companies as "financial institutions."

Section 503 of the GLB Act requires that financial institutions must provide their customers with a notice of their privacy policies and practices. Section 502 prohibits these financial institutions from disclosing nonpublic personal information about a consumer to nonaffiliated third parties unless the institutions satisfy various disclosure and opt-out requirements and the consumer has not elected to opt out of the disclosure. The final GLB Privacy Rule was effective November 13, 2000 and implemented the requirements. Full compliance was required by July 1, 2001. The National Association of Insurance Commissioners (NAIC) asked the FTC to clarify the boundary of Federal and State jurisdiction over privacy regulations, and ensure that the financial Privacy Rules under the GLB Act are compatible with the Privacy Rules relating to medical information that were issued by the Secretary of the Department of Health and Human Services (HHS) under HIPPA.

The FTC ruled that financial institutions may be covered both by this Privacy Rule and by the regulations disseminated by HHS under the authority of sections 262 and 264 (and possibly others) of HIPAA once those regulations are finalized. Based on the final Privacy Rule, there are areas of overlap between HIPAA and the GLB financial Privacy Rules.

For example, under the proposed HIPAA regulations, consumers must provide affirmative authorization before a covered institution may disclose medical information in certain instances, and under the GLB financial Privacy Rules, institutions need only provide consumers with the opportunity to opt out of disclosures. In this case, the FTC anticipates that compliance with the affirmative authorization requirement, consistent with the procedures required under HIPAA, satisfies the opt-out requirement under the financial Privacy Rules.

Timeline

HHS published a proposed rule on privacy standards on November 3, 1999. On December 29, 2000, HHS published the final rule establishing privacy standards. The final rule had an effective date of February 26, 2001. On February 26, 2001, HHS delayed the final rule's effective date to meet a statutory requirement for

Congressional review. On April 14, 2001, HHS published a notice indicating that it would be adopting the December 29, 2000 regulations with a new effective date of April 14, 2001.

Although the HIPAA privacy regulations went into effect on April 14, 2001, no entity is required to comply with any standard or implementation regulation in the regulations until 24 months (or 36 months for small health plans) after that date, which makes the compliance date April 14, 2003.

As for Business Associate Contracts, covered entities have one additional year, until April 2004, instead of April 2003, to make certain that business associate contracts comply with HIPAA. The extra year does not apply to

◆ Small health plans

◆ Oral or other agreements that are not in writing

◆ New agreements entered into after the effective date of the transition rule's provisions

Contracts in all such areas must be in place by April 14, 2003.

To qualify for the extension, the agreements must be in place on the date the transition provisions take effect and must require modification or renewal before April 14, 2003. The exception to this is the contract that automatically renews without any change or action by the parties.

As a practical matter, providers and other covered entities need to use the remaining time to take those actions necessary to bring their policies, procedures, and processes, as well as contracts, into compliance and to publish their Notice of Privacy Policies as required under the regulations. Where possible, HIPAA privacy programs need to be implemented in a manner that ensures maximum operational flexibility.

Given the scale and scope of implementing HIPAA privacy compliance programs, there is not time to wait for all relevant regulations to stabilize. At this point, the best that you can do is minimize the impact of last minute changes on your schedule and budget.

The regulations protect individuals from the use or disclosure of health information held electronically, on paper, or in any other form by a covered entity. Any use or disclosure of protected health information by the covered entity, including use for treatment of patients, marketing, medical research, and most other activities, are prohibited unless the use or disclosure complies with the HIPAA regulation.

Key Terminology

This section reviews key terminology used in the Privacy Rule.

Individually Identifiable Health Information

Individually Identifiable Health Information (IIHI) is health information that is a subset of health information, including demographic information collected from an individual, and:

◆ Is created or received by a health care provider, health plan, employer, or clearinghouse

◆ Relates to the past, present, or future physical or mental health condition of an individual; the provision of health care to an individual; or the past, present, or future payment for the provision of health care to an individual

◆ Identifies the individual, or there is a reasonable basis to believe the information can be used to identify the individual

Patient Identifiable Information

Identifiers within health information, which could be used to identify an individual would constitute patient identifiable information (PII), may include, for example, any one of the following.

◆ The individual's name

◆ City or county where the individual lives

◆ Zip code

◆ Social Security Number

◆ Finger print

◆ Telephone number

◆ Medical record number or fax number

The Privacy Rule lists a number of other identifiers. Thus, any health information maintained by a covered entity where the individual could, in any possible way, be identified, needs to be treated as individually identifiable health information.

Protected Health Information

Any patient identifiable information is now Protected Health Information (PHI) regardless of the media form it is or was in. HIPAA—Data may be at rest or in transit. At rest can mean data that is

- Accessed
- Stored
- Processed
- Maintained

In transit can mean data that is transmitted in any form.

The final Privacy Rule establishes the privacy safeguard standards that covered entities must meet. The requirements are flexible and scalable to account for the nature of each entity's business, size, and resources. Covered entities generally will have to

- **Adopt written privacy procedures.** These include a description of who has access to protected information, how it will be used within the entity, and when the information can be disclosed. Covered entities also need to take steps to ensure that their business associates protect the privacy of health information.
- **Train employees and designate a privacy officer.** Covered entities need to train their employees in their privacy procedures and must designate an individual to be responsible for ensuring the procedures are followed.

Deidentified Information (DII)

Once the personal identifiers have been removed from a data set, the information is not individually identifiable and can be disclosed without consent or authorization of the individuals. The Privacy Rule refers to such information as *deidentified* and to the process of removing identifying information as *deidentification*.

If deidentified information is *re-identified* then the information again becomes subject to the use and disclosure requirements that apply to any PHI.

The information needed to match records with specific individuals, called the *keys*, is considered PHI and subject to the use and disclosure requirements that apply to any other PHI.

HIPAA specified two alternative tests for concluding that information is deidentified:

- ◆ A person with "appropriate knowledge and experience" determines that the information cannot be used to identify the person described by the information.

- ◆ Certain specified identifying data elements have been removed, and the covered entity has no actual knowledge that the information could be used to identify a person described by the information. This is the "safe harbor" method.

For information to be regarded as deidentified the following identifiers of the individual or of relatives, employers, and household members of the individual must be removed:

- ◆ Names.

- ◆ All geographic subdivisions smaller than a State, including street address, city, county, precinct, zip code, and their equivalent geocodes. However, the initial three digits of a zip code may remain on the information if, according to current publicly available data from the Bureau of the Census, the geographic unit formed by combining all zip codes with the same three initial digits contains more than 20,000 people, and the initial three digits for all such geographic units containing 20,000 or fewer people is changed to 000.

- ◆ All elements of dates (except year) for dates directly relating to an individual, including birth date, dates of admission and discharge from a health care facility, and date of death. For persons age 90 and older, all elements of dates (including year) that would indicate such age must be removed, except that such ages and elements may be aggregated into a single category of "age 90 or older."

- ◆ Telephone numbers.

- ◆ Fax numbers.

- ◆ Electronic mail addresses.

- ◆ Social Security Numbers.

- ◆ Medical record numbers.

- ◆ Health plan beneficiary numbers.

- ◆ Account numbers.

- ◆ Certificate or license numbers.

- ◆ Vehicle identifiers and serial numbers, including license plate numbers.

- ◆ Device identifiers and serial numbers.

- ◆ Web Universal Resource Locators (URLs).

- ◆ Internet Protocol (IP) address numbers.

- ◆ Biometric identifiers, including fingerprints and voiceprints.

- ◆ Full face photographic images and any comparable images.

- ◆ Any other unique identifying number, characteristic, or codes.

Deidentification Safe Harbor List

For safe harbor to apply, you must be able to answer "True" to all statements identified in Table 3.3.

Table 3.3 Safe Harbor Application

| True _____ | False _____ | Covered entity does not have actual knowledge that information could be used alone or in combination with other reasonably available information to re-identify the individual. |

| True _____ | False _____ | The following identifiers of the individual or of relatives, employers, or household members of the individual have been removed or are not present: |

_____ 1. Names

_____ 2. All geographic subdivisions smaller than a state, including street address, city, county, precinct, zip code, and their equivalent geocodes

Except for the initial three digits of a zip code if according to currently available data from the Bureau of the Census

The geographic unit formed by combining all zip codes with the same three initial digits contains more than 20,000 people

The initial three digits of a zip code for all such geographic units containing 20,000 or fewer people are changed to 000

(continued)

Table 3.3 Safe Harbor Application *(continued)*

_____ 3. All elements of dates (except year) or dates relating to an individual, including birth date, admission date, discharge date, date of death;

And all ages over 89, except that such ages and elements may be aggregated into a single category of age 90 or older

_____ 4. Telephone numbers

_____ 5. Fax numbers

_____ 6. Electronic mail addresses

_____ 7. Social Security Numbers

_____ 8. Medical record numbers

_____ 9. Health plan beneficiary numbers

_____ 10. Account numbers

_____ 11. Certificate/license numbers

_____ 12. Vehicle identifier and serial numbers, including license plate numbers

_____ 13. Device identifiers and serial numbers

_____ 14. Web Universal Resource Locators (URLs)

_____ 15. IP address numbers

_____ 16. Biometric identifiers, including fingerprints and voiceprints

_____ 17. Full face photographic images and any comparable images

_____ 18. Any other unique identifying number, characteristic, or code

Deidentified data might contain a key that allows the covered entity that created it to re-identify the record. This re-identification code or number cannot be derived from any identifiable fields in the Safe Harbor list.

Limited Data Set

The final modifications to the Privacy Rule defined a *limited data set* as a data set that must have certain identifying fields removed and may contain a limited number of fields that might identify a person.

A limited data set can be used for research, public health, or other health care operations purposes as long as the covered entity removes certain specific fields.

A limited data set is information that excludes the following direct identifiers of the individual, or of relatives, employers or household members of the individual:

◆ Names

◆ Postal address information, other than town or city, state, and zip code

◆ Telephone numbers

◆ Fax numbers

◆ Electronic mail addresses

◆ Social Security Numbers

◆ Medical record numbers

◆ Health plan beneficiary numbers (such as Medicaid Prime Numbers)

◆ Account numbers

◆ Certificate/license numbers

◆ Vehicle identifiers and serial numbers, including license plate numbers

◆ Web Universal Resource Locators (URLs)

◆ Internet Protocol (IP) address numbers

◆ Biometric identifiers, including finger and voice prints

◆ Full face photographic images and any comparable images

Dates related to the individual are not prohibited as content. So birth date, admission date, and discharge date could be included in the limited data set. Address information fields, aside from street address, are likewise not prohibited. But all of the parts of the street address are restricted. So the name of the street, without of the house number, is still prohibited.

A characteristic that distinguishes a limited data set from the safe harbor deidentified data set is that the limited data set does not allow the inclusion of a re-identification code. So there is no mechanism to allow the disclosing covered entity to re-identify the limited data set records they create.

The minimum necessary standard applies to limited data sets. If the requesting party asks for birth date and the covered entity does not agree it is needed for the stated use of the data set, then the covered entity must limit the content.

Data Use Agreement

The disclosing covered entity must also develop a *data use agreement* with the recipient of the data. In this agreement the recipient would promise to

- Limit their use of the limited data set to research, public health, and other health care operations
- Limit who could use or receive the data
- Agree not to re-identify the data

Use and Disclosure

Use and disclosure are two fundamental concepts in the HIPAA Privacy Rule. They are different concepts. "Use" refers to sharing, employing, applying, utilizing, examining, or analyzing individually identifiable health information by employees or other members of an organization's work force.

Information is used when it moves inside an organization.

"Disclosure" is defined as the release, transfer, provision of access to, or divulging in any matter information outside the entity holding the information.

Information is disclosed when it is transmitted between or among organizations. Under HIPAA, "use" limits the sharing of information within a covered entity, while "disclosure" restricts the sharing of information outside an entity holding the information.

Thus, information is used if a physician discusses the information with a nurse within the physician's practice. Information is disclosed when the physician discusses the information with the insurance company.

The Privacy Rule requires a patient's permission for PHI to be used or disclosed.

Routine Disclosures

HIPAA does not require the review and approval of every routine disclosure of PHI. For routine or reoccurring requests for information disclosure, the policies and procedures may be standard protocols. An example is the release of information to a medical transcription service. The covered entity can establish protocols for handling the routine disclosure of PHI.

A covered entity must adopt and implement policies and procedures governing routine disclosures that identify

- The types of PHI to be disclosed
- The types of persons who would receive the PHI
- The conditions that would apply to such disclosure

Non-Routine Disclosures

Providers and other covered entities are required to develop reasonable criteria for reviewing requests for non-routine disclosure of PHI. The criteria should identify the minimum amount of PHI that is needed to accomplish the purpose of the request. The criteria should be used to approve, approve in part, or disapprove requests.

These policies and procedures must specifically require justification for the disclosure of an entire medical record. Note that when an entire medical record is disclosed in the absence of such justification, the act is presumed to be a violation of the Privacy Rule.

Non-routine requests for disclosures of PHI must be reviewed individually. Each one requires a specific authorization unless the regulations allow it.

Payment

As provided for by the Privacy Rule, a covered entity may use and disclose protected health information (PHI) for payment purposes. *Payment* is a defined term that encompasses the various activities of health care providers to obtain payment or be reimbursed for their services, and for a health plan to obtain premiums to fulfill their coverage responsibilities and provide benefits under the plan and to obtain or provide reimbursement for the provision of health care.

In addition to the general definition, the Privacy Rule provides examples of common payment activities, which include, but are not limited to

- Determining eligibility or coverage under a plan and adjudicating claims
- Risk adjustments
- Billing and collection activities
- Reviewing health care services for medical necessity, coverage, justification of charges, and the like

- Utilization review activities
- Disclosures to consumer reporting agencies (limited to specified identifying information about the individual, his or her payment history, and identifying information about the covered entity)

Fair Credit Reporting Act (FCRA)

The Privacy Rule's definition of "payment" includes disclosures to consumer reporting agencies. These disclosures, however, are limited to the following PHI about the individual:

- Name and address
- Date of birth
- Social Security Number
- Payment history
- Account number

In addition, disclosure of the name and address of the health care provider or health plan making the report is allowed. The covered entity may perform this payment activity directly or may carry out this function through a third party, such as a collection agency, under a business associate arrangement.

HHS is not aware of any conflict in the consumer credit reporting disclosures permitted by the Privacy Rule and FCRA. The Privacy Rule permits uses and disclosures by the covered entity or its business associate as may be required by FCRA or other law. Therefore, HHS does not believe there would be a conflict between the Privacy Rule and legal duties imposed on data furnishers by FCRA.

Fair Debt Collection Practices Act

The Privacy Rule permits covered entities to continue to use the services of debt collection agencies. Debt collection is recognized as a payment activity within the payment definition. Through a business associate arrangement, the covered entity may engage a debt collection agency to perform this function on its behalf.

Disclosures of information, which would include a portion of PHI, to collection agency have to be made under a business associate agreement (which is presented later) and include restrictions on what PHI could be disclosed and how the collection agency could use the information. Such disclosures are governed by the minimum necessary requirements.

HHS is not aware of any conflict between the Privacy Rule and the Fair Debt Collection Practices Act. Where a use or disclosure of PHI is necessary for the covered entity to fulfill a legal duty, the Privacy Rule would permit such use or disclosure as required by law.

Payment is broadly defined as activities by health plans or health care providers to obtain premiums or obtain or provide reimbursements for the provision of health care. The activities specified are by way of example and are not intended to be an exclusive listing. Billing, claims management, collection activities, and related data processing are expressly included in the definition of payment.

Obtaining information about the location of the individual is a routine activity to facilitate the collection of amounts owed and the management of accounts receivable, and, therefore, constitutes a payment activity. The covered entity and its business associate also have to comply with any limitations placed on location information services by the Fair Debt Collection Practices Act.

Disclosure and Use for Treatment

A covered entity can use PHI for its own treatment purposes and can disclose PHI to another covered entity or health care provider for the treatment purposes of the entity that receives the information. The other health care provider does not need to be a covered entity.

 NOTE

Q: Can direct treatment providers, such as a specialist or hospital, to whom a patient is referred for the first time, use PHI to set up appointments or schedule surgery or other procedures before the patient receives their notice?

A: Yes, covered entities and other health care professionals can use or disclose PHI for an individual's treatment.

Disclosure and Use for Payment

A provider receives payment for the medical services that it renders from the patient, directly, or from a health plan on behalf of the patient. Health insurers also receive premiums from employers for the coverage the insurer provides to health plan members.

A covered entity can use PHI for its own payment activities and can disclose PHI to another covered entity or health care provider for the payment activities of the entity that receives the information. The other health care provider does not need to be a covered entity.

Under HIPAA regulations, payment refers to almost every activity that is related to establishing coverage and making payment for services covered by a health plan, including

- Eligibility determination
- Determination of coverage
- Adjudication of claims, including subrogation
- Adjustment of premium payments to reflect the risk of enrolled persons
- Billing
- Claims management
- Medical data processing
- Medical review
- Utilization review, including prior authorization

Disclosure and Use for Health Care Operations

Typically, a covered entity can use PHI in its own health care operations without obtaining an individual's authorization. This does not imply that any employee can use any information for any purpose.

Health care operations are limited to using PHI information for the following activities:

- Health care quality related operations activities
  - Quality assessment and improvement activities
  - Education and provider credentialing and certification
- Non–health care quality related operations activities
  - Underwriting, rating, and other insurance-related functions
  - Medical review, legal services, and auditing functions
  - Business planning and development
  - Business management and general administrative activities
- Compliance with privacy requirements

- Customer service
- Internal grievance procedures
- Sale, transfer, merger, or consolidation of all or part of a covered entity with another covered entity, or that afterward will become a covered entity; and due diligence relating to such activity creating deidentified health information
- Fund-raising for the benefit of the covered entity
- Marketing for which an individual authorization is not required

A covered entity can disclose protected health information to another covered entity for health care operations activities of the entity that receives the information, if both entities have a relationship with the individual who is the subject of the protected health information being requested, and the disclosure is for health care quality related operations activities like the following:

- Fraud and abuse investigations
- Quality assessment and improvement activities
- Education and provider credentialing and certification

A covered entity that participates in an organized health care arrangement can disclose protected health information about an individual to another covered entity that participates in the organized health care arrangement for any health care operations activities of the organized health care arrangement.

Mandatory Disclosures

The Privacy Rule requires disclosure of information only under two circumstances:

- To permit individuals to review and copy information about themselves
- In connection with enforcement of the rule

This implies that

- A covered entity cannot refuse to make a PHI that is collected, received, or maintained available to an individual except under very specific conditions.
- A covered entity cannot refuse to make PHI available to an oversight agency that has the legal authority to enforce the privacy protections. The covered entity does not need an individual's authorization to make such a disclosure.

Notice, Consent, and Authorization

Notice, Consent, and Authorization are the documents that a health care provider must maintain to "Use" or "Disclose" Protected Health Information.

Notice refers to a covered entity's Notice of Privacy Practices.

Consent refers to an optional consent by an individual for use or disclosure of PHI for TPO purposes. An individual's consent may not be obtained to permit use or disclosure that is not otherwise permitted or required by the regulations.

An Authorization allows use and disclosure of PHI for purposes other than TPO:

◆ Covered entities must obtain the individual's authorization to make uses or disclosures for purposes other than TPO.

◆ An Authorization must be written in specific terms.

◆ An Authorization can allow use and disclosure of PHI by the covered entity seeking the authorization or by a third party.

Table 3.4 examines the characteristics of Notice, Consent, and Authorization documents.

Table 3.4   Privacy Rule Related Documents

Notice (Required)	Consent (Optional)	Authorization (Required)
A general consent for the use and disclosure of information for treatment, payment, or health care operations.	Consent allows for the use and disclosure of PHI only for the practice's TPO purposes.	Authorization allows use and disclosure of PHI for purposes other than TPO.
The Notice must be written in plain, simple language.	It is written in general terms.	An Authorization must be written in specific terms.
Specific authorizations for uses and disclosures that are not covered by the consent.	It refers to the Notice of Privacy Practices for further information on the covered entity's privacy practices.	It can allow use and disclosure of PHI by the covered entity seeking the authorization or by a third party.
The Notice must specify an effective date.	It allows use and disclosure of PHI by the covered entity seeking the consent and not by other persons.	Covered entities must obtain the individuals' authorization to make uses or disclosures not covered by the consent requirements.
A Notice of Privacy Practices	Health care providers will be looking to obtain consent, as will health plans and health care clearinghouses	

A Consent cannot be used to allow a disclosure that otherwise requires an Authorization. For instance, a non-routine disclosure requires a specific Authorization. A general consent form for this purpose would be non-compliant.

Record Keeping

Covered entities must keep records of all

- Written acknowledgements of receipt of Notice
- Consents
- Authorizations
- Disclosures

Disclosures that are allowed by the Notice or by an Authorization do not need to be recorded for purposes of HIPAA compliance. A covered entity may still want to record these disclosures for its own business purposes, but it does not need to report them to an individual or an HHS auditor.

The records must be retained in either paper or electronic form for a minimum of six years.

Notice Requirement: Notice of Privacy Practices

All covered entities must provide individuals with a Notice that summarizes their privacy practices.

Notices are intended to provide a general explanation of the individual's rights under the federal regulations.

 NOTE

Q: Can a pharmacist use PHI to fill a prescription that was telephoned in by a patient's physician if the patient is a new patient to the pharmacy and has not yet received, or acknowledged, the pharmacy's Notice?

A: Yes, covered entities and other health care professionals can use or disclose PHI for an individual's treatment.

Core Elements of a Notice

There are several mandatory requirements for a Notice:

- The Notice must be written in plain, simple language.
- The Notice must prominently include specific language. The "header" of the Notice must read as follows: "This Notice describes how medical information about you may be used and disclosed and how you can get access to this information. Please review carefully."
- The Notice must describe the covered entities uses and disclosures of PHI. For example, if an entity wants to contact individuals for certain specific activities, it must list those activities in the notice. These activities include
  - Providing appointment reminders.
  - Describing or recommending treatment alternatives.
  - Providing information about health-related benefits and services that may be of interest to the individual.
  - Soliciting funds to benefit the covered entity.
- The Notice must describe an individual's rights under the Privacy Rule. This includes the rights of the individual to
  - Request restrictions on certain uses and disclosures.
  - Receive confidential communication of PHI.
  - Inspect and copy PHI.
  - Amend PHI.
  - Obtain an accounting of disclosures of PHI.
- The Notice must describe the covered entity's duties. This includes specifically stating that the entity is legally obligated to
  - Maintain the privacy of PHI.
  - Provide the Notice of Privacy Practices.
  - Abide by the terms of the Notice.
- The Notice must describe how to register complaints concerning suspected violations of privacy rights with the entity.
- The Notice must specify a point of contact.
- The Notice must specify an effective date.

Changes to Notice

The Notice must also state that the entity reserves the right to change its privacy practices and apply revised privacy practices to PHI. If the Notice does not include this reservation, the entity cannot change its privacy policies and apply them retroactively. If an entity does change its policies and applies the new policies retrospectively, it must provide individuals with a revised Notice.

Activity in Notice

If the Notice does not include a specific activity, then it cannot use or disclose protected health information for that activity without obtaining an individual's Authorization.

Providers with a Direct Treatment Relationship

Health care providers with a direct treatment relationship to an individual are required to

- ◆ Post the Notice at their physical delivery site, if applicable, in a clear and prominent location
- ◆ Make a copy of their Notice available for the individual to take with him
- ◆ Make a good faith attempt to obtain a written acknowledgement of receipt of the Notice from the individual

When the direct treatment provider conducts emergency treatment, they should supply their Notice as soon as reasonably practicable after the emergency treatment situation. Exceptions are made for emergency care providers like ambulance services and ER physicians who might only have contact with an individual for the emergency encounter itself.

Health Plans

Health care plans must make the Notice required by this section available on request to any person, and a health plan must provide Notice

- ◆ No later than their compliance date
- ◆ Thereafter, at the time of enrollment to individuals who are new enrollees

- ◆ Within 60 days of a material revision to the notice, to individuals then covered

- ◆ No less frequently than once every three years, the health plan must notify individuals then covered by the plan of the availability of the Notice and how to obtain the Notice

A health plan satisfies these requirements if the Notice is provided to the named insured of a policy under which coverage is provided to the named insured and one or more dependents.

If a health plan has more than one Notice, it satisfies the requirements by providing the Notice that is relevant to the individual or other person requesting the Notice.

First Interaction

The first time an individual request services, the Notice must be provided automatically. So, for example, the first time an individual interacts with an Internet pharmacy, the system must generate an electronic version of the Notice and deliver that to the individual.

Electronic Notice

A covered entity that maintains a Web site that provides information about the covered entity's customer services or benefits must prominently post its Notice on the Web site and make the Notice available electronically through the Web site.

A covered entity can provide the Notice to an individual by e-mail, if the individual agrees to electronic Notice and such agreement has not been withdrawn. If the covered entity knows that the e-mail transmission has failed, a paper copy of the Notice must be provided to the individual. Provision of electronic Notice by the covered entity will satisfy the provision requirements when done in a timely manner.

If the first service delivery to an individual is delivered electronically, the covered health care provider must provide an electronic Notice automatically and contemporaneously in response to the individual's first request for service. However, a health care provider with a direct treatment relationship must still make a good faith attempt to obtain a written acknowledgement of receipt of the Notice.

The individual who is the recipient of an electronic Notice retains the right to obtain a paper copy of the Notice from a covered entity upon request.

Joint Notice

Covered entities that participate in organized health care arrangements may comply by a joint Notice, provided that

- They agree to abide by the terms of the Notice with respect to PHI created or received by the covered entity as part of its participation in the organized health care arrangement.

- The joint Notice meets the requirements except that the statements required may be altered to reflect the fact that the Notice covers more than one covered entity.

- The Notice describes with reasonable specificity the covered entities to which the joint Notice applies.

- The Notice describes with reasonable specificity the service delivery sites to which the joint Notice applies.

- If applicable, it states that the covered entities participating in the organized health care arrangement will share protected health information with each other, as necessary, to carry out treatment, payment, or health care operations relating to the organized health care arrangement.

Documentation

A covered entity must document compliance with the Notice requirements by retaining copies of the Notices issued and, if applicable, any written acknowledgments of receipt of the Notice or documentation of good faith efforts to obtain such written acknowledgment for at least six years after they were last effective.

Consent (Optional)

Under HIPAA regulations, covered entities are permitted to obtain consent for TPO, if they wish, but there is no requirement that a consent be obtained. However if a covered entity chooses to obtain an individual's consent, it may not be obtained to permit use or disclosure that is not otherwise permitted or required by the regulations.

 NOTE

After the 2002 Privacy Rule modifications, obtaining a Consent became optional.

Consent and State Law

State law may impose additional requirements for a Consent and consent forms on covered entities.

Consent Revocation

A Consent can be revoked at any time. The revocation of a Consent must be received in writing.

Authorization

An Authorization is a more customized document that gives covered entities permission to use specified PHI for specified purposes, which are generally other than TPO, or to disclose PHI to a third party specified by the individual. Covered entities cannot condition treatment or coverage on the individual providing an Authorization. An Authorization is more detailed and specific than a Consent. It covers only the uses and disclosures and only the PHI stipulated in the Authorization; it has an expiration date, and, in some cases, it also states the purpose for which the information can be used or disclosed.

An Authorization is required for use and disclosure of PHI not otherwise allowed by the rule. In general, this means an Authorization is required for purposes that are not part of TPO and not described in

- ◆ Uses and disclosures that require an opportunity for the individual to agree or to object
- ◆ Uses and disclosures for which an Authorization or an opportunity to agree or to object is not required

All covered entities, not just direct treatment providers, must obtain an Authorization to use or disclose PHI for these purposes.

For example, a covered entity would need an Authorization from individuals to sell a patient mailing list, to disclose information to an employer for employment decisions, or to disclose information for eligibility for life insurance. A covered entity never needs to obtain both an individual's consent and authorization for a single use or disclosure.

However, a provider might need to obtain an Authorization from the same patient for different uses or disclosures. For example, an obstetrician might, under the

Authorization obtained from the patient, send an appointment reminder to the patient, but would need an additional Authorization from the patient to send her name and address to a company marketing a diaper service.

Individual Authorization

Covered entities can use or disclose protected health information with the individuals' authorization for any lawful purpose. A standard form would be established for this purpose. Each Authorization must specify the information to be disclosed, who would get the information, and when the Authorization would expire. Individuals can revoke an Authorization at any time.

Core Data Elements and Required Statements

All Authorizations must contain a core set of data elements. These include

- A specific and meaningful description of the information to be used or disclosed.
- The name or other specific identification of the person(s), or class of persons, authorized to make the requested use or disclosure.
- The name or other specific identification of the person(s), or class of persons, to whom the covered entity may make the requested use or disclosure.
- A description of each purpose of the requested use or disclosure. The statement "at the request of the individual" is a sufficient description of the purpose when an individual initiates the Authorization and does not, or elects not to, provide a statement of the purpose.
- An expiration date or an expiration event that relates to the individual or the purpose of the use or disclosure. The following statements meet the requirements for an expiration date or an expiration event if the appropriate conditions apply:
  - The statement "end of the research study" or similar language is sufficient if the Authorization is for a use or disclosure of protected health information for research.
  - The statement "none" or similar language is sufficient if the Authorization is for the covered entity to use or disclose protected health information for the creation and maintenance of a research database or research repository.

- A statement of the individual's right to revoke the Authorization in writing and the exceptions to the right to revoke, together with a description of how the individual may revoke the Authorization and a reference to the covered entity's notice.
- The ability or inability to condition treatment, payment, enrollment, or eligibility for benefits on the authorization, by stating either
  - The covered entity may not condition treatment, payment, enrollment, or eligibility for benefits on whether the individual signs the Authorization.
  - The consequences to the individual of a refusal to sign the Authorization when the covered entity can condition treatment, enrollment in the health plan, or eligibility for benefits on failure to obtain such Authorization.
- A statement that information used or disclosed pursuant to the Authorization may be subject to re-disclosure by the recipient and no longer be protected by the Privacy Rule.
- Signature of the individual and date.
- If the Authorization is signed by a personal representative of the individual, a description of such representative's authority to act for the individual.
- A valid Authorization must be written in plain language according to the guidelines for Notices.
- The covered entity must provide the individual with a copy of the signed Authorization.

Defective Authorizations

An Authorization is not valid if the document submitted has any of the following defects:

- The expiration date has passed or the expiration event is known by the covered entity to have occurred.
- The Authorization has not been filled out completely, with respect to a core element or required statement.
- The Authorization is known by the covered entity to have been revoked.

- The Authorization violates the prohibition on conditioning treatment on the individual signing the authorization.
- Any material information in the Authorization is known by the covered entity to be false.

Prohibition on Conditioning of Authorizations

A covered entity cannot condition the provision to an individual of treatment, payment, enrollment in the health plan, or eligibility for benefits on the provision of an Authorization, except

- A covered health care provider can condition the provision of research-related treatment on provision of an Authorization for the use or disclosure of protected health information for such research.
- A health plan can condition enrollment in the health plan or eligibility for benefits on provision of an Authorization requested by the health plan prior to an individual's enrollment in the health plan, if
  - The Authorization sought is for the health plan's eligibility or enrollment determinations relating to the individual or for its underwriting or risk rating determinations.
  - The Authorization is not for a use or disclosure of psychotherapy notes.
- A covered entity can condition the provision of health care that is solely for the purpose of creating protected health information for disclosure to a third party on provision of an Authorization for the disclosure of the protected health information to such third party.

Authorization for Disclosure and Use

A written Authorization is required before PHI can be used or disclosed for any purpose other than treatment, payment, or health care operations (TPO).

An Authorization differs from a Consent in at least two ways:

- It describes specific uses and disclosures of specific elements of PHI.
- It permits disclosure and use by the covered entity that obtains the Authorization, or by one or more identified third parties such as research physicians.

An Authorization obtained for one purpose does not authorize the use or disclosure of PHI for any other purpose. The covered entity can disclose and use the information only as described in the Authorization.

Revocations

Individuals may revoke an Authorization, but revocations must be in writing.

Compound Authorizations

An Authorization for use or disclosure of protected health information cannot be combined with any other document to create a compound Authorization, except as follows:

- An Authorization for the use or disclosure of protected health information for a specific research study can be combined with any other type of written permission for the same research study, including another Authorization for the use or disclosure of protected health information for such research or a Consent to participate in such research.
- An Authorization for a use or disclosure of psychotherapy notes can only be combined with another Authorization for a use or disclosure of psychotherapy notes.
- An Authorization, other than an Authorization for a use or disclosure of psychotherapy notes, can be combined with any other such Authorization, except when a covered entity has conditioned the provision of treatment, payment, enrollment in the health plan, or eligibility for benefits on the provision of one of the Authorizations.

Authorization and Express Legal Permission

The Privacy Rule permits a covered entity to continue to use or disclose health information, that it has on the compliance date pursuant to an Authorization or express legal permission obtained from an individual prior to the compliance date.

Final Privacy Rule Impact

The final Privacy Rule clarifies the authorization requirements to the Privacy Rule to, among other things, eliminate separate authorization requirements for covered entities. Patients have to grant permission in advance for each type of non-routine use or disclosure, but providers do not have to use different types of forms. These modifications also consolidate and streamline core elements and notification requirements.

Key Parties Impacted

This section examines the Privacy Rule in the context of

- Individuals
- Health care providers and payers
  - Direct treatment relationships
  - Indirect treatment relationships
- Parents and minors
- Business associates
- Hybrid covered entities
- Employers
- Organized health care arrangements (OCHA)

Individuals

The standards established in the regulations provide extensive rights to individuals with regard to the protected health information held by the covered entity. These protections include the general requirement that a patient should be notified of their privacy rights, in accordance with the regulations, before a covered entity uses or discloses protected health information to carry out treatment, payment, or health care operations.

Individuals have the following rights:

- Access to their own information, consistent with certain limitations.
- Receive an accounting of disclosures that have been made of their PHI for up to six years prior to the date of requesting such accounting.
- Submit complaints if they believe or suspect that information about them has been improperly used or disclosed, or if they have concerns about the privacy policies of the organization.

- That the organization restricts uses and disclosures of their individual information while carrying out treatment, payment activities, or health care operations.
- To receive information from the entity by alternative means, such as mail, e-mail, fax, or telephone, or at alternative locations.
- Request an amendment of their health care information. The individual may have reason to believe that the health care information maintained by the organization is either not accurate or complete.

In addition, any permitted use or disclosure must only be of "the minimum necessary to accomplish the intended purpose of the use, disclosure, or request." The minimum necessary requirement, however, has certain exceptions, such as disclosures to or requests by a health care provider for treatment.

These broad patient consent requirements mean that health care providers and other covered entities must begin formulating their policies and procedures now so that the appropriate consents are in place when the regulations go into effect.

The Privacy Rule provides individuals with the right to request that the covered entity restrict how protected health information is used or disclosed to carry out treatment, payment, or other health care operations. The covered entity, however, is not required to agree to the requested restrictions.

Individuals are also provided the right of access to inspect and obtain a copy of their own protected health information.

Exclusions from Right of Access

This right of access does not extend to

- Psychotherapy notes
- Information compiled in reasonable anticipation of, or for use in, a civil, criminal, or administrative action or proceeding
- A research project that the individual consented to that is still in progress
- An individual denied access to the information under the Privacy Act
- An inmate in a correctional facility where the covered entity is a correctional facility or provider acting under the direction of the correctional

facility, where providing access to the information would endanger other inmates or correctional employees

Individuals also have the right to have a covered entity amend protected health information about the individual that is maintained by the covered entity, with limited exceptions.

Request for Amendment

If the covered entity accepts the request for amendment of health care information, it must

- Make the required amendment to the PHI or records that contain the information to be amended
- Inform the individual that the amendment was accepted
- Ask the individual to identify persons who should be notified of the amendment
- Obtain the individual's permission to contact those persons
- Make a reasonable effort to inform the following two groups of the amendment:
  - Persons identified by the individual
  - Persons, including business associates, to whom it has disclosed the information who could be predicted to use the information to the detriment of the individual

If the covered entity denies the request for amendment, it

- Must provide a written denial notice
- Must permit the individual to submit a written statement disagreeing with the denial and giving the basis for the disagreement
- May write a rebuttal to the disagreement and provide a copy of the rebuttal to the individual
- Must append the following to the record containing the disputed information:
  - Request for amendment
  - Denial of amendment

- Statement of disagreement
- Written rebuttal

In any subsequent disclosure of the PHI contained in the disputed record, the covered entity must include

- Request for amendment that was submitted by the individual or an accurate summary of the request
- The denial of the request for amendment
- Any statement of disagreement submitted, or a reasonable summary of the statement
- The covered entity's rebuttal of the statement of disagreement
- This information must be submitted as part of any standard transaction

Accounting of Disclosures

Individuals also are given the right to request and receive an accounting, in a form that meets regulatory requirements, of the disclosures of their protected health information by the covered entity, with certain exceptions. Covered entities must maintain records regarding these disclosures of protected health information.

The federal commentary that accompanied the regulation states that an audit trail must be kept to be able to inform the patient which information was sent to which recipients. This information, in turn, enables the individuals to exercise certain other rights under the rule, such as the rights to inspection and amendment.

The federal regulation also allows individuals to monitor how covered entities are complying with the rule.

Disclosures that follow the guidelines of the covered entity's Notice of Privacy Practices, or that were made using a signed Authorization, do not need to be recorded for this accounting. In both situations the individual has had the opportunity to be informed of the disclosure.

Limits on Medical Record Use and Release

With few exceptions, an individual's health information can only be used for her health care and related purposes unless the individual specifically authorizes its use for another purpose.

◆ **Ensuring that health information is not used for non-health purposes.**
Health information covered by the rule generally cannot be used for
purposes not related to health care—such as disclosures to employers
to make personnel decisions, or to financial institutions—without
explicit authorization from the individual.

◆ **Clear, strong protections against marketing.** The final Privacy Rule set
new restrictions and limits on the use of patient information for marketing purposes. The proposed modifications would explicitly require covered entities to first obtain the individual's specific authorization before
sending that person any marketing materials.

◆ **Providing the minimum amount of information necessary.** In general,
uses or disclosures of information are limited to the minimum necessary
for the purpose of the use or disclosure. This provision does not apply to
the disclosure of medical records for treatment purposes because physicians, specialists, and other providers need access to the full record to
provide quality care.

Health Care Providers and Payers

Under the Privacy Rule, providers and payers are required to implement basic
administrative procedures to protect health information. Among them:

◆ Develop a Notice of Privacy Practice

◆ Allow individuals to inspect and copy their protected health information

◆ Develop a mechanism for accounting for all disclosures made for
purposes other than treatment, payment, or health care operations

◆ Allow individuals to request amendments or corrections to their
protected health information

◆ Designate a privacy official

◆ Provide privacy training to members of its workforce who would have
access to protected health information

◆ Implement physical and administrative safeguards to protect health
information from intentional or accidental misuse

◆ Establish policies and procedures to allow individuals to log complaints
about the entity's information practices, and maintain a record of any
complaints

- ◆ Develop a system of sanctions for members of the workforce and business partners who violate the entity's policies
- ◆ Have available documentation regarding compliance with the requirements of the regulation
- ◆ Develop methods for disclosing only the minimum amount of protected information necessary to accomplish any intended purpose
- ◆ Develop and use contracts that ensure that business partners also protect the privacy of identifiable health information

The Privacy Rule distinguishes between providers who have direct and indirect treatment relationships with individuals.

Providers should develop policies and procedures for denying an individual's request for access to PHI. The policies and procedures should identify the individual or conditions under which an individual will not be given access to his or her records.

Direct Treatment Relationships

HIPAA considers direct treatment relationships to exist when the provider delivers health care without relying on the orders of another provider and communicates the results of diagnostic or other procedures directly to the patient. An example is the primary care physician or family practitioner.

Keep in mind that a face-to-face encounter between a provider and a patient does not constitute a direct treatment relationship, and that the absence of such an encounter does not rule out a direct treatment relationship.

Further, the specialization of the physician or other provider does not determine whether relationships are direct or indirect. A sub-specialist who assists another physician would probably have an indirect relationship with the patient. However, if that same sub-specialist assumed primary responsibility for managing the care of the patient, he or she would assume a direct treatment relationship.

When providers have direct treatment relationships with individuals, HIPAA requires that they must

- ◆ Provide the individual with a Notice of Privacy Practices that describes the uses of PHI

- ◆ Make a good faith effort to obtain a written acknowledgement of receipt of their Notice of Privacy Practices from the individual to whom the Noticed was provided

- ◆ Obtain specific written authorization for any disclosure or use of PHI other than for the purposes of treatment, payment, or in health care operations

- ◆ Make reasonable steps to preserve the confidentiality of certain communications of PHI when requested to do so by an individual

- ◆ Provide access to the PHI that it has collected and maintains, and make reasonable efforts to correct possible errors in this information when requested to do so by an individual

- ◆ Establish procedures to receive complaints relating to the handling of PHI

- ◆ Establish agreements or contracts with business associates that specify the PHI that will be disclosed to them for specified business purposes and that require the business associates to treat that information in the same manner as the provider

- ◆ Disclose PHI to law enforcement and other government agencies that are legally entitled to obtain the information

Indirect Treatment Relationships

HIPAA considers indirect treatment relationships to be ones in which the provider delivers treatment or performs procedures according to the orders of another provider and communicates the results to another provider who in turn communicates the results to the patient. For example, a fertility physician who performs diagnostic procedures on the orders of another physician and communicates results back to the ordering physician.

HIPAA basically requires the same things from providers in indirect relationships as it does from those in direct relationships. The key differences are

- ◆ A Notice of Privacy Practices is required only when requested by the individual.

- There is no requirement to obtain a written acknowledgement of receipt of its Notice of Privacy Practice.
- The provider must disclose and use PHI for treatment, payment, and health care operations in accordance with its Notice of Privacy Practices.

Parents and Minors

The Privacy Rule provides individuals with certain rights with respect to their personal health information, including the right to obtain access to and to request amendment of health information about themselves. These rights rest with that individual, or with the personal representative of that individual. In general, a person's right to control protected health information (PHI) is based on that person's right (under state or other applicable law, for example, tribal or military law) to control the health care itself.

Because a parent usually has authority to make health care decisions about his or her minor child, a parent is generally a personal representative of his or her minor child under the Privacy Rule and has the right to obtain access to health information about his or her minor child. This would also be true in the case of a guardian or other person acting *in loco parentis* of a minor.

There are exceptions in which a parent might not be the personal representative with respect to certain health information about a minor child. In the following situations, the Privacy Rule defers to determinations under other laws that the parent does not control the minor's health care decisions and, thus, does not control the PHI related to that care:

- When state or other law does not require consent of a parent or other person before a minor can obtain a particular health care service, and the minor consents to the health care service, the parent is not the minor's personal representative under the Privacy Rule.

For example, when a state law provides an adolescent the right to consent to mental health treatment without the consent of his or her parent, and the adolescent obtains such treatment without the consent of the parent, the parent is not the personal representative under the Privacy Rule for that treatment. The minor may choose to involve a parent in these health care decisions without giving up his or her right to control the related health information. Of course, the minor may always have the parent continue to be his or her personal representative even in these situations.

State Law

In addition to the provisions tying the right to control information to the right to control treatment, the Privacy Rule also states that it does not preempt state laws that specifically address disclosure of health information about a minor to a parent. This is true whether the state law authorizes or prohibits such disclosure. Thus, if a physician believes that disclosure of information about a minor would endanger that minor, but a state law requires disclosure to a parent, the physician may comply with the state law without violating the Privacy Rule.

Similarly, a provider may comply with a state law that requires disclosure to a parent and would not have to accommodate a request for confidential communications that would be contrary to state law.

Children's Rights

The Privacy Rule does not address consent to treatment, nor does it preempt or change state or other laws that address consent to treatment. The rule addresses access to health information, not the underlying treatment.

Even though the parent cannot provide consent to the treatment, under the Privacy Rule, the parent is still the child's personal representative. This is not so only when the minor provided consent (and no other consent is required) or the treating physician suspects abuse or neglect or reasonably believes that releasing the information to the parent will endanger the child.

Personal Representatives

A personal representative is an individual who is legally authorized to make decisions related to health care on behalf of an individual. Examples of personal representatives include

- Court-appointed guardians for non-competent adults
- Persons who have been granted power of attorney

The authority of the personal representative may be limited to specific decisions. A personal representative may consent to or authorize the use or disclosure of another person's PHI under certain circumstances. A personal representative can also exercise the right of that other individual to inspect, copy, or correct PHI in the possession of a covered entity.

Minors

Generally, a minor is not able to consent to or authorize disclosure of PHI. It is the minor's parent or legal guardian who does so on behalf of the minor. However, the minor is permitted to exercise the rights of an individual under HIPAA if one of the following is true:

◆ The minor is not legally required to obtain the consent of a parent or guardian to receive treatment, and the minor has not requested that a parent or guardian be treated as a legal representative.

◆ The minor can legally obtain treatment without the consent of a parent or guardian, and the minor (or a court or a lawfully authorized person) has consented to treatment.

Business Associates

The HIPAA privacy regulations affect the disclosures by covered entities of protected health information to their business associates.

The definition of "business associate" casts a broad net over the parties with which covered entities contract or otherwise deal in their operations. The preamble, which accompanies the regulation, explains that the regulations extend the Privacy Rule to a covered entity's arrangements with their business associates, in part, to prevent covered entities from circumventing the rules by contracting out the performance of various functions.

By law, the Privacy Rule applies only to health plans, health care clearinghouses, and certain health care providers. In today's health care system, however, most health care providers and health plans do not carry out all of their health care activities and functions by themselves; they require assistance from a variety of contractors and other businesses.

In allowing providers and plans to give PHI to these "business associates," the Privacy Rule conditions such disclosures on the provider or plan obtaining, typically by contract, satisfactory assurances that the business associate will use the information only for the purposes for which he was engaged by the covered entity, will safeguard the information from misuse, and will help the covered entity comply with the covered entity's duties to provide individuals with access to health information about them and a history of certain disclosures (for example, if the business associate maintains the only copy of information, it must promise to cooperate with the covered entity to provide individuals access to information upon request).

PHI may be disclosed to a business associate *only* to help the providers and plans carry out their health care functions—not for independent use by the business associate.

So to summarize, a business associate is a person or entity who provides certain functions, activities, or services for or to a covered entity, involving the use and/or disclosure of PHI. A business associate is not a member of the health care provider, health plan, or other covered entity's workforce. A health care provider, health plan, or other covered entity can also be a business associate to another covered entity.

The Privacy Rule also includes exceptions. The business associate requirements do not apply to covered entities who disclose PHI to providers for treatment purposes—for example, information exchanges between a hospital and physicians with admitting privileges at the hospital.

The Privacy Rule does not "pass through" its requirements to business associates or otherwise cause business associates to comply with the terms of the rule. The assurances that covered entities must obtain prior to disclosing PHI to business associates create a set of contractual obligations far narrower than the provisions of the rule to protect information generally and help the covered entity comply with its obligations under the rule. For example, covered entities do not need to ask their business associates to agree to appoint a privacy officer, or develop policies and procedures for use and disclosure of PHI.

HIPAA gives the Secretary of HHS the authority to directly regulate health care providers, health plans, and health care clearinghouses. It also grants the Department of HHS explicit authority to regulate the uses and disclosures of PHI maintained and transmitted by covered entities. Therefore, HHS has the authority to condition the disclosure of PHI by a covered entity to a business associate on the covered entity's having a contract with that business associate.

Examples of business associate–related services follow:

◆ Legal
◆ Actuarial
◆ Consulting
◆ Administration accreditation

- Financial services
- Data aggregation
- Accounting

Privacy Violations of Business Associates

A health care provider, health plan, or other covered entity is not liable for privacy violations of a business associate. Covered entities are not required to actively monitor or oversee the means by which the business associate carries out safeguards or the extent to which the business associate abides by the requirements of the contract.

Moreover, a business associate's violation of the terms of the contract does not, in and of itself, constitute a violation of the rule by the covered entity. The contract must obligate the business associate to advise the covered entity when violations have occurred.

If the covered entity becomes aware of a pattern or practice of the business associate that constitutes a material breach or violation of the business associate's obligations under its contract, the covered entity must take reasonable steps to cure the breach or to end the violation. Reasonable steps vary with the circumstances and nature of the business relationship.

If such steps are not successful, the covered entity must terminate the contract if feasible. The rule also provides for circumstances in which termination is not feasible, for example, where there are no other viable business alternatives for the covered entity. In such circumstances where termination is not feasible, the covered entity must report the problem to the department.

Only if the covered entity fails to take these kinds of steps described above is it considered to be out of compliance with the requirements of the rule.

Business Associate Contract (BAC)

To make disclosures of protected health information to a business associate, a covered entity must have in place a written Business Associate Contract (BAC) or written arrangement with the business associate to document that the covered entity has obtained satisfactory assurance that the business associate will appropriately safeguard the protected health information. Specific provisions in these contracts are required.

This obligation requires that health care providers and other covered entities begin now to review their contractual relationships with business associates and amend them so that the covered entity will be in compliance with the privacy regulations when they go into effect. Covered entities have until April 14, 2004 to bring their business associate contracts into compliance with the Privacy Rule. The additional year to negotiate compliant contracts was granted as part of the final modifications to the Privacy Rule on August 14, 2002.

A Business Associate Contract must do two things:

- Specify the PHI to be disclosed and the uses that may be made of that information

- Impose security, inspection, and reporting requirements on the business associate

The BAC must describe the purpose of any permitted uses or disclosures of PHI and indicate the reasons and types of persons or entities to whom the information may be disclosed.

The business associate can be authorized to do the following:

- Use and disclose PHI as necessary for proper management and to meet its legal obligations. The business associate must also give reasonable assurances that the information will be kept confidential and that any breaches to confidentiality will be reported to the covered entity.

- Provide data aggregation services to the covered entity. *Data aggregation* is the process of combining information from a variety of sources to provide comparative or other management information. Data aggregation must conform to certain requirements that protect the confidentiality of PHI.

Exemptions

Two types of organizations are exempted from the definition of a business associate: conduits and financial institutions.

Conduits include entities that pass along PHI such as the U.S. Postal Service, Federal Express, Internet service providers, and other similar services. Conduits transport information but do not have access to it except on a random or infrequent basis.

A financial institution refers to firms that process consumer-related financial transactions. This includes banks that process payments by debit cards, credit cards, or other payment cards; clears checks; initiates or processes electronic funds transfers, or conducts any other activity that directly facilitates or effects the transfer of funds or compensation for health care—all such entities are not regarded as business associates. However, if a collection agency is retained for addressing issues related to delinquent patients, then the collection agency is regarded as a business associate.

In addition, Business Associate Contracts are not necessary between health care providers to conduct treatment.

Hybrid Covered Entities

A hybrid entity is an entity

◆ In which some aspect of the entity engages in activities that trigger HIPAA-covered entity status, which means engaging in functions that make an entity a covered entity such as providing health care, paying for health care, or performing a clearinghouse function

◆ That designates one or more health care components within the entity

The Privacy Rule provides special treatment of hybrid covered entities. The Privacy Rule permits any covered entity to be a hybrid entity if it is a single legal entity that performs both covered and non-covered functions, regardless of whether the non-covered functions represent the entity's primary function, a substantial function, or even a small portion of the entity's activities. Covered entities that qualify as hybrid entities may choose whether or not they want to be considered hybrid entities. To be a hybrid entity, a covered entity that otherwise qualifies must designate its health care component. If it does not designate a health care component, then the entire entity is considered to be a covered entity.

The final Privacy Rule permits any entity that performs covered and non-covered functions to elect to use the hybrid entity provisions and provides the entity additional discretion in designating its health care components.

The Privacy Rule imposes the requirement that a hybrid covered entity must ensure that the health care component of the covered entity complies with the applicable requirements of the Privacy Rule. The hybrid entity must ensure that

- The health care component does not disclose PHI to another component of the hybrid covered entity, where that disclosure would be prohibited if the sender and receiver were in separate and distinct legal entities.

- A component of a hybrid entity acts like a business associate to the health care component, as if the health care component was a separate entity, and only uses or discloses PHI for the functions that are analogous to business associate functions.

- A workforce member of the covered entity who performs health care component functions and other functions for the hybrid entity does not use PHI from the health care component for any other purpose prohibited by the Privacy Rule.

Employers

The final Privacy Rule clarifies that employment records maintained by a covered entity in its capacity as an employer are excluded from the definition of protected health information. The modifications do not change the fact that individually identifiable health information created, received, or maintained by a covered entity in its health care capacity is protected health information.

Organized Health Care Arrangements (OCHA)

There are five types of organized health care arrangements (OCHA) in which PHI may be shared for purposes of joint management and operations:

- A clinically integrated care setting in which individuals typically receive health care from more than one provider. An example would be a hospital in which attending physicians must share clinical information on patients with each other and with the hospital.

- An organized system of health care in which more than one provider participates, described to the public as joint arrangements in which the participants share in certain joint activities.

- An arrangement between a group health plan and a health insurer or HMO with respect to such plan, but only with respect to PHI that relates to individuals who are or have been participating in the plan.

- An arrangement among multiple group health plans maintained by the same sponsor.

- An arrangement among multiple group health plans maintained by the same plan sponsor and the health insurance issuers or HMOs that establish or manage those plans

Minimum Necessary

The Privacy Rule generally requires covered entities to take reasonable steps to limit the use or disclosure of, and requests for, protected health information (PHI) to the minimum necessary to accomplish the intended purpose.

In every case HIPAA requires that the use and disclosure of PHI be limited to the minimum necessary to accomplish the intended or specified purpose.

The minimum necessary provisions do not apply to the following:

- Disclosures to or requests by a health care provider for treatment purposes
- Disclosures to the individual who is the subject of the information
- Uses or disclosures made pursuant to an authorization requested by the individual
- Uses or disclosures required for compliance with the standardized HIPAA transactions
- Disclosures to the Department of Health and Human Services (HHS) when disclosure of information is required under the rule for enforcement purposes
- Uses or disclosures that are required by other laws

In practice, the minimum necessary requirement should lead to compartmentalization of medical records so that one portion of the record may be readily disclosed for one purpose without compromising the privacy of the entire record. Compartmentalization may appear burdensome, but it should not be. It can be accomplished by adopting simple, standard protocols for categorizing and labeling portions of a record. Keeping the standard categorization protocols simple is the key to the implementation success for many organizations. At the outset, the concept of categorization should be easy for everyone to understand.

Compartmentalization is a common method for individuals to handle non-medical information about themselves. One of the contributors of this course material, for example, maintains a professional biography that is available in numerous electronic databases to anyone else in the world. It contains information that he chooses to make public: his educational credentials, the professional organizations he belongs to, and his areas of professional expertise. Yet there is much personal information about him that he chooses to make available to his friends but not the general public, and there is a layer of even more intimate information that he makes available only to his family.

Finally, there is medical information that he makes available only to his doctor and legal information that he makes available only to his lawyer, both categories of which he expects to be kept confidential and used only as needed. In effect, each of us utilizes a "minimum necessary" standard as we go through life disclosing information about ourselves to others.

The minimum necessary standard is a linchpin for the rest of the Privacy Rule. Its implementation begins with the creation of a data classification scheme that is appropriate for your environment. In general terms there are subsets or buckets of health information that are either related to other buckets or not. Determining what is and is not related is the key to being able to painlessly apply the minimum necessary standard. If the entire record is in one bucket, more effort is required to limit access to information.

What are the anticipated benefits of the minimum necessary standard? The minimum necessary standard benefits patients in the same way that the Privacy Rule as a whole does, by bolstering the patient's control of his or her medical information, thereby advancing the goal of medical confidentiality. This benefit is not merely abstract. Clearer privacy protections for sensitive health information encourages patients to be candid with their doctors, and that leads to better health care.

PHI Uses, Disclosures, and Requests

For uses of PHI, the policies and procedures must identify the persons or classes of persons within the covered entity who need access to the information to carry out their job duties, the categories or types of PHI needed, and conditions appropriate to such access. For example, hospitals may implement policies that permit doctors, nurses, or others involved in treatment to have access to the entire medical record, as needed. Case-by-case review of each use is not required. Where the entire medical record is necessary, the covered entity's policies and procedures must state so explicitly and include a justification.

For routine or recurring requests and disclosures, the policies and procedures may be standard protocols and must limit PHI disclosed or requested to the minimum necessary for that particular type of disclosure or request. Individual review of each disclosure or request is not required.

For non-routine disclosures, covered entities must develop reasonable criteria for determining, and limiting disclosure to, only the minimum amount of PHI necessary to accomplish the purpose of a non-routine disclosure. Non-routine disclosures must be reviewed on an individual basis in accordance with these criteria. When making non-routine requests for PHI, the covered entity must review each request in order to ask for only that information reasonably necessary for the purpose of the request.

Reasonable Reliance

In certain circumstances, the Privacy Rule permits a covered entity to rely on the judgment of the party requesting the disclosure as to the minimum amount of information that is needed. Such reliance must be reasonable under the particular circumstances of the request. This reliance is permitted when the request is made by

◆ A public official or agency for a disclosure permitted under the rule

◆ Another covered entity

◆ A professional who is a workforce member or business associate of the covered entity holding the information

◆ A researcher with appropriate documentation from an Institutional Review Board (IRB) or Privacy Board

The Privacy Rule does not require such reliance, however, and the covered entity always retains discretion to make its own minimum necessary determination for disclosures to which the standard applies.

Reasonable Effort

The Privacy Rule requires a covered entity to make reasonable efforts to limit use, disclosure of, and requests for PHI to the minimum necessary to accomplish the intended purpose. To allow covered entities the flexibility to address their unique circumstances, the rule requires covered entities to make their own assessment of what PHI is reasonably necessary for a particular purpose, given the characteristics of their business and workforce, and to implement policies and procedures accordingly.

The minimum necessary standard is intended to make covered entities evaluate their practices and enhance protections as needed to prevent unnecessary or inappropriate access to PHI. It is intended to reflect and be consistent with, not override, professional judgment and standards.

Assessment Tasks

To prevent unnecessary and inappropriate access to PHI the entity needs to analyze the flow of PHI throughout the organization and outside. This will require a review of current policies and procedures and a subsequent analysis of the same to introduce changes in the workplace to be in compliance with HIPAA Privacy Rule requirements. The following assessment tasks should be completed to make sure the entity prevents unnecessary or inappropriate access to PHI:

1. Catalog or otherwise document all routine PHI-related communications— regardless of their transmission medium (oral, paper, file, fax, data entry, automated data transfers, and so on).

2. Assume that 80 percent or more of your PHI-dependent communications result from some relatively small fraction of your complete catalog of all routine PHI-related communications. Focus on that highest-impact fraction first.

3. Identify and document the subset of a given person's PHI required to satisfy each of the selected routine communications. Assume that not all PHI is required to satisfy each type of routine communication.

4. Review the existing policies, procedures, and training to ensure that for each routine communication, only the minimum required PHI is passed.

5. Document any exceptions for risk analysis and, where required, remediation. Escalate all exceptions and anomalies to the Privacy Compliance Officer.

6. After reviewing the highest-impact communications and determining which require change, build a project plan to remediate them (include acquiring funding and resources required for project success).

7. Execute the initial remediation plan.

8. Review, identify, and document the subset of a given person's PHI required to satisfy each of the rest of the routine communications. Assume that not all PHI is required to satisfy each type of routine communication. Quickly rule out further analysis of any that are obviously compliant.

9. Review the existing policies, procedures, and training to ensure that for each of the remaining routine communications, only the minimum required PHI is passed.

10. Document any exceptions for risk analysis and, where required, remediation. Escalate all exceptions and anomalies to the Privacy Compliance Officer.

11. After reviewing the remaining communications and determining which require change, build a project plan to remediate them (include acquiring funding and resources required for project success).

12. Execute the plan.

Routine Communications to Consider

Consider the situation of the following types of health care organizations: hospitals, ambulatory care centers, home health care providers, long-term care facilities, physicians practices/clinics, and rehabilitation facilities. These health care organizations typically include the following types of PHI-relevant routine communications:

- **Admissions—third-party payers** (any of whom will use your PHI in communications with employers, third-party benefit managers, marketers/database developers, and others):
  - Managed care organizations
  - Traditional fee-for-service insurers
  - Other third-party payers
  - Pharmacy benefit administrators
  - Health plan administrators
- Admissions—patient care areas
- Patient care areas—patient account billing

- ◆ Patient care areas—internal "hospital" functional departments:
  - Case management and utilization review
  - Dietary
  - Laboratory
  - Pharmacy
  - Radiology
  - Physical therapy
  - Respiratory therapy
  - Discharge planning
- ◆ Patient care areas—information services:
  - IS professionals
  - Data warehouses
  - Line-of-business systems
  - Data analysis
  - Transaction Support (internal and external)
- ◆ Information services—patient accounts billing
- ◆ Information services—internal "hospital" functional departments (may also support all the functional departments in a previous set of bullets above):
  - Disease registries
  - Risk management
  - Quality management/outcomes
  - Transcription
  - Epidemiology
- ◆ Internal "hospital" functional departments—external entities:
  - County and/or state health departments
  - State disease registries
  - State data commissions
  - Contract outcomes management databases

◆ The "hospital"—accreditation and review organizations:
- American Osteopathic Association
- Joint Commission on Accreditation of Health Care Organizations
- State surveyors
- Peer review organizations

Health Care Operations and Minimum Necessary

The definition of health care operations in the Rule provides for "conducting training programs in which students, trainees, or practitioners in areas of health care learn under supervision to practice or improve their skills as health care providers."

Covered entities can shape their policies and procedures for minimum necessary uses and disclosures to permit medical trainees access to patients' medical information, including entire medical records.

Disclosure and Use for Treatment

The primary purpose of any health care delivery organization is medical treatment. The job of a provider is to diagnose and treat patients' medical conditions. The function of a health insurer or health plan is to help its beneficiaries pay for or finance medical treatment.

Disclosures for treatment purposes (including requests for disclosures) between health care providers are explicitly exempted from the minimum necessary requirements.

The Privacy Rule provides the covered entity with substantial discretion as to how to implement the minimum necessary standard, and appropriately and reasonably limit access to the use of identifiable health information within the covered entity.

The Privacy Rule also recognizes that the covered entity is in the best position to know and determine who in its workforce needs access to personal health information to perform their jobs. Therefore, the covered entity can develop role-based access policies that allow its health care providers and other employees, as appropriate, access to patient information, including entire medical records, for treatment purposes.

Disclosures to Third Parties

The Privacy Rule exempts from the minimum necessary requirements most uses or disclosures that are authorized by an individual. This includes authorizations covered entities may receive directly from third parties, such as life, disability, or casualty insurers pursuant to the patient's application for or claim under an insurance policy.

For example, if a covered health care provider receives an individual's authorization to disclose medical information to a life insurer for underwriting purposes, the provider is permitted to disclose the information requested on the authorization without making any minimum necessary determination.

However, minimum necessary does apply to authorizations requested by the covered entity for its own purposes.

Disclosure to Federal and State Agencies

The minimum necessary determination to disclose to federal or state agencies, such as the Social Security Administration (SSA) or its affiliated state agencies, must be authorized by an individual and, therefore, is exempt from the minimum necessary requirements. Further, use of the provider's own authorization form is not required. Providers can accept an agency's authorization form as long as it meets the requirements of the rule.

For example, disclosures to SSA (or its affiliated state agencies) for purposes of determining eligibility for disability benefits are currently made subject to an individual's completed SSA authorization form. After the compliance date, the current process may continue subject only to modest changes in the SSA authorization form to conform to the requirements.

Disclosure of Entire Medical Record

The Privacy Rule does not prohibit use, disclosure, or requests of an entire medical record. A covered entity can use, disclose, or request an entire medical record, without a case-by-case justification, if the covered entity has documented in its policies and procedures that the entire medical record is the amount reasonably necessary for certain identified purposes.

For uses, the policies and procedures would identify those persons or classes of persons in the workforce that need to see the entire medical record and the conditions (if any) that are appropriate for such access. Policies and procedures for routine disclosures and requests and the criteria used for non-routine disclosures identify the circumstances under which disclosing or requesting the entire medical record is reasonably necessary for particular purposes. In making non-routine requests, the covered entity can also establish and utilize criteria to assist in determining when to request the entire medical record.

The Privacy Rule does not require that a justification be provided with respect to each distinct medical record. No justification is needed in those instances where the minimum necessary standard does not apply, such as disclosures to or requests by a health care provider for treatment or disclosures to the individual.

Where should the line be drawn in determining what is reasonably necessary? By definition, there is no single answer to this question. Organizations and their internal processes are different from each other. The line must be drawn in each instance by what individuals learned about their privacy obligations in training, the application of common sense, and by reference to the fundamental purpose of the Privacy Rule. That said, the adoption of strong privacy policies at the outset of an entity's compliance with the rules obviates the need for anguished deliberation each time a request for information is made.

The original intent of the legislation was that those policies should draw a bright line in favor of confidentiality and should give life to each of the two words in the standard: minimum and necessary. The policy should prompt quick consideration of two basic questions: how much information is needed to fulfill the purpose of this request? Conversely, are we about to provide information that is not necessary to fulfill the purpose of this request? Sometimes the answer is obvious.

For example, when an insurance company requests documentation that the patient was treated for a broken arm, it is not necessary to provide information about the patient's treatment for a sexually transmitted disease. Other times the answers to the minimum necessary questions are less clear. Simple, easy-to-train policies will help minimize the delay and cost of making these kinds of decisions.

HIPAA Transactions Standards

The Privacy Rule exempts from the minimum necessary standard any uses or disclosures that are required for compliance with the applicable requirements of the subchapter for Transactions. This includes all data elements that are required or required by a particular situation in the standard transactions.

However, in many cases, covered entities have significant discretion as to the information included in these transactions. The minimum necessary standard does apply to those optional data elements.

Office Space Design

The basic standard for minimum necessary uses requires that covered entities make reasonable efforts to limit access to PHI to those in the workforce that need access based on their roles in the covered entity.

It is generally not necessary to consider facility redesigns as necessary to meet the reasonableness standard for minimum necessary uses. As HHS has made clear, the minimum necessary standard does not require soundproof rooms, nor does it prevent doctors from having access to all the medical history needed for the provision of effective health care. However, covered entities might need to make certain adjustments to their facilities to minimize access, such as isolating and locking file cabinets or records rooms, or providing additional security, such as passwords, on computers maintaining personal information.

Covered entities should also take into account their ability to configure their record systems to allow access to only certain fields, and the practicality of organizing systems to allow this capacity.

For example, it might not be reasonable for a small, solo practitioner who has largely a paper-based records system to limit access of employees with certain functions to only limited fields in a patient record, while other employees have access to the complete record. Alternatively, a hospital with an electronic patient record system might reasonably implement such controls, and, therefore, may choose to limit access in this manner to comply with the rule.

Medical Charts and X-Ray Light Boards

The minimum necessary standards do not require that covered entities prohibit the maintenance of medical charts at bedside or that empty prescription vials be shredded or that X-ray light boards be isolated. Covered entities must, in accordance with other provisions of the Privacy Rule, take reasonable precautions to prevent inadvertent or unnecessary disclosures.

For example, while the Privacy Rule does not require that X ray boards be totally isolated from all other functions, it does require covered entities to take reasonable precautions to protect X rays from being accessible to the public.

Request for More Than Minimum Necessary PHI

If there is a request for more than the minimum necessary PHI, the Privacy Rule requires a covered entity to limit the disclosure to the minimum necessary as determined by the disclosing entity. Where the Privacy Rule permits covered entities to rely on the judgment of the person requesting the information, and if such reliance is reasonable despite the covered entity's concerns, the covered entity can make the disclosure as requested.

Nothing in the Privacy Rule prevents a covered entity from discussing its concerns with the person making the request, and negotiating an information exchange that meets the needs of both parties. Such discussions occur today and may continue after the compliance date of the Privacy Rule.

Policies and Procedures

Policies and procedures must be developed to restrict the use of PHI to the minimum necessary information for the performance of specific functions or duties. Policies must include procedures that

- Identify the persons or classes of persons in the entity's workforce who need access to PHI to carry out their duties
- Identify the category or categories of PHI to which each person or class of persons needs access
- Identify the conditions that apply to such access

For example, the policy might grant all persons involved in treatment access to an entire medical record. Further, when a covered entity requests disclosure of PHI by another covered entity, it must

- Describe the purpose of the request
- Limit the information that it requests to the minimum necessary for the stated purpose

Providers should make sure their policies and procedures require justification for the disclosure of the contents of an entire medical record to anyone who is not an employee.

Impact of Final Privacy Rule

The final Privacy Rule exempts from the minimum necessary standards any uses or disclosures for which the covered entity has received an authorization. The Privacy Rule previously exempted only certain types of authorizations from the minimum necessary requirement, but since the Privacy Rule only has one type of authorization, the exemption is now applied to all authorizations. Minimum necessary requirements are still in effect to ensure an individual's privacy for most other uses and disclosures.

The Department of HHS clarifies in the preamble that the minimum necessary standard is not intended to impede disclosures necessary for workers' compensation programs.

Oral Communications

The Privacy Rule applies to individually identifiable health information in all forms:

◆ Electronic

◆ Written

◆ Oral

◆ Any other

Coverage of oral (spoken) information ensures that information retains protections when discussed or read aloud from a computer screen or a written document. If oral communications were not covered, any health information could be disclosed to any person, so long as the disclosure was spoken.

Providers and health plans understand the sensitivity of oral information. For example, many hospitals already have confidentiality policies and concrete procedures for addressing privacy, such as posting signs in elevators that remind employees to protect patient confidentiality.

General Requirements

The general requirements for oral communications are as follows:

Covered entities must reasonably safeguard protected health information (PHI)—including oral information—from any intentional or unintentional use or disclosure that is in violation of the rule.

They must have in place appropriate administrative, technical, and physical safeguards to protect the privacy of PHI.

"Reasonably safeguard" means that covered entities must make reasonable efforts to prevent uses and disclosures not permitted by the rule. However, reasonable safeguards are not expected to guarantee the privacy of PHI from any and all potential risks. In determining whether a covered entity has provided reasonable safeguards, the Department of HHS will take into account all the circumstances, including the potential effects on patient care and the financial and administrative burden of any safeguards.

Covered entities must have policies and procedures that reasonably limit access to and use of PHI to the minimum necessary given the job responsibilities of the workforce and the nature of their business.

The minimum necessary standard does not apply to disclosures, including oral disclosures, among providers for treatment purposes.

Many health care providers already make it a practice to ensure reasonable safeguards for oral information—for instance, by speaking quietly when discussing a patient's condition with family members in a waiting room or other public area, and by avoiding using patients' names in public hallways and elevators.

Protection of patient confidentiality is an important practice for many health care and health information management professionals; covered entities can build upon those codes of conduct to develop the reasonable safeguards required by the Privacy Rule.

Conversations

The Privacy Rule is not intended to prohibit providers from talking to each other and to their patients. Provisions of this rule requiring covered entities to implement reasonable safeguards that reflect their particular circumstances and exempting treatment disclosures from certain requirements are intended to ensure that providers' primary consideration is the appropriate treatment of their patients. It is also understood that overheard communications are unavoidable.

For example, in a busy emergency room, it might be necessary for providers to speak loudly to ensure appropriate treatment. The Privacy Rule is not intended to prevent this appropriate behavior. The following practices are permissible, if reasonable precautions are taken to minimize the chance of inadvertent disclosures to others who may be nearby (such as using lowered voices, talking apart):

- Health care staff may orally coordinate services at hospital nursing stations.

- Nurses or other health care professionals may discuss a patient's condition over the phone with the patient, a provider, or a family member.

- A health care professional may discuss lab test results with a patient or other provider in a joint treatment area.

- Health care professionals may discuss a patient's condition during training rounds in an academic or training institution.

Office Environment

The Privacy Rule does not require structural changes be made to facilities. Covered entities must have in place appropriate administrative, technical, and physical safeguards to protect the privacy of PHI. "Reasonable safeguards" mean that covered entities must make reasonable efforts to prevent uses and disclosures not permitted by the Privacy Rule.

The Department of HHS does not consider facility restructuring to be a requirement under this standard. In determining what is reasonable, the Department of HHS takes into account the concerns of covered entities regarding potential effects on patient care and financial burden.

For example, the Privacy Rule does not require the following types of structural or systems changes:

- Private rooms

- Soundproofing of rooms

- Encryption of wireless or other emergency medical radio communications, which can be intercepted by scanners

- Encryption of telephone systems

Covered entities must provide reasonable safeguards to avoid prohibited disclosures. The Privacy Rule does not require that all risk be eliminated to satisfy this standard. Covered entities must review their own practices and determine what steps are reasonable to safeguard their patient information.

The following are examples of the types of adjustments or modifications to facilities or systems that might constitute reasonable safeguards:

♦ Pharmacies could ask waiting customers to stand a few feet back from a counter used for patient counseling.

♦ Providers could add curtains or screens to areas where oral communications often occur between doctors and patients or among professionals treating patients.

♦ In an area where multiple patient-staff communications routinely occur, use of cubicles, dividers, shields, or similar barriers may constitute a reasonable safeguard. For example, a large clinic intake area may reasonably use cubicles or shield-type dividers, rather than separate rooms.

Patient Access to Oral Information

The Privacy Rule requires covered entities to provide individuals with access to PHI about themselves that is contained in their designated record sets. The term *record* in the term *designated record set* does not include oral information; rather, it connotes information that has been recorded in some manner.

The rule does not require covered entities to tape or digitally record oral communications, nor to retain digitally or tape recorded information after transcription. But if such records are maintained and used to make decisions about the individual, they may meet the definition of *designated record set*.

For example, a health plan is not required to provide a member access to tapes of a telephone advice line interaction if the tape is only maintained for customer service review and not to make decisions about the member.

Documentation of Oral Communications

The Privacy Rule does not require covered entities to document any information, including oral information, that is used or disclosed for treatment, payment, or health care operations (TPO).

However, the Privacy Rule does include documentation requirements for some information disclosures for other purposes. For example, some disclosures must be documented to meet the standard for providing a disclosure history to an individual upon request. Where a documentation requirement exists in the

Privacy Rule, it applies to all relevant communications, whether in oral or some other form.

For example, if a covered physician discloses information about a case of tuberculosis to a public health authority as permitted by the Privacy Rule, then he or she must maintain a record of that disclosure regardless of whether the disclosure was made orally by phone or in writing.

Health-Related Marketing

The Privacy Rule addresses the use and disclosure of protected health information (PHI) for marketing purposes in the following ways:

- Defines what is "marketing" under the Privacy Rule.
- Removes from that definition certain treatment or health care operations activities.
- Set limits on the kind of marketing that can be done as a health care operation.
- Requires individual authorization for all other uses or disclosures of PHI for marketing purposes.

Defining Marketing

The Privacy Rule defines marketing as "a communication about a product or service, a purpose of which is to encourage recipients of the communication to purchase or use the product or service."

In recommending treatments, providers and health plans advise us to purchase goods and services. The overlap between treatment, health care operations, and marketing is unavoidable. Instead of creating artificial distinctions, the rule imposes requirements that do not require such distinctions. Specifically,

- If the activity is included in the Privacy Rule's definition of marketing, the rule's provisions restricting the use or disclosure of PHI for marketing purposes apply, whether or not that communication also meets the rule's definition of treatment, payment, or health care operations. For these communications, the individual's authorization is required before a covered entity can use or disclose PHI for marketing unless one of the exceptions to the authorization requirement applies.

♦ The Privacy Rule exempts certain activities from the definition of marketing. If an activity falls into one of the definition's exemptions, the marketing rules do not apply. In these cases, covered entities can engage in the activity without first obtaining an authorization if the activity meets the definition of treatment, payment, or health care operations.

Communications That Are Not Marketing

The Privacy Rule carves out activities that are not considered marketing under this definition. In recommending treatments or describing available services, health care providers and health plans are advising consumers to purchase goods and services. To prevent any interference with essential treatment or similar health-related communications with a patient, the Privacy Rule identifies the following activities as not subject to the marketing provision, even if the activity otherwise meets the definition of marketing.

Written communications for which the covered entity is compensated by a third party are not carved out of the marketing definition.

Thus, a covered entity is not "marketing" when it

♦ Describes the participating providers or plans in a network. For example, a health plan is not marketing when it tells its enrollees about which doctors and hospitals are preferred providers, which are included in its network, or which providers offer a particular service. Similarly, a health insurer notifying enrollees of a new pharmacy that has begun to accept its drug coverage is not engaging in marketing.

♦ Describes the covered entity's own health-related products or services. For example, informing a plan enrollee about drug formulary coverage is not marketing. Offering an insured an upgrade in coverage or different combinations of deductibles and co-payments is not marketing. Neither is telling your patients about a new laser surgery machine that will let you correct their vision more accurately.

♦ Conducts case management or care coordination for the individual.

♦ Offers health-related products or services. For example, many health plans offer value added services like discounts on vitamins or health club memberships. These are allowed as long as they are not pass throughs. That is, the discount should be greater than what the public at large can get.

. Furthermore, it is not marketing for a covered entity to use an individual's PHI to tailor a health-related communication to that individual, when the communication is

- ◆ Part of a provider's treatment of the patient and for the purpose of furthering that treatment. For example, recommendations of specific brand-name or over-the-counter pharmaceuticals or referrals of patients to other providers are not marketing.

- ◆ About general health topics. For instance, dietary advice to avoid heart problems or the importance of exercise to good health.

- ◆ Made in the course of managing the individual's treatment or recommending alternative treatment. For example, reminder notices for appointments, annual exams, or prescription refills are not marketing. Similarly, informing an individual who is a smoker about an effective smoking-cessation program is not marketing, even if someone offers that program other than the provider or plan making the recommendation.

Limitations on Marketing Communications

If a communication is marketing, a covered entity can use or disclose PHI to create or make the communication, pursuant to any applicable consent obtained, only in the following circumstances:

- ◆ It is a face-to-face communication with the individual. For example, sample products might be provided to a patient during an office visit.

- ◆ It involves products or services of nominal value. For example, a provider can distribute pens, toothbrushes, or key chains with the name of the covered entity or a health care product manufacturer on it.

For all other communications that are marketing under the Privacy Rule, the covered entity must obtain the individual's authorization to use or disclose PHI to create or make the marketing communication.

The Privacy Rule prohibits health plans and covered health care providers from giving PHI to third parties for the third party's own business purposes, lacking authorization from the individuals. Under the statute, this regulation cannot govern contractors directly.

Business Associates and Marketing

Disclosure of PHI for marketing purposes is limited to disclosure to business associates that undertake marketing activities on behalf of the covered entity. No other disclosure for marketing is permitted. Covered entities may not give away or sell lists of patients or enrollees without obtaining an Authorization from each person on the list.

As with any disclosure to a business associate, the covered entity must obtain the business associate's agreement to use the PHI only for the covered entity's marketing activities. A covered entity cannot give PHI to a business associate for the business associate's own purposes.

Selling or Disclosing PHI

The preceding provisions impose limits on the use or disclosure of PHI for marketing that does not exist in most states today. For example, the Privacy Rule requires a patient's authorization for the following types of uses or disclosures of PHI for marketing:

- ◆ Selling PHI to third parties for their use and re-use. Under the Rule, a hospital or other provider cannot sell names of pregnant women to baby formula manufacturers or magazines.
- ◆ Disclosing PHI to outsiders for the outsiders' independent marketing use. Under the rule, doctors cannot provide patient lists to pharmaceutical companies for those companies' drug promotions.

These activities can occur today with no Authorization from the individual. In addition, for the marketing activities that are allowed by the Privacy Rule without an Authorization from the individual, the Privacy Rule requires covered entities to offer individuals the ability to opt out of further marketing communications.

Similarly, under the business associate provisions of the Rule, a covered entity cannot give PHI to a telemarketer, door-to-door salesperson, or other marketer it has hired unless that marketer has agreed by contract to use the information only for marketing on behalf of the covered entity. And, of course, each name given must have a signed Authorization allowing the marketing effort. Today, there may be no restrictions on how marketers re-use information they obtain from health plans and providers.

Telemarketing

Under the Privacy Rule, a covered entity must obtain the individual's authorization to do any marketing. This includes telemarketing.

The telemarketer must be a business associate under the Privacy Rule, which means that it must agree by contract to use the information only for marketing on behalf of the covered entity, and not to market its own goods or services (or those of another third party).

The caller must identify the covered entity that is sponsoring the marketing call, and the caller must provide individuals the opportunity to opt out of further marketing.

Authorization for Use or Disclosure

An Authorization for use or disclosure of PHI for marketing is always required, unless one of the following two exceptions apply:

- ◆ The marketing occurs during an in-person meeting with the patient (for example, during a medical appointment).
- ◆ The marketing concerns products or services of nominal value.

A covered entity must also state in the Authorization when they are compensated (directly or indirectly) for making the communication.

Affect on Other State and Federal Marketing Laws

The Privacy Rule does not amend, modify, or change any rule or requirement related to any other federal or state statutes or regulations regarding

- ◆ Anti-kickback
- ◆ Fraud and abuse
- ◆ Self-referral statutes or regulations

Final Privacy Rule Impact

The final Privacy Rule requires a covered entity to obtain an individual's prior written authorization to use his or her protected health information for marketing purposes except for a face-to-face encounter or a communication involving a promotional gift of nominal value.

HHS defines marketing to distinguish between the types of communications that are and are not marketing, and makes clear that a covered entity is prohibited from selling lists of patients and enrollees to third parties or from disclosing protected health information to a third party for the marketing activities of the third party, without the individual's authorization. The Privacy Rule clarifies that doctors and other covered entities communicating with patients about treatment options or the covered entity's own health-related products and services are not considered marketing. For example, health care plans can inform patients of additional health plan coverage and value-added items and services, such as discounts for prescription drugs or eyeglasses.

Research

The Privacy Rule establishes the conditions under which protected health information (PHI) can be used or disclosed by covered entities for research purposes. A covered entity can always use or disclose for research purposes health information which has been deidentified.

The Privacy Rule also defines the means by which individuals/human research subjects are informed of how medical information about themselves will be used or disclosed and their rights with regard to gaining access to information about themselves, when such information is held by covered entities. Where research is concerned, the Privacy Rule protects the privacy of individually identifiable health information, while at the same time ensuring that researchers continue to have access to medical information necessary to conduct vital research.

Currently, most research involving human subjects operates under the Common Rule (codified for the Department of Health and Human Services (HHS) at Title 45 Code of Federal Regulations Part 46) and/or the Food and Drug Administration's (FDA) human subjects protection regulations, which have some provisions that are similar to, but more stringent than and separate from, the Privacy Rule's provisions for research.

HHS does not believe that the Privacy Rule will hinder medical research. Indeed, patients and health plan members should be more willing to participate in research when they know their information is protected.

For example, in genetic studies at the National Institutes of Health (NIH), nearly 32 percent of eligible people offered a test for breast cancer risk decline to take it.

The overwhelming majority of those who refuse cite concerns about health insurance discrimination and loss of privacy as the reason. The Privacy Rule both permits important research and, at the same time, encourages patients to participate in research by providing much needed assurances about the privacy of their health information.

The Privacy Rule requires some covered health care providers and health plans to change their current practices related to documenting research uses and disclosures. It is possible that some covered health care providers and health plans may conclude that the rule's requirements for research uses and disclosures are too burdensome and will choose to limit researchers' access to PHI.

For example, unlike the Privacy Rule, the Common Rule requires Institutional Review Board (IRB) review for all research proposals under its purview, even if informed consent is to be sought. The Privacy Rule requires documentation of IRB or Privacy Board approval only if patient authorization for the use or disclosure of PHI for research purposes is to be altered or waived.

Using and Disclosing PHI for Research

In the course of conducting research, researchers may create, use, and/or disclose individually identifiable health information. Under the Privacy Rule, covered entities are permitted to use and disclose PHI for research with individual authorization, or without individual authorization under limited circumstances set forth in the Privacy Rule.

Research Use/Disclosure without Authorization

To use or disclose PHI without an Authorization by the research participant, a covered entity must obtain one of the following:

◆ Documentation that an alteration or waiver of research participants' authorization for use/disclosure of information about them for research purposes has been approved by an Institutional Review Board (IRB) or a Privacy Board. This provision of the Privacy Rule might be used, for example, to conduct records research, when researchers are unable to use de-identified information and it is not practicable to obtain research participants' authorization.

or

- Representations from the researcher, either in writing or orally, that the use or disclosure of the PHI is solely to prepare a research protocol or for similar purposes preparatory to research, that the researcher will not remove any PHI from the covered entity, and representation of that PHI for which access is sought is necessary for the research purpose. This provision might be used, for example, to design a research study or to assess the feasibility of conducting a study.

  or

- Representations from the researcher, either in writing or orally, that the use or disclosure being sought is solely for research on the PHI of decedents, that the PHI being sought is necessary for the research, and, at the request of the covered entity, documentation of the death of the individuals about whom information is being sought.

A covered entity may use or disclose PHI for research purposes pursuant to a waiver of authorization by an IRB or Privacy Board provided it has obtained documentation of all of the following:

- A statement that the alteration or waiver of authorization was approved by an IRB or Privacy Board that was composed as stipulated by the Privacy Rule

- A statement identifying the IRB or Privacy Board and the date on which the alteration or waiver of authorization was approved

- A statement that the IRB or Privacy Board has determined that the alteration or waiver of authorization, in whole or in part, satisfies the following eight criteria:

  - The use or disclosure of PHI involves no more than minimal risk to the individuals.

  - The alteration or waiver will not adversely affect the privacy rights and the welfare of the individuals.

  - The research could not practicably be conducted without the alteration or waiver.

  - The research could not practicably be conducted without access to and use of the PHI.

  - The privacy risks to individuals whose PHI is to be used or disclosed are reasonable in relation to the anticipated benefits, if any, to the individuals, and the importance of the knowledge that may reasonably be expected to result from the research.

- There is an adequate plan to protect the identifiers from improper use and disclosure.

- There is an adequate plan to destroy the identifiers at the earliest opportunity consistent with conduct of the research, unless there is a health or research justification for retaining the identifiers or such retention is otherwise required by law.

- There are adequate written assurances that the PHI will not be reused or disclosed to any other person or entity, except as required by law, for authorized oversight of the research project, or for other research for which the use or disclosure of PHI would be permitted by this subpart.

◆ A brief description of the PHI for which use or access has been determined to be necessary by the IRB or Privacy Board

◆ A statement that the alteration or waiver of authorization has been reviewed and approved under either normal or expedited review procedures as stipulated by the Privacy Rule

◆ The signature of the chair or other member, as designated by the chair, of the IRB or the Privacy Board, as applicable

Research Use/Disclosure with Individual Authorization

The Privacy Rule also permits covered entities to use and disclose PHI for research purposes when a research participant authorizes the use or disclosure of information about him or herself. Today, for example, a research participant's authorization will typically be sought for most clinical trials and some records research. In this case, documentation of IRB or Privacy Board approval of a waiver of authorization is not required for the use or disclosure of PHI.

To use or disclose PHI created from a research study that includes treatment (for instance, a clinical trial), additional research-specific elements must be included in the authorization form required, which describes how PHI created for the research study will be used or disclosed.

For example, if the covered entity/researcher intends to seek reimbursement from the research subject's health plan for the routine costs of care associated with the protocol, the Authorization must describe types of information that are provided to the health plan. This Authorization can be combined with the traditional informed consent document used in research.

The Privacy Rule permits, but does not require, the disclosure of PHI for specified public policy purposes. With few exceptions, the covered entity/researcher may choose to limit its right to disclose information created for a research study that includes treatment to purposes narrower than those permitted by the Privacy Rule, in accordance with his or her own professional standards.

Waiver Criteria

Under the Privacy Rule, IRBs and Privacy Boards need to use their judgment as to whether the waiver criteria have been satisfied. Several of the waiver criteria are closely modeled on the Common Rule's criteria for the waiver of informed consent and for the approval of a research study. Thus, it is anticipated that IRBs already have experience in making the necessarily subjective assessments of risks and benefits.

While IRBs or Privacy Boards may reach different determinations, the assessment of the waiver criteria through this deliberative process is a crucial element in the current system of safeguarding research participants' privacy. The entire system of local IRBs is, in fact, predicated on a deliberative process that permits local IRB autonomy. The Privacy Rule builds upon this principle; it does not change it. In addition, for multisite research that requires PHI from two or more covered entities, the Privacy Rule permits covered entities to accept documentation of IRB or Privacy Board approval from a single IRB or Privacy Board.

Conditions for Enrollment in a Research Study

The Privacy Rule does not address conditions for enrollment in a research study. Therefore, the Privacy Rule in no way prohibits researchers from conditioning enrollment in a research study on the execution of an authorization for the use of pre-existing health information.

Database for Research Purposes

A covered entity can use or disclose PHI without individuals' authorizations for the creation of a research database, provided the covered entity obtains documentation that an IRB or Privacy Board has determined that the specified waiver criteria were satisfied.

PHI maintained in such a research database could be used or disclosed for future research studies as permitted by the Privacy Rule—that is, for future studies in which an individual Authorization has been obtained or where the Privacy Rule would permit research without an Authorization, such as pursuant to an IRB or Privacy Board waiver.

IRBs and Privacy Boards

Recognizing that some institutions may not have an *Institutional Review Board* (IRB), or that some IRBs might not have the expertise needed to review research that requires consideration of risks to privacy, the Privacy Rule permits the covered entity to accept documentation of waiver of authorization from an alternative body called a Privacy Board—which could have fewer members, and members with different expertise than IRBs.

In addition, for research that is determined to be of no more than minimal risk, IRBs and Privacy Boards can use an expedited review process, which permits covered entities to accept documentation when only one or more members of the IRB or Privacy Board have conducted the review.

The covered entity or the recipient researcher could create the IRB or Privacy Board, or it could be an independent board.

The Privacy Rule requires documentation of waiver approval by either an IRB or a Privacy Board, not both.

Privacy Rule and Common Rule

Where both the Privacy Rule and the Common Rule apply, both regulations must be followed. The Privacy Rule regulates only the content and conditions of the documentation that covered entities must obtain before using or disclosing PHI for research purposes.

Patients Right To Inspect

With few exceptions, the Privacy Rule gives patients the right to inspect and obtain a copy of health information about themselves that is maintained in a designated record set.

A *designated record set* is a group of records that a covered entity uses to make decisions about individuals, and includes a health care provider's medical records and billing records, and a health plan's enrollment, payment, claims adjudication, and case or medical management record systems. Research records or results maintained in a designated record set are accessible to research participants unless one of the Privacy Rule's permitted exceptions applies.

One of the permitted exceptions applies to PHI created or obtained by a covered health care provider/researcher for a clinical trial. The Privacy Rule permits the individual's access rights in these cases to be suspended while the clinical trial is in progress, provided the research participant agreed to this denial of access when consenting to participate in the clinical trial. In addition, the health care provider/researcher must inform the research participant that the right to access PHI will be reinstated at the conclusion of the clinical trial.

Clinical Laboratory Improvements Amendments of 1998 (CLIA)

The Privacy Rule does not require clinical laboratories that are also covered health care providers to provide an individual access to information if the Clinical Laboratory Improvements Amendments of 1998 (CLIA) prohibits them from doing so. CLIA permits clinical laboratories to provide clinical laboratory test records and reports only to "authorized persons," as defined primarily by state law.

The individual who is the subject of the information is not always included as an authorized person. Therefore, the Privacy Rule includes an exception to individuals' general right to access PHI about themselves if providing an individual such access would be in conflict with CLIA.

In addition, for certain research laboratories that are exempt from the CLIA regulations, the Privacy Rule does not require such research laboratories, if they are also a covered health care provider, to provide individuals with access to PHI because doing so may result in the research laboratory losing its CLIA exemption.

Privacy Rule's Authorization and Common Rule's Informed Consent

Under the Privacy Rule, a patient's Authorization is used for the use and disclosure of PHI for research purposes. In contrast, an individual's Informed Consent as required by the Common Rule and FDA's human subjects regulations is a consent to participate in the research study as a whole, not simply a consent for the research use or disclosure of PHI.

For this reason, there are important differences between the Privacy Rule's requirements for an individual Authorization and the Common Rule's and FDA's requirements for Informed Consent. Where the Privacy Rule, the Common Rule, and/or FDA's human subjects regulations are applicable, each of the applicable regulations needs to be followed.

Final Privacy Rule Impact

The final Privacy Rule facilitates researchers' use of a single combined form to obtain Informed Consent for the research and Authorization to use or disclose protected health information for such research. The final Privacy Rule also clarifies the requirements relating to a researcher obtaining an IRB or Privacy Board waiver of authorization by streamlining the privacy waiver criteria to more closely follow the requirement of the Common Rule, which governs federally funded research. The transition provisions have been expanded to prevent needless interruption of ongoing research.

Government Access to Health Information

Under the Privacy Rule, government-operated health plans and health care providers must meet substantially the same requirements as private ones for protecting the privacy of individual identifiable health information. For instance, government-run health plans, such as Medicare and Medicaid, must take virtually the same steps to protect the claims and health information that they receive from beneficiaries as do private insurance plans or health maintenance organizations (HMO).

In addition, all federal agencies must also meet the requirements of the Privacy Act of 1974, which restricts what information about individual citizens—including any personal health information—can be shared with other agencies and with the public.

The only new authority for government involves enforcement of the Privacy Rule itself. To ensure covered entities protect patients' privacy as required, the rule provides that health plans, hospitals, and other covered entities cooperate with the

Department of Health and Human Services' efforts to investigate complaints or otherwise ensure compliance. The Department of HHS Office for Civil Rights (OCR) is responsible for enforcing the privacy protections and access rights for consumers under this rule.

Medical Records to Government

The Privacy Rule does not require a physician or any other covered entity to send medical information to the government for a government database or similar operation. In addition, the Privacy Rule does not require or allow any new government access to medical information, with one exception: It does give OCR the authority to investigate complaints and to otherwise ensure that covered entities comply with the Privacy Rule.

OCR has been assigned the responsibility of enforcing the Privacy Rule. As is typical in many enforcement settings, OCR may need to look at how a covered entity handled medical records and other personal health information. The Privacy Rule limits disclosure to OCR of information that is "pertinent to ascertaining compliance."

OCR maintains stringent controls to safeguard any individually identifiable health information that it receives. If covered entities could avoid or ignore enforcement requests, consumers would not have a way to ensure an independent review of their concerns about privacy violations under the rule.

Government Enforcement Process

An important ingredient in ensuring compliance with the Privacy Rule is the Department's responsibility to investigate complaints that the rule has been violated and to follow up on other information regarding noncompliance. At times, this responsibility entails seeing personal health information, such as when an individual indicates to the Department of HHS that they believe a covered entity has not properly handled their medical records.

What information would be needed depends on the circumstances and the alleged violations. The Privacy Rule limits OCR's access to information that is "pertinent to ascertaining compliance." In some cases, no personal health information would be needed. For instance, OCR might need to review only a business contract to determine whether a health plan included appropriate language to protect privacy when it hired an outside company to help process claims.

Examples of investigations that may require OCR to have access to protected health information (PHI) include

- ◆ Allegations that a covered entity refused to note a request for correction in a patient's medical record, or did not provide complete access to a patient's medical records to that patient.
- ◆ Allegations that a covered entity used health information for marketing purposes without first obtaining the individual's authorization when required by the rule. OCR may need to review information in the marketing department that contains personal health information, to determine whether a violation has occurred.

Law Enforcement Agencies

The Privacy Rule does not expand current law enforcement access to individually identifiable health information. In fact, it limits access to a greater degree than currently exists. Today, law enforcement officers obtain health information for many purposes, sometimes without a warrant or other prior process. The Privacy Rule does establish new procedures and safeguards to restrict the circumstances under which a covered entity can give such information to law enforcement officers.

For example, the Privacy Rule limits the type of information that covered entities can disclose to law enforcement, absent a warrant or other prior process, when law enforcement is seeking to identify or locate a suspect. It specifically prohibits disclosure of DNA information for this purpose, absent some other legal requirements such as a warrant.

Similarly, under most circumstances, the Privacy Rule requires covered entities to obtain permission from persons who have been the victim of domestic violence or abuse before disclosing information about them to law enforcement. In most states, such permission is not required today.

Where state law imposes additional restrictions on disclosure of health information to law enforcement, those state laws continue to apply. This Privacy Rule sets a national floor of legal protections; it is not a set of "best practices."

Even in those circumstances when disclosure to law enforcement is permitted by the Privacy Rule, the rule does not require covered entities to disclose any information.

Some other federal or state law may require a disclosure, and the Privacy Rule does not interfere with the operation of these other laws. However, unless some other law requires the disclosure, covered entities should use their professional judgment to decide whether to disclose information, reflecting their own policies and ethical principles. In other words, doctors, hospitals, and health plans could continue to follow their own policies to protect privacy in such instances.

Public Health

All states have laws that require providers to report cases of specific diseases to public health officials. The Privacy Rule allows disclosures that are required by law. Furthermore, disclosures to public health authorities who are authorized by law to collect or receive information for public health purposes are also permissible under the Privacy Rule. To do their job of protecting the health of the public, it is frequently necessary for public health officials to obtain information about the persons affected by a disease. In some cases they may need to contact those affected to determine the cause of the disease to allow for actions to prevent further illness.

The Privacy Rule continues to allow for the existing practice of sharing PHI with public health authorities who are authorized by law to collect or receive such information to aid them in their mission of protecting the health of the public. Examples of such activities include those directed at the reporting of disease or injury, reporting deaths and births, investigating the occurrence and cause of injury and disease, and monitoring adverse outcomes related to food, drugs, biological products, and dietary supplements.

Federal Privacy Act of 1974

The Privacy Act of 1974 protects personal information about individuals held by the federal government. Covered entities that are federal agencies or federal contractors that maintain records that are covered by the Privacy Act not only must obey the Privacy Rule's requirements but also must comply with the Privacy Act.

Example Scenarios

In this section we review scenarios as they relate to use, disclosure, and business associates.

Use and Disclosure Scenarios

Under HIPAA, use limits the sharing of information within a covered entity, while disclosure restricts the sharing of information outside an entity holding the information.

Thus, information is used if a physician discusses the information with a nurse within the physician's practice. Information is disclosed when the physician discusses the information with the insurance company.

The challenge is to determine who is inside and outside of your box. It can be different for each organization. A smaller physician's office with fewer staff has to rely more on outside the box resources, where a large hospital may have enough staff employed in their organization to seldom go outside the box. Looking at various types of health care organizations, we can see why there is some confusion in this area.

Table 3.5 shows Scenario 1, a small physician's office with two doctors, three nurses, and three office staff.

Table 3.5   Small Physician's Office

Inside the Box (Use)	Outside the Box (Disclose)
Doctors	Hospital
Nurses	Lawyer
Office staff	Accountant
Patient	Building owner
	Cleaning service
	Laboratory
	Computer system vendor
	Insurance company
	Medicare
	Medicaid
	Collection agency

There are a few ways to get out of becoming HIPAA compliant. A physician's practice may be exempt from the HIPAA standards in either of the following scenarios:

◆ It does not submit electronic transactions (because it takes no forms of insurance or submits only paper or otherwise), and it does not accept Medicare patients.

◆ It accepts Medicare but has less than 10 full-time employees, and does not submit electronic transactions (because it takes no forms of insurance or submits only paper or otherwise).

A physician's practice must submit Medicare claims electronically by October 16, 2003, unless the practice has less than 10 full-time employees. This is a new mandate from the Administrative Simplification Compliance Act passed in December 2001. Many small physician offices hear this criterion and say, "Good, I have less than 10 full-time employees, therefore I don't have to comply with HIPAA." Or they say, "I don't take Medicare patients so I don't have to comply with HIPAA." These are not accurate assumptions. If a physician practice submits any of the transactions listed above in electronic form, or a third party does so on its behalf, the practice must still comply with the HIPAA standards regardless of the size of the practice.

The following scenario has less than 10 employees but would still be required to be HIPAA compliant.

Table 3.6 shows Scenario 2—Long Term Care Center with 10 nurses, 60 health aids, 4 social workers, 10 maintenance staff, 8 administrative staff, and 15 volunteers.

Table 3.7 shows Scenario 3—Large Hospital Complex with four locations throughout the state. The doctors work out of 10 clinics, a nursing school, and a hospice. They have 8,000 employees including a Board of Directors, nurses, doctors, laboratory, maintenance, housekeeping, security, information technology, food service, volunteers, social workers, business office, billing, accounts payable, and accounts receivable.

Table 3.6 Long Term Care Center

Inside the Box (Use)	Outside the Box (Disclose)
Doctors	Ambulance Service
Nurses	Hospital
Health aids	Laboratory
Social workers	Food service contractor
Maintenance staff	Beautician
Volunteers	Lawyer
Administrative staff	Accountant
Patient	Clergy
	Computer system vendor
	Security guard services
	Marketing services vendor
	Insurance company
	Medicare
	Medicaid
	Collection agency

Table 3.7 Large Hospital Complex

Inside the Box (Use)	Outside the Box (Disclose)
All 8,000 employees	Ambulance service
Patient	Lawyer
	Clergy
	Insurance company
	Medicare
	Medicaid
	Collection agency

Anyone who is designated outside the box requires a Business Associate Contract (BAC). The HIPAA privacy regulations affect the disclosures by covered entities of protected health information to their business associates.

Business Associate Scenario

The definition of business associate casts a broad net over the parties with which covered entities contract or otherwise deal in their operations. The preamble, which accompanies the regulation, explains that the regulations extend the Privacy Rule to a covered entity's arrangements with their business associates (in part) to prevent covered entities from circumventing the Privacy Rule by contracting out the performance of various functions.

By law, the Privacy Rule applies only to health plans, health care clearinghouses, and certain health care providers. In today's health care system, however, most health care providers and health plans do not carry out all of their health care activities and functions by themselves; they require assistance from a variety of contractors and other businesses.

In allowing providers and plans to give PHI to these business associates, the Privacy Rule conditions such disclosures on the provider or plan obtaining, typically by contract, satisfactory assurances that the business associate will use the information only for the purposes for which he was engaged by the covered entity, will safeguard the information from misuse, and will help the covered entity comply with the covered entity's duties to provide individuals with access to health information about them. They must also provide a history of certain disclosures (for example, if the business associate maintains the only copy of information, it must promise to cooperate with the covered entity to provide individuals access to information upon request).

PHI may be disclosed to a business associate only to help the providers and plans carry out their health care functions—not for independent use by the business associate.

So to summarize, a business associate is a person or entity who provides certain functions, activities, or services for or to a covered entity, involving the use and/or disclosure of PHI. A business associate is not a member of the health care provider, health plan, or other covered entity's workforce. A health care provider, health plan, or other covered entity also can be a business associate to another covered entity.

Many questions arise about the other residents of a Long Term Care (LTC) facility or other patients in a hospital. They may see things or overhear things but they are not a part of the patients' health care so they are not in or outside of the box. Other patients are bystanders observing a patient event. What they have to say about a patient's treatment based on what they have seen is not relevant to a health care professional's diagnosis. There is no Business Associate Contract (BAC) needed for other patients or residents who may witness a patient event.

Even if your business associate is authorized to have access to PHI the Covered Entity is required to only give them the minimum necessary PHI to complete their responsibility.

As stated earlier, there are no templates telling the covered entity who is in or out of the box, what information is to be disseminated, or who they can share PHI with. The goal of HIPAA is to protect the rights of individuals by protecting their medical information from anyone who does not directly effect the treatment, payment, or health care operations of the patient, while allowing the health care community to provide the highest possible quality care.

Summary

Former President Clinton probably stated it best when he said that the HHS rule "has been carefully crafted for this new era, to make medical records easier to see for those who should see them, and much harder to see for those who shouldn't."

The Privacy Rule is among the most sweeping privacy laws in the history of the United States. All covered entities need to initiate a thorough review of existing privacy practices and clearly analyze the gaps that exist so that remediation steps may be launched to bring the practice into compliance.

The final Privacy Rule mandates the following requirements:

◆ Health plans and health care providers must inform their patients/ beneficiaries of their business practices concerning the use and disclosure of health information.

- Direct health care providers must supply their Notice of Privacy Practices to their patients. These providers must also make a good-faith effort to get a written acknowledgement of the receipt of the Notice from their patients. This allows routine treatment, payment, and health care operations to proceed. A separate, specific Authorization is required for non-routine disclosures.

- Patients are granted the opportunity to request restrictions on the use and disclosure of their health information.

- Within 60 days of a request, patients are entitled to a disclosure history identifying all entities that received health information unrelated to treatment or payment.

- Patients also have a right to review and copy their own medical records and have the corresponding right to request amendments or corrections to potentially harmful errors within the record.

- Health care providers and health plans are required to create privacy-conscious business practices, which include the requirement that only the minimum amount of health information necessary is disclosed.

- Business practices should ensure the internal protection of medical records, employee privacy training and education, and the creation of a mechanism for addressing patient privacy complaints.

- The designation of an enterprise privacy officer or HIPAA compliance officer.

- Overall, covered entities are encouraged to use deidentifiable information whenever possible. Once information is in a deidentifiable form, it is no longer subject to the privacy regulation restrictions.

Lastly, here's something to remember as one thinks about the Privacy Rule: What I see here, what I hear here, when I leave here, will remain here.

Lesson 4

This chapter focuses on HIPAA's Security Rule, the security of health care information, systems, and the infrastructure in general. It covers the following topics:

- The scope of the final HIPAA Security Rule
- Threats and attacks to which health care enterprises are vulnerable
- Key security terminology and concepts
- HIPAA Security Rule's design objectives
- HIPAA Security Rule's core domain areas
- Administrative Safeguards implementation specifications
- Physical Safeguards implementation specifications
- Technical Safeguards implementation specifications
- Scenario: A sample TCP/IP security policy review

Security Standards

Title II of the Health Insurance Portability and Accountability Act (HIPAA) includes requirements for security standards. The proposed Security Rule was published on August 12, 1998. The Security Rule describes the security requirements that health care entities need to follow in order to be in compliance with the Administrative Simplification portion of HIPAA Title II. The Final Security Rule was published in the Federal Register on February 20, 2003.

This Final Rule adopts standards for the security of electronic protected health information to be implemented by health plans, health care clearinghouses, and certain health care providers. According to HHS, the use of the security standards will improve the Medicare and Medicaid programs and other federal and private health programs, and the effectiveness and efficiency of the health care industry in general by establishing a level of protection for certain electronic health information.

The confidentiality of health information is threatened not only by the risk of improper access to stored information, but also by the risk of interception during electronic transmission of the information.

 NOTE

> Covered entities are required to comply with the security standards no later than 24 months after they are published as a final Security Rule. Small health plans have to comply with the security standards no later than 36 months following their publication as a final Security Rule. Covered entities, with the exception of small health plans, must comply with the requirements of the final Security Rule by April 21, 2005. Small health plans must comply with the requirements of the final Security Rule by April 21, 2006.

The final Security Rule establishes standards for the security of individual health information and electronic signature use by covered entities (health plans, health care clearinghouses, and health care providers). Covered entities must use the security standards to develop and maintain the security of all electronic individual health information.

The proposed Security Rule did not require the use of an electronic signature, but specifies the standard for an electronic signature that must be followed if such a signature is used. If an entity elects to use an electronic signature, it must comply with the Electronic Signature Standard. However, the final Security Rule adopts only security standards. The Final Rule for electronic signatures will be published at a later date. Hence, we only include a brief description of the proposed Electronic Signature Rule in this chapter. Electronic transmissions include transactions using all media, even when the information is physically moved from one location to another using magnetic tape, disk, or compact disc (CD) media. Transmissions over the Internet, extranet (using Internet technology to link a business with information only accessible to collaborating parties), leased lines, dial-up lines, and private networks are all included.

The Security Rule is applicable to all health care information electronically maintained or used in an electronic transmission, regardless of format (standard transaction or a proprietary format). The Security Rule makes no distinction between internal corporate entity communication or communication external to the corporate entity.

The Security Rule was defined in terms of implementation specifications that enable businesses in the health care industry to select the technology that best meets their business requirements while still allowing them to comply with the standards.

The Security Rule allows individual health care industry businesses to ascertain the level of security information that is needed. The confidentiality level associated with individual data elements concerning health care information determines the appropriate security application to be used. The Security Rule defines the requirements to be met to achieve the privacy and confidentiality goal, but each business entity, driven by its business requirements, can decide what techniques and controls provide appropriate and adequate electronic data protection. This allows data collection and the paperwork burden to be as low as is feasible.

The Threat

The May 20, 2002 issue of *Information Week Magazine* reported extensively about security managers trying to prepare for the next blended threat attack to business systems. Blended attacks are based on a virus or worm that spreads through or attacks security vulnerabilities commonly found in applications and operating systems. Many industry analysts report that preparation appears to be prudent activity.

According to Richard Mogull, speaking at the Spring 2002 Gartner Group Symposium, "100 percent of organizations connected to the Internet will experience undirected attacks in the next six months, (*and*) 20 percent will experience a directed internal or external attack." Mr. Mogull went on to say that "80 percent of organizations are vulnerable to a cyber attack due to well-known problems and poor security culture."

Types of Attacks

1. Virus attacks
2. Denial of service attacks
3. Unauthorized access
4. Laptop theft
5. Network abuse
6. Theft of proprietary information
7. Sabotage

The threat to businesses has never been greater, and gaps in the infrastructure provide opportunities for malicious, relentless, 24 x 7 x 365, attacks from professional hackers worldwide. This applies to all industries and sectors. The threat to the health care and insurance industry is in particular very significant because of the increasing dependence upon electronic medical records and transactions.

Sanjay Kumar, CEO of Computer Associates, stated in the May 27, 2002 issue of *VAR Business* that there is a massive opportunity emerging in the areas of desktop protection and application security. The desktop and applications are more vulnerable than ever before. Trustworthy computing is now the mantra at Microsoft for good reason; weaknesses in application security have been exploited to penetrate enterprise networks and systems.

There are three factors fueling the drive for health care businesses to make security an enterprise and an executive priority:

- Protecting health care business infrastructure from threats
- Health care business transformation to e-business
- HIPAA legislation

Businesses worldwide lose three billion dollars yearly in lost productivity due to testing, cleaning, and deploying patches to computer systems. Blended attacks are based on threats from viruses and worms. A virus attaches itself to an executable file while a worm spreads through memory and disk space. *Information Week* reports that a successful virus strike costs individual businesses from one hundred thousand to one million dollars a year in cleanup and related costs. Threats today do have a real and immediate impact on business revenue and costs.

 NOTE

The challenge for all health care businesses today is to establish a secure infrastructure.

Security is only as strong as the weakest link, and all gaps in the security infrastructure are opportunities for malicious attacks. Security is today a business infrastructure issue. It is an essential and required component for all businesses.

Each year, the Computer Security Institute and the San Francisco Federal Bureau of Investigation's (FBI) Computer Intrusion Squad conduct and publish the

"Computer Crime and Security Survey." The trends established in the 1990s continue:

- 90 percent of respondents (primarily large corporations and government agencies) detected computer security breaches within the last 12 months.

- 80 percent acknowledged financial losses due to computer breaches.

- 44 percent (223 respondents) were willing and/or able to quantify their financial losses. These 223 respondents reported $455,848,000 in financial losses.

- As in previous years, the most serious financial losses occurred through theft of proprietary information (26 respondents reported $170,827,000) and financial fraud (25 respondents reported $115,753,000).

- For the fifth year in a row, more respondents (74 percent) cited their Internet connection as a frequent point of attack than cited their internal systems as a frequent point of attack (33 percent).

- 34 percent reported the intrusions to law enforcement. (In 1996, only 16 percent acknowledged reporting intrusions to law enforcement.)

Respondents detected a wide range of attacks and abuses. The following is a small sample of attacks and abuses:

- 40 percent detected system penetration from the outside.

- 40 percent detected denial-of-service attacks.

- 78 percent detected employee abuse of Internet access privileges (for example, downloading pornography or pirated software or inappropriate use of e-mail systems).

- 85 percent detected computer viruses.

For the fourth year, CSI asked some questions about electronic commerce over the Internet. Here are some of the results:

- 98 percent of respondents have Web sites.

- 52 percent conduct electronic commerce on their sites.

- 38 percent suffered unauthorized access or misuse on their Web sites within the last 12 months. 21 percent said that they didn't know if there had been unauthorized access or misuse.

- 25 percent of those acknowledging attacks reported from 2 to 5 incidents. 39 percent reported 10 or more incidents.
- 70 percent of those attacked reported vandalism (only 64 percent in 2000).
- 55 percent reported denial of service (60 percent in 2000).
- 12 percent reported theft of transaction information.

The threats are real. Patrice Rapalus, CSI Director, remarked in April 2002 that the Computer Crime and Security Survey had served as a reality check for industry and government:

> Over its seven-year life span, the survey has told a compelling story. It has underscored some of the verities of the information security profession, for example that technology alone cannot thwart cyber attacks and that there is a need for greater cooperation between the private sector and the government. It has also challenged some of the profession's "conventional wisdom," for example that the "threat from inside the organization is far greater than the threat from outside the organization" and that "most hack attacks are perpetrated by juveniles on joyrides in cyberspace."

> Over the seven-year life span of the survey, a sense of the "facts on the ground" has emerged. There is much more illegal and unauthorized activity going on in cyberspace than corporations admit to their clients, stockholders, and business partners or report to law enforcement. Incidents are widespread, costly, and commonplace. Post-9/11, there seems to be a greater appreciation for how much information security means not only to each individual enterprise but also to the economy itself and to society as a whole.

> Hopefully, this greater appreciation will translate into increased staffing levels, more investment in training, and enhanced organizational clout for those responsible for information security.

Given the health care industry's dependence on computers, data storage, and data communications, this research is relevant to everyone involved in HIPAA security compliance work. Executive Assistant Director (EAD) Bruce J. Gebhardt, former Special Agent In-Charge FBI San Francisco, stresses the need for cooperation between the government and the private sector that the annual survey reflects.

The United States' increasing dependency on information technology to manage and operate our nation's critical infrastructures provides a prime target to would-be cyber-terrorists. Now, more than ever, the government and private sector need to work together to share information and be more cognitive of information security so that our nation's critical infrastructures are protected from cyber-terrorists.

Threats exist, but to address them, we must establish a foundation of common vocabulary.

Types of Threats

Security threats to a system may be classified as accidental or intentional and can be active or passive.

Accidental threats are those that exist with no premeditated intent. An example of an accidental threat may be if a user powers off a system and when it re-boots, the system is in single-user (privileged) mode—now the user can do anything he/she wants on the system. *Intentional threats* may range from casual examination of computer or network data to sophisticated attacks using special system knowledge.

Passive threats are those that, if realized, would not result in any modification to any information contained in the system(s) and where neither the operation nor the state of the system changes. For example, a user runs the snoop application from their system and listens in (filters) on packets exchanged between two nodes on the network. In this example, even if the user captures a copy of these network packets to analyze data exchanged, there is no change to the original packet sent by the source to the destination system. The intruder or malicious user can easily capture and store any protected clear text data passing between devices on your network. This type of potential disclosure is one of the reasons that encryption is so important to HIPAA compliance.

Alteration of information or changes to the state or the operation of the system is defined as an *active threat* to a system. An example would be an unauthorized user modifying a system's routing tables.

Types of Attacks and Attackers

Systems that exist on a network may be subject to specific types of attacks. For example, in a *masquerade* (also referred to as *spoofing*), one entity pretends to be a different entity. An entity can be a user, a process, or a node on the network. Typically, a masquerade is used with other forms of an active attack such as replay and modification of messages—a *message* is a packet or packets on the network.

Hacking and attacking are rising significantly with the profile of the attacker changing as a consequence of better funding and easier access to tools and resources.

A *replay* occurs when a message, or part of a message, is repeated to produce an unauthorized effect.

Modification of a message occurs when the content of a data transmission is altered without detection and results in an unauthorized effect.

Denial of service occurs when an entity fails to perform its proper function or acts in a way that prevents other entities from performing their proper functions. This type of attack may involve suppressing traffic or generating extra traffic. The attack might also disrupt the operation of a network, especially if the network has relay entities that make routing decisions based on status reports received from other relay entities.

Insider attacks occur when legitimate users of a system behave in unintended or unauthorized ways. Most known computer crimes involved insider attacks that compromised the security of a system.

The techniques that might be used for *outsider attacks* include wiretapping, intercepting emissions, masquerading as authorized users of the system, and bypassing authentication or access control mechanisms.

A *trapdoor* is added to a system when an entity of that system is altered to allow an attacker to produce an unauthorized effect on command or at a predetermined event or a sequence of events. A trapdoor is a backdoor into the system. It is analogous to the situation where the front door is locked (you use a good, cryptic password for the root account on a Linux system), but the windows are open (no passwords are defined for some end-user accounts, and by accessing these accounts you have access to root owned superuser ID (SUID) applications).

When introduced to the system, a *Trojan horse* has an unauthorized function in addition to its authorized function. For example, an end-user account is accessed by an unauthorized individual and she places a file with the same name as a system command (such as `ls` or `cp`) so that whenever that command was executed, it also e-mailed a copy of the `/etc/passwd` file to a remote user.

Some relatively common examples of these various attacks and attackers follow:

◆ A virus or other malicious code introduced via e-mail, scripts, or downloads during Web browsing, accessing floppy disks from external sources, untrusted CD-ROMs, restoring from external tapes, and so on.

◆ Unauthorized local login into secure computers via valid, but inappropriately accessed, usernames and passwords and then reading, modifying, or deleting data in a manner that was not approved by the owner of the computer resource.

◆ Unauthorized network login into secure computers via valid, but inappropriately accessed, usernames and passwords, or via unsecured services/applications, and then reading, modifying, or deleting data in a manner that was not approved by the owner of the computer resource.

◆ Unauthorized physical access to, or tampering with network devices that results in intentional or inadvertent power-off or other damage, or in the loss of data integrity.

◆ Inappropriate or unauthorized access to data by a user when there were inadequate file protections.

◆ Tampering with data in transit resulting in the loss of data assurance (where you receive data without traceability).

◆ Tampering with data in transit resulting in the loss of integrity of confidential corporate data.

◆ Theft of removable media, such as disks and tapes.

◆ Intentional or inadvertent loss of electric power.

Definition and Terminology

HIPAA will result in the deployment of security technology to protect patient, medical information, and health care–related transactions. This section focuses on security implications of the Administrative Simplification (AS) portions of HIPAA Title II. The HIPAA Administrative Simplification Title is the launch pad for e-security initiatives for electronic and secure medical information.

Defining Security

Security is generally defined as having controls, countermeasures, and procedures in place to ensure the appropriate protection of information assets and control access to valued resources. Therefore, the object of security is often to counter identified threats and to satisfy relevant security policies and assumptions. Security professionals tend to view security in at least two different ways—both as a concept and as a "state." In either case, "security" is never far from "risk." Risk—real, potential, and imagined—is the force driving investments in security.

Professionals in different fields often misunderstand each other when attempting to communicate about issues related to security and risk. Because HIPAA security remediation requires the effort and cooperation of individuals and teams from a variety of backgrounds, it is vital to establish a shared understanding of what security and risk mean.

In the 1990s, seven governmental organizations from Canada, France, Germany, The Netherlands, United Kingdom, and the United States worked together to create what is now known as the "Common Criteria."[1]

The Common Criteria defines the general security context or concept in the following manner:

> Security is concerned with the protection of assets from threats, where the threats are categorized as the potential for abuse of protected assets. All categories of threats should be considered; but in the domain of security greater attention is given to those threats that are related to malicious or other human activities.[2]

Security is minimizing the vulnerability of assets and resources. An *asset* is defined as anything of value. *Vulnerability* is any weakness that could be exploited to violate a system or the information it contains. A *threat* is a potential violation of security.

Figure 4.1 describes the concept with a deceptively simple block diagram.

In the Common Criteria model, owners include all those who are accountable for or place value upon the assets in question. Threat agents, real and presumed, may also place value on the assets, yet seek to abuse or damage them in a manner

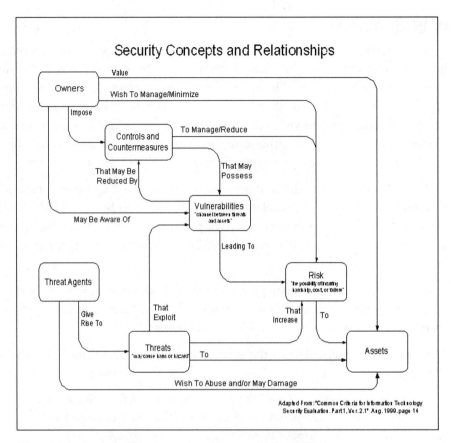

Figure 4.1 *Common Criteria security concepts and relationships.*

contrary to the interests of the owners. Owners assume that the threats may impair the assets in a way that reduces their value.

Asset owners analyze the possible and probable threats to decide which of them apply to their environment. This is often called a *risk assessment*. Every infrastructure is imperfect, and therefore includes vulnerabilities. The results or this threat-and-vulnerability scenario are understood as risks. Performing this analysis helps owners select controls and countermeasures to resist the risks and reduce them to an acceptable level.

Controls and countermeasures are imposed to reduce vulnerabilities. Additionally, controls and countermeasures help to meet security policies established by the owners of the assets or by their proxies. Human endeavor remaining imperfect, residual vulnerabilities remain after controls and countermeasures are in place. Threat agents may exploit these residual vulnerabilities. This represents the residual level of risk to the assets.

 NOTE

The key to enabling effective security is to achieve the appropriate level or residual risk.

Risk-mitigating controls and countermeasures represent an expense. Not all information has the same value to an organization. At some level of investment in risk mitigation, the expense exceeds the value of the asset. Somewhere prior to that point is an appropriate balance of investment and assumption of remaining risk (see Figure 4.2).

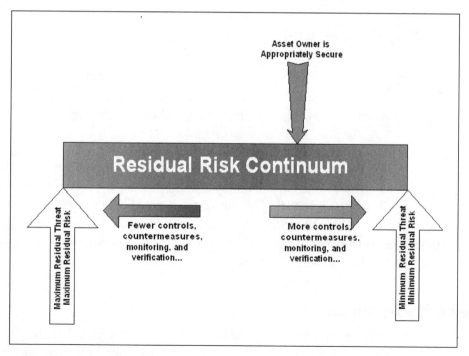

Figure 4.2 *Security and risk continuum.*

Using the preceding description of security, it should not be difficult to visualize that security can also be viewed as a given context along a risk continuum. The context is bounded by more or less risk, more or fewer remaining vulnerabilities, and more or less money to fund risk-mitigating controls and countermeasures. Business leaders, especially chief financial officers, often talk about achieving an appropriate level of risk at an acceptable cost. Extremely difficult technical, procedural, logistical, and financial issues aside, that is just what security is all about.

Within this context, HIPAA security implementation leads to the establishment of an appropriately secure, trusted infrastructure that benefits both patients and providers. "Appropriate" security, then, requires risk assessment so that the organization better understands the relevant threats and risks. Only then can an organization do something about them. One of the most effective ways to ensure that you can achieve even a threshold level of consistency over time is to design each of your risk management/security efforts around a set of formal security/risk management policies. That way, when technical experts sit down to perform system configurations or when auditors begin to review your infrastructure and operations, they have specific goals in mind—goals that you can often measure their achievement against.

So, security is relative. It depends on a lot of variables.

 NOTE

Two key variables are the threats/risks and the value of the assets that are at risk.

Value can be defined many ways. Sometimes an information asset has a given value to the organization, but should that information be inappropriately revealed to the public or the organization's competitors, it would have a negative impact on the organization far greater than its simple sales value. Because of the negative value of information, health care organizations generally need to carefully manage access to the data for which they are responsible.

Security Services

Security services that might be supported by a health care enterprise include authentication, access control, data confidentiality, data integrity, and non-repudiation. Each is discussed in detail within the following sections.

Authentication

Authentication is the process of proving your identity. A system needs to authenticate users to a degree appropriate for the level of risk/threat that an authenticated user represents. Authentication is typically the first step in gaining access to the system. Typing a username and a password is an example of authenticating yourself as a user on the system. Kerberos is an example of a network authentication protocol designed to provide strong authentication for client/server applications by using secret-key cryptography. The Kerberos protocol uses strong cryptography so that a client can prove his or her identity to a server (and vice versa) across an insecure network connection. Kerberos infrastructure provides a well-documented foundation for application developers to develop high-confidence authentication systems.

Access Control

Access control relates to what resources a user or service can access on the system or network. It provides protection against the unauthorized use of resources accessible using network protocols. Permissions for files, directories, and processes relate to the area of access control—who has access to these resources (objects) on the system.

Data Confidentiality

Data confidentiality relates to secrecy of data on the system and network. It protects your data from passive threats and provides for the protection of data from unauthorized disclosure. Data confidentiality services include connection confidentiality, connectionless confidentiality, selective field confidentiality, and traffic flow confidentiality.

Data Integrity

Data integrity provides protection against active threats. Data integrity services include connection integrity with recovery, connection integrity without recovery, selective field connection integrity, and selective field connectionless integrity.

Non-repudiation

Repudiation is defined as the denial by one of the entities involved in a communication of having participated in all or part of the communication.

Non-repudiation services may take one or both of two forms: non-repudiation with proof of origin or non-repudiation with proof of delivery.

Security Mechanisms

Security mechanisms implement security services. There are two types, pervasive and specific. Both are discussed in detail in the following sections.

Specific Security Mechanisms

Specific security mechanisms may be incorporated into an appropriate layer to provide some of the security services described earlier. The following list provides examples of specific security mechanisms:

- Encipherment (encryption)
- Digital signatures
- Access control mechanisms
- Data integrity mechanisms
- Authentication
- Traffic padding
- Notarization

Encipherment can be used to provide confidentiality of either data or traffic flow information. It also is used to verify the integrity of data or of a specific traffic flow. When *clear text* data is effectively encrypted for a specific destination or party, then only that party should be able to cost effectively decrypt that data. If that data were tampered with or otherwise corrupted between the time it was encrypted and the receiver's attempt to decrypt it, the receiver would be unable to effectively restore that data to clear text. Encipherment is often also called *encryption*.

Digital signatures, especially when used in combination with encipherment, have the following properties:

- The ability to verify the author, date, and time of the signature
- The ability to authenticate the contents at the time of the signature
- Signature verification by third parties, in case of dispute

Access control mechanisms might be involved at the origin or any intermediate point to determine if the sender is authorized to communicate with the recipient or to use the resources. Mechanisms might be based on authentication information such as passwords, security labels, duration of access, time of access, or route of attempted access. *Data integrity mechanisms* include time stamping, sequence numbering, or cryptographic chaining, all of which may be used to provide integrity of a single data unit or field and the integrity of a stream of data units or fields.

Authentication information such as passwords, use of characteristics or possessions of the entity, digital signature, or notarization is another technique that can be applied. *Traffic padding* might be used to provide various levels of protection against traffic analysis.

Each instance of communication might use a digital signature, encipherment, and integrity mechanisms as appropriate to the service being provided by the notary. Properties such as data origin, time, and destination can be assured by the provision of a *notarization* mechanism.

Pervasive Security Mechanisms

Pervasive security mechanisms are not specific to any particular security service and are in general directly related to the level of security required. Pervasive security mechanisms include

- Trusted functionality
- Security labels
- Audit trail
- Security recovery

Trusted functionality might be used to extend the scope of or establish the effectiveness of other security mechanisms. *Security labels* might be used to indicate sensitivity level. Labels are additional data associated with the data transferred or may be implied by the use of a specific key to encipher data. *An audit trail* permits detection and investigation of breaches of security. The logging or recording of information is considered to be a security mechanism. *Security recovery* deals with requests from mechanisms—for example, event handling and management functions, and takes recovery action as the result of applying a set of rules.

Key HIPAA Security Terminology

Systems today are more vulnerable to attacks, break-ins, and viruses than ever before. This is partly because more individuals within organizations have access to corporate information systems than ever before. Further, with health care businesses increasingly connecting to the Internet, security threats are not just internal but external—threats today are truly global in nature. There must be complete top management support and funding to secure health care records, transactions, and systems.

The following list defines key security terminology:

- **Access.** Refers to the ability or the means necessary to read, write, modify, or communicate data/information or otherwise make use of any system resource.

- **Access Control.** Refers to a method of restricting access to resources, allowing only privileged entities access. Types of access control include, among others:
  - Mandatory Access Control
  - Discretionary Access Control
  - Time-of-day, Classification
  - Classification

- **Access Control List.** A list of entities, together with their access rights, that are authorized to have access to a resource.

- **Accountability.** Property that ensures that entity actions may be traced uniquely to the entity.

- **Active Threat.** Threat of a deliberate unauthorized change in the state of the system.

- **Authentication.** Refers to the corroboration that an entity is the one claimed.

- **Authentication Exchange.** Mechanism used to ensure the identity of an entity by means of information exchange.

- **Authentication Information.** Information used to ensure validity of a claimed entity.

- **Authorization.** Granting of rights, including those based on access rights.

- **Availability.** Property of being accessible and usable upon demand by an authorized entity.

- **Channel.** Information transfer path.

- **Ciphertext.** Data produced through encipherment; the semantic content of the resulting data is not available.

- **Clear text.** Intelligible data, the semantic content of which is available.

- **Confidentiality.** Property that information is not made available or disclosed to unauthorized individuals, entities, or processes.

- **Contingency Plan.** Refers to a plan for responding to a system emergency. The plan includes performing backups, preparing critical facilities that can be used to facilitate continuity of operations in the event of an emergency, and recovering from a disaster.

- **Credentials.** Data transferred to establish the claimed identity of an entity.

- **Cryptanalysis.** The analysis of a cryptographic system or its inputs and outputs to derive confidential variables or sensitive data, including clear text.

- **Cryptography.** This determines the methods used in encipherment and decipherment; attack on a cryptographic principle, means, or method is cryptanalysis.

- **Data Integrity.** Property that data has not been altered or destroyed in an unauthorized manner.

- **Decipherment.** The reversal of a corresponding reversible encipherment.

- **Decryption.** See decipherment.

- **Denial of Service.** Prevention of authorized access to resources or the delaying of time-critical operations.

- **Digital Signature.** Data appended to, or a cryptographic transformation of, a data unit that allows the recipient of the data unit to prove its source and integrity and protect against forgery (for example, by the recipient).

- **Encryption or Encipherment.** Refers to transforming confidential plaintext into ciphertext to protect it. An encryption algorithm combines plain text with other values called *keys* or *ciphers*, so that the data becomes unintelligible.

Once encrypted, data can be stored or transmitted over unsecured lines. Decrypting data reverses the encryption algorithm process and makes the plaintext available for further processing. The Encryption is the cryptographic transformation of data to produce ciphertext.

- **End-to-End Encipherment.** Encipherment of data within or at the source and system, with the corresponding decipherment occurring only with or at the destination end system.

- **Identity-based Security Policy.** A security policy on the identities or attributes of users, a group of users, or entities acting on behalf of the users and the resources or objects to which they have access.

- **Key.** A sequence of symbols that controls the operation of encipherment and decipherment.

- **Key Management.** The generation, storage, distribution, deletion, archiving, and application of keys in accordance with a security policy.

- **Link-by-link Encipherment.** The individual application of encipherment to data on each link of a communications system; therefore, data will be in clear text form in relay entities.

- **Manipulation Detection.** A mechanism used to detect whether a data unit has been modified (accidentally or intentionally).

- **Masquerade.** The pretense by an entity to be a different entity.

- **Non-repudiation.** Denial by one of the entities involved in a communication of having participated in all or part of the communication.

- **Notarization.** The registration of data with a trusted third party that allows the later assurance of accuracy of its characteristics, such as content, origin, time, and delivery.

- **Passive Threat.** The threat of unauthorized disclosure of information without changing the state of the system.

- **Password.** Confidential authentication information, usually composed of a string of characters.

- **Peer-entity Authentication.** The corroboration that a peer entity in an association is the one claimed.

- **Physical Security.** The measures used to provide physical protection of resources against deliberate and accidental threats.

- **Privacy.** The right of individuals to control or influence what information related to them may be collected and stored, and by whom and to whom that information may be disclosed.

- **Role-based Access Control (RBAC).** RBAC is an alternative to traditional access control models (for example, discretionary or non-discretionary access control policies) that permits the specification and enforcement of enterprise-specific security policies in a way that maps more naturally to an organization's structure and activities.

  With RBAC, rather than attempting to map an organization's security policy to a relatively low-level set of technical controls, such as access control lists, each user is assigned to one or more predefined roles, each of which has been assigned the various privileges needed to perform that role.

- **Routing Control.** The application of rules during the process of routing so as to chose or avoid specific networks, links, or relays.

- **Rule-based Security Policy.** A security policy based on global rules imposed on all users. the The rules usually rely on a comparison of the sensitivity of the resources being accessed and the possession of corresponding attributes of users, a group of users, or entities acting on behalf of users.

- **Security Audit.** An independent review or examination of system records or activities to test for adequacy of system controls, to ensure compliance with established policy and operations procedures, to detect breaches in security, and to recommend any indicated changes in control, policy, and procedures.

- **Security Audit Trail.** Data collected and potentially used to facilitate a security audit.

- **Security Label.** The marking bound to a resource (may be a data unit) that names or designates the security attributes of that resource.

- **Security Policy.** The set of criteria for the provision of security services.

- **Security Service.** A service, provided by a layer of communicating open systems, that ensures adequate security of the systems or data transfers.

- **Selective Field Protection.** The protection of specific fields within a message that is to be transmitted.

- **Sensitivity.** The characteristic of a resource that implies its value or importance and may include its vulnerability.

- **Signature.** *See* Digital Signature.

- **Threat.** A potential violation of security.

- **Token.** Refers to a physical item necessary for user identification when used in the context of authentication. (For example, an electronic device that can be inserted in a door or a computer system to obtain access.)

- **Traffic Analysis.** The inference of information from observation of traffic flows (presence, absence, amount, direction, and frequency).

- **Traffic Flow Confidentiality.** A confidentiality service to protect against traffic analysis.

- **Trusted Functionality.** That which is perceived to be correct with respect to some criteria, such as established by a security policy.

- **User-Based Access.** Refers to a security mechanism used to grant users of a system access based upon the identity of the user.

HIPAA Security Requirements

The final Security Rule outlines the requirements in three major categories:

- Administrative safeguards
- Physical safeguards
- Technical safeguards

The administrative safeguards category forms the foundation on which the other standards depend. Covered entities are required to implement administrative, physical, and technical safeguards. These entities must ensure that data are protected, to the extent feasible, from inappropriate access, modification, dissemination, and destruction.

The proposed Security Rule had identified four security standards, or categories, and the electronic signature standard. The four categories in the proposed Security Rule were

- Administrative procedures
- Physical safeguards

- ◆ Technical security services
- ◆ Technical security mechanisms

Security Rule Implementation Specifications

The proposed Security Rule contained multiple proposed requirements and implementation features. In the final Security Rule, the term *requirement* is replaced with *standard* and the term *implementation feature* is replaced with *implementation specification.*

In the final Security Rule, the implementation specification may either be required implementation specifications or addressable implementation specifications. The concept of addressable implementation specifications is to provide covered entities additional flexibility with respect to compliance with the security standards. A covered entity does one of the following for addressable implementation specifications:

- ◆ Implement one or more of the addressable implementation specifications
- ◆ Implement one or more alternative security measures
- ◆ Implement a combination of both
- ◆ Not implement either an addressable implementation specification or an alternative security measure

After its own risk analysis, risk mitigation strategy, an assessment of what security measures may already be in place, and the cost of implementation the covered entity must decide:

- ◆ If a given addressable implementation specification is determined to be reasonable and appropriate, the covered entity must implement it.
- ◆ If a given addressable implementation specification is determined to be an inappropriate and/or unreasonable security measure for the covered entity, but the standard cannot be met without implementation of an additional security safeguard, the covered entity may implement an alternate measure that accomplishes the same end as the addressable implementation specification.
- ◆ An entity that meets a given standard through alternative measures must document the decision to not implement the addressable implementation specification, the rationale behind that decision, and the alternative safeguard implemented to meet the standard.

A covered entity may also decide that a given implementation specification is simply not applicable (that is, neither reasonable nor appropriate) to its situation and that the standard can be met without implementation of an alternative measure in place of the addressable implementation specification. In this scenario, the covered entity must document the decision not to implement the addressable specification, the rationale behind that decision, and how the standard is being met.

For example, under the information access management standard, an access establishment and modification implementation specification reads: "implement policies and procedures that, based upon the entity's access authorization policies, establish, document, review, and modify a user's right of access to a workstation, transaction, program, or process." It is possible that a small practice, with one or more individuals equally responsible for establishing and maintaining all automated patient records, will not need to establish policies and procedures for granting access to that electronic protected health information because the access rights are equal for all of the individuals.

Approach and Philosophy

The HIPAA security standards are designed to be

- ◆ **Comprehensive.** They cover all aspects of security safeguards, including Access:
  - Identification
  - Authentication
  - Access control
  - Accountability and non-repudiation
  - Integrity
  - Communications
  - Administration
- ◆ **Technology neutral.** Standards can be implemented using a broad range of off-the-shelf and user-developed technologies and security solutions
- ◆ **Scalable.** The goals of the regulations can be achieved by entities of all sizes, from single practitioners to large multinational health care organizations

The regulations explicitly recognize that very small organizations will be able to satisfy the requirements with less elaborate approaches than larger, more complex organizations.

Security Principals

Security of health information is especially important when health information can be directly linked to an individual. For example, confidentiality is threatened not only by the risk of improper access to electronically stored information, but also by the risk of interception during electronic transmission of the information.

The Security Rule consists of security standards that a health care entity must address to safeguard the confidentiality, integrity, and availability of its electronic data. It also describes the implementation specifications that must be present to satisfy each requirement. As mentioned previously, the central principals of security are confidentiality, integrity, and availability.

Security-related impairment generally includes, but is not limited to, "damaging disclosure or the asset to unauthorized recipients (*loss of confidentiality*), damage to the asset through unauthorized modification (*loss of integrity*), or unauthorized deprivation of access to the asset (*loss of availability*)."

 NOTE

Confidentiality prevents unauthorized disclosure of sensitive information. Integrity prevents unauthorized modification of systems and information. Availability prevents disruption of service and productivity.

The Security Rule requires that each health care entity engaged in electronic maintenance or transmission of health information assess potential risks and vulnerabilities to the individual health data in its possession in electronic form, and develop, implement, and maintain appropriate security measures. Most importantly, these measures must be documented and kept current.

Security Rule Selection Criteria

The selection criteria for the Security Rule included these factors:

◆ **Improve the efficiency and effectiveness of the health care system.** The Security Rule needs to be integrated with the electronic transmission of health care information to improve the overall effectiveness of the health care system. This integration would assure that electronic health care information would not be accessible to any unauthorized person or organization, but would be both accurate and available to those who are authorized to receive it.

◆ **Be consistent and uniform with the other HIPAA standards and, secondly, with other private and public sector health data standards.** The Security and Electronic Signature Standards were developed after a comprehensive review of existing standards and guidelines, with significant input by a wide range of industry experts. The standards map well to existing standards and guidelines.

◆ **Be technologically independent of computer platforms and transmission protocols.** The Security and Electronic Signature Standards have been defined in terms of requirements that would allow businesses in the health care industry to select the technology that best meets their business requirements while still allowing them to comply with the standards.

◆ **Keep data collection and paperwork burdens on users as low as is feasible.** The Security and Electronic Signature Standards enables individual health care industry businesses to ascertain the level of security information that is needed. The confidentiality level associated with individual data elements concerning health care information determines the appropriate security application to be used. The Security Rule defines the requirements to be met to achieve the privacy and confidentiality goal, but each business entity, driven by its business requirements, must decide what techniques and controls provide appropriate and adequate electronic data protection. This enables data collection and the paperwork burden to be as low as is feasible.

◆ **Incorporate flexibility to adapt more easily to changes in the health care infrastructure and information technology**. A technologically neutral security standard is more adaptable to changes in infrastructure and information technology.

HIPAA Security

This section categorizes all HIPAA security requirements for ease of understanding and reading clarity.

Administrative Safeguards (164.308)

Administrative safeguards are administrative actions, policies, and procedures, to manage the selection, development, implementation, and maintenance of security measures to protect electronic PHI and to manage the conduct of the covered entity's workforce in relation to the protection of that information.

These administrative safeguards include the following nine standards:

◆ Security Management Process
◆ Assigned Security Responsibility
◆ Workforce Security
◆ Information Access Management
◆ Security Awareness and Training
◆ Security Incident Procedures
◆ Contingency Plan
◆ Evaluation
◆ Business Associate Contracts and Other Arrangements

As part of the administrative safeguards requirement, for example, an organization must perform a risk analysis and develop a sanctions policy. Table 4.1 summarizes information on the Administrative Safeguards' standards and their associated required and addressable implementation specifications.

Table 4.1   Administrative Safeguards

Standards	Implementation Specifications	R = Required, A = Addressable
Security Management Process	Risk Analysis	R
	Risk Management	R
	Sanction Policy	R
	Information System Activity Review	R
Assigned Security Responsibility		R
Workforce Security	Authorization and/or Supervision	R
	Workforce Clearance Procedure	A
	Termination Procedures	A
Information Access Management	Isolating Health Care Clearinghouse Function	R
	Access Authorization	A
	Access Establishment and Modification	A
Security Awareness and Training	Security Reminders	A
	Protection from Malicious Software	A
	Login Monitoring	A
	Password Management	A
Security Incident Procedures	Response and Reporting	R
Contingency Plan	Data Backup Plan	R
	Disaster Recovery Plan	R
	Emergency Mode Operation Plan	R
	Testing and Revision Procedure	A
	Applications and Data Criticality Analysis	A
Evaluation		R
Business Associate Contracts and Other Arrangements	Written Contract or Other Arrangement	R

Each of these nine standards is discussed in detail in the following sections.

Security Management Process (Standard)

The objective of this standard is to implement policies and procedures to prevent, detect, contain, and correct security violations.

Security management process refers to the creation, administration, and oversight of policies to address the full range of security issues and to ensure the prevention, detection, containment, and correction of security violations.

The security management process includes the establishment of accountability, management controls (policies and education), electronic controls, physical security, and penalties for the abuse and misuse of its assets (both physical and electronic) that includes all of the following implementation features:

- Risk Analysis (Required)
- Risk Management (Required)
- Sanction Policy (Required)
- Information System Activity Review (Required)

In the final Security Rule, risk analysis, risk management, and sanction policy have been adopted as required implementation specifications although some of the details have been changed, and the proposed internal audit requirement has been renamed as "information system activity review" and incorporated as an additional implementation specification.

Each of these features is discussed in the following sections.

Risk Analysis (Required)

The objective is to conduct an accurate and thorough assessment of the potential risks and vulnerabilities to the confidentiality, integrity, and availability of electronic protected health information held by the covered entity.

Risk analysis is a process whereby relevant assets and relevant threats are identified, and cost-effective security/control measures are identified or engineered to effectively balance the costs of various security/risk mitigation/control measures against the losses that would be expected if these measures were not in place. Threats and risks are real. Each entity needs to identify and prioritize risks and threats.

Risk Management (Required)

The objective is to implement security measures sufficient to reduce risks and vulnerabilities to a reasonable and appropriate level.

Security professionals generally define risk management as a process for identifying, selecting, and implementing controls, countermeasures, reporting, and verification to achieve an appropriate level of risk at an acceptable cost. Effective risk management requires leadership and accountability—without these key individual attributes, a risk management exercise is generally doomed.

Someone must be accountable and have the ability to make complex and often difficult decisions. This individual will ultimately determine what level of threat and risk is "appropriate" and "acceptable." This individual is also generally able to allocate resources for achieving the target levels.

Sanction Policy (Required)

The objective is to apply appropriate sanctions against workforce members who fail to comply with the security policies and procedures of the covered entity.

Sanction policy addresses statements regarding disciplinary actions that are communicated to all employees, agents, and contractors. Examples include

- Verbal warning
- Notice of disciplinary action placed in personnel files
- Removal of system privileges
- Termination of employment
- Contract penalties

Sanction policies and procedures must include employee, agent, and contractor notice of civil or criminal penalties for misuse or misappropriation of health information and must make employees, agents, and contractors aware that violations may result in notification to law enforcement officials and regulatory, accreditation, and licensure organizations.

The sanction policy is a required implementation specification because

- The statute requires covered entities to have safeguards to ensure compliance by officers and employees.
- A negative consequence to noncompliance enhances the likelihood of compliance.

♦ Sanction policies are recognized as a usual and necessary component of an adequate security program.

The type and severity of sanctions imposed, and for what causes, must be determined by each covered entity based on its security policy and the relative severity of the violation.

Information System Activity Review (Required)

The objective is to implement procedures to regularly review records of information system activity, such as audit logs, access reports, and security incident tracking reports.

The extent, frequency, and nature of reviews would be determined by the covered entity's security environment.

> **NOTE**
>
> The key objective for internal review is that the entity must implement an ongoing review of system activity, identify and investigate potential security violations, and take appropriate security action.

Assigned Security Responsibility (Standard)

The objective is to identify the security official who is responsible for the development and implementation of the policies and procedures required by this subpart for the entity.

Assigned security responsibility is the practice established by management to administer and supervise the execution and use of security measures to protect data, and to manage and supervise the conduct of the workforce in relation to the protection of data.

The final Security Rule requires that the final responsibility for a covered entity's security must be assigned to one official to ensure accountability. More than one individual may be given specific security responsibilities, especially within a large organization, but a single individual must be designated as having the overall responsibility for the security of the entity's electronic PHI. Depending on the size of the organization and other factors, it is possible for the same person to fill the role for both security and privacy.

NOTE

The key objective for assigned security responsibility is that the entity must assign responsibility for management and supervision of security to a specific individual. This individual must have sufficient accountability and authority to drive out the types of changes that HIPAA can require of, or inflict upon, health care organizations and on their interactions with others in the industry.

Workforce Security (Standard)

The objective is to implement policies and procedures to ensure that all members of its workforce have appropriate access to electronic protected health information and to prevent those workforce members who do not have access from obtaining access to electronic protected health information.

This standard addresses requirements for a covered entity's workforce that has access to any sensitive information. This area includes the following implementation specifications:

◆ Authorization and/or supervision (addressable)

◆ Workforce clearance procedure (addressable)

◆ Termination procedures (addressable)

This standard results in assurances that all personnel with access to electronic PHI have the required access authority as well as the appropriate clearances.

Authorization and/or Supervision (Addressable)

The objective is to implement procedures for the authorization and/or supervision of workforce members who work with electronic protected health information or in locations where it might be accessed.

Workforce Clearance Procedure (Addressable)

The objective is to implement procedures to determine that the access of a workforce member to electronic protected health information is appropriate.

Termination Procedures (Addressable)

The objective is to implement procedures for terminating access to electronic protected health information when the employment of a workforce member ends.

Termination procedures are documented instructions, which include appropriate security measures for the ending of an employee's employment or an internal/external user's access.

Termination procedures are relevant for any covered entity with employees because of the risks associated with the potential for unauthorized acts by former employees, such as acts of retribution or use of proprietary information for personal gain.

 NOTE

The key objective for workforce security is that the entity must limit access to health information to authorized individuals.

Information Access Management (Standard)

The objective is to implement policies and procedures for authorizing access to electronic protected health information that are consistent with the applicable requirements of this standard.

Information access management covers documented policies and procedures for granting different levels of access to health care information to authorized personnel. This standard is consistent with the Privacy Rule minimum necessary requirements for use and disclosure of PHI. Restricting access to those persons and entities with a need for access is a basic tenet of security. As a consequence of the implementation of this standard, the risk of inappropriate disclosure, alteration, or destruction of information is minimized.

The implementation specifications defined for information access management are

- ◆ Isolating Health Care Clearinghouse Function (Required)
- ◆ Access Authorization (Addressable)
- ◆ Access Establishment and Modification (Addressable)

The implementation will be dependent and influenced by factors, such as the size and scale of operations of the covered entity. For example, a fully automated covered entity spanning multiple locations and involving hundreds of employees may determine it has a need to adopt a formal policy for access authorization, while a small provider may decide that a desktop operating procedure will meet the specification.

Isolating Health Care Clearinghouse Function (Required)

If a health care clearinghouse is part of a larger organization, the clearinghouse must implement policies and procedures that protect the electronic PHI of the clearinghouse from unauthorized access by the larger organization.

Access Authorization (Addressable)

The objective is to implement policies and procedures for granting access to electronic protected health information, for example, through access to a workstation, transaction, program, process, or other mechanism. Information-use policies and procedures that establish the rules for granting access, for example, to a terminal, transaction, program, process, or some other user.

Access Establishment and Modification (Addressable)

The objective is to implement policies and procedures that, based upon the entity's access authorization policies, establish, document, review, and modify a user's right of access to a workstation, transaction, program, or process. Access establishment is about security policies and rules that determine an entity's initial right of access to a terminal, transaction, program, process, or some other user. Access modification is about security policies and rules that determine the types of, and reasons for, modification to an entity's established right of access to a terminal, transaction, program, process, or some other user.

 NOTE

The key objective for information access management is that the entity must establish policies and procedures for granting levels of access for all personnel authorized to access health information and how access is granted or modified.

Security Awareness and Training (Standard)

The objective is to implement a security awareness and training program for all members of its workforce (including management). The implementation specifications for security awareness and training include

- ◆ Security reminders (addressable)
- ◆ Protection from malicious software (addressable)
- ◆ Login monitoring (addressable)
- ◆ Password management (addressable)

Training implies education concerning the vulnerabilities of the health information in an entity's possession and ways to ensure the protection of that information. The final Security Rule requires training of the workforce as reasonable and appropriate to carry out their functions in the facility.

Security awareness training is a critical activity, regardless of the organization's size. The amount and type of training is dependent upon an entity's configuration and security risks. Business associates must be made aware of security policies and procedures, whether through contract language or through other means. Covered entities are not required to provide training to business associates or anyone else that is not a member of their workforce.

Each individual who has access to electronic PHI must be aware of the appropriate security measures to reduce the risk of improper access, uses and disclosures. Training is not a one-time type of activity, but rather an ongoing, evolving process as an entity's security needs and procedures change. Training may be tailored to job need if the covered entity so desires. The initial training must be carried out by the compliance date.

Security Reminders (Addressable)

These are periodic security updates to members of the workforce.

Protection from Malicious Software (Addressable)

These are procedures for guarding against, detecting, and reporting malicious software.

Login Monitoring (Addressable)

These are procedures for monitoring login attempts and reporting discrepancies.

Password Management (Addressable)

These are procedures for creating, changing, and safeguarding passwords.

 NOTE

The key objective for training is that the entity must require security training for all personnel, including management, and implement an ongoing communications program with personnel about security issues and concerns.

Security Incident Procedures (Standard)

The objective is to implement policies and procedures to address security incidents. Security incident procedures are documented instructions for reporting security incidents.

The defined implementation specification in this standard is Response and Reporting (Required).

The final Security Rule emphasizes that documenting and reporting incidents, as well as responding to incidents, are an integral part of a security program.

Whether a specific action is considered a security incident, the specific process of documenting incidents, what information should be contained in the documentation, and what the appropriate response should be is dependent upon an entity's environment and the information involved. An entity should be able to rely upon the information gathered in complying with the other security standards, for example, its risk assessment and risk management procedures and the privacy standards, to determine what constitutes a security incident in the context of its business operations.

Note that internal reporting is an inherent part of security incident procedures. This regulation does not specifically require any incident reporting to outside entities. External incident reporting is dependent upon business and legal considerations. Improper network activity should be treated as a security incident because, by definition, it represents an improper instance of access to or use of information.

Response and Reporting (Required)

Identify and respond to suspected or known security incidents; mitigate, to the extent practicable, harmful effects of security incidents that are known to the covered entity; and document security incidents and their outcomes.

 NOTE

The key objective for security incident procedures is that the entity must adopt and implement procedures for timely reporting of incidents of security.

Contingency Plan (Standard)

The objective is to establish (and implement as needed) policies and procedures for responding to an emergency or other occurrence (for example, fire, vandalism, system failure, and natural disaster) that damages systems that contain electronic protected health information.

A contingency plan is the only way to protect the availability, integrity, and security of data during unexpected negative events. Data are often most exposed in these events, since the usual security measures may be disabled, ignored, or not observed.

Contingency planning includes the following implementation specifications:

- ◆ Data Backup Plan (Required)
- ◆ Disaster Recovery Plan (Required)
- ◆ Emergency Mode Operation Plan (Required)
- ◆ Testing and Revision (Addressable)
- ◆ Applications and Data Criticality Analysis (Addressable)

 NOTE

The key objective of the contingency plan is that the entity must establish and implement contingency plans to ensure the integrity, confidentiality, and availability of its health information during and after an emergency.

Each of these implementation specifications is discussed in the following sections.

Data Backup Plan (Required)

The objective is to establish and implement procedures to create and maintain retrievable exact copies of electronic protected health information. A data backup plan is a documented and routinely updated plan to create and maintain, for a specific period of time, retrievable exact copies of information. Successful data backup and restores are sometimes dependent on business processes and batch activities. Carefully test all critical backups and restores on a schedule related to the criticality of success to the organization.

Disaster Recovery Plan (Required)

The objective is to establish (and implement as needed) procedures to restore any loss of data. A disaster recovery plan contains a process enabling an enterprise to restore any loss of data in the event of fire, vandalism, natural disaster, or system failure. It is important to invest in relatively realistic testing of your disaster recovery plan. Build this effort into your budgets and schedules, then guard these resources because they must work effectively when called upon.

An overall security contingency plan covers this area of security.

Emergency Mode Operation Plan (Required)

The objective is to establish (and implement as needed) procedures to enable continuation of critical business processes for protection of the security of electronic protected health information while operating in emergency mode. An emergency mode operation plan contains a process enabling an enterprise to continue to operate in the event of fire, vandalism, natural disaster, or system failure. In a manner similar to disaster recovery planning, budget for and schedule required resources for effective emergency mode operation plan testing.

An overall security contingency plan covers this area of security.

Testing and Revision Procedures (Addressable)

The objective is to implement procedures for periodic testing and revision of contingency plans. Testing and revision procedures are documented procedures for processing of periodic testing of written contingency plans to discover weaknesses and the subsequent process of revising the documentation, if necessary. These written testing and feedback mechanisms are the key to successful testing, as mentioned earlier.

Applications and Data Criticality Analysis (Addressable)

The objective is to assess the relative criticality of specific applications and data in support of other contingency plan components. It is an entity's assessment of the sensitivity, vulnerabilities, and security of its programs and information it receives, manipulates, stores, and/or transmits. This procedure begins with an application and data inventory. (This application and data inventory is required for identifying and categorizing the value of the company's assets, for performing vulnerability and risk analysis, and for a variety of audit-related activities.)

Evaluation (Required)

The objective of this standard is to perform a periodic technical and non-technical evaluation, based initially upon the standards implemented under this rule. Subsequently, it is based in response to environmental or operational changes affecting the security of electronic protected health information.

It is required that covered entities periodically conduct an evaluation of their security safeguards to demonstrate and document their compliance with the entity's security policy and the requirements of the Security Rule.

Covered entities must assess the need for a new evaluation based on changes to their security environment since their last evaluation, for example, new technology adopted or responses to newly recognized risks to the security of their information.

This evaluation can be performed internally or by an external accrediting agency, which would be acting as a business associate. The evaluation would be to both technical and non-technical components of security.

A small provider might be able to self-certify through industry-developed check lists. The evaluation process must be thorough and complete to be sure that the provider's environment is not vulnerable to threats and attacks.

 NOTE

The entity must evaluate that it meets the security standards and associated implementation specifications.

Business Associate Contract or Other Arrangements (Standard)

A covered entity may permit a business associate to create, receive, maintain, or transmit electronic protected health information on the covered entity's behalf, only if the covered entity obtains satisfactory assurances that the business associate will appropriately safeguard the information.

This standard does not apply with respect to

♦ The transmission by a covered entity of electronic protected health information to a health care provider concerning the treatment of an individual.

♦ The transmission of electronic protected health information by a group health plan or an HMO or health insurance issuer on behalf of a group health plan to a plan sponsor.

♦ The transmission of electronic protected health information from or to other agencies providing the services when the covered entity is a health plan that is a government program providing public benefits.

A covered entity that violates the satisfactory assurances it provided as a business associate of another covered entity will be in non-compliance with the standards and implementation specifications.

Covered entities that electronically exchange information must enter into a contract or other arrangement with persons or entities that meet the definition of a business associate.

The covered entity must obtain satisfactory assurances from the business associate that it will appropriately safeguard the information in accordance with the requirements of the Security Rule.

Prudent organizations implement periodic audits and scans to verify that the agreements are implemented effectively and remain viable. Because the health services industry is characterized by change, your company's security depends upon effective positive verifications that each and every business partner contract or agreement remains in force.

NOTE

The key objective is that the entity establish a business associate contract or other agreement with each organization with which it exchanges data electronically, protecting the security of all such data.

Physical Safeguards (164.310)

Physical safeguards are physical measures, policies, and procedures to protect a covered entity's electronic information systems and related buildings and equipment from natural and environmental hazards and unauthorized intrusion.

Physical safeguards include physical security access, card access solutions, paper destruction procedures, and computer room access, as shown in Table 4.2.

Table 4.2   Safeguards

Standards	Implementation Specifications	R = Required, A = Addressable
Facility Access Controls	Contingency Operations	A
	Facility Security Plan	A
	Access Control and Validation Procedures	A
	Maintenance Records	A
Workstation Use		R
Workstation Security		R
Device and Media Controls	Disposal	R
	Media Re-use	R
	Accountability	A
	Data Backup and Storage	A

Physical safeguard standards include

- Facility Access Controls
- Workstation Use
- Workstation Security
- Device and Media Controls

Facility Access Controls (Standard)

The objective of this standard is to implement policies and procedures to limit physical access to its electronic information systems and the facility or facilities in which they are housed while ensuring that properly authorized access is allowed.

The implementation specifications of facility access controls are

- Contingency Operations (Addressable)
- Facility Security Plan (Addressable)
- Access Control and Validation Procedures (Addressable)
- Maintenance Records (Addressable)

Contingency Operations (Addressable)

The objective is to establish (and implement as needed) procedures that allow facility access in support of restoration of lost data under the disaster recovery plan and emergency mode operations plan in the event of an emergency.

Facility Security Plan (Addressable)

The objective is to implement policies and procedures to safeguard the facility and the equipment therein from unauthorized physical access, tampering, and theft.

Access Control and Validation Procedures (Addressable)

The objective is to implement procedures to control and validate a person's access to facilities based on his role or function, including visitor control and control of access to software programs for testing and revision.

Maintenance Records (Addressable)

The objective is to implement policies and procedures to document repairs and modifications to the physical components of a facility that are related to security (for example, hardware, walls, doors, and locks).

Workstation Use (Standard)

The objective is to implement policies and procedures that specify the proper functions to be performed, the manner in which those functions are to be performed, and the physical attributes of the surroundings of a specific workstation or class of workstation that can access electronic protected health information.

Workstation Security (Standard)

The objective is to implement physical safeguards for all workstations that access electronic protected health information, to restrict access to authorized users.

Device and Media Controls (Standard)

The objective is to implement policies and procedures that govern the receipt and removal of hardware and electronic media that contain electronic protected health information into and out of a facility, and the movement of these items within the facility.

The implementation specifications of device and media controls are

- ◆ Disposal
- ◆ Media re-use
- ◆ Accountability
- ◆ Data backup and storage

Disposal (Required)

The objective is to implement policies and procedures to address the final disposition of electronic protected health information, and/or the hardware or electronic media on which it is stored.

Media Re-use (Required)

The objective is to implement procedures for removal of electronic protected health information from electronic media before the media are made available for re-use.

Accountability (Addressable)

The objective is to maintain a record of the movements of hardware and electronic media and any person responsible therefore.

Data Backup and Storage (Addressable)

The covered entity must create a retrievable, exact copy of electronic protected health information, when needed, before movement of equipment.

Technical Safeguards (164.312)

Technical safeguards refer to the technology and the policy and procedures for its use that protect electronic PHI and control access to it. The Technical Safeguard Standards follow and are shown in Table 4.3.

- ◆ Access Control
- ◆ Audit Controls
- ◆ Integrity
- ◆ Person or Entity Authentication
- ◆ Transmission Security

Access Control (Standard)

The objective is to implement technical policies and procedures for electronic information systems that maintain electronic protected health information to allow access only to those persons or software programs that have been granted access rights.

The implementation specifications of the access control standard are

- ◆ Unique User Identification (Required)
- ◆ Emergency Access Procedure (Required)
- ◆ Automatic Logoff (Addressable)
- ◆ Encryption and Decryption (Addressable)

Table 4.3   Technical Safeguard Standards

Standards	Implementation Specifications	R = Required, A = Addressable
Access Control	Unique User Identification	R
	Emergency Access Procedure	R
	Automatic Logoff	A
	Encryption and Decryption	A
Audit Controls		R
Integrity	Mechanism to Authenticate Electronic PHI	A
Person or Entity Authentication		R
Transmission Security	Integrity Controls	A
	Encryption	A

Access control generally requires some form of authentication. Authentication, the process of "proving" your identity, identifies a user to an application. A system needs to authenticate users to a degree appropriate for the level of risk or threat that an authenticated user represents. While verifying the expenses for the inventory of cleaning supplies may require a simple username and password (something you know), remote access to patient histories in a mental illness treatment clinic may require a username, password, and biometric scan (something you know, something you are).

Context-based access is an exception to standard authentication, and is often related to enforced workflow. For example, you may not be able to access the master patient information DB/2 database directly because it is restricted except when interacting with specifically authorized application transactions. In this case, you may be able to log on to the patient management system and access screens of information or print reports about a specific patient, but you would be unable to use a desktop query tool to perform a SELECT against any tables in the database, even if your SELECT returns exactly the same data.

Unique User Identification (Required)

The objective is to assign a unique name and/or number for identifying and tracking user identity. Digital signatures, soft tokens, and biometrics, as well as other mechanisms may be used to implement this requirement.

Emergency Access Procedure (Required)

The objective is to establish (and implement as needed) procedures for obtaining necessary electronic protected health information during an emergency.

Automatic Logoff (Addressable)

The objective is to implement electronic procedures that terminate an electronic session after a predetermined time of inactivity.

Encryption and Decryption (Addressable)

The objective is to implement a mechanism to encrypt and decrypt electronic protected health information. The use of file encryption is an acceptable method of denying access to information in files or directories. Encryption provides confidentiality, which is a form of control. The use of encryption for the purpose of access control of data at rest should be based upon an entity's risk analysis.

Audit Controls (Standard)

The objective is to implement hardware, software, and/or procedural mechanisms that record and examine activity in information systems that contain or use electronic protected health information.

Integrity (Standard)

The objective is to implement policies and procedures to protect electronic protected health information from improper alteration or destruction.

The implementation specification defined for the Integrity Standard is the Mechanism to Authenticate Electronic PHI (Addressable).

Mechanism to Authenticate Electronic PHI (Addressable)

The objective is to implement electronic mechanisms to corroborate that electronic protected health information has not been altered or destroyed in an unauthorized manner.

Person or Entity Authentication (Standard)

The objective is to implement procedures to verify that a person or entity seeking access to electronic protected health information is the one claimed.

Transmission Security (Standard)

The objective is to implement technical security measures to guard against unauthorized access to electronic protected health information that is being transmitted over an electronic communications network.

The Transmission Security Standard includes the following implementation specifications:

- ◆ Integrity Controls (Addressable)
- ◆ Encryption (Addressable)

Integrity Controls (Addressable)

The objective is to implement security measures to ensure that electronically transmitted electronic protected health information is not improperly modified without detection until disposed of.

Encryption (Addressable)

The objective is to implement a mechanism to encrypt electronic protected health information whenever deemed appropriate.

Organizational Requirements (164.314)

This includes the Standard, Business associate contracts or other arrangements. A covered entity is not in compliance with the standard if the covered entity knew of a pattern of an activity or practice of the business associate that constituted a material breach or violation of the business associate's obligation under the contract or other arrangement, unless the covered entity took reasonable steps to cure the breach or end the violation, as applicable. If such steps were unsuccessful,

- ◆ Terminate the contract or arrangement, if feasible.
- ◆ If termination is not feasible, report the problem to the Secretary (HHS).

The required implementation specifications associated with this standard are

◆ Business Associate Contracts

◆ Other Arrangements

Business Associate Contracts

The contract between a covered entity and a business associate must provide that the business associate will

◆ Implement administrative, physical, and technical safeguards that reasonably and appropriately protect the confidentiality, integrity, and availability of the electronic protected health information that it creates, receives, maintains, or transmits on behalf of the covered entity

◆ Ensure that any agent, including a subcontractor, to whom it provides such information agrees to implement reasonable and appropriate safeguards to protect it

◆ Report to the covered entity any security incident of which it becomes aware

◆ Authorize termination of the contract by the covered entity, if the covered entity determines that the business associate has violated a material term of the contract.

Other Arrangements

When a covered entity and its business associate are both governmental entities, the covered entity is in compliance if

◆ It enters into a memorandum of understanding with the business associate.

◆ Other law (including regulations adopted by the covered entity or its business associate) contains requirements applicable to the business associate.

If a business associate is required by law to perform a function or activity on behalf of a covered entity or to provide a service described in the definition of business associate, the covered entity may permit the business associate to create, receive, maintain, or transmit electronic protected health information on its behalf to the extent necessary to comply with the legal mandate without meeting the requirements of this section. All of this is provided that the covered entity attempts in good faith to obtain satisfactory assurances as required and documents the attempt and the reasons that these assurances cannot be obtained.

The covered entity may omit from its other arrangements authorization of the termination of the contract by the covered entity, if such authorization is inconsistent with the statutory obligations of the covered entity or its business associate.

Group Health Plan

Except when the only electronic protected health information disclosed to a plan sponsor is disclosed as authorized, a group health plan must ensure that its plan documents provide that the plan sponsor will reasonably and appropriately safeguard electronic protected health information created, received, maintained, or transmitted to or by the plan sponsor on behalf of the group health plan.

The plan documents of the group health plan must be amended to incorporate provisions to require the plan sponsor to

- Implement administrative, physical, and technical safeguards that reasonably and appropriately protect the confidentiality, integrity, and availability of the electronic protected health information that it creates, receives, maintains, or transmits on behalf of the group health plan
- Ensure that the adequate separation required is supported by reasonable and appropriate security measures
- Ensure that any agent, including a subcontractor, to whom it provides this information agrees to implement reasonable and appropriate security measures to protect the information
- Report to the group health plan any security incident of which it becomes aware

Policies, Procedures and Documentation Requirements (164.316)

This requirement includes two standards:

- Policies and Procedures Standard
- Documentation Standard

Policies and Procedures Standard

A covered entity must implement reasonable and appropriate policies and procedures to comply with the standards and implementation specifications. This standard is not to be construed to permit or excuse an action that violates any other standard, implementation specification, or other requirements of this subpart. A covered entity may change its policies and procedures at any time, provided that the changes are documented and are implemented in accordance with this subpart.

Documentation Standard

A covered entity must maintain the policies and procedures implemented to comply with this subpart in written (which may be electronic) form. If an action, activity, or assessment is required to be documented, the covered entity must maintain a written (which may be electronic) record of the action, activity, or assessment.

The implementation specifications of the documentation standard are

- ◆ Time Limit (Required)
- ◆ Availability (Required)
- ◆ Updates (Required)

Time limit (Required)

Retain the documentation required for six years from the date of its creation or the date when it last was in effect, whichever is later.

Availability (Required)

Make documentation available to those persons responsible for implementing the procedures to which the documentation pertains.

Updates (Required)

Review documentation periodically, and update as needed, in response to environmental or operational changes affecting the security of the electronic protected health information.

Electronic Signatures (Proposed Rule Only)

The proposed Security Rule includes recommendations for, but does not require, the use of electronic signatures for any of the HIPAA transactions. The Security Rule adopts only security standards. The Final Rule for electronic signatures will be published at a later date.

Although the HIPAA proposed Security Rule does not mandate a particular technology, the requirements do call for the use of a particular type of electronic signature, namely digital signatures based on cryptography. This is in order to meet the requirement for non-repudiation, which currently can only be met with digital signatures.

For this proposed rule, if a digital signature is employed, the following three implementation features must be implemented:

- Message integrity
- Non-repudiation
- User authentication

The following are the suggested implementation features:

- Message integrity
- Non-repudiation
- User authentication
- Ability to add attributes
- Continuity of signature capability
- Counter signatures
- Independent verifiability
- Interoperability
- Multiple signatures
- Transportability

NOTE

The proposed Security Rule does not mandate the use of electronic signatures; however, if electronic signatures are used, they must be digital signatures.

An electronic signature is the attribute affixed to an electronic document to bind it to a particular entity. An electronic signature

- ◆ Secures the user authentication (proof of claimed identity) at the time the signature is generated
- ◆ Creates the logical manifestation of a signature (including the possibility for multiple parties to sign a document and have the order of application recognized and proven); supplies additional information such as time stamp and signature purpose specific to that user
- ◆ Ensures the integrity of the signed document to enable transportability of data, interoperability, independent verifiability, and continuity of signature capability

Verifying a signature on a document verifies the integrity of the document and associated attributes and verifies the identity of the signer. There are several technologies available for user authentication, including

- ◆ Passwords
- ◆ Cryptography
- ◆ Biometrics

Implementation Features

Based on the requirements of the proposed Security Rule, if a health care entity uses electronic signatures, the signature method must assure all of the following features:

- ◆ **Message integrity**. The assurance of unaltered transmission and receipt of a message from the sender to the intended recipient.
- ◆ **Non-repudiation**. Strong and substantial evidence of the identity of the signer of a message, and of message integrity, sufficient to prevent a party from successfully denying the origin, submission, or delivery of the message and the integrity of its contents.
- ◆ **User authentication**. The provision of assurance of the claimed identity of an entity.

If an entity uses electronic signatures, the entity may also use, among others, any of the following implementation features:

- **Ability to add attributes.** One possible capability of a digital signature technology; for example, the ability to add a time stamp as part of a digital signature.

- **Continuity of signature capability.** The concept that the public verification of a signature must not compromise the ability of the signer to apply additional secure signatures at a later date.

- **Counter signatures.** The capability to prove the order of application of signatures. This is analogous to the normal business practice of counter-signatures, where a party signs a document that has already been signed by another party.

- **Independent verifiability.** The capability to verify the signature without the cooperation of the signer.

- **Interoperability.** The applications used on either side of a communication between trading partners and/or between internal components of an entity are able to read and correctly interpret the information communicated from one to the other.

- **Multiple signatures.** With this feature, multiple parties are able to sign a document. Conceptually, multiple signatures are simply appended to the document.

- **Transportability.** The ability of a signed document to be transported over an insecure network to another system, while maintaining the integrity of the document, including content, signatures, signature attributes, and (if present) document attributes.

Digital Signatures

The standard for electronic signature as per the proposed Security Rule is a digital signature—an electronic signature based upon cryptographic methods of originator authentication, computed by using a set of rules and parameters so that the identity of the signer and the integrity of the data can be verified.

Some large health plans, health care providers, and health care clearinghouses that currently exchange health information between trading partners may already have security systems and procedures in place to protect the information from unauthorized access. Some entities may already support digital signatures and may just need to verify that their own enterprise security requirements are, in fact, met.

Scenario: Enterprise TCP/IP Security Policy

As discussed earlier, the HIPAA Security Rule requires that a covered entity must implement reasonable and appropriate policies and procedures to comply with the standards and implementation specifications. In this section we review some key elements of an enterprise Transmission Control Protocol/Internet Protocol (TCP/IP) security policy. An enterprise TCP/IP security policy typically includes the following core elements:

◆ Defining the security perimeter based on an organization's network topology and security requirements

◆ Developing a customized security policy based on business and application requirements

◆ Deploying firewall system(s) to implement the specifications of the organization's security policy

Questions to Address to Create TCP/IP Security Policy Document

A number of areas need to be reviewed in the process of developing an organization's TCP/IP Security Policy document. Some questions that need to be addressed include:

◆ What is the objective or motivation for this document in your organization?

◆ Who is the intended audience for this document? In other words, to whom will this document be distributed? Will all or some parts of this document be distributed?

- How frequently will this document be revised?
- Who is responsible for updating the document?
- Are there recommendations in the document that will be enforced?
- Identify the security philosophy that best reflects the belief of the organization.
- Which firewall systems are used to secure your connection to the Internet?
- What is the firewall system and network architecture?
- What is your policy for in-bound access to systems? Which specific protocols will be allowed to access nodes on your internal network?
- What is your policy on out-bound access to nodes on the Internet? Which specific protocols will be allowed to establish outbound connections to nodes on the Internet?
- Do you have remote offices or branches that connect to the home office? If yes, is the remote office directly connected to the Internet or is their access to the Internet through the home office?
- Are there external networks that are not trusted? Are there external networks that do need access to your internal network via the Internet?
- Where are your key servers such as Web server, DNS server, FTP server, located on the network?
- Does your firewall architecture define where Internet servers are configured on the network?
- What is your policy on consultants and contractors that may have privileged access to systems and networks?
- What is your policy on employees that are no longer with the organization—how do you ascertain that they have no access, privileged or unprivileged, to system resources on the network?

Security Perimeter

The security perimeter identifies what parts of the network and which systems are trusted and thus do not require any security services. The enterprise security team must clearly identify restricted network segments as well as the de-militarized zone (DMZ).

Template: For Your Enterprise TCP/IP Security Policy

Every organization must develop its own customized security policy. Typically, an enterprise TCP/IP security policy is over 50 pages in length. Its objective is to describe corporate policy for each and every protocol and network device that communicates on the enterprise network. Each section of the security policy document must cover three areas:

- ◆ Overview (of the protocol)
- ◆ Recommendation (for use of the protocol on the enterprise network)
- ◆ Reasoning (justifying the recommendation)

A customized enterprise TCP/IP security policy document typically includes sections such as those identified in the following example:

Executive Summary

    Overview

    Internal and External Networks

Security Philosophy

Scope and Deployment

    Audience

    Compliance

How to Use the Security Policy Document

    Document Changes and Feedback

Network Services

    Minimal IP Requirements

    Routing Protocols

        BGP

        IGRP

            EIGRP

        OSPF

            Authentication

        RIP

            RIP-2 or OSPF

ICMP

ICMP Netmask Requests

ICMP Timemap Requests

Transport Layer

TCP/UDP Port 7—ECHO

TCP Port 11—SYSTAT

TCP Port 15—NETSTAT

TCP/UDP Port 19—CHARGEN

TCP/UDP Ports 20 and 21—FTP

Authenticate FTP

Anonymous FTP

TCP/UDP Port 22—SSH

TCP/UDP Port 23—Telnet

TCP/UDP Port 25—SMTP

TCP Port 43—WHOIS

TCP/UDP Port 53—DNS

UDP Port 69—TFTP

TCP Port 79—Finger

TCP Port 80—HTTP

TCP Ports 109 and 110—POP

TCP/UDP Port 111—RPC's Portmapper

TCP Port 119—NNTP

TCP Port 123—NTP

TCP Port 143—IMAP

UDP Ports 161 and 162—SNMP

TCP Port 389—LDAP

TCP Port 512—REXEC

TCP Port 513—RWHO

TCP Port 514—RLOGIN, RSH

Kerberos

TCP Port s 6000-6063—X Window Systems Parameters

Internet Relay Chat (IRC) Prohibited

I Seek YOU (ICQ) Prohibited

Recommendations for Enterprise TCP/IP Security Policy

To secure IP devices and data on an enterprise, businesses must strongly consider the following:

◆ Using encryption as much as possible to protect data

◆ Using strong authentication mechanisms including tokens, smart cards, and biometrics

◆ Using firewall(s) to secure critical segments

◆ Disabling all services that are not in uses or services that have use of which you are not sure

◆ Using wrappers around all services to log their usage as well as to restrict connectivity

For each request that a system needs to service, the host must authenticate the user's identity and then provide access based on the user's privileges or rights.

The following sections summarize recommendations for some key network protocols and services.

TCP/UDP Ports 20-21—FTP

In numerous FTP releases an attacker could potentially use the PORT command to connect to sites through the host and bounce the connection. Do not allow Proxy connection; instead, implement FTP in passive mode or upgrade to the latest version of FTP server.

◆ Disable FTP default accounts; they allow attackers easy access to remote systems.

◆ Disable the CHMOD command on FTP servers. The CHMOD command executed on a server may be used by attackers to modify files or replace files with Trojans.

◆ Ensure that FTP daemons do not reveal the true path to the FTP user's home directory. The FTP user's home directory may provide an attacker with information about the structure of the user's file system.

◆ Do not allow writeable FTP directories. Writeable FTP directories may be used as drop points for unauthorized content and may also be used for denial-of-service attacks.

◆ Use a one-time password and encryption to protect passwords and the login session. FTP packets are vulnerable to packet sniffing because the username, password, and the entire session is transmitted in clear text on the network.

◆ A writeable anonymous FTP server may lead to denial-of-services or possibly hidden directories for unauthorized activities. Do not grant write permission to anonymous FTP accounts. If depository directories are required

- Create the correct home directories for exclusive use of **ftpd**; place actual files into the FTP home directories (not symbolic links).

- Create a special FTP account that points to the FTP home directory

- Alter the FTP password file to contain entries only for **root** and **FTP**; change the Group file to contain only the FTP Group.

- Apply the appropriate owners to the directory, and apply correct permissions to all directories and files.

- Secure any open repository directories so they cannot be used as drop points. For example, create a directory that is writeable but not readable.

- Automatically check for viruses, and then move any files that remain in the depository after a specified period of time into another directory that is not accessible by anonymous FTP users.

- Enable a file quota on the FTP user.

TCP/UDP Port 19—CHARGEN

Disable the Chargen port. Chargen returns a packet with 0 to 512 characters chosen randomly; there is no restriction on what may be in the packet. This port has been used for denial-of-service attacks.

TCP/UDP Port 22 SSH

Implement secure shell (SSH) as a secure alternative to the following services:

◆ FTP

◆ Telnet

◆ "r" commands (rlogin, rcp, rsh)

◆ Encryption for securing X Window sessions

SSH encrypts the entire session and is a secure alternative to services that are transmitted in clear text over the network.

◆ Ensure that SSHD servers and clients are updated to the latest version. Some older versions of SSHD have multiple security weaknesses that may allow a hacker to execute arbitrary commands on the SSH server, or subvert an encrypted SSH channel with arbitrary data. Other attacks may exploit race conditions to steal another user's credentials.

◆ Do not allow .rhosts authentication and use only RSA and RHOST-RSA. The .rhosts authentication relies on trusted host names that can be defeated by DNS cache poisoning and IP spoofing.

Border Gateway Protocol (BGP)

Private Autonomous System (AS) numbers must be removed before sending updates to the global BGP mesh. Private AS numbers range from 64512 to 65535. If the AS_PATH includes both private and public AS numbers, BGP does not remove the private AS numbers.

Internet Control Messages Protocol (ICMP) Netmask

Block ICMP netmask requests into sensitive networks. ICMP netmask requests provide the hacker with a better map of your subnet architecture. Blocking unnecessary ICMP types prevents information disclosure about network layouts.

ICMP Timemap

Block ICMP Timemap requests into sensitive requests. An ICMP time stamp request allows an attacker to accurately determine the target's clock state. An attacker can then attack certain time-based pseudo–random number generators and the authentication systems that rely on them.

TCP/UDP Port 7 ECHO

Disable the ECHO port. This service echoes back any character sent to it. It is used primarily for testing. The service can be spoofed into sending data from one service on one machine to another service on another machine. This action causes an infinite loop and creates a denial-of-service attack.

TCP Port 11 SYSTAT

Disable the SYSTAT service. This port may be configured on devices to respond with the output of **who** or **w** commands. Information provided includes user-names, login times, and origination hosts—these may be used to target specific attacks against your systems.

TCP Port 15 NETSTAT

Disable the NETSTAT service. This allows remote users connected to the NET-STAT port to view networking status, including services running and connected clients of the network.

TCP/UDP Port 23—Telnet

This prevents default access to the Telnet default account.

Use one-time passwords and encryption. An accessible default Account through Telnet allows attackers easy access to the remote system. Telnet sessions are vul-nerable because the username, password, and the entire session are transmitted as clear text on the network. Another concern is that an attacker can hijack a session that is in progress.

TCP/UDP Port 25—SMTP

The following points must be kept in mind for Port 25:

- ◆ Encrypt basic authentication to prevent passwords from being transmit-ted in clear text. By default an SMTP session is sent as clear text on the network.

- ◆ Implement encryption to secure SMTP communication. By default an SMTP session is sent as clear text on the network.

- ◆ Configure all SMTP servers to force all mail messages to either originate or terminate locally. An attacker can use e-mail to obscure their identity while sending a large amount of junk e-mail.

- ◆ Limit message size, session size, number of messages, and recipients per message when capabilities are available. This limitation can greatly reduce denial-of-service attacks.

◆ Check a user's `.forward` files to determine if any of them allow messages to be piped to other programs or scripts. The ability to pipe the delivered message to programs or scripts can produce dangerous results. An attacker sending the message could take advantage of the vulnerability because these programs or scripts may contain security holes.

◆ Disable the extended HELO (EHELO). SMTP servers that support EHELO will release useful information for potential attackers.

◆ Disable mail aliases for decode and uudecode. Older mail transfer agents commonly include a configuration to include an alias for the decode user. All mail sent to this user is sent to the uudecode program, which automatically converts and stores files. The configuration could allow an attacker to remotely overwrite files on the system.

◆ Disable `EXPN` and `VRFY` commands. `EXPN` and `VRSY` allow an attacker to determine if an account exists on a system, provide significant assistance to a brute force attack on user accounts.

◆ Configure SMTP server to validate host names. The lack of authorization could allow users to more easily forge mail from your server.

TCP Port 43 – WHOIS

Disable the WHOIS service, which is typically regarded as an unnecessary service.

TCP/UDP Port 53—DNS

Update to the latest version of DNS and apply the latest DNS security fixes. Older versions of DNS are vulnerable to denial-of-service and spoofing attacks.

◆ Do not allow BIND servers to remotely query for its version. BIND servers permit remote users to query their version numbers. The information could allow an attacker to remotely query computers for vulnerable versions of BIND.

◆ Disable DNS server inverse queries. The Inverse Query (Iquery) feature supported on some DNS servers should be disabled. An attacker can use the feature to obtain a zone transfer.

◆ Limit zone transfers to a list of hosts. Zone transfers identify every machine registered with the DNS server and can be used by attackers to better understand the layout of your network.

◆ Always negotiate a secure, dynamic update for Dynamic DNS (DDNS). DDNS dynamic update without authentication permits an attacker to perform denial-of-service or spoofing attacks.

UDP Port 69—TFTP

To disable the TFTP service is potentially dangerous and typically unnecessary. TFTP has no authentication process. An attacker can gain access to the password file.

◆ Set restrictions to only allow files to be transferred to or from certain restricted directories. Due to poor security of the TFTP protocol, this restriction can minimize the impact of the risk.

◆ Authenticate file transfers where available. The TFTP security key authentication provides basic security controls that can enhance the security of this protocol.

TCP Port 79—Finger

Disable the Finger service. The finger service or daemon is available to anybody on the network. Finger makes it easy for intruders to get a list of users on the system, which increases the chance of a system break-in.

TCP Port 80—HTTP

Devices that use HTTP port for device administration must implement the basic security setting; the password must be set for Administrator. Without basic security settings, anyone connected to the port can alter the system settings without proper authentication.

TCP Ports 109 and 110—POP

The following points must be kept in mind for ports 109 and 110:

◆ The POP3 default Account must not be accessible.

◆ Implement the APOP option for user authentication.

◆ Use a version of POP that can work with Kerberos. An accessible default Account through POP3 allows attackers easy access to remote systems.

- Use the APOP option. The client program does not send the USER and PASS commands; instead, it sends a APOP command that contains the use name and a 128-bit MD5 hash code of the time stamp and a secret pass phrase that is known to both the user and the POP server.

- Kerberos is a secure authentication protocol.

TCP/UDP Port 111—RPC's Portmapper

Use Portmapper to improve logging and provide access to control lists. The standard portmapper assumes that security will be handled by the servers, and allows any network client to communicate with any RPC server.

- Do not use NFS for restricted data. The security of NFS relies heavily upon who is allowed to mount the volumes that a server exports, and whether or not they are exported read-only. Improperly configured access permission on exported volumes can permit an attacker to gain access to critical files.

- Do not use NFS on a public Web server. If the mountd daemon is running over a non-reserved port, this daemon is vulnerable to port hijacking.

- The mountd daemon must operate on a reserved port. Exported file systems to other domains pose a serious concern and should be evaluated carefully.

- Do not export file systems to a domain other than their own. Applying strong control over NFS can reduce the security risk associated with the protocol.

- Never export a root file system.

- Create a separate partition for file systems that you intend to export.

- Do not self-reference on an NFS server in its own exports file.

- Do not allow the exports file to contain a localhost entry.

- Export file systems only to a list of hosts that require them.

- Export only to a fully qualified host name.

- Ensure the exports list does not exceed 256 characters.

- Export file systems as read-only whenever possible.

- ◆ Disable the RPC.Ruserd service. Ruserd can expose the system to unwanted intelligence-gathering activity, producing similar results to finger output.

- ◆ Disable the RPC.Rstatd service. Rstatd provides information on system statistics including statistics on the CPU, virtual memory, network uptime, and hard drive. Although exposure may not pose a great risk, there is no good reason to provide it for public access.

- ◆ Disable the RPC.Walld service. This process allows remote users to send messages to all users on the network. It may allow an attacker to jam up terminals with illegible text.

TCP Port 143—IMAP

Disable anonymous access to IMAP. If anonymous access to IMAP is enabled, an attacker could connect and possibly access confidential data. An attacker also can perform a denial-of-services attack by creating folders and large files on the victim's system.

TCP Port 119—NNTP

Disable the NNTP service. If the service is required, a detailed security plan must be developed for review of associated risks. NNTP's security can be bypassed through IP spoofing or through DNS attacks. A compromised NNTP service may not represent a serious security risk—however an unauthorized individual may be able to read or post Usenet articles without permission—and may reveal confidential information.

TCP Port 123—NTP

Use NTP only in a very controlled environment. NTP was not designed to resist attacks. Some versions of NTP can be fooled into making significant and erroneous changes to the system's clock. If an attacker can change your system clock, a replay attack can be attempted, system log files will no longer accurately give the correct time, and batch jobs may not execute.

UDP Ports 161 and 162—SNMP

The Simple Network Management Protocol (SNMP) lacks authentication capabilities (especially older versions). SNMP vulnerabilities include masquerading, information modification, message sequence and timing modifications, and information disclosure.

- Use SNMP version 2. It supports secure capabilities. SNMPv2 specifications support Digest Authentication protocol for authentication and data integrity using a 128-bit MD5 message digest. Symmetric Privacy protocol for privacy is the protocol using DES to protect the content.

- Rename the default community string to a value that is hard to guess. Community strings provide authentication for SNMPv1. This makes it a little difficult for attackers to access information or maliciously alter a device.

- Implement access lists for SNMP. Access lists can be used to prevent SNMP messages from traversing certain router interfaces.

- Configure an agent that supports RMON queries to restrict unauthorized access. An active RMON probe can remotely monitor applications, network traffic, and users.

TCP Port 389—LDAP

The following points must be kept in mind for Port 389:

- Disable the **cn=config** entry or allow only authorized users to view the entry. An attacker can obtain information about the LDAP server, accessing the LDAP configuration. The information can show the back-end system used. An attacker can use the information for malicious activity.

- Disable the **cn=monitor** entry or allow only authorized users to view the entry. An attacker can obtain information about the LDAP server, accessing the monitor. The information revealed includes LDAP server version, the number of backbends, and who is logged on. An attacker can use the information for malicious activity.

- Disable the **cn=schema** entry or allow only authorized users to view the entry. An attacker can obtain information about the LDAP server, accessing the LDAP schema. The schema information reveals all attributes of an object hidden or non-readable attributes. An attacker can use the information for malicious activity.

◆ Do not allow the NULL base in an LDAP search and disable the NULL bind entry, or control the entity with Access Control Lists. An attacker can run a search that returns information on naming context and supported controls.

TCP Port 512—REXEC

Disable the REXEC services. Use SSH. It uses the `.rhosts` file for authentication; passwords and subsequent sessions are transmitted in clear text, and no logging is performed.

TCP Port 513—RWHO

Disable the RWHO services. This is generally an unnecessary service.

TCP Port 514—RLOGIN, RSH

Disable the RLOGIN/RSH services. It uses the **.rhosts** file for authentication; passwords and subsequent sessions are transmitted in clear text, and no logging is performed. The vulnerability could allow remote attackers to log in as root without being prompted for a password. Use SSH as a replacement for these services.

UDP Port 520—Route

Disable the Route services. This application exchanges routing table updates to other systems on the network. It allows an attacker to eavesdrop on all communications of the compromised host.

TCP Port 540—UUCP

Disable the UUCP services. UUCP over TCP presents a security risk because UUCP passwords and contents are sent unencrypted.

Kerberos

Implement Kerberos version V and do not use Kerberos version IV. The Kerberos IV KDC does not clear some internal buffers. A remote hacker can send a malformed packet to the KDC that will cause it to leak the username of the last request. Also, the KDC enables anyone to request a ticket-granting ticket, certain parts of the ticket are known, and the ticket is encrypted with the user's password. The attackers can mount a brute force attack on the KDC.

TCP Ports 6000-6063 X Windows

X Window System has no concept of privilege. If you can access a display, you can create windows, read the screen's contents, kill any window or any resource, record most of the X windows events including key strokes, and send fake events.

- ◆ Configure the Autolock X Windows Screen. To prevent the risk of abuse of an unattended system use the screen lock capability. The available protection for X protocol include

  - **Host-based access control (xhost) only.** This offers minimal security features and is sufficient for a workstation or a single user environment. In this environment every one trusts everyone. The security can be bypassed by spoofing the IP address. Use the **xhost** command to control permission to write to the display. Limit the users or systems that can write to the X Windows display to prevent any network sniffing and keystroke insertion attacks.

  - **Xauth for authentication using XDM-AUTHORIZATION or SUN-DES. Authorization Protocol (xauth).** It allows access control per user instead of per host. It creates a virtual X server on the machine where it runs, and it prompts the user for each connection. The following system options exist:

    - MIT-MAGIC-COOKIE: Uses shared plain text cookies and exchanges and transmits cookies in clear text. Can be eavesdropped by a potential attacker.

    - XDM-AUTHORIZATION: Uses secure DES-based private keys.

    - SUN-DES: Is based on Sun's secure RPC system.

- ◆ Implement MIT-KERBEROS-5 as an X authentication mechanism. The X protocol does not have any notion of Windows operating permissions nor does it limit what a client may do. If a program can connect to a display, it has full run of the screen. A Kerberos authorization system can make use of the hook in the libraries and the server to provide additional security models.

◆ For XDM-AUTHORIZATION and SUN-DES, a user may have to transfer the keys because it is hard to use with different user IDs. The keys must be secured, requiring strong ACL protections. Stolen keys may be used from anywhere.

◆ For securing XDM communications implement SSH to protect X authentication for X terminals. The XDM protocol is responsible for the assignment of the X server sessions to logged-on users. The security features of XDM are very similar to the X protocol itself. The transmission of UNIX-user credentials that takes place when a new user logs on at the X server is in clear text. This is a problem with X terminals where the X server and XDM reside on different workstations.

◆ Approve external IRC service on a case-by-case basis. IRC permits real-time communication between many different people on different systems. Messages can be automatically forwarded from one system to another. Because these systems permit unrestricted communication between users on the Internet, they create an excellent opportunity for social engineering. Most IRCs require users to create an account with a username and a password that they use for their internal accounts. Some of the IRC clients may contain intentional security holes and back doors. It is difficult to determine if a client program has backdoors built-in.

◆ Do not permit ICQ services. ICQ is a program that lets you know when contacts are also online on the Internet, so you may then page and chat with them. Due to the lack of security features of the protocol, some ICQ applications allow users to add others to their contact list without the permission of others, crack passwords, and other malicious effects. ICQ has been the source of holes that allowed an attacker to transfer data from the ICQ user's system. ICQ has been the target of denial-of-service and is vulnerable to message spoofing.

Remote Desktop Protocol (RDP)

RDP is based on the ITU T.120 protocol. It is platform independent as well as independent of the underlying network and transport layer. The screen content is basically transferred as bitmaps from server to client. Mouse and keyboard events are transferred from client to servers.

Use 128-bit high encryption to encrypt all packets in both directions. Low encryption only protects packets from client to server; medium encryption encrypts all packets, but only with 40-bit RC4.

Other Remote Control Software

Ensure implementations of other remote control software are secure. Review on a case-by-case basis. Each remote control software introduces its own set of vulnerabilities. Review protocols used and associated with each software carefully.

Game servers

Prohibit game servers on the network. Game servers such as Quake and Doom are typically for multi-users on multiple platforms, including Linux, Solaris, and Windows. Game servers have been widely known to contain numerous security holes and consume valuable network bandwidth.

Firewalls

Install firewall systems to isolate networks that contain sensitive systems and information. Firewalls are still the foremost protection against external attacks. A well-maintained and well-configured firewall will stop most casual or inexperienced hackers.

Network Intrusion Detection System (IDS)

Install network IDS to monitor sensitive network or host-based IDS to protect sensitive hosts. IDS may be used to automatically and intelligently detect intrusion attempts in real-time. An IDS with reporting and analysis tools enables administrators to detect spot ping sweeps and port scans before a hacker can break into any system.

Scan and Test for Network Vulnerabilities

Run regular security scanning and testing on key network segments and systems. Small changes in networks, such as new services, new operating systems, or new service packs, can open vulnerabilities that were once secure. Regular scanning and testing can locate and identify vulnerabilities before hackers can exploit them.

IPSec

Implement IPSec to protect vulnerable network services. IPSec can protect against both external and internal attacks. IPSec works below the transport layer, so its security services are transparently inherited by applications. It supports security services such as integrity, authentication, and confidentiality without the requirement to upgrade applications or train users.

Kerberos

Use Kerberos for authentication: you need to go above and beyond simple operating system–based usernames and passwords for authentication.

Biometrics

Consider using fingerprint-based biometrics solutions for authentication. This is one of the more secure forms of authentication. It is increasingly a cost-effective way to strongly authenticate a user.

Public Key Infrastructure (PKI)

Implement a PKI to bring trust to your IT infrastructure. PKI enables you to integrate your suppliers, customers, and employees to share, exchange and access data securely. PKI applications include digital signature and digital certificates.

Summary

The core objective of HIPAA is to protect individuals from the unapproved and unwarranted release of information related to their personal health. The focus of the HIPAA Privacy Rule is to address the intentional release of health-related information. Its purpose is to restrict the disclosure and use of the information to entities approved in advance by the individual. "Intentional release" is generally defined as outside the bounds of reasonable and diligent attempts to prevent such release. The security standards are intended to support the protection of electronic information protected by the Privacy Rule.

This chapter reviewed the objective of HIPAA's Security Rule to address the unintentional release of health-related information of the individual. The Security Rule addresses the steps that the covered entity must take to prevent the unintentional:

♦ Disclosure
♦ Destruction
♦ Corruption

The Security Rule also addresses disclosure, destruction, and corruption of PHI maintained or transmitted by

- Health plans
- Health care providers
- Health care clearinghouses

The identification of solutions to meet the requirements of the Security Rule must take into account

- HIPAA Security Rule requirements (implementation specifications that must be supported by the health care enterprise)
- Threats to the entity
- Requirements related to the Privacy Rule such as flow of PHI and business associates

The final Security Rule establishes the minimum level of security that covered entities must meet.

Footnotes

1. The ISO/IEC is now continuing the development and maintenance of the Common Criteria under the ISO/IEC 15408 international standard.
2. "Common Criteria for Information Technology Security Evaluation." Part 1, Ver. 2.1. Aug. 1999. page 13. <http://www.commoncriteria.org/docs/PDF/CCPART1V21.PDF>

Lesson 5

**Getting Started
with HIPAA
Transactions**

After reading this chapter, you will be able to

◆ Understand what a HIPAA transaction is and how to plan and convert the current system to HIPAA compliance

◆ Understand the framework for Microsoft's BizTalk Accelerator for HIPAA product

◆ Analyze transaction set identifiers, data segments, and schemas

◆ Examine document specification and mapping

◆ Examine the document processing path and tracking

◆ Understand the framework for Sybase's HIPAA Studio product

This chapter examines the implementation of the electronic processing of HIPAA documents and data. It introduces HIPAA transactions and demonstrates how to create a plan to become compliant as per the new requirements, and also shows the HIPAA Academy E-Accelerator methodology, a series of steps to be performed for achieving compliance. Finally, it leads you through a review of the transactions framework of two products, Microsoft's BizTalk Accelerator and Sybase's HIPAA Studio. The chapter does not specifically endorse these products, but uses them as references to help make key points about the HIPAA transactions framework.

HIPAA Transactions

A transaction is the exchange of health information between various health care providers, for example, doctors, health insurance companies, laboratories, clearing-houses, and so on. One of the primary objectives of HIPAA, the Health Insurance Portability and Accountability Act of 1996, was to address the deficiencies in business processes within the health care industry.

Currently, the health care industry has no fixed standards for collecting, storing, exchanging, or filing health care related information. Different organizations are using their own various (sometimes proprietary) formats for conducting day-to-day business. No standard or control exists that can ensure information exchange between different providers and payers is compliant with each other. Security or protection of the data exchange also follows no norms, risking exposure of the personal protected health information (PHI).

Figure 5.1 depicts two problem scenarios:

- The sender is sending information in a different sequence of data elements (service type code, diagnosis code, entity ID) than the receiver expects it to be in. This becomes a problem when the application software at the receiving end reads the first few characters as entity ID instead of service type code.

- The sender and receiver use different sets of diagnosis codes. For example, the sender might use SP001 for throat infection where as the receiver might refer TI001 for throat infection. This leads to the overheads of converting first the sender's code to the receiver's code sets and then after the adjudication process, converting it back to the code set understandable to the sender.

As the transactions take the shape of electronic formats over the paper-based exchange of information, it becomes inevitable to adopt standards that all the providers, payers, clearinghouses, billing services, and other entities systematically follow.

This is where HIPAA Title II, Administrative Simplification subsection F comes into play. It intends to reduce the costs and administrative burdens of health care by making possible the standardized, electronic transmission of many administrative and financial transactions that are currently performed on paper, and to provide an appropriate level of protection for the medical data on which the transactions are based.

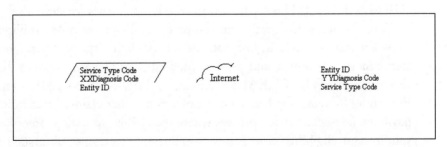

FIGURE 5.1 *An example of code information exchanged between the sender and receiver.*

EDI Issues

Today the health care industry uses many different forms of electronic data interchange (EDI), which does not necessarily mean X12N EDI; it refers to flat files that are based on a recommended data set and modified for individual partners' needs. More than 400 different electronic formats are in use spanning across various transactions.

Even though the majority of hospital claims are filed electronically, very few claims use the X12N 837(s), few more use the 835 for claims payment and remittance advice; but this too is rare, and most of the time eligibility is determined by a phone call.

In today's environment, it is not unusual to have many legacy environments, whether you are a provider, a payer, or another entity. Existing systems may have to deal with many of the 400 EDI formats that are in use, and the entities may require multiple systems just to handle this environment, which is expensive.

As a result of HIPAA, all major U.S. health care entities soon must be able to send electronic administrative information by using EDI in a single standard. Providers, payers, and other entities—such as clearinghouses that use administrative transactions (for example, claims and eligibility)—must be able to exchange information in a uniform standard format using approved implementation guides by October 16, 2002. Secondary claims will be easier to make because coordination of benefits information can also be sent in a standardized manner. This standard EDI transaction and implementation also delivers additional required fields and data elements.

Healthy Health Insurance (HEALS)

This section discusses a fictitious company called Healthy Health Insurance or "HEALS" in short. This company provides health insurance through its own network of providers. Currently, the company handles around one million transactions per month, such as, but not limited to, eligibility inquiry/response, claim status inquiry/response, and prior authorizations. The Information Technology Department (ITD) of HEALS maintains a software called TAPS (Transactions Processing System) that batches and uploads provider claims for adjudication and payment. (*Adjudication* is a process where the claims are settled after checking the validity and eligibility criteria and application of various rules, such as out of pocket maximum, deductions, and so on.)

Problem Statement

Being a covered entity as per the HIPAA law, HEALS has to comply with various requirements of meeting HIPAA standards, which are very different from the approach used by TAPS today. For example:

- HIPAA formats data in looping structures with variable length fields by the use of identifiers, while TAPS formats data by assigning it to specific fixed-length fields in a flat file.

- A current TAPS claim contains around 3,000 data elements, while a HIPAA compliant claim must contain around 28,000 data elements.

These gaps between the current system and the new HIPAA requirements make it too expensive in terms of time, dollars, and resources to remediate the current TAPS to accept and process HIPAA-compliant transactions directly from users. Therefore, a solution is needed to modify the TAPS as minimally as possible by implementing a front-end/middleware solution between providers and the TAPS back end.

HEALS has hired your company to provide solutions as per the HIPAA requirements to provide the following functionality:

- Provide a Web application front end for providers to submit HIPAA-compliant electronic transactions.

- Receive in-bound HIPAA transactions and translate data from the in-bound transaction into a native format that the TAPS can recognize and process.

- Pass and receive native format transactions to/from TAPS.

- Build a HIPAA-compliant out-bound transaction by translating the TAPS transaction and rejoining it to previously stored data.

- Forward HIPAA-compliant outgoing transactions to providers.

To achieve these objectives of HIPAA compliance, let's see some of the available tools.

E-Accelerator Methodology

The HIPAA Academy E-Accelerator methodology is a four phase methodology developed and owned by HIPAA Academy. HIPAA Academy developed this methodology through their long involvement in HIPAA training and specifically consultative engagements around the HIPAA transaction standards.

This methodology defines four steps towards achieving HIPAA compliance; these four steps are

- ◆ Planning
- ◆ Analyzing
- ◆ Remediating
- ◆ Auditing

Step 1: Planning

The first step to implement the mandated transaction standards of the Health Insurance Portability and Accountability Act of 1996 (HIPAA) is to plan the approach to the system compliance as per the existing scenario and HIPAA requirements.

 NOTE

Planning is the most important phase of any project.

In this phase various activities take place:

- ◆ **Scope defining.** When defining the scope of the project, you should create a list of all the transactions that are currently in use. All the systems, the software, the transaction component, or any user systems that need to be checked or changed are listed. Output from this activity is a scope document that contains areas that are likely to be affected by the HIPAA laws and that needs to be checked and modified (if required) for HIPAA compliance. Identification of the business processes that correspond to HIPAA transactions is also done.

- ◆ **Risk Assessment.** During risk assessment, you should identify compliance hindrances, for example, for a set of current code in a transaction that does not have data dictionary available; this can be a potential risk that could delay the project. Output from this phase is the risk report that outlines the problematic issues that could lead to pushing of the timelines.

- ◆ **Timelines.** After the scope document and risk assessment documents are prepared, you should assess them in order to form the project schedule. This will generate an approximate date when the compliance can be achieved.

Step 2: Analyze

Various activities performed under this step are

- **Gap Analysis.** During a gap analysis, the X12N Implementation Guides adopted under HIPAA are compared with the legacy environment. The output of this activity is a match/no-match report having HIPAA data analysis gaps.

  This gap analysis report contains a comparison between HIPAA transactions and legacy records that lists

  - Legacy system fields those are no longer required.
  - Data elements that are new in the HIPAA transaction and do not have any equivalent value coming from the legacy system record.
  - Identification of the identifiers and codes, which are new in the HIPAA transaction.

- **Data Mapping.** The goal of data mapping is to identify

  - Where each legacy field will fit in the HIPAA transaction.
  - Any HIPAA required data elements that are not stored in the legacy system and, thus, need to have a specified default value or logic of extracting the value from the legacy record. These data elements must be developed, derived, or defaulted for the resultant transaction to be HIPAA compliant.
  - Any legacy system data elements that have no place to be sent in the HIPAA transaction are identified, then assessed to see if they are important from the adjudication process or required from the current process point of view.
  - Any legacy system data elements that need to be longer to support HIPAA byte lengths. HIPAA mandates that no data be truncated. So if data is received via a HIPAA transaction that is longer than the current field where it should be stored and that data would ever need to be sent back out in another HIPAA transaction, then the longer length must be accommodated.
  - All local codes that must be converted to standard codes.

To achieve the data mapping goals, the following tasks are to be completed:

- Identify the legacy system data records (tables) that contain the relevant data elements for each transaction.
- Load the legacy record layout (field names, data types, byte lengths) into the gap analysis software, like Microsoft's BizTalk accelerator for HIPAA
- Match all the legacy record fields to a place to be sent in the HIPAA transaction, based upon HIPAA implementation guides and discussions with legacy system data content experts.
- Identify any HIPAA required data elements that are not stored in the legacy system.
- Document any known special processing logic needed to convert data during implementation.
- Generate a report out of the gap analysis tool to document all of the above.

Step 3: Remediation

During this phase, the gaps that were identified in the gap analysis data mapping report are closed. Various tools and technologies can be used for the creation and usage of the data mapping. This process is an ongoing process, incorporating changes when they happen.

 NOTE

Unlike the Y2K date problem that required a one-time solution, HIPAA solutions will be like a moving target and require constant analysis as changes occur.

◆ Depending upon the existing system, the solution might vary from creating a middle-tier component that does the data conversion from one format to another, to adding the missing information with the predetermined data elements, or feeding of the standard code from the HIPAA-compliant code set pool equivalent to the legacy system code.

- ◆ Another solution deployment requires creation of a front end that accepts data as per the transaction's Implementation Guide specification. This eliminates the process of conversion all together since the new solution does the needed validation checks before accepting the values during runtime.

Step 4: Auditing

This phase is a follow-up phase to ensure the continued compliance with the HIPAA law.

- ◆ As mentioned previously, HIPAA compliance is like a moving target and is an ongoing process that will take several years to address. The industry will continue to evolve in this area, and attention to new issues will become a significant part of every health care organization's operations. Auditing of the solution to verify continued compliance becomes an important activity that needs to be done periodically.

- ◆ The checklists created in step1 can be used to perform audits, and if needed, as amendments or new requirements (for example, the standard for claims attachment) come in effect, steps 1 to 3 can be performed again for incorporating the changes.

Microsoft's BizTalk Accelerator Components

Microsoft BizTalk Accelerator is an automation solution to quickly deploy and easily manage, track, and maintain health transactions. BizTalk Accelerator permits organizations to integrate HIPAA functionality into their existing information systems and business processes.

 NOTE

Microsoft BizTalk Accelerator was created specifically to provide health care organizations with a solution that can be deployed quickly and easily to support schemas that specifically address HIPAA transaction set requirements.

Key Components

The key components of the BizTalk Accelerator for HIPAA are

◆ Schemas for all the 12 X12N HIPAA transaction sets in the Implementation Guides provided by the Washington Publishing Company (WPC)

◆ A runtime parser

◆ Documentation, including content licensed from WPC and based on the X12N HIPAA Implementation Guides

Advantages

(Information source: Microsoft Corporation)

◆ **Support and Accurate schemas.** HIPAA regulations have been captured into a set of 12 schemas, or forms sets, produced by the Washington Publishing Company (WPC). The BizTalk Accelerator integrates these schemas with the transaction routing and tracking capabilities of the Microsoft BizTalk Server.

◆ **Tracking.** Microsoft BizTalk Server includes document tracking and analysis functionality that enable organizations to observe and analyze their data flow and business processes in real time. This provides accurate records of both total transactions and specific fields, enabling health care companies to respond quickly and easily to government audits, in addition to providing better business management.

◆ **Sustainability.** HIPAA transaction requirements will change and evolve. Through its partnership with WPC, Microsoft will make new schemas available immediately after the new implementation guides are published, giving health care organizations extra time to meet new implementation deadlines.

◆ **Integration.** Rapidly build and deploy secure, reliable business processes within and between organizations. The tools and services in Microsoft BizTalk Server help businesses quickly integrate applications regardless of operating system, programming model, or programming language, while minimizing the amount of custom coding and maintenance needed.

◆ **Giving businesses control over their claims process.** BizTalk Accelerator for HIPAA enables organizations to define and monitor meaningful metrics that allow them insight into the operational health of their businesses. Plus, powerful business process automation offers more control over the claims process. And the accelerator can be set to monitor a Health care Claims Request (837) and tie it to any series of Health care Claims Payment/Advice transactions (835).

In most cases, this chapter will describe in detail all the necessary steps for the installation of the HIPAA Academy software solution. The following system requirements are necessary before implementing solutions using BizTalk Accelerator.

A computer must have the following hardware:

◆ At least P-II 400 megahertz (MHz) of CPU, and preferably 933 megahertz (MHz) Intel Pentium III Xeon or more

◆ A minimum of 256 MB of memory; preferably 1 gigabyte (GB) of RAM

◆ At least an 18 GB hard drive—the more GB the better

◆ CD-ROM drive

◆ Network adapter card of 100 megabits

◆ VGA or Super VGA monitor

◆ Microsoft mouse or compatible pointing device

A computer must also have the following software:

◆ **Software.** Windows 2000 Application Center or Data center version with SP2 or Windows XP

◆ **Web Server.** IIS 5.0 with the following hot fixes:
  • Windows 2000 Pre-SP3 Hot fix for IIS (Q294831)
  • Windows 2000 15 Aug 2001 Cumulative Patch for IIS (Q301625, MS01-044)

◆ **Database Server.** SQL Server 7.0 with SP 3 or SQL Server 200.0 (SQL Server 2000 is recommended due to its native support for XML.)

◆ **Biz Talk Server.** Biz Talk Server 2000 with the Accelerator for HIPAA component.

- ◆ **COM+Services.** These are an integral part of Windows 2000; make sure to check the Message Queuing Services check box in the Windows Components Wizard.

- ◆ **XML Parser.** MSXML 3.0 with SP2, which installs automatically when installing BizTalk Server

 NOTE

Problems are known to occur with the installation of Microsoft BizTalk Accelerator on a Windows XP platform, many of which have documented solutions. However, to ensure optimal functionality, Windows 2000 is the recommended platform because it is the operating system on which Microsoft BizTalk Server 2000 was developed.

Service Pack 2 (PK2) is an update to the Windows 2000 operating system and must be installed in order for the computer system to support BizTalk Accelerator functionality. SP2 can be downloaded from the Microsoft Windows 2000 Web site (http://www.microsoft.com/windows2000).

You should install Microsoft Windows 2000 Professional version only if your computer is a terminal in a network.

For servers or standalone systems Windows 2000 advanced Server version is recommended. Windows 2000 or Windows XP must be installed with the NTFS (New Technology File System) file partition. It offers features such as local file security, data compression, and encryption for transaction-oriented systems.

Windows 2000 or XP must also be installed with message queuing capability and Internet Information Service (IIS) software. Both of these can be installed either during initial installation of Windows or as modifications to the current installation.

Message queuing software provides BizTalk Accelerator the capability to transmit and monitor large volumes of e-messages while maintaining the integrity of the contents of each. IIS software formats messages in compliance with Internet protocols (for example, http, and ftp).

Microsoft's SQL Server

Microsoft SQL Server 7.0 and Microsoft SQL Server 2000 is the database management program adopted for the HIPAA Academy software solution. SQL Server is a complete database system that rapidly handles data transactions and delivery. When the BizTalk Accelerator processes transactions, they are produced as forms by SQL Server, and the data supporting or arising from such transactions are stored, maintained, and retrieved by SQL Server.

Transactions and database queries are passed to and received from SQL using an advanced Structured Query Language, a popular standard database instruction set.

- ◆ SQL Server must be installed on your computer before BizTalk Server is installed.
- ◆ SQL Server 7.0 must be installed with SP3, while SQL Server 2000 must be installed with SP1.
- ◆ If you are installing BizTalk Server and SQL Server on separate computers, the BizTalk Server service account must have system administrator permissions on both computers.

Microsoft's BizTalk Server 2002

BizTalk Server 2002 is the network server software the HIPAA Academy has selected for its server engine. This powerful network manager integrates internal applications with Internet transportability while ensuring secure data transfer among geographically separated agencies. This provides agencies network security in the generation, routing, and tracking of transactions. To health care agencies it provides a means of implementation of HIPAA regulations and ensures quick, easy compliance with federal mandates.

The BizTalk Server 2002 installation process creates the following databases on the SQL Server:

Name of the Database	Purpose of the Database
InterchangeBTM	The BizTalk Messaging Management database
InterchangeSQ	The Shared Queue database
InterchangeDTA	The Tracking database
XLANG	The Orchestration Persistence database

BizTalk Server 2002 is available in two editions:

◆ The Standard Edition integrates large numbers of internal applications with up to 10 external trading partners at a time.

◆ The Enterprise Edition supports unlimited internal applications with unlimited trading partners over the Internet.

Both of these versions are fully operable with the BizTalk Accelerator for HIPAA.

Table 5.1 shows the features and functions of the major software modules embedded in BizTalk Server. The features are organized based on categories such as Administration or Document Tracking.

Table 5.1   Major Software Modules Embedded in BizTalk

Feature	Function
Administration	Used for managing queues, transports, and services
BizTalk Servers Administration	Create and manage servers and server groups
BizTalk Orchestration Services	Configure global server group properties, such as the location for the Shared Queue database and the Tracking database
	Configure server settings
	Configure and manage receive functions
	View and manage document queues
	Programmatically access the XLANG Scheduler System Manager, group managers, XLANG schedule instances, and XLANG ports
Document Tracking	Track message and schedule activity
BizTalk Document Tracking	Track the progress of documents processed by Microsoft BizTalk Server 2002
	Search for, display, view, and save complete copies of any interchange or document processed by BizTalk Server 2002
	Create queries to extract essential information from the Tracking database in an easy-to-view format
	Extract, store, and analyze important user-defined data from within documents

Table 5.1   Major Software Modules Embedded in BizTalk *(continued)*

Feature	Function
Orchestration Design	A visual environment for business process modeling
BizTalk Orchestration Designer	Create drawings that describe business processes, and programmatically implement these drawings within an integrated design environment
	Compile XLANG schedule drawings into XLANG schedules
	Define the flow of data between messages within business processes
Messaging	Used to specify and manage business relationships
BizTalk Messaging Manager	Manage the exchange of data locally or remotely using BizTalk Messaging Manager
	Manage the exchange of data programmatically using the BizTalk Messaging Configuration object model
	Create and manage channels, messaging ports, document definitions, envelopes, organizations, and distribution lists
XML Tools	An Extensible Style sheet Language Transformation (XSLT) component
BizTalk Editor	Define business document schemas
BizTalk Mapper	Create and manage document specifications
	Create records and fields, and set their properties
	Map records and fields from a source specification to records and fields of a destination specification
	Use functions to implement powerful data-transformation functionality
Deployment	Rapidly enable your trading partners by using SEED packages to make your configurations available through the Internet
BizTalk SEED Wizard	
HIPAA Specific	A component that translates HIPAA (X12) files into Extensible Markup Language (XML) files
BizTalk Accelerator for HIPAA parser	BizTalk Server-specific XML schemas that are created by using BizTalk Editor
HIPAA-specific document specifications	

BizTalk Accelerator for HIPAA

An accelerator is a companion program that streamlines functions and operations in a main driver program. The BizTalk Accelerator for HIPAA was designed to harness the capabilities of BizTalk Server 2002 while abbreviating the end users' interface with the computer system or network.

 NOTE

Washington Publishing Company (WPC) is the exclusive publisher of HIPAA Implementation Guides. These are 12 manuals that describe transactions common to health service providers.

These transactions comprise basic templates, called *schemas*, which form the bulk of documents and procedures necessary for HIPAA compliance. The schemas, in turn, have been translated into BizTalk Server 2002 methods, which are supervised by the BizTalk Accelerator for HIPAA.

The end result of integrating BizTalk Accelerator for HIPAA with the other software elements in the HIPAA Academy software solution is the creation of a complete operating environment with a schema data set, which can be easily implemented, engaged, and updated. The WPC updates the HIPAA Implementation Guides standards and mandates evolve, and Microsoft continually updates and tests new and existing schemas.

Microsoft Visio 2002

The BizTalk Server 2002 Orchestration Designer is an internal function that interfaces with drawing and diagramming software to produce flow diagrams of business processes and transactions. BizTalk Accelerator for HIPAA incorporates Microsoft Visio 2002 for this purpose. Microsoft Visio is a standalone product that tightly integrates with other Microsoft products.

Microsoft's Application Center 2000

The Application Center facilitates the deployment capabilities of BizTalk Accelerator for HIPAA. The Microsoft Application Center 2000 is a deployment tool that manages Internet and other communication functions for the BizTalk Accelerator for HIPAA. Its basic operational domain is an entity called a *cluster*, a collection of computers and servers in a single operating unit. Stated simply, the Application Center manages and synchronizes the activity of multiple programs and transactions running simultaneously.

Like the SQL Server, the Application Center must be installed before installing the BizTalk Server.

HIPAA Data and Schemas

Microsoft BizTalk Accelerator for HIPAA translated the WPC's Implementation Guides into twelve schemas, or templates, which correspond to the 12 basic transactions addressed by the Implementation Guides. WPC will continue to produce the Implementation Guides, and Microsoft will in turn produce new schemas for the BizTalk Accelerator.

Though each schema addresses a unique transaction in the health care repertoire, there are several characteristics they all have in common, including

- Formatting rules for all transaction sets
- The communication protocols
- The formatting of headers and trailers

Headers and *trailers* are delimiters marking the beginning and ending of transactions. A *transaction set* refers to the collection of all of the data segments in a schema. Examples of data segments are header control segments, patient identification and health data segments, health care procedures segments, and trailer control segments.

Transaction Set Identifiers

The BizTalk Accelerator for HIPAA refers to each schema by a unique identifier. This identifier is used to maintain the integrity of HIPAA data as it is transported over communication lines from one computer or network to another. Schema identifiers have the following format: TSXXXYY.

TS stands for Transaction Set, XXX is the X12N Transaction Set ID, and YY is a suffix identifying unique features of ambiguous Transaction Set IDs.

Examples:

- ◆ **TS834A1** Health Care and Enrollment Transaction Set
- ◆ **TS837Q1** Health Care Claim—Professional
- ◆ **TS837Q2** Health Care Claim—Dental

Apart from having these unique identifiers, Table 5.2 shows all 11 HIPAA transaction sets along with the template filenames supported by the BizTalk Accelerator.

Table 5.2 HIPAA Transaction Sets

Transaction Number	Description	Filename
270	Health Care Eligibility/Benefit Inquiry	270_V1_wpc.xml
271	Health Care Eligibility/Benefit Information Response	271_V1_wpc.xml
276	Health Care Claim Status Request	276_V1_wpc.xml
277	Health Care Claim Status Response	277_V1_wpc.xml
278	Health Care Services Review— Request for Review and Response	278Request_V1_wpc.xml
		278Response_V1_wpc.xml
820	Payroll Deducted and Other Group Premium Payment for Insurance Products	820_V1_wpc.xml
834	Benefit Enrollment and Maintenance	834_V1_wpc_multiple.xml
		834_V1_wpc_single.xml
835	Health Care Claim Payment/Advice	835_V1_wpc_multiple.xml
		835_V1_wpc_single.xml
837	Health Care Claim: Institutional	837Institutional_V1_wpc_multiple.xml
		837Institutional_V1_wpc_single.xml
837	Health Care Claim: Dental	837Dental_V1_wpc_multiple.xml
		837Dental_v1_wpc_single.xml
837	Health Care Claim: Professional	837Professional_v1_wpc_multiple.xml
		837Professional_v1_wpc_single.xml

Data Segments

Data segment identifiers also serve to maintain data integrity. In the transmission of large amounts of data from one network to another, the transaction set is broken down into discrete units called *data segments*, which are transmitted independent of one another. It is the task of the communication server on each of the networks to either break down the transaction set before sending the data or to reconstruct it after receiving all of the segments. To identify a data segment, tracking code is appended to the transaction set identifier.

A complete transaction is comprised of a transmittable message that adheres to strict formatting rules. Data segments are grouped in a consistent, logical order dictated by the ASC X12 standard for data transmission. The segments are organized into functional groups in which related segments are bundled together. The functional groups are then packaged into a pair of envelopes. These envelopes are simply character strings that identify the beginning and ending of data transmission protocol and interchange segments.

The inside envelope containing the functional groups is called the interchange envelope, which contains information the network server requires to decode the message. The outer envelope is called a communications envelope, which includes a communications transport protocol, which identifies the beginning and ending of a transmission.

The remainder of this section describes the fields, which must be filled in on the various HIPAA transaction sets. These fields are the information required by health care service providers in administering services to patients. These fields are what the end user would consider his or her bread-and-butter responsibilities. Most of the details of data communications discussed in the previous paragraphs are usually totally transparent to the end user because they are information that is handled by or for the communications servers. It doesn't appear on the visible transaction, but there may be times in which a familiarity with the preceding nomenclature is useful in tracking transactions.

HIPAA Transaction Sets (Schemas)

Each of the HIPAA schemas is comprised of hundreds of fields. Many of these are the protocol, interchange, and envelope codes that are invisible to the end user. Health care service providers aren't required to provide all fields. When an agency's documents (such as claims or enrollment forms) are mapped to the schemas, the final transaction need only include certain fields required by HIPAA and other fields deemed appropriate by the submitter of the transaction. The HIPAA schemas are flexible in that they include large numbers of fields the architects of the legislation anticipated would be potentially useful to health care agencies. In the mapping process, users define the fields they will incorporate into their documents.

A word about HIPAA vernacular is appropriate before continuing. HIPAA architects define an entity called a hierarchical level (HL) into which is grouped information for the various participants in a transaction. The collection of fields that comprise a hierarchical level is referred to as a _loop_.

♦ On the 837 schemas, the hierarchical level for information about the submitter is referred to as the `SubmitterName`.

♦ The loop includes the fields `EntityIdentifierCode`, `EntityTypeQualifier`, `SubmitterLastOrOrganization`, `SubmitterFirstfName`, and so on.

The simplest way to understand how data is organized in the schemas is to examine a data tree as displayed in BizTalk Editor. Several of the hierarchical levels have been expanded to illustrate how loops are organized and are shown in Figures 5.2, 5.3, 5.4, and 5.5.

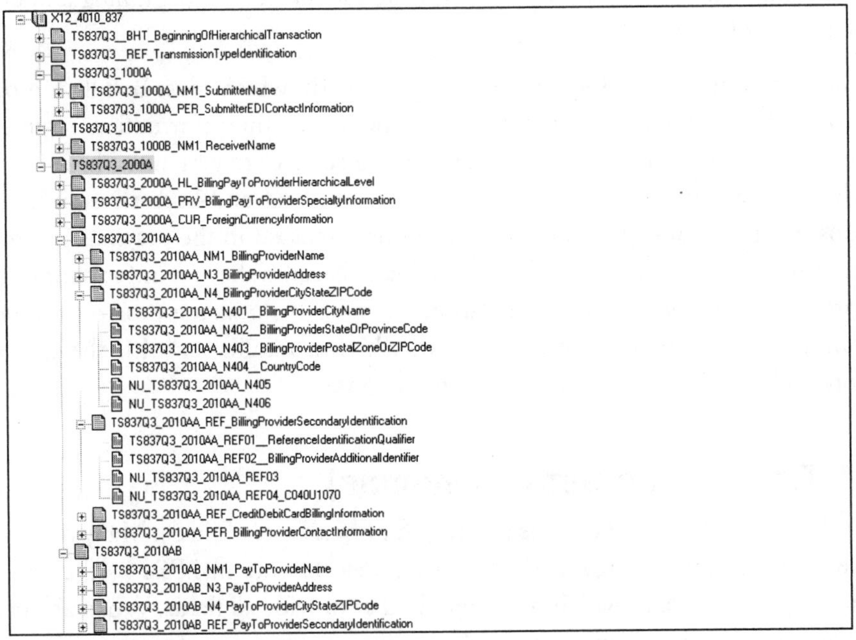

FIGURE 5.2 _Hierarchical levels, part 1._

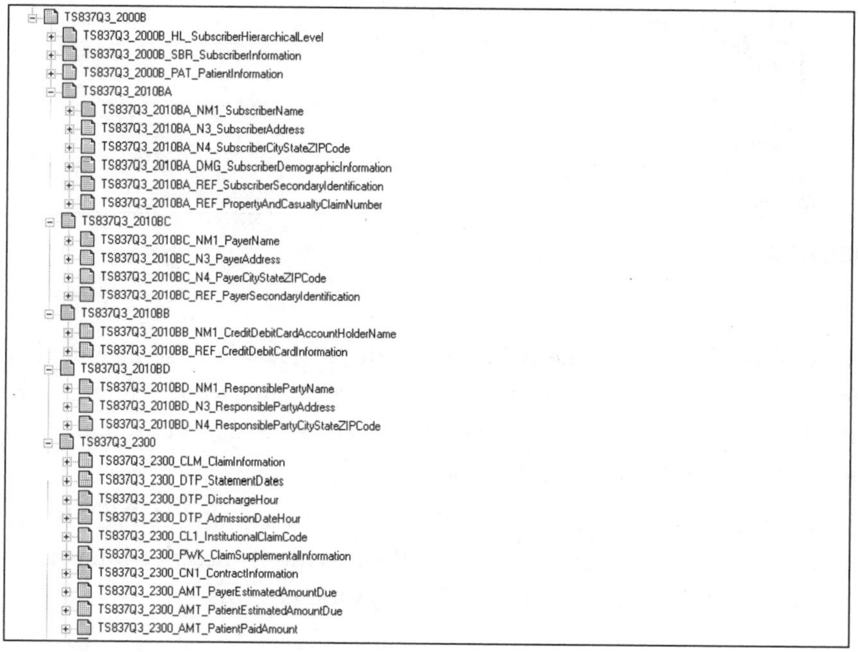

FIGURE 5.3 *Hierarchical levels, part 2.*

FIGURE 5.4 *Hierarchical levels, part 3.*

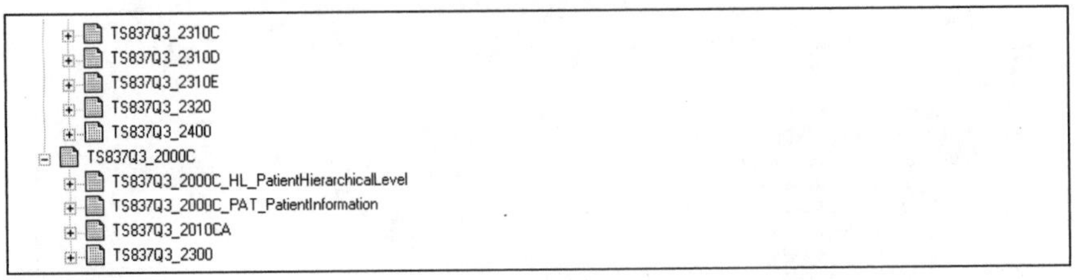

```
    ⊞  TS837Q3_2310C
    ⊞  TS837Q3_2310D
    ⊞  TS837Q3_2310E
    ⊞  TS837Q3_2320
    ⊞  TS837Q3_2400
 ⊟  TS837Q3_2000C
    ⊞  TS837Q3_2000C_HL_PatientHierarchicalLevel
    ⊞  TS837Q3_2000C_PAT_PatientInformation
    ⊞  TS837Q3_2010CA
    ⊞  TS837Q3_2300
```

FIGURE 5.5 *Hierarchical levels, part 4.*

Many of the loops in some of the hierarchical levels look similar in that they require identical fields. Several of the data segments require foreign currency information. These segments are included to allow providers to submit claims for services received in foreign countries.

Further details for each of these schemas are available in the HIPAA Implementation Guides. The Implementation Guides specifically describe limits and guidance on what submitters can include on the various forms.

Representing Data and Documents

One of HIPAA's legislated standards is that electronically transmitted health care information must conform to a single, universally readable language and character code. A *character code* is simply a definition of digital input to represent keyboard characters as they are entered into a computer. For example, when a computer user types the letter B, the computer interprets this as a string of 0s and 1s that uniquely identify the letter. After all, in accomplishing all of its processing, all a computer has to work with is electrical circuits.

A computer has millions of circuits. If a circuit is closed, electricity flows through it. The presence of electricity means the circuit is "on" and the computer associates the value 1 with it. If a circuit is open, it is said to be "off" and it has a value of 0. Each character on the keyboard is represented by a string of 0s and 1s. A position in this string is called a *bit*. So, a string like 0110 has 4 bits, as does 1011. 11001100 is a string of 8 bits. There are many different character codes in the world, some that use eight bits to represent each keyboard character, some use 9, and others 24 or 36.

To impose full integration and portability throughout the health care system, HIPAA mandated the adoption of one of these character sets for the transmission of data. This character set is known as *ASCII (Accredited Standards Committee)*.

To further facilitate speed and security in the transmission of data as it travels over communications lines, such as telephone lines, coaxial cables (just like your cable TV), or radio waves (for satellite transmission), HIPAA mandates the use of a single electronic communication standard technology. This technology is called the *Electronic Data Interchange* (EDI). A committee called the *American National Standards Institute* (ANSI) regulates EDI standards.

The designator for the data transmission technology is ANSI X12 EDI (or just X12). These standards specify formats for data transmission, which include, among other things, how data is coded so computers can tell where one transmitted message ends and the next one begins.

 NOTE

The term EDI does not necessarily mean X12N EDI; it can refer to flat files that are based on a recommended data set and modified for individual partners' needs.

In addition to character codes and transmission codes, computers operate with code on another level. This level is referred to as the language of computers. It refers to coded lines of instructions that computers decode to determine what to do with all of the 0s and 1s being thrown at them. The language adopted by BizTalk Server is known as *XML* which stands for *eXtensible Markup Language*. Listing 5.1 is an example of one of the 12 HIPAA XML transactions.

Listing 5.1 HIPAA schema in XML

```xml
<?xml version="1.0" ?>
- <!--
 Generated by using BizTalk Editor on Mon, Aug 06 2001 05:42:11 PM
--->
- <!--
 Microsoft Corporation (c) 2000 (http://www.microsoft.com)
--->
<Schema name="X12_4010_837" b:BizTalkServerEditorTool_Version="1.0" b:root_
reference="X12_4010_837" b:schema_type="837" b:version="1.0" b:is_envelope="no"
b:standard="X12" b:standards_version="4010" b:subdocument_break="yes"
xmlns="urn:schemas-microsoft-com:xml-data" xmlns:b="urn:schemas-microsoft-
com:BizTalkServer" xmlns:d="urn:schemas-microsoft-com:datatypes">
```

```
--<b:SelectionFields />
<ElementType name="X12_4010_837" content="eltOnly" model="closed">
--<b:RecordInfo structure="delimited" delimiter_type="inherit_record"
field_order="postfix" count_ignore="yes" />
--<element type="TS837Q3__BHT_BeginningOfHierarchicalTransaction" maxOccurs="1"
minOccurs="1" />
--<element type="TS837Q3__REF_TransmissionTypeIdentification" maxOccurs="1"
minOccurs="1" />
--<element type="TS837Q3_1000A" maxOccurs="1" minOccurs="1" />
--<element type="TS837Q3_1000B" maxOccurs="1" minOccurs="1" />
--<element type="TS837Q3_2000A" maxOccurs="*" minOccurs="1" />
--</ElementType>
<ElementType name="TS837Q3__REF_TransmissionTypeIdentification" content="empty"
model="closed">
--<description>Transmission Type Identification</description>
<b:RecordInfo tag_name="REF" structure="delimited"
delimiter_type="inherit_field" field_order="prefix" count_ignore="no">
<b:Rule subjects="any">
--<b:Subject name="@TS837Q3__REF02__TransmissionType
```

All of this probably sounds rather confusing to those whose interface with computers has always been the handling of data by programs that seem to kick on all by themselves when the computer is turned on. The good news is that health care workers, providers, and agents don't have to know anything about character codes, EDI, and XML.

The BizTalk HIPAA Accelerator takes care of all that for you! These details are included only because you will encounter the terms as you proceed to learn how to use the HIPAA Academy's software solution. Furthermore, in your everyday conduct of HIPAA-related business, you will encounter file extensions like xml and folder names like X12 and ANSI. Though you may not understand the finer details about what's really happening, you will at least be able to associate a context with these abbreviations.

The next logical step in understanding the BizTalk Accelerator for HIPAA is to visualize the overall flow of documents and data as they move through cyberspace in the form of transactions. Look at the flow diagram in Figure 5.6. This shows the path followed by a transaction from the time it is generated, perhaps in the form of a paper document, until it is delivered to the end user.

```
<?xml version="1.0" ?>
- <!--
Generated by using BizTalk Editor on Mon, Aug 06 2001 05:42:11 PM
  -->
- <!--
Microsoft Corporation (c) 2000 (http://www.microsoft.com)
  -->
-               <Schema name='X12_4010_837 "
   b:BizTalkServerEditorTool_Version ="1.0"
   b:root_reference ='X12_4010_837 " b:schema_type='837'
   b:version ='1.0" b:is_envelope='no" b:standard='X12"
   b:standards_version ='4010" b:subdocument_break='yes"
   xmlns ='urn:schemas-microsoft-com:xml-data"
   xmlns:b ='urn:schemas-microsoft-com:BizTalkServer "
   xmlns:d ='urn:schemas-microsoft-com:datatypes'>
   <b:SelectionFields />
-    <ElementType name='X12_4010_837 " content='eltOnly"
     model='closed'>
            <b:RecordInfo           structure='delimited"
     delimiter_type ='Inherit_record " field_order='postfix"
     count_ignore ='yes" />
                                      <element
     type='TS837Q3__BHT_BeginningOfHierarchicalTransactio
     n" maxOccurs='1" minOccurs='1" />
                                      <element
     type='TS837Q3__REF_TransmissionTypeIdentification   "
     maxOccurs='1" minOccurs='1" />
       <element     type='TS837Q3_1000A " maxOccurs='1"
     minOccurs='1" />
       <element     type='TS837Q3_1000B " maxOccurs='1"
     minOccurs='1" />
       <element     type='TS837Q3_200 0A" maxOccurs='*"
     minOccurs='1" />
   </ElementType>
-                                      <ElementType
     name ='TS837Q3__REF_TransmissionTypeIdentification   "
     content='empty" model='closed'>
     <description>Transmission Type Identification </description>
-    <b:RecordInfo tag_name='REF" structure='delimited"
     delimiter_type ='Inherit_field " field_order='prefix"
     count_ignore ='no'>
   - <b:Rule subjects ='any'>
                                  <b:Subject
     name ='@TS837Q3__REF02__TransmissionType
```

FIGURE 5.6 *HIPPA schema in XML.*

The transaction originates as a hard copy that must be manually entered into a computer terminal or as a digital transaction, perhaps through a Web page. In either case, the document enters the transaction process in the form of a computer file. If the file is already formatted as an XML document, it is ready to be processed by the BizTalk Server. Unfortunately, there are a myriad of file formats that computer programs generate for documents and data files. You may have heard of some of these.

One of the most popular is the ASCII format, usually referred to as a text or .txt file. Other formats include the .doc format familiar to Microsoft Office users, HTML for Web pages, and EDI for data interchange processes. The simplest type of file format is the flat file, in which data records and fields are bounded by commas or some other character or delimiter. Flat files pass data without regard for the type of information being carried; everything is just 0s and 1s until a delimiter is encountered.

BizTalk Server 2002 processes deal exclusively with XML files. Data entering the system in any format other than XML must be transformed into an XML document. This is done with tools called parsers. BizTalk Server 2002 comes fully equipped with its own set of parsers for converting text files, HTML files, and others into XML.

 NOTE

BizTalk Accelerator for HIPAA parser is a component that translates HIPAA (X12N) files into *Extensible Markup Language* (XML) files.

When a transaction has been parsed, processed, and transmitted to its destination, it may have to be converted from XML back to its original form or into another file format used by the destination computer's other programs. A serializer is the tool used for converting from XML to other formats. Serializing is essentially the reverse of parsing. Once the transaction has been serialized, it can be passed to the destination computer's control for further processing (such as printing a document) or storage.

In Figure 5.7 each step is covered in moderate detail, but before we can understand how the pieces in the total process fit together, we have to examine three tasks that must be accomplished before the BizTalk Accelerator for HIPAA can run. These are document specification, document mapping, and orchestration.

Documents entering the BizTalk Server process represent data that are organized in a way that is meaningful to the user. Meaningful in this context means the type of data provided (numeric, text, dates, currency, and so on) and the order in which it is arranged.

Let's try to understand this by way of analogy. Ancient Egyptians wrote in two different scripts, the demotic script and hieroglyphics. Demotic was the common script used for everyday administrative business. Hieroglyphics was the ceremonial, pictographic script the Egyptians used to record historic and political events on their monuments. These monuments have survived until the present day, but the language was totally lost through time.

For centuries the hieroglyphics were just pictures in stone and the demotic script was just lines of characters with no meaning. In 1799, a French military officer in Napoleon's army on a military expedition in Egypt discovered an interesting artifact in the city of Rosetta, near Alexandria. The artifact was a stone on which was written a message in three different scripts—Egyptian demotic, Egyptian hieroglyphics, and ancient Greek. Fortunately, ancient Greek was a language that many scholars of the day understood, including Jean-Francois Champollion.

By translating the Greek, Champollion was able to decipher the other two scripts and give Egyptologists the tools to crack the secrets of ancient Egyptian life and history.

In our analogy, let ASCII be a character code used to generate a document. These are the hieroglyphics in the preceding story. When the document is passed to our computer, it is unrecognizable to the BizTalk Server until it is translated into an XML document (Greek by analogy). Now we have the capability to give meaning to our document. But the document only has meaning if the data in the document are presented in the proper order and form.

The French archaeologists were able to translate the words represented by the hieroglyphic characters, but these words told the stories of Egypt only if they were arranged in the proper order.

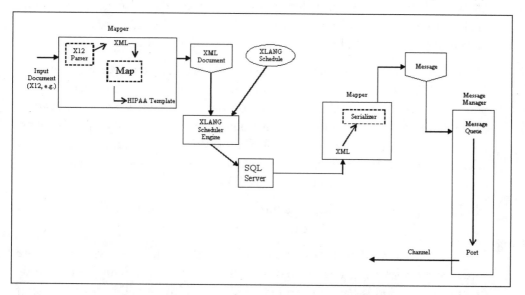

FIGURE 5.7 *The BizTalk Accelerator for HIPAA transaction handling process.*

NOTE

The words "drove," "chariot," "victory," "his," "Ramses," and "to" tell very little until they are rearranged to form the sentence "Ramses drove his chariot to victory."

In the same way, data passed in files means little if it doesn't appear in the order we are expecting it.

Database managers use two entities to organize data, records, and fields, which also are adopted for the organization of data files in BizTalk Server. It is the responsibility of the user to ensure that data entering the BizTalk Server, whether as ASCII, EBCDIC, XS3, or whatever character code, is organized into predefined records and fields. A *record* represents the collection of data in a transaction. Records are comprised of fields. Again, an analogy will make this clearer. Consider how a telephone book is organized. Each entry corresponds to a person and contains the person's last name, first name, street address, and telephone number. The complete entry for John Doe is called a record. His record consists of the four fields: Last Name, First Name, Street Address, and Telephone Number.

Data type is an attribute, which describes the form a field can take. For example, Last Name in a phone book must be presented in the form of letters. Multiple letters grouped together in a single field are called strings. Thus, "John Doe" is string data type. Other data types include numeric, currency, date, and so on. An example of a field requiring numeric data type would be the "Quantity" field in an inventory transaction. The "Price" field in an invoice requires currency data.

Before introducing a document into the BizTalk Server system, you must describe how the data is organized. This allows the Server to recognize the contents of your document after it is parsed. The description you create is known as a *specification*. BizTalk Server includes a tool to help you create your document specifications. This tool is a function of the BizTalk Editor. With the BizTalk editor you can define your records and the fields they contain. Figure 5.8 shows a payment document as it would appear in the BizTalk Editor window.

In Figure 5.8, the hierarchical structure is depicted in the left panel and the record or field attributes in the right panel.

Notice that the window has two panes. The one on the left displays the structure tree for the document. The name of the transaction corresponding to this document specification is Payment, and it is indicated with a small icon at the top of

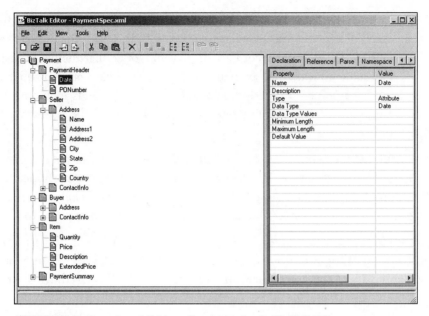

FIGURE 5.8 *Records and fields as they appear in the BizTalk Editor.*

the structure tree that looks like a ledger book. The records in this document are indicated with an icon that looks like a green sheet of paper. The fields are indicated with a blue sheet of paper. Notice that each record and field has a name.

For example, the `PaymentHeader` record has two fields named `Date` and `PONumber`. This tells us that each payment transaction entered into our system will have a header, which includes a date and purchase order number.

Notice, also, that some records are actually embedded within records. For example, just beneath the `PaymentHeader` record is a record called Seller with two other records named `Address` and `ContactInfo` embedded within. The embedding of records within records creates a node, in this case the Seller node. At the bottom, or lowest level, of each node is a list of fields.

NOTE

The arrangement of records and nodes in the form of a structure tree is called a *hierarchy*.

Now look at the right pane in the BizTalk Editor. This is where the user defines what each record or field looks like and represents. In this case, the properties of the Date field in the Payment record are displayed. Notice that the list of attributes describes in detail what the data will look like. It contains blocks in which the field is given a name and a description, followed by other fields including data type and minimum and maximum field lengths. Not all of the properties are required for every field.

The BizTalk Editor permits the user to fully describe a variety of data characteristics. Figure 5.8 illustrates the Declaration tab in the right pane, but notice there are five other tabs that can be used to describe other features. There's even a tab to describe how BizTalk Server should parse the data when converting it to XML.

Figure 5.9 is a similar to Figures 5.2–5.5, showing HIPAA transaction set 837— Health Care Claim: Professional displayed in BizTalk Editor. Because of its length, only part of the hierarchical structure tree can be displayed. Most of the

FIGURE 5.9 *Hierarchical structure tree of HIPAA transaction set 837— Health Care Claim: Professional.*

nodes are collapsed. When all of the nodes and records are expanded, the structure displays hundreds of fields. Most of the transactions you deal with day to day will not be this long.

Document Mapping

As you can see, the specification of a HIPAA schema is a formidable task. Fortunately, the WPC (Washington Publishing Company) has already created all 12 of the HIPAA schemas. These are the heart of the BizTalk Accelerator for HIPAA. They include all of the fields specified by the WPC Implementation Guides. HIPAA standards and regulations detail an exhaustive number of nodes and fields in an attempt to anticipate a diversity of scenarios. Most of the fields are optional input.

As the HIPAA transaction processes in your organization, you will match fields in your transaction documents with those on the HIPAA schemas. This is the process called *document mapping*. BizTalk Server then takes the document map you create and generates another XML document, which represents your transaction in HIPAA compliant format.

 NOTE

To map your documents, you use the BizTalk Mapper tool.

The Mapper window has three panels:

- ◆ The left panel is where the document specification appears.
- ◆ The middle panel has the quasi-horizontal lines that transect the window panels join fields on the provider's claim document with their corresponding fields on the HIPAA transaction set.
- ◆ The right panel is where the HIPAA template to which you are mapping your fields appears.

Figure 5.10 illustrates the mapping of a medical service provider's claim document to a HIPAA transaction set 837—Health Care Claim: Professional.

The Mapper is quite simple to use because the links between the two schemas are secured simply by dragging a field from one panel and dropping it onto its corresponding field in the other panel.

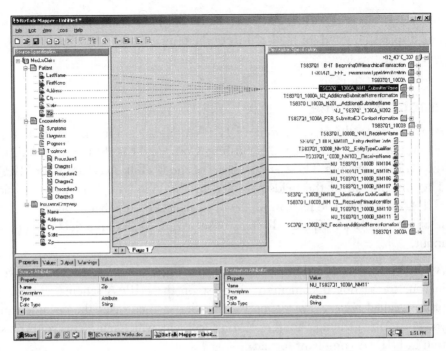

FIGURE 5.10. *BizTalk Mapper in the process of mapping a health claim to the HIPAA transaction set 837—Health Care Claim: Professional.*

The result of the mapping process is the creation of another XML file, which contains the information to link the fields in both schemas. This information is used by the BizTalk Mapper to create yet another XML file representing the document required by the user on the receiving end. In this case, the receiver document must be HIPAA-compliant, which is why we mapped our input schema to the HIPAA schema.

Orchestration

The movement of health transactions through a complex computer system is accomplished by a sequence of steps that must occur in a logically defined order. If one of these steps is accomplished in the wrong order, the transaction will not be handled correctly. Each of these steps is referred to as a *process*. After an incoming health services document has been parsed and mapped appropriately, it must be routed through the system under the guidance of a roadmap called the XLANG schedule. However, this is only possible if the XLANG schedule has been properly created before the document arrives. The XLANG schedule is constructed using the BizTalk Orchestration Designer.

Orchestration is a powerful feature provided by BizTalk Server that provides the most flexible approach to integrating business process logic with new and existing applications and systems. It is a method for defining the exchange of messages between the software applications that make up the system.

In the HIPAA Academy software solution, orchestration is performed with the use of Microsoft Visio 2000 diagramming software. The BizTalk Orchestration Designer, as an imbedded program, executes Visio 2000.

The Orchestration Designer designs the workflow of the BizTalk Server message, handling processes by separating process definition from implementation. The definition phase involves the identification of the discrete processes that make up the overall message-handling task. Figure 5.11 is a flow diagram that illustrates how the BizTalk Orchestration Designer builds the XLANG schedule.

Before building the XLANG schedule, you need to do some planning. Remember, the XLANG schedule serves as a director of activity in the transaction process. To direct your documents properly, you need to determine where you are going and how you will get there. First, you should determine your starting point, that is, which document are you processing?

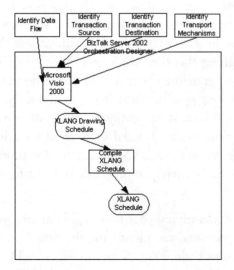

FIGURE 5.11 *Process flow in the development of an XLANG schedule using BizTalk Orchestration Designer.*

NOTE

If you were entering a claim into the system, the BizTalk Server would process it differently than it would a payment transaction. This is what is referred to as the *transaction source.*

Next, you need to identify the transaction destination. Where is it going and in what format must it arrive to be meaningful to the recipient?

To deliver the formatted document to the recipient, it must be passed through a channel. Though the channel is the last element in any BizTalk Server process, it must be included early during the planning. A channel represents a path in the overall process that joins discrete tasks (or sub-processes) in the larger picture.

It might simply be the passing of data from one program element to another (for example, from Visio 2000 to BizTalk Orchestration Designer) or the passing of data between computers (a communications channel). If the data is to pass through a communication channel, it must enter and leave the channel through a port. So, during the planning phase, we need to know which communication channels we intend to use. Because channels may take different forms during different phases of the execution of a program, we will refer to the collection of all of these various forms as *transport mechanisms.*

The last step in the planning phase is to define the *data flow.* This refers to a path the data will follow as it moves from one sub-process to another. Each sub-process will be joined to other sub-processes by channels indicated with arrows. You should avoid the temptation of designing this flow while you draw it in Visio 2000. You should sketch the flow on paper before opening BizTalk Orchestration Designer. This will assist you in identifying possible flaws in the design early. If a flaw is built into the Visio 2000 design files, it can easily become part of your XLANG schedule. In some cases, a process can proceed undeterred for a long time before a flawed condition is triggered in the XLANG schedule. Do yourself and your system managers a great service by giving considerable thought to your design before you start to code it.

Once you have performed the tasks of identifying your sources, identifying your destination, identifying transport mechanisms, and identifying the data flow, you are ready to begin drawing your design in Visio 2000. Notice in Figure 5.11 that all of the phases of the design task provide input to the drawing phase.

When the BizTalk Orchestration Designer is executed, Visio 2000 appears as a pane inside the Orchestration Designer window (see Figure 5.11). If you have Visio 2000 running on your computer, open it now and notice the similarities between it and Figure 5.12. Though they look similar, there are obvious differences in the window appearance. This is because Figure 5.12 shows Visio 2000 as it runs embedded in BizTalk Orchestration Designer.

The obvious question you might ask is "If BizTalk Orchestration Designer uses Visio 2000 to diagram the flow process, why not just use Visio 2000 and eliminate the Orchestration Designer?" The answer is that the Orchestration Designer adds to the process capabilities that Visio 2000 doesn't possess. After the process diagram is completed in the Visio 2000 overlay, BizTalk Orchestration Designer deconstructs the process step-by-step and compiles the XLANG schedule. This is a powerful capability! This means that the BizTalk Orchestration Designer actually translates the flow diagram in a machine-coded process that will execute on the BizTalk Server.

The wonderful thing about the BizTalk Accelerator for HIPAA is that this all occurs almost transparent to the users. All you need to do is design the process flow and the communication components and BizTalk Orchestration Designer do the rest. Let's see how it works.

In Figure 5.12 you see two panels within the Visio 2000 pane. The panel on the left is titled Use Flowchart Shapes to Draw a Business Process. This is called the Process Panel or *Flowchart Panel*. The right panel is labeled Use Implementation Shapes to Implement Ports. This is called the *Implementation Panel*.

In the Flowchart Panel you see a list of flowchart symbols on the far left edge of the window. These symbols can be dragged and dropped onto the Flowchart Panel to depict the processes and entities that form the transaction process being designed. Arrows can be added to indicate channels through which the processing flows. Figure 5.13 is an example of a completed flow diagram from the BizTalk Server online documentation manual. If you would like to learn more about this tool, you can refer to the online manual.

After the process flow has been designed, the communication ports for message handling must be specified. Certain actions in the process flow diagram must be coupled with messaging services provided by the BizTalk Messaging Manager. Messaging service is a concurrent process that continually runs in the background with all other BizTalk Server processes. BizTalk Messaging Service continually

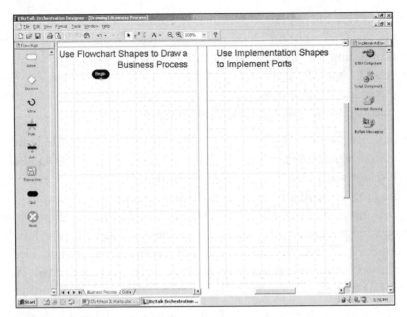

FIGURE 5.12 *BizTalk Orchestration Designer with Visio 2000 embedded.*

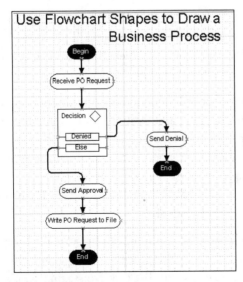

FIGURE 5.13 *The design of a process created in the BizTalk Orchestration Designer.*

monitors the status of incoming and outgoing messages as well as the movement from one process to another in the XLANG schedule.

Let's suppose that in our transaction, an 837—Health Care Claim moves from the parser to the Mapper. This is a movement that must be monitored by the Messaging Manager. Such movement between two sub-processes is automatically configured by the XLANG compiler from the Process Flow Diagram (left-hand panel in the Orchestration Designer). This is referred to as *internal communications* because it takes place solely within a single computer system.

External communication flow, transfer of documents between at least two server systems, is depicted on the Implementation Panel of the Orchestration Designer. It is here that you specify ports and channels through which documents will flow into and out of the BizTalk Server (to or from other servers or to or from input and output devices). When a HIPAA-compliant document must be shipped externally (for example, from one agency to another), it is sent to a port that transfers it to a channel.

To understand what is happening in the Orchestration Designer, one must understand the two ways the word *port* is used.

 NOTE

A *port* refers to a technology that carries out the communication process. It doesn't refer to a physical port through which the documents and data travel.

The technologies refer to software and hardware that manage the transfer of data. In our case, the ports will be directed to the Messaging Manager. It is the function of the Messaging Manager to direct the documents to a physical port. In other words, the Implementation Panel models the communication process whereas the Messaging Manager controls the communication process.

Figure 5.14 depicts a complete transaction process in which document flow is depicted between the processing and the communications through logical ports, which bridge the implementation panel and the Flowchart Panel. The benefit in using the Orchestration Designer is apparent in the ease with which the design is accomplished. The message ports and channels are configured graphically on the implementation page by dragging and dropping icons from the right side of the Visio 2000 pane.

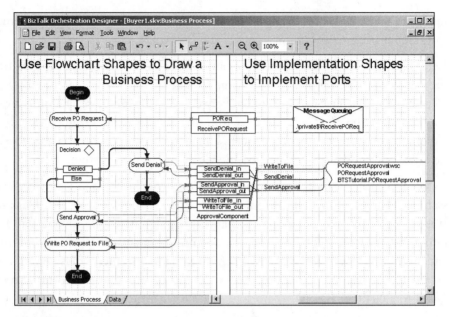

FIGURE 5.14 *Integration of flowchart and implementation in the BizTalk Orchestration Designer.*

In Figure 5. 14, the data flow is described in the left panel and the communication flow is depicted in the right panel.

Concurrent with the layout of the flowchart and implementation diagrams, BizTalk Orchestration Designer also diagrammed the data structure and flow. You can see the data layout by clicking on the data tab on the bottom edge of the Orchestration Designer (see Figure 5.15).

The data page displays every message and data port created on the business page. The data flow indicates the connection between source document and destination document with arrows joining the two. As you design the document flow between message ports and the processes on the business page, Orchestration Designer is configuring the data communication plan for documents entering and leaving the BizTalk Server.

Remember, however, that BizTalk Orchestration Designer uses Visio 2000 merely to diagram processes and data flow. The diagrams simply represent the procedures for handling documents. They don't really do anything. To accomplish any tasks at all, the diagrams must be translated into some vehicle for actually processing the documents. This vehicle is the XLANG schedule and the act of translating is

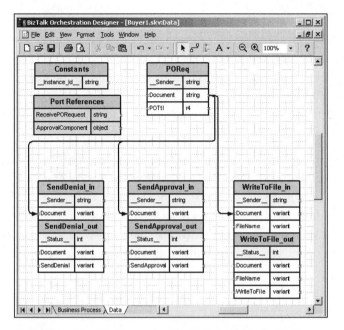

FIGURE 5.15 *The Data tab of BizTalk Orchestration Designer.*

what we call *compiling*. The XLANG schedule is actually an executable program written in XML. So is the XML produced? All you do with the BizTalk Orchestration Designer is diagram the processes and communication paths.

The word *compile* in computer programming vernacular refers to the process of taking code written in a high-level computer language (such as C++ or PASCAL) and converting (or translating) it into machine language, the instructions a computer understands. This is basically the arrangement of 0s and 1s that open and close circuits in the precise order and with the precise timing to accomplish the desired tasks.

XML is the language that BizTalk Server uses to interface between the programmer and the machine. That's right, a programmer. When you create the XLANG flow diagrams, you are creating the skeleton of a computer program. Even as you put these diagrams together, the BizTalk Orchestration Designer begins constructing your program. That's how it is able to put together the data elements on the data page while you develop the business page. When you finish diagramming your process, you send the completed diagram to the compiler to complete the conversion of your design into machine language.

Refer back to Figure 5.11. Recall that when you plan out the procedures for processing a document, you define the source transaction, the destination transaction, the transport mechanisms, and the data flow. Next you execute BizTalk Orchestration Designer, which simultaneously executes its own variation of Visio 2000. The output of Visio 2000 is a flow diagram of the process you defined for handling the transaction. This diagram is represented on Figure 5.11 as the XLANG Drawing Schedule.

Notice that at this point we are still in the BizTalk Orchestration Designer, but we are finished with Visio 2000. When you issue the command from the File menu to Make XLANG, the BizTalk Orchestration Designer takes the XLANG drawing and converts into an XML document, which it passes to the XLANG compiler. After the XML code is compiled (translated), the compiler generates the XLANG schedule. Now you have machine code that is capable of processing your document.

 NOTE

A key concept in the operation of the BizTalk Accelerator for HIPAA is that a different XLANG schedule must be created for each type of transaction that is processed by the BizTalk Server.

This is true regardless of the direction from which the transaction enters the system. In other words, you must have a unique XLANG schedule for each category of transaction coming into your computer (for instance, one each for 278—Health Care Services Review—Request for Review, 278—Health Care Services Review—Response to Request for Review, 837—Health Care Claim—Professional, 837—Health Care Claim—Dental, and so on).

The BizTalk Server stores these XLANG schedules in files with extensions of .skx. When a transaction enters the BizTalk Server, the proper XLANG schedule is invoked by the XLANG Scheduler Engine to process the documents. The Scheduler Engine creates an instance of the XLANG schedule. An *instance* is a copy of the XLANG schedule, which is associated with a unique transaction. This *instantiation* leads its associated transaction through the BizTalk Server. The XLANG Scheduler Engine executes an instantiation and monitors its status until it leaves the Server. When the transaction leaves the Server through a port, the instantiation ceases to exist.

BizTalk Accelerator for HIPAA— Execution and Tracking

Now that a set of XLANG schedules has been created, it is time to set the BizTalk Server into motion. Refer again to Figure 5.6. Begin by submitting a transaction into the BizTalk Server. For the purpose of this walkthrough, consider a transaction in which the computer system receives a document in X12 format. Again, this could be a document, which originates in any format.

For example, if a health services agent entered the contents of the document directly into the computer through the keyboard, it may be put into a word processing file in text (.txt) format. On the other hand, it may come in electronically through a communications port, perhaps from the Internet.

The first stop for our transaction, once it is absorbed into the BizTalk Server, is the BizTalk Mapper. The Mapper identifies the document's format as X12, and then selects the appropriate parser to convert the document to XML.

After the transaction is converted to XML, the messaging manager selects the appropriate HIPAA overlay to match with the transaction. The Mapper associates the fields from the XML document with those from the matching HIPAA standard. You previously identified these fields when you created the links using the Messaging Manager during the designing process. When the fields are properly associated, the Messaging Manager creates a new XML document representing the transaction in both a HIPAA-compliant document and a format that is capable of being processed by the BizTalk Server.

Next, the XML-formatted HIPAA transaction is passed to the XLANG Scheduler Engine. The engine retrieves the XLANG schedule, which matches the HIPAA transaction being processed, and executes it. The XLANG schedule validates the fields and routes the messages according to the flow that you defined with the Orchestration Designer. If the transaction meets all of the criteria you specified in your flowcharts, then the contents of the transaction are passed onto the SQL Server for archiving in the database. From the SQL server, the message is accessible to other processes in the BizTalk Server cycle.

Though the data flow diagram indicates movement from the XLANG engine to the SQL Server, this doesn't mean the XLANG Schedule has been terminated. Remember, the schedule doesn't terminate until the message leaves the BizTalk Server through a data port. The XLANG Scheduler Engine executes the

XLANG Schedule, which is the function of the engine; the schedule continues to guide the document through the system. In moving your data from the engine to the SQL Server, Figure 5.6 implies only that the engine has done its job even though the schedule continues to run.

From this point on, the document is accessible to other processes in the cycle through the SQL Server. The SQL Server is basically a database manager, though a rather sophisticated one. When other programs and processes interface with the database, they do so in the Structured Query Language (SQL), a standardized database language that provides commonality between the SQL Server and other database systems. Once again, SQL is totally transparent to you, the end user. When you invoke the database through BizTalk Server, the BizTalk Server communicates with the SQL Server. You don't have to.

An archive of your transaction in the SQL Server database implies that the document has passed all of the conditions for HIPAA compliance imposed by the HIPAA schema, as well as conditions that your agency also imposed on transactions. For example, the HIPAA template ensured that your data meets the structure and format imposed by HIPAA legislation. When you created your flowchart during the orchestration phase, you imposed criteria defined by your agency. Both sets of criteria must be met before the transaction is archived in the database.

Having processed and verified your transaction, BizTalk Server is ready to prepare a transmittal copy to send to the recipient. In the case of the 837—Health Care Claim, the recipient is more than likely an insurance company's claims processor. Before it is sent, BizTalk Server converts the transaction into the format specified by the recipient. This is the format recognizable to the recipient's computer system. In our case, incoming documents are in X12 format. Our recipient might be expecting it in X12, .txt, or some other format.

Still under the guidance of the XLANG schedule, the transaction is moved to the Messaging Manager. The Messaging Manager receives the transaction (still in XML), selects the proper serializer, and translates the message into the required format and character set. Now we have resident within the HIPAA Accelerator for BizTalk system two copies of the same transaction. One copy is in XML, stored in the SQL Server and accessible by the BizTalk Server. The other is in our intended recipient's format, ready for transmission. This copy is stored in the Messaging Manager's Message Queue.

NOTE

The message queue is a holding area for messages as they wait to be transmitted.

Once the transaction is safely delivered to the Messaging Manager, the XLANG schedule terminates. It is the Messaging Manager's responsibility to identify a port through which to transmit the documents to the recipient.

There are many reasons why a message would be queued for transmission. It all has to do with synchronous and asynchronous messaging. Synchronous messaging occurs when the sender's and the recipient's computer systems are both running at the same time. The recipient is in a sense waiting for us to send a transaction. In this case, the resident time in the queue is minimal. On the other hand, if the recipient's server is down (turned off or broken down), their system is inaccessible by ours. In this case, the message will has to remain in the queue until our server determines that the recipient's server is up and running. This situation is continuously monitored by the Messaging Manager, which sends out a poll at regular intervals.

A *poll* is simply a "knock on the door" by one computer to another. The sending computer issues a sequence of bits called an *ack*. If the receiving computer is up, it returns another sequence called a *nack*. If the other system is down, nothing comes back. Once our server receives a nack, the Messaging Manager sends the message out through the port into the channel.

 NOTE

Polling is a process to prepare the communication channel between the sending and receiving computers.

The Messaging Manager also has other duties to perform. As transactions are placed into the Message Queue they are disassembled into units called *packets*. In the process of transmitting electronic messages over communications channels, data integrity is often compromised. This means bits (the 0s and 1s) can be *lost* or *flipped* as they pass between two points. Losing bits means that messages may get truncated and parts of the complete transmission just disappear. Flipping bits occurs when a 0 is changed to a 1 or vice versa.

The longer the path (the greater the distance) between the sender and receiver, the greater the threat. Data compromise can occur through natural physical phenomena (for instance a thunderstorm somewhere along the communication path between the two computer systems) or by interference from hackers. In either case, the communications industry has devised methods for protecting data integrity. One of these methods is to break large messages up into small, easy-to-manage packets. The Messaging Manager keeps track of all of these packets and sends them out through the ports as the opportunities become available. It is the responsibility of the receiving computer system to reconstruct the packets into their original form.

With the sending of a message out through a port, it would seem that the processing cycle on the originating computer system is complete. However, such is not the case. Even though the original document has left the server, BizTalk continues to track the document.

Document Tracking

The lifetime of a transaction extends beyond the delivery point. It is usually necessary to maintain a history of transactions because most transactions require and generate replies or actions. For example, health service recipients (patients) require statements from their health service providers summarizing claims progress and financial records for income tax purposes. Also, claim progress is often traced by submission of a 276—Health Care Claim Status Request followed by a 277—Health Care Claim Status Notification, both of which require a full history of a transaction along with attendant transactions.

BizTalk has a built-in transaction tracking system. BizTalk maintains a history of all transactions, which includes parsing and mapping information, processing steps, serialization, and message routing, as well a copy of the transaction itself. Tracking information is maintained in the Document Tracking Activity (DTA) database on not only the transaction originator's computer but on the computers of all recipients.

The DTA database in the HIPAA Academy software solution is stored on the SQL Server. Because most health service agencies and providers will probably generate a great number of transactions each month, it is important to have some way of maintaining the histories without jeopardizing the performance of the

SQL Server and its database. This requires meticulous database discipline, which BizTalk Server also provides.

In addition to including software to effectively store transactions histories, BizTalk Server also includes database maintenance software, which allows for the deletion of expired or outdated information from the online database. However, though the online database is purged of extraneous records, health service agencies are required to maintain a permanent history of transactions. This can be accomplished by regularly backing up the database and maintaining a permanent archival of the histories.

The document tracking function of BizTalk Server is a Web-based activity. This provides the capability of tracking documents from any computer with Internet access. This has some real advantages if you stop to think about it. For example, it permits agencies to track their documents without using resources currently taxed by the online, real-time BizTalk Server. It also permits the sharing of transaction audits with other authorized agencies through the use of the Internet. Figure 5.16 is a picture of the Web-based BizTalk Document Tracking interface.

Document tracking is accomplished through the execution of database queries. The user specifies the criteria and executes the query. In the background, the

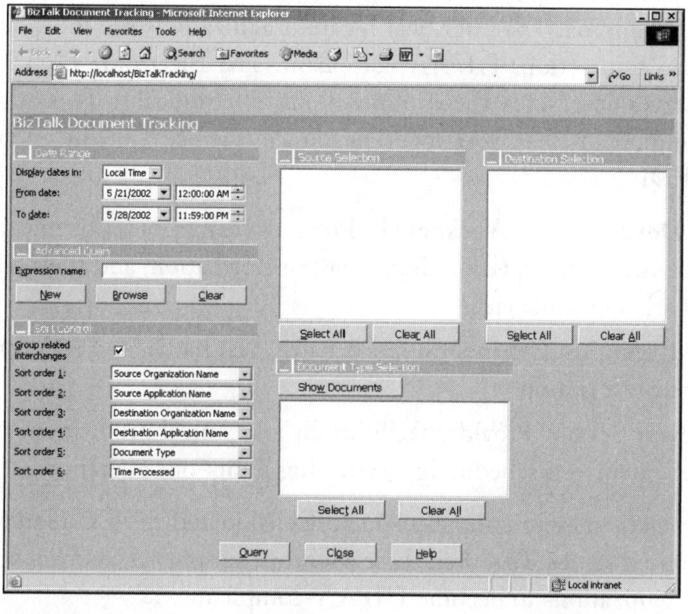

FIGURE 5.16 *Web-based BizTalk Document Tracking interface.*

BizTalk document tracker translates the criteria into SQL database instructions, again removing that level of complexity from the end user.

Sybase HIPAA Studio

(Reference: EDI server data sheet, Sybase Inc.)

Sybase also has an application product that provides message management coupled with comprehensive security to facilitate HIPAA compliance. Though the recommended Sybase HIPAA Studio application collection is analogous to the components adopted for the Microsoft BizTalk solution, the Sybase system is operating system independent. By operating Sybase HIPAA Studio in conjunction with Sybase Enterprise Portal, the server achieves the added benefit of exploiting the Internet as a way of achieving connectivity between providers.

The SYBASE based HIPAA Accelerator consists of three components:

◆ HIPAA-compliant X12 standards

◆ HIPAA compliance maps for each X12 transaction

◆ A suite of compliant test data

Together these components are known as the HIPAA Studio. The HIPAA Studio is an integrated approach to offer health care organizations the tools needed to make their data transactions HIPAA-compliant. The Electronic Data Interchange (EDI) server integrates these transactions electronically. This product includes three components that work together to meet the needs of any organization processing EDI:

◆ **ECMap Development Workbench.** Provides management of trading partners, business rules, versioning, data transformation, and their relationships and dependencies

◆ **ECRTP Execution Engine.** Supports batch, fast batch, and real-time data format integration

◆ **EC Gateway Server.** Provides facilities for job control production scripting and event-driven scheduling, permitting lights-out operations

The HIPAA Accelerator is an enhancement to ECMap and the EC Gateway, a message management server. Together, these solutions simplify the efforts needed for health care organizations to become HIPAA-compliant.

NOTE

Compliance maps contained within Sybase HIPAA Accelerator enable users to verify that their transactions conform to the implementation guides, which are fully open and allow the user to add, delete, or change compliance rules as the customer sees fit.

The Adapter Suite for EDI has a flexible architecture that can be configured to meet widely different customer requirements. It uses a modular approach that can be configured to fit small, midsized, and large enterprise architectures. Companies that exchange EDI business documents with their trading partners use a Messaging service called MQSeries.

Broadly speaking, the Sybase HIPAA Studio components perform the same functions as those of the Microsoft BizTalk Accelerator for HIPAA, although the distribution of functions differs, as illustrated in Table 5.3.

Table 5.3 Application Function Comparison between BizTalk and HIPAA Studio

Application Function	Microsoft BizTalk Solution	Sybase HIPAA Studio
Transaction Mapping	BizTalk Editor	ECMap
	BizTalk Mapper	ECMap
Process Flow Design	BizTalk Orchestration	ECMap
Execution of Process Flow	BizTalk XLANG Scheduler Engine	ECRTP Execution Engine
Data Parsing	BizTalk Messaging Manager	ECRTP Execution Engine
Message Managing and Routing	BizTalk Messaging Manager	EC Gateway
HIPAA Server add-on	BizTalk Accelerator for HIPAA	Sybase HIPAA Accelerator
Transaction Tracking	BizTalk Document Tracking and Messaging Manager	EC Gateway and Sybase Enterprise Portal

The functions performed by the Microsoft BizTalk component in the middle column are analogous to those performed by the corresponding application in the Sybase HIPAA Studio component on the right.

Just as the BizTalk Accelerator for HIPAA is an add-on to the Microsoft BizzTalk Server, the Sybase HIPAA Accelerator is an add-on to ECMap and the EC Gateway, formerly marketed under the name PaperFree.

ECMap

The ECMap application program enables seamless transformation of large volumes of data between health care agencies. ECMap operates in an environment called the Development Workbench, which provides tools to allow the transfer of information across multiple document format boundaries.

The following features are supported by ECMap:

♦ The transformation of health care transactions to and from X12, XML, and HTML and other popular formats.

♦ Any-to-Any Mapping, whereby standard and proprietary formats require no pre-processing to map them directly to or from the database. In other words, ECMap allows for field mapping to HIPAA templates.

♦ Process Flow Diagramming is accomplished with ECMap's internal graphical user interface. ECMap's business rule and flow logic design is driven by the fact that data messages, while based on standards, are context sensitive. For example, an incoming transaction may require eligibility verification for health plan members, credit authorization with suppliers, or other steps to complete the integration into business applications. These rules and associated flow logic are easily created within ECMap's graphical user interface and shared between maps, reducing development time significantly

♦ Compilation of the flow logic diagram into an executable file to be run by the ECRTP Execution Engine.

These roles correspond to analogous roles of field matching performed by BizTalk Mapper, process flow design performed by BizTalk Orchestration Designer, and document parsing performed by BizTalk Messaging Manager in Microsoft's solution.

Another feature of ECMap is the Web Application Development capability to create powerful, interactive Web applications with ease. ECMap empowers users to collect data from the Web or a database and create HTML forms at high speed.

Though BizTalk Server 2002 does not support Web application development internally, the Application Center add-on, in combination with BizTalk Application Integration Components, provides this capability.

Standard or Proprietary Formats

ECMap's database already contains many standardized semantic data object definitions from published standards such as ANSI X12, UN/EDIFACT, and HL7. Other industry standards like UCS, VICS for ANSI X12, and EANCOM in UN/EDIFACT are easily supported by the standards database in the ECMap Development Workbench. The ECMap Development Workbench also allows the modification of the supplied standards database for modifying the standard definition to support trading partner requirements. Implementation guides can easily be added into the ECMap standards database via the SEF import utility. This simplifies the creation of trading partner–specific data transformations. The ACORD (property and casualty insurance standard) and NCPDP (pharmaceutical industry) definitions are easily supported in the ECMap Development Workbench by defining their layouts as sequential or delimited file types and using the "any-to-any" mapping capability native in ECMap.

ECMap, XML, and HTML Support

The ECMap Development Workbench provides a fast and easy way to Web-enable any application by supporting HTML Web page and XML data formats. ECMap supports the mapping of any supported format, EDI standards, sequential, delimited, and database to and from XML and HTML, including mapping XML to/from HTML. ECMap facilitates the integration of back-end application data with HTML Web pages through its ability to read and write HTML and through its capabilities to access, update, and/or create application data, thus simplifying integration. XML is supported by ECMap, making mapping of XML to and from HTML Web pages easy to accomplish.

ECRTP Engine

(Reference: Successfully Negotiating the HIPAA Maze, A Sybase, Inc. Health Care Report on Complying with Administrative Simplification & Security Mandates)

The ECRTP Engine is the Sybase analogue to the XLANG Scheduler Engine of the BizTalk HIPAA Accelerator. It performs the following operations:

- ◆ **Data Transformation.** ECRTP converts data to or from back-end data sources, permitting high speed integration to business applications. ECRTP can collect data from the Web or a database and create HTML at high speed.

- ◆ **Portal Empowerment.** ECRTP allows end users to permit trading partners to access multiple business applications across the Internet for data viewing or data collecting.

- ◆ **Performance and Scalability.** Health care organizations can permit trading partners real-time access to multiple back-end business systems simultaneously, allowing more informed business decisions.

Let's look at these operations one at a time and place them into the context of HIPAA transactions. The first operation (Data Transformation) refers to data parsing and conversion of documents from source formats (.txt, .doc, and so on) into X12 standards and XML formats. This function is performed by the Messaging Manager in BizTalk, so the correspondence of functions illustrated in Table 5.3 is not truly one-to-one (for example, it cannot be said that BizTalk Messaging Manager is equivalent in operation to EC Gateway, nor BizTalk XLANG Scheduler Engine to ECRTP Engine). What is true, however, is that both solutions result in equivalent HIPAA compliance.

Portal Empowerment refers to the ECRTP engine's capability to perform in consonant with the Sybase Enterprise Portal to deliver secure, Web-based portability to HIPAA transactions.

The third ECRTP engine capability, Performance and Scalability, addresses the ability of the Sybase HIPAA Accelerator to permit delivery and receipt of transactions to and from all required partners regardless of their legacy systems and document standards. This is true even if the respective partners use different operating systems and application solutions. This feature also facilitates the requirements of tracking the status and history of transactions.

The HIPAA Accelerator

The HIPAA Accelerator add-on to the Sybase EDI Server is strikingly similar to the BizTalk Accelerator for HIPAA. In fact, the underlying solution is really the same for both Sybase and Microsoft—start with an existing server application and augment it with HIPAA generic products. Both application giants provide documentation on the HIPAA X12 standards along the 12 transaction schemas, which are electronically imported to the server applications so users can map the required fields of the HIPAA transaction templates to their own transaction forms.

The Sybase HIPAA Studio uses ECMap to map the fields of the user agency transaction against the HIPAA X12 schema. The output, as with BizTalk, is an XML form, which is picked up by the processor engine.

Sybase markets their HIPAA Accelerator as a tool, which, in addition to facilitating HIPAA compliance, verifies compliance with the use of compliance checking maps.

The maps generated by HIPAA Studio enable an organization to process information following HIPAA's Transaction Rule requirements specified in the implementation guides.

"These maps are generated from within HIPAA Studio to verify conformity to the implementation guides. These are baseline compliance maps to which specific rules can be added. The rules further narrow down the implementation guides to allow for business logic and flow. Rules may be created, for example, to validate information such as member numbers, provider numbers, and dates of birth versus dates of service from a cross-reference table," (*Health Care Insurance Portability and Accountability Act (HIPAA): An Industry White Paper*).

Among the necessary functions of compliance map checking is the HIPAA mandated requirement that all Medicare intermediaries must obtain translators that validate the syntax compliance for the X12N 837 transactions, such as alpha numeric, field length, valid qualifiers, mandatory loops and segments, as well as appropriate segments within a given loop. These compliance-checking maps are the XLANG schedules generated by BizTalk Accelerator for HIPAA.

Sybase Enterprise Portal

Enterprise application really refers to distributing network capabilities over the Internet. In this way, the Internet functions as the connection between distributed workstations. This saves network managers the need to manage and control the delivery of network transactions and products. All they need to do is provide access to the Internet through an Internet server or gateway. Again, BizTalk Server achieves enterprise application technology by the integration of BizTalk Messaging Manager with Microsoft Application Center.

Sybase, on the other hand, does so by integrating the HIPAA Accelerator with its popular Enterprise Portal. The Enterprise Portal provides security for HIPAA compliance through encryption, single sign-on, authentication, and electronic signatures. For the purposes of this book, it is sufficient to understand that Enterprise Portal provides secure, efficient network connectivity through the use of Web pages.

EC Gateway

EC Gateway is an enterprise message management server. In the Sybase HIPAA Accelerator it integrates with ECRTP to provide a seamless message management solution designed for high volume environments. ECRTP can transform messages into any application-specific data format, and thus serves as the entry and departure points of HIPAA transaction processing.

EC Gateway can also interface directly with IBM MQSeries, so it can put and get data from a queue. And via ECRTP, EC Gateway is able to interface with e-Biz Integrator and MQSI. These capabilities allow implementation of a flexible solution to address a wide range of customer integration requirements.

Process Scripting

The process component is the heart of EC Gateway. Using a GUI, users can easily define a series of actions to be performed; this series is called a *process*. A process can trigger an array of powerful actions, including compliance checking; e-mail; encryption; fax; communications; and if/then/else, page, or message routing. Processes can be called from the scheduler.

Scheduler

Scheduler is a feature-rich component. Scheduler detects and executes based on file presence or change and job presence or absence. In addition, the scheduler can invoke a process or another program, permitting keystroke emulation for complete program execution.

Data Communication

The communication component enables users to set up complex communication paths with a large number of trading partners, utilizing the automated communication script recording features. Asynchronous and FTP communication protocols are supported. The EC Gateway provides connectivity to third-party software and secures SMTP communication. The EC Gateway can utilize the Internet to support trading partner to trading partner communication and VAN connectivity.

Mailbox Services

EC Gateway provides a flexible mailbox component. Mailboxes can be customized to meet your organizational needs. EC Gateway mailbox services permit both EDI and non-EDI messaging. Mailboxes can be configured to support internal and external messaging. Mailboxes can be unique to a trading partner or a communications path. In addition, mailboxes permit routing of EDI data.

Trading Partner Management

The trading partner component offers a full array of trading partner administration services that allow fast addition of new trading partners and modification of existing trading partners. The trading partner database can be maintained in any ODBC-compliant database. This open system enables users to access the trading partner database from their applications. The trading partner database is common to both EC Gateway and ECRTP, eliminating the need to develop a separate trading partner management system.

Log/Archive/Restore

These components support the auditing and archiving requirements of mission-critical production data. The log is an ODBC database that enables users to access the information from their applications. Information posted to the log allows for system activity reporting and error tracking. Archive allows users to save any file at any time into a user-specified location. Restore allows archived data to be restored to its original state for reprocessing, retransmission, or analysis.

Reporting

EC Gateway provides a comprehensive reporting component that utilizes all logged information. Management reports include activity reporting on a daily, monthly, or annual basis for all messages in the system. Exception reporting allows for easy isolation of errors in any phase of the message production process. Many other reports are available for operational and system definition documentation requirements.

Document Processing Path

Figure 5.17 depicts the process flow that carries a document from delivery to transmission in the Sybase HIPAA Accelerator. The process has two starting points. The EDI Server is initially invoked for the designing of a map, which will be used to match fields on the input transaction with the HIPAA X12 schema. This is indicated along the top of the flowchart. The output from the mapping process is an XML document describing the records and fields along with the processing steps.

The flow moves from the mapping process to the lower portion of the flowchart. The Sybase Server waits for the arrival of a document to process. The incoming document is converted from its original format into X12 EDI format. Then the document is sent to message queue where it waits to be processed. When the server allocates time for the processing of this document, it is first copied into the legacy database.

 NOTE

A *legacy database* is any database supported by the computer's operating system. In our analysis of the Sybase HIPAA Accelerator, we have not endorsed any specific application database.

After the contents of the document have been securely stored in the database, a copy is transferred to the ECRTP Engine. The engine then retrieves the appropriate map for processing the document.

After the document has been appropriately processed, its contents are updated in the database, and the outgoing message is sent to the message queue to await transmission to its recipient agencies.

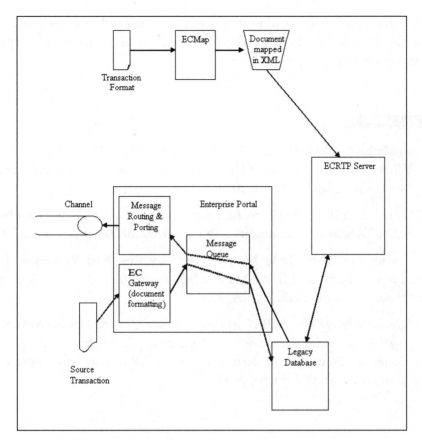

FIGURE 5.17 *The Sybase HIPAA Studio transaction handling process.*

Notice that the role of the Enterprise Portal is as a host to the EDI Server for the input and output functions of the message handling phase.

Figure 5.17 depicts the progression of a transaction from the point at which it enters the Sybase EDI Server until it leaves through a communication port.

Summary

This chapter described the application industry's solution to HIPAA compliance. Microsoft has produced its BizTalk Accelerator product specifically tailored for developing HIPAA transactions-related applications. Microsoft's BizTalk Accelerator for HIPAA is a powerful automation solution for quick deployment and seamless integration with existing information systems and business processes. Sybase has developed the Sybase HIPAA Studio a solution, which is not dependent on Windows-based systems.

References

Healthcare Insurance Portability and Accountability Act (HIPAA): An Industry White Paper. White paper by New Era of Networks, online Web-based documentation (http://www.sybase.com/products), 2002.

HIPAA Studio: HIPAA Accelerator and EDI Server. White Paper by New Era of Networks, online Web-based documentation (http://www.sybase.com/products), 2002.

Lowe, David, Xin Chen, Todd Mondor, Tomislav Rus, Ned Rynearson, Ben Smith, Steve Wright, and Tom Xu. *BizTalk Server, The Complete Reference:* Osborne/McGraw-Hill, Berkeley, CA, 2002.

Successfully Negotiating the HIPAA Maze, A Sybase, Inc. Healthcare Report on Complying with Administrative Simplification & Security Mandates. White paper by New Era of Networks, online Web-based documentation (http://www.sybase.com/products), 2002.

Lesson 6

**Getting Started
with HIPAA Privacy**

HIPAA

After reading this chapter you will be able to:

- Describe HIPAA Privacy Rule's administrative requirements
- Identify responsibilities of the Privacy Officer
- Examine the flow of PHI within and outside an organization
- Identify the steps involved in conducting an assessment and gap analysis
- Analyze the requirements for business associates and step through the model Business Associates Contract published by the Office for Civil Rights (OCR)
- Step through a scenario for compliance with the Privacy Rule for a small physician's or dentist's office
- Review sample privacy compliance documents such as Notice of Privacy Practices and Authorization
- Examine sample privacy policy documents

Administrative Requirements

In this section, we examine the administrative requirements that organizations need to review for compliance with the HIPAA Privacy Rule. We address requirements in the areas of assigned responsibility, policies and procedures, as well as safeguards for Protected Health Information (PHI).

The key steps that a business needs to consider to meet HIPAA Privacy Rule requirements are

- Administrative requirements
  - Assigned responsibility
  - Development of policies and procedures
  - Safeguards
  - Documentation

- Training
- Complaints
- Sanctions
- Mitigation
- No intimidation acts
- No waiver of rights
- Identify and assess organization PHI
- Analyze gaps in current policies
- Adjust organizational processes
- Negotiate Business Associate Contracts (BACs)

There are several administrative requirements that relate to the Privacy Rule. These include

- Assigned responsibility
  - Privacy Officer
  - Contact person for complaints
  - Development of policies and procedures
    - Notice of Privacy Practices
    - Consent (optional)
    - Authorization
- Safeguards
  - Administrative
  - Technical
  - Physical
- Documentation
  - Creation
  - Maintenance
- Training
  - Overview of HIPAA privacy requirements
  - Overview of HIPAA security requirements
  - PHI policies and procedures
- Complaints
  - Process
  - Documentation

◆ Sanctions
- Policy
- Documentation
◆ Mitigation
◆ No intimidation acts
◆ No waiver of rights

The following sections discuss these requirements in depth to further understand the core issues related to the identified areas.

Assigned Responsibility

An organization must designate a Privacy Officer and a contact person or office for complaints and the Notice of Privacy Practices.

Smaller organizations might assign these responsibilities to the same person, or these might be separate functions handled by different individuals in larger organizations. The Privacy Rule requires that one individual have principal privacy responsibility. This individual has a number of responsibilities, including identifying business associates and negotiating business associate contracts.

The contact person for complaints must be clearly identified in the Notice of Privacy Practices document. These designations must be documented in the organization's privacy policies and procedures manual.

Development of Policies and Procedures

The development of policies and procedures is required because these documents establish the framework for members of the workforce to be in compliance with the Privacy Rule. Keep in mind that if there is an audit or an investigation, then the privacy policies and procedures manual will be among the first things to be probed.

It is recommended that you consult with legal counsel on the development of the policies and agreements required by HIPAA.

The organization must develop Notice of Privacy Practices and clearly communicate information such as patient's rights, the point of contact for complaints, and details related to the use and disclosure of the patient data. Other documents that need to be developed include the Authorization form, as well as policies such as sanctions, termination, security, and others.

Safeguards

Complying with the safeguards requirements and minimum necessary requirements is required for the incidental use and disclosure permission contained in the final Privacy Rule. Overheard conversations are permitted if the incidental disclosure permission conditions are met.

The Privacy Rule provides that the organization must have appropriate administrative, technical, and physical safeguards to protect the privacy of PHI. The organization must reasonably safeguard PHI and make reasonable efforts to prevent any intentional or unintentional use or disclosure that is in violation of the Privacy Rule. HHS has indicated that these safeguards are intended to prevent uses and disclosures that are in violation of the Privacy Rule, as well as prevent accidental disclosures. Only intended individuals must have access to PHI information.

Documentation

The organization must initiate projects and activities for the creation and maintenance of HIPAA Privacy Rule–related documentation. The policies and procedures developed by the organization must be maintained in written or electronic form—we would recommend both. Where required by the legislation, communication must be in writing and procedures for the maintenance of such documentation need to be established. Organizations are required to maintain the records for six years from the date the record was created or the date when it was last in effect, whichever is later. Keep in mind that there are special documentation requirements for group health plans. The Secretary of HHS has the right to inspect records, thus you need to establish internal procedures for supporting such communications.

Training

An organization must train all members of its workforce on the policies and procedures related to PHI that are required by the HIPAA Privacy Rule—to the extent necessary and appropriate for the members of its workforce to carry out their functions. Training should be provided to each member of the workforce and completed no later than April 14, 2003. Members of the workforce include employees, volunteers, and trainees.

The training provided must address

◆ Privacy protections

◆ Security protections

◆ Organizations' privacy policies, procedures, and other documentation. such as those related to safeguards

One of the biggest challenges facing organizations is the delivery of training to all employees. Organizations need to be able to identify several different training options. The best way to get started is to deliver HIPAA Awareness training. Such training is a short one to two hour overview of the HIPAA legislation and its core requirements as it directly relates to the organization. This training may then be followed with more extensive training for all members of the HIPAA implementation team and others who may be involved with the initiatives within the enterprise. The organization must document that training has been provided. Although certification of skills and knowledge is not required, we strongly encourage the organization to consider all employees being certified with the objective of establishing PHI literacy. The goal is to have a minimal common body of knowledge across the enterprise as it directly relates to HIPAA, and certification is a way to validate skills.

The documentation of training delivered must be maintained for six years. The training must include information as it directly relates to the organization—such as the Notice of Privacy Practices and other forms created, list of business associates, and other agreements that may have been created.

Complaints

There are two key areas that need to be addressed in the context of individuals who might complain about the organizations' policies and procedures as required by the Privacy Rule. These are process and documentation.

The organization must designate a point of contact who will receive all complaints on its behalf. The Notice of Privacy Practices must specifically advise patients of their complaint rights under the Privacy Rule.

Sanctions

The organization must develop a sanctions policy that describes the specific actions against members of its workforce who fail to comply with internal policies and procedures. The organization must also document all information on sanctions that have been applied.

Mitigation

The organization must mitigate to the extent possible any harmful effect that it knows about, due to a use or disclosure of PHI in violation of its policies and procedures or requirements that have been established. Privacy breaches by a business associate may trigger the mitigation duties and responsibilities. Mitigation policies should include steps to remedy any harm caused by the mistake and further prevent that mistake from occurring again.

No Intimidation Acts

The organization cannot intimidate, threaten, coerce, discriminate against, or take other retaliatory action against any patient for the exercise of any right under the HIPAA Privacy Rule, including filing of a complaint.

This includes the organization not taking any action against any individual for filing a complaint, testifying, assisting with an investigation, or opposing any practice or act by the organization that would be regarded as unlawful by the HIPAA Privacy Rule legislation. This applies if the individual or person believes that the practice is unlawful, the manner of opposition is reasonable, and that the person's actions do not involve a disclosure of PHI in violation of the HIPAA Privacy Rule.

No Waiver of Rights

An organization may not require, as a condition of TPO or eligibility of benefits, that an individual waive his or her right to make complaints to the Secretary of HHS.

HIPAA Privacy Officer Responsibilities

The HIPAA Privacy Officer is responsible for overseeing all ongoing activities related to the development, implementation, maintenance, and adherence to the organization's policies and procedures covering the privacy of, and access to, all patient's PHI in compliance with federal and state laws and the health care organizations' information privacy practices. The HIPAA Privacy Officer typically reports to the individual responsible for compliance, Board of Directors, or Corporate compliance officer. A HIPAA Privacy Officer typically has knowledge and experience in information privacy laws, access, release of information, and release control technologies.

The responsibilities of a HIPAA Privacy Officer include

- Privacy policy development and implementation
- Maintenance of privacy policy

Both of these responsibilities are discussed in detail in the following sections.

Privacy Policy Development and Implementation

Compliance with the Privacy Rule requires the development of privacy policies as well as procedures. The Privacy Officer is typically involved in guiding the development effort of such policies and their implementation across the organization and has the following responsibilities.

- Provides development guidance and assists in the identification, implementation, and maintenance of privacy policies and procedures in coordination with organization management and administration and legal counsel
- Reviews all system-related information security plans throughout the organization's network to ensure alignment between security and privacy practices, and acts as a liaison to the information systems department
- Develops, reviews, and publishes the practice's privacy notice to the general public as required under federal and state law
- Conducts or ensures conduction of initial privacy training and orientation for all employees, volunteers, medical and professional staff, contractors, alliances, business associates, and other appropriate third parties

- Establishes and administers a process for receiving, documenting, tracking, investigating, and taking action on all complaints concerning the organization's privacy policies and procedures
- Establishes a mechanism to track access to protected health information within the organization to an extent as required by law

Key Responsibilities

The Privacy Officer leads an organization's compliance efforts in several areas, such as review and development of business associate contracts and risk assessment as well as reviews and investigations as required. In this section we review some key responsibilities of the Privacy Officer.

- Participates in the development, implementation, and ongoing compliance monitoring of all trading partner and business associate agreements to ensure all privacy concerns, requirements, and responsibilities are addressed
- Ensures compliance with privacy practices and consistent application of sanctions for failure to comply with privacy policies for all individuals in the organization's workforce, extended workforce, and for all business associates, in cooperation with Human Resources, the information security officer, administration, and legal counsel as applicable
- Performs initial and periodic risk assessments or "privacy audits" and conducts related ongoing compliance monitoring activities to ensure compliance
- Works with key departments to ensure the practice has and maintains appropriate privacy and confidentiality consent, authorization forms, information notices and materials reflecting current organization, and legal practices and requirements.
- Maintains current knowledge of applicable federal and state privacy laws and accreditation standards, and monitors advancements in information privacy technologies to ensure organizational adaptation and compliance
- Cooperates with the Office for Civil Rights, the HHS, other legal entities, and organization officers in any compliance reviews or investigations

Flow of PHI

As part of compliance efforts in meeting HIPAA regulation requirements, it is critical to identify and track the flow of PHI throughout the organization as well as identify other organizations that may come into contact with the enterprise PHI.

The areas that need to be reviewed closely include the following:

1. Defining exactly what Patient Identifiable Information (PII) is
   - How information is handled
     - Created
     - Modified
     - Reviewed
     - Transferred
     - Received from another department within the organization
     - Received from another organization
     - Disclosed to individuals/entities outside the enterprise
     - Maintained

2. Tracking the flow of PII
   - Creation of new information
     - What is created?
     - Who creates the information?
   - What is modified?
     - Who modifies the information?
   - What is reviewed?
     - Who reviewed the information?
     - What is the purpose of the review?
   - What information is transferred within the organization?
     - Who transfers the information?
     - How is the information transferred?
   - What information is received from within the organization?
     - Who receives it?
     - How is it received?
     - What is done with the information?

- ◆ What information is received from outside the organization?
  - Who receives it?
  - How is it received?
  - What is done with the information?
- ◆ From what other sources is information received?
  - What is received?
  - Who receives it?
  - How is it received?
  - What is done with the information?
- ◆ To what sources is information disclosed (outside the organization)?
  - Who is the person/organization to which information is disclosed?
  - What is released?
  - Who is releasing the information?
  - What is the purpose of the disclosure?
  - How is the information released?
  - How is the release/disclosure authorized?
  - Where is the information maintained?
  - How long is it maintained?
  - How is it discarded/destroyed?
- ◆ What information is maintained by the organization?
  - How is it maintained (in what format)?
  - Where is it maintained?
  - How long is it maintained?
  - How is it discarded/destroyed?

3. Aggregate patient data (grouped patient information/data that does not identify individual patients)
   - ◆ Does the organization handle aggregate patient data in any of the following ways?
     - Create new aggregate data
     - Review aggregate data by others
     - Transfer aggregate data to another department within the organization

- Receive aggregate data from another department within the organization
- Receive aggregate data from persons or entities outside the organization
- Disclose aggregate data to persons or entities outside the organization

◆ Create new aggregate data
  - What is created?
  - Who creates this information?

◆ Review aggregate data
  - What is reviewed?
  - Who reviews the information?
  - What is the purpose of the review?

◆ Transfer aggregate data to another department within the organization
  - What is transferred?
  - Who transfers it?
  - How is it transferred?

◆ Receive aggregate data from another department within the organization
  - What is received?
  - Who receives it?
  - How is it received?
  - What is done with the information?

◆ Receive aggregate data from persons or entities outside the organization
  - What is received?
  - Who receives it?
  - How is it received?
  - What is done with the information?

◆ Disclose aggregate data to persons or entities outside the organization
  - Who is the person/organization to which information is disclosed?
  - What is released?
  - Why is the information released?

- How is the information released?
- How is the release/disclosure authorized?
- Where is the information maintained?
- How long is it maintained?
- How is it discarded/destroyed?

Scenario: Releasing PHI to Third Parties

This scenario examines what happens when your organization receives a request for your patient's PHI from a third party. These are steps that need to be taken before PHI is released to third parties:

1. Receiving the request
2. Patient's permission
3. Review of information requested
4. Preparing information requested
5. Sending the information requested

Each of these steps is discussed in detail in the following sections.

Step 1: Receiving the Request

Upon receipt of a request for PHI the covered entity needs to use established written procedures and policies to verify the identity and authority of the requestor when the covered entity does not know the person requesting the PHI. For most disclosures, it is necessary to verify the authority for the request by taking reasonable steps to determine that the request is lawful.

Step 2: Patient's Permission

This is a critical step. Here verification needs to be made that the patient has provided the appropriate permissions for the information to be disclosed. If the reason for the request for PHI does not relate to TPO then the appropriate authorizations must be in place before any information may be disclosed.

Step 3: Review of Information Requested

Here the focus is on the minimum necessary element of the privacy rule. Generally, the information that needs to be disclosed should be limited to the information required for the third party to perform the activity or service. In some cases, it may be necessary for the Privacy Officer or the treating physician to review the information to verify that it meets the minimum necessary standard.

Keep in mind that an Authorization can override the minimum necessary standard. If the Authorization along with the request is for the entire medical record, then you can disclose the entire record.

Step 4: Preparing Information Requested

Your organization is responsible for making sure that disclosures are not made to unauthorized individuals or organizations. The procedures for disclosures should include steps that the staff is responsible for to make sure information will only be disclosed to the extent necessary to the permitted recipient.

If the disclosure is based on an Authorization from the patient then the Authorization should include information about where this disclosure needs to be sent. This information also should include a fax or mailing address of the permitted recipient.

Step 5: Sending the Information Requested

There are two key steps here that need to be verified:

- ◆ The requestor's identity and authority
- ◆ Limit the disclosure to the minimum necessary, if applicable

At this point the information may be sent. Upon sending this information, each disclosure needs to be documented and recorded.

Assessment and Gap Analysis

Assessment is a critical step towards establishing the foundation or baseline of information required for subsequent steps associated with HIPAA compliance projects. It provides a baseline, a foundation, of where the organization is and positions the enterprise for gap analysis. Assessment and gap analysis are typically the first two steps that any organization needs to complete before initiating any remediation initiatives. In this section we take a close look at key steps involved in assessment and gap analysis, with particular emphasis on identifying the flow of PHI within and outside the enterprise.

Assessment

At a high level there are a number of critical areas that need to be investigated during the process of an assessment. These areas include

- ◆ Summary of business scope and objectives
- ◆ Identification of business policies, risks, and vulnerabilities
- ◆ Inventory of infrastructure technology
- ◆ Assessment of business and technical skills, capabilities, and limitations

For example, the area of security assessment is the first critical step towards managing HIPAA compliance and enterprise security and maintaining a corporate security policy that addresses threats to business assets and resources.

The assessment initiative result in interviews with key managers and staff members at your organization to understand what policies and controls may be in place.

An assessment report typically includes information that addresses the following areas:

- ◆ Review of the organizations
  - • Policies
  - • Documents
  - • Practices
  - • Procedures
- ◆ Flow of PHI
- ◆ Review of contracts
- ◆ Review of communication programs

The assessment phase will require the organization to review closely the internal and external flow of PHI, which is then analyzed in the gap analysis phase. The assessment phase also results in a complete inventory of existing policies, documents, practices, and procedures. Finally, the assessment phase results in identifying and documenting all key elements of the organization's technical infrastructure.

Gap Analysis

After assessment, gap analysis is the next step that any organization working to be compliant with the HIPAA regulations will need to execute. Gap analysis provides information about the level of compliance with each applicable requirement of HIPAA's Privacy Rule. It identifies the policies, documents, practices, and procedures that meet these requirements as well as the policies, documents, practices, and procedures that do not meet the HIPAA Privacy Rule requirements. The gap analysis information can then be used to prioritize HIPAA compliance initiatives.

A gap analysis report typically includes information that addresses the following areas:

- Comparison of the organization's practices to HIPAA requirements in the areas of
  - Use and disclosure
  - Business associates
  - Minimum necessary
  - Administration, enforcement, and complaint process
  - Individual rights
  - Special requirements
- Identification of compliant and non-compliant
  - Policies
  - Documents
  - Practices
  - Procedures
- Recommendations
  - Strategic framework
  - Priorities
  - Implementation challenges

Gap analysis is preceded by a site assessment and followed by remediation initiatives to close gaps that have been identified. The process of conducting the gap analysis will lead to several interviews and review of current policies and documents.

Table 6.1 provides a template that may be used for capturing and recording information related to critical privacy and security areas.

Table 6.1   HIPAA Privacy Gap Analysis

#	Item	PHI Info	Location	Gap Info	Gap Status	Policy Impact	Resolution	Date
1.								
2.								
3.								
4.								
5.								

The column on Gap Status may have the following responses:

♦ Yes

♦ No

♦ Partial

♦ NA

The Gap Status response is based on that particular item's status with require-ments defined in the HIPAA Privacy Rule. The Policy Impact column captures information if this item requires a change to HIPAA-related policies. The Reso-lution column is useful for determining the full scope of remediation projects that may need to be launched as a result of gaps that have been identified.

This document next needs to be prioritized based on business needs and available resources.

Gap analysis is a qualitative process where certain results may be subjective. Judgment is an important part of the process.

Business Associates

The term business associates refers to organizations or entities that are involved in services that require the disclosure of PHI to the service provider. There are a few key steps that an organization must follow to address the Privacy Rule requirements related to business associates. First, the organization needs to identify the entities that are business associates.

There are two questions that need to be asked as you determine which organizations are possibly business associates of the enterprise:

◆ Does the entity provide services for your organization?

◆ Does all such service performed require access to PHI?

An example is a billing service that submits claims to insurance carriers.

Once you have determined the list of business associates that meets the criteria defined, the next step is to establish appropriate assurances in the written agreement. The Business Associate Contract (BAC) should address the following key points:

◆ Limit use and disclosures of PHI as permitted by state or federal law

◆ Limit the use and disclosure of PHI to terms of the contract

◆ Bind all business associate agents and subcontractors to the contract

◆ Business associates must report all unauthorized uses and disclosures to your organization

◆ Your organization must be permitted to take "reasonable steps" to correct any misuse of PHI, including canceling the contract without penalty

All Business Associate Contracts (BACs) must be stored safely as they may be required for audit or other compliance activities.

The final phase of addressing business associates is to monitor their performance. Your organization needs to be sure that if business associates disclose PHI without proper authorization, then you are positioned to take reasonable steps to correct the misuse. Keep in mind that in determining if a covered entity is properly monitoring business associates, HHS will consider if a reasonable person should have known of any inappropriate disclosures.

It is the responsibility of the Privacy Officer to determine new relationships with entities that may be business associate relationships and then require them to enter into a Business Associate Contract. The Privacy Officer must review all BACs.

Business Associate Contracts

Business Associates Contracts address the core issue of protecting a patient's privacy of his or PHI. Key sections of the Business Associate Contract (BAC) are

- ◆ The business associate agrees to protect PHI
- ◆ Assurances to provider that the business associate
  - Will not use or disclose PHI information except as provided in contract
  - Agreement applies to subcontractors and other entities that access PHI
  - Has met minimum safeguards to protect unauthorized use or disclosure
  - Will report any instance of misuse or unauthorized disclosure
  - Will communicate any alteration to PHI to provider
  - Knows that termination of the BAC results in return or destruction of PHI information
  - Knows that if there is a violation, then provider may inform HHS or other federal or state agencies
  - Is aware that HHS or its agent may inspect practices, policies, and documents related to PHI
- ◆ Policies and procedures meet minimum privacy and security standards defined

Model Business Associate Contract Provisions

The Department of Health and Human Services provides these model Business Associate Contract provisions in response to numerous requests for guidance. This is only model language. These provisions are designed to help covered entities more easily comply with the Business Associate Contract requirements of the Privacy Rule. However, use of these model provisions is not required for compliance with the Privacy Rule. The language may be amended to more accurately reflect business arrangements between the covered entity and the business associate.

These or similar provisions may be incorporated into an agreement for the provision of services between the entities, or they may be incorporated into a separate business associate agreement. These provisions only address concepts and requirements set forth in the Privacy Rule and alone are not sufficient to result in a binding contract under state law and do not include many formalities and substantive provisions that are required or typically included in a valid contract. Reliance on this model is not sufficient for compliance with state law and does not replace consultation with a lawyer or negotiations between the parties to the contract.

Furthermore, a covered entity may want to include other provisions that are related to the Privacy Rule but that are not required by the Privacy Rule. For example, a covered entity may want to add provisions in a Business Associate Contract for the covered entity to be able to rely on the business associate to help the covered entity meet its obligations under the Privacy Rule. In addition, there may be permissible uses or disclosures by a business associate that are not specifically addressed in these model provisions. For example, the Privacy Rule does not preclude a business associate from disclosing protected health information to report unlawful conduct in accordance with Sec. 164.502(j). However, there is not a specific model provision related to this permissive disclosure. These and other types of issues need to be worked out between the parties. The Privacy Officers from both organizations, the covered entity, and the business associate need to identify in as much clarity as possible the handling of PHI while in the possession of the business associate. This will include provisions if the business associate becomes aware of any type of violation, for example.

Words or phrases contained in brackets are intended as either optional language or as instructions to the users of these model provisions and are not intended to be included in the contractual provisions.

Definitions (Alternative Approaches)

Catch-all Definition

Terms used, but not otherwise defined, in this Agreement shall have the same meaning as those terms in 45 CFR 160.103 and 164.501.

Examples of specific definitions:

(a) **Business Associate.** *Business Associate* shall mean [Insert Name of Business Associate].

(b) **Covered Entity.** *Covered Entity* shall mean [Insert Name of Covered Entity].

(c) **Individual.** *Individual* shall have the same meaning as the term *individual* in 45 CFR 164.501 and shall include a person who qualifies as a personal representative in accordance with 45 CFR 164.502(g).

(d) **Privacy Rule.** *Privacy Rule* shall mean the Standards for Privacy of Individually Identifiable Health Information at 45 CFR part 160 and part 164, subparts A and E.

(e) **Protected Health Information.** *Protected Health Information* shall have the same meaning as the term *protected health information* in 45 CFR 164.501, limited to the information created or received by Business Associate from or on behalf of Covered Entity.

(f) **Required By Law.** *Required By Law* shall have the same meaning as the term *required by law* in 45 CFR 164.501.

(g) **Secretary.** *Secretary* shall mean the Secretary of the Department of Health and Human Services or his designee.

Obligations and Activities of Business Associate

(a) Business Associate agrees to not use or further disclose Protected Health Information other than as permitted or required by the Agreement or as Required By Law.

(b) Business Associate agrees to use appropriate safeguards to prevent use or disclosure of the Protected Health Information other than as provided for by this Agreement.

(c) Business Associate agrees to mitigate, to the extent practicable, any harmful effect that is known to Business Associate of a use or disclosure of Protected Health Information by Business Associate in violation of the requirements of this Agreement. [This provision may be included if it is appropriate for the Covered Entity to pass on its duty to mitigate damages by a Business Associate.]

(d) Business Associate agrees to report to Covered Entity any use or disclosure of the Protected Health Information not provided for by this Agreement.

(e) Business Associate agrees to ensure that any agent, including a subcontractor, to whom it provides Protected Health Information received from, or created or received by Business Associate on behalf of Covered Entity, agrees to the same restrictions and conditions that apply through this Agreement to Business Associate with respect to such information.

(f) Business Associate agrees to provide access, at the request of Covered Entity, and in the time and manner designated by Covered Entity, to Protected Health Information in a Designated Record Set to Covered Entity or, as directed by Covered Entity, to an Individual to meet the requirements under 45 CFR 164.524. [Not necessary if business associate does not have protected health information in a designated record set.]

(g) Business Associate agrees to make any amendment(s) to Protected Health Information in a Designated Record Set that the Covered Entity directs or agrees to pursuant to 45 CFR 164.526 at the request of Covered Entity or an Individual, and in the time and manner designated by Covered Entity. [Not necessary if business associate does not have protected health information in a designated record set.]

(h) Business Associate agrees to make internal practices, books, and records relating to the use and disclosure of Protected Health Information received from, or created or received by Business Associate on behalf of, Covered Entity available to the Covered Entity, or at the request of the Covered Entity to the Secretary, in a time and manner designated by the Covered Entity or the Secretary, for purposes of the Secretary determining Covered Entity's compliance with the Privacy Rule.

(i) Business Associate agrees to document such disclosures of Protected Health Information and information related to such disclosures as would be required for Covered Entity to respond to a request by an Individual for an accounting of disclosures of Protected Health Information in accordance with 45 CFR 164.528.

(j) Business Associate agrees to provide to Covered Entity or an Individual, in time and manner designated by Covered Entity, information collected in accordance with Section [Insert Section Number in Contract Where Provision (i) Appears] of this Agreement, to permit Covered Entity to respond to a request by an Individual for an accounting of disclosures of Protected Health Information in accordance with 45 CFR 164.528.

Permitted Uses and Disclosures by Business Associate

General Use and Disclosure Provisions (alternative approaches)

Specify Purposes:

Except as otherwise limited in this Agreement, Business Associate may use or disclose Protected Health Information on behalf of, or to provide services to, Covered Entity for the following purposes, if such use or disclosure of Protected Health Information would not violate the Privacy Rule if done by Covered Entity: [List Purposes.]

Refer to Underlying Services Agreement:

Except as otherwise limited in this Agreement, Business Associate may use or disclose Protected Health Information to perform functions, activities, or services for, or on behalf of, Covered Entity as specified in [Insert Name of Services Agreement], provided that such use or disclosure would not violate the Privacy Rule if done by Covered Entity.

Specific Use and Disclosure Provisions [only necessary if parties wish to allow Business Associate to engage in such activities]

(a) Except as otherwise limited in this Agreement, Business Associate may use Protected Health Information for the proper management and administration of the Business Associate or to carry out the legal responsibilities of the Business Associate.

(b) Except as otherwise limited in this Agreement, Business Associate may disclose Protected Health Information for the proper management and administration of the Business Associate, provided that disclosures are required by law, or Business Associate obtains reasonable assurances from the person to whom the information is disclosed that it will remain confidential and used or further disclosed only as required by law or for the purpose for which it was disclosed to the person, and the person notifies the Business Associate of any instances of which it is aware in which the confidentiality of the information has been breached.

(c) Except as otherwise limited in this Agreement, Business Associate may use Protected Health Information to provide Data Aggregation services to Covered Entity as permitted by 42 CFR 164.504(e) (2) (i) (B).

Obligations of Covered Entity

Provisions for Covered Entity to Inform Business Associate of Privacy Practices and Restrictions [provisions dependent on business arrangement].

(a) Covered Entity shall provide Business Associate with the notice of privacy practices that Covered Entity produces in accordance with 45 CFR 164.520, as well as any changes to such notice.

(b) Covered Entity shall provide Business Associate with any changes in, or revocation of, permission by Individual to use or disclose Protected Health Information, if such changes affect Business Associate's permitted or required uses and disclosures.

(c) Covered Entity shall notify Business Associate of any restriction to the use or disclosure of Protected Health Information that Covered Entity has agreed to in accordance with 45 CFR 164.522.

Permissible Requests by Covered Entity

Covered Entity shall not request Business Associate to use or disclose Protected Health Information in any manner that would not be permissible under the Privacy Rule if done by Covered Entity. [Include an exception if the Business Associate will use or disclose protected health information for, and the contract includes provisions for, data aggregation or management and administrative activities of Business Associate.]

Term and Termination

(a) **Term.** The Term of this Agreement shall be effective as of [Insert Effective Date], and shall terminate when all of the Protected Health Information provided by Covered Entity to Business Associate, or created or received by Business Associate on behalf of Covered Entity, is destroyed or returned to Covered Entity, or, if it is infeasible to return or destroy Protected Health Information, protections are extended to such information, in accordance with the termination provisions in this Section.

(b) **Termination for Cause.** Upon Covered Entity's knowledge of a material breach by Business Associate, Covered Entity shall provide an opportunity for Business Associate to cure the breach or end the violation and terminate this Agreement [and the _____ Agreement/sections _____ of the _____ Agreement] if Business Associate does not cure the breach or end the violation within the time specified by Covered Entity, or immediately terminate this Agreement [and the _____ Agreement/sections _____ of the _____ Agreement] if Business Associate has breached a material term of this Agreement and cure is not possible. [Bracketed language in this provision may be necessary if there is an underlying services agreement. Also, opportunity to cure is permitted, but not required by the Privacy Rule.]

(c) **Effect of Termination.** (1) Except as provided in paragraph (2) of this section (c), upon termination of this Agreement, for any reason, Business Associate shall return or destroy all Protected Health Information received from Covered Entity, or created or received by Business Associate on behalf of Covered Entity. This provision shall apply to Protected Health Information that is in the possession of subcontractors or agents of Business Associate. Business Associate shall retain no copies of the Protected Health Information.

(2) In the event that Business Associate determines that returning or destroying the Protected Health Information is infeasible, Business Associate shall provide to Covered Entity notification of the conditions that make return or destruction infeasible. Upon mutual agreement of the Parties that return or destruction of Protected Health Information is infeasible, Business Associate shall extend the protections of this Agreement to such Protected Health Information and limit further uses and disclosures of such

Protected Health Information to those purposes that make the return or destruction infeasible, for so long as Business Associate maintains such Protected Health Information.

Miscellaneous

(a) **Regulatory References.** A reference in this Agreement to a section in the Privacy Rule means the section as in effect or as amended, and for which compliance is required.

(b) **Amendment.** The Parties agree to take such action as is necessary to amend this Agreement from time to time as is necessary for Covered Entity to comply with the requirements of the Privacy Rule and the Health Insurance Portability and Accountability Act, Public Law 104-191.

(c) **Survival.** The respective rights and obligations of Business Associate under Section [Insert Section Number Related to "Effect of Termination"] of this Agreement shall survive the termination of this Agreement.

(d) **Interpretation.** Any ambiguity in this Agreement shall be resolved in favor of a meaning that permits Covered Entity to comply with the Privacy Rule.

Sample Business Associate Terms Rider

This Business Associates Terms Rider is included here for reference purposes only. It is a draft document. Please consult a legal professional for the development of a Business Associates Contract that meets the requirements for your business or organization. It originated from the State of Oregon Department of Human Services.

BUSINESS ASSOCIATE TERMS RIDER

This Business Associate Terms Rider ("Rider") amends and supplements that certain _____ contract no. _____ [insert name and contract number of underlying services contract] ("Agreement") between _____("Agency") and _____("Contractor").

RECITALS

A. Contractor uses and/or discloses Protected Health Information in the performance of its obligations under the Agreement; and

B. The Health Insurance Portability and Accountability Act of 1996, Public Law 104-191 ("HIPAA") and its implementing Privacy Rule, 45 CFR Parts 160 and 164, require that Agency, as a Covered Entity, obtain satisfactory assurances from its business associates, as that term is defined in the Privacy Rule, that they will comply with the business associate requirements set forth in 45 CFR 164.502(e) and 164.504(e). Contractor (hereafter "Business Associate") is a business associate of Agency and desires to provide such assurances with respect to the performance of its obligations under the Agreement; and

C. Both Agency and Business Associate are committed to current and future compliance with the standards set forth in the Privacy Rule, as it may be amended from time to time, in the performance of their obligations under the Agreement.

NOW, THEREFORE, for mutual and valuable consideration, the parties agree as follows:

AGREEMENT

The parties agree that the following terms and conditions shall apply to the performance of their obligations under the Agreement, effective April 14, 2003. Capitalized terms used, but not otherwise defined in this Rider, shall have the same meaning as those terms in the Privacy Rule.

1. SERVICES. Pursuant to the Agreement, Business Associate provides certain services for or on behalf of Agency, as described in the Agreement, that involve the use and disclosure of Protected Health Information. Business Associate may make use of Protected Health Information to perform those services if authorized in the Agreement and not otherwise limited or prohibited by this Rider, the Privacy Rule, and other applicable federal or state laws or regulations. All other uses of Protected Health Information are prohibited.

2. OBLIGATIONS AND ACTIVITIES OF BUSINESS ASSOCIATE.

(a) Business Associate agrees to not use or disclose Protected Health Information other than as permitted or required by the Agreement as amended by this Rider, as permitted by the Privacy Rule, or as Required By Law.

(b) Business Associate agrees to use appropriate safeguards to prevent use or disclosure of the Protected Health Information other than as provided for by the Agreement, as amended by this Rider.

(c) Business Associate agrees to mitigate, to the extent practicable, any harmful effect that is known to Business Associate of a use or disclosure of Protected Health Information by Business Associate in violation of the requirements of the Agreement, as amended by this Rider.

(d) Business Associate agrees to report to Agency, as promptly as possible, any use or disclosure of the Protected Health Information not provided for by the Agreement, as amended by this Rider, of which it becomes aware.

(e) Business Associate agrees to ensure that any agent, including a subcontractor, to whom it provides Protected Health Information received from, or created or received by Business Associate on behalf of Agency, agrees to the same restrictions and conditions that apply through the Agreement, as amended by this Rider, to Business Associate with respect to such information.

(f) Business Associate agrees to provide access, at the request of Agency, and in the time and manner designated by Agency, to Protected Health Information in a Designated Record Set, to Agency or, as directed by Agency, to an Individual in order to meet the requirements under 45 CFR 164.524.

(g) Business Associate agrees to make any amendment(s) to Protected Health Information in a Designated Record Set that the Agency directs or agrees to pursuant to 45 CFR 164.526 at the request of Agency or an Individual, and in the time and manner designated by Agency.

(h) Business Associate agrees to make internal practices, books, and records, including policies and procedures and Protected Health Information, relating to the use and disclosure of Protected Health Information received from, or created or received by Business Associate on behalf of Agency, available to Agency or to the Secretary, in a time and manner designated by Agency or the Secretary, for purposes of the Secretary determining Agency's compliance with the Privacy Rule.

(i) Business Associate agrees to document such disclosures of Protected Health Information and information related to such disclosures as would be required for Agency to respond to a request by an Individual for an accounting of disclosures of Protected Health Information in accordance with 45 CFR 164.528.

(j) Business Associate agrees to provide to Agency or an Individual, in time and manner to be designated by Agency, information collected in accordance with Section 2(i) of this Rider, to permit Agency to respond to a request by an Individual for an accounting of disclosures of Protected Health Information in accordance with 45 CFR 164.528.

3. PERMITTED USES AND DISCLOSURES BY BUSINESS ASSOCIATE.

(a) **General Use and Disclosure Provisions.** Except as otherwise limited or prohibited by this Rider, Business Associate may use or disclose Protected Health Information to perform functions, activities, or services for, or on behalf of, Agency as specified in the Agreement and this Rider, provided that such use or disclosure would not violate the Privacy Rule if done by Agency or the minimum necessary policies and procedures of Agency.

(b) **Specific Use and Disclosure Provisions.**

(1) Except as otherwise limited in this Rider, Business Associate may use Protected Health Information for the proper management and administration of the Business Associate or to carry out the legal responsibilities of the Business Associate.

(2) Except as otherwise limited in this Rider, Business Associate may disclose Protected Health Information for the proper management and administration of the Business Associate, provided that disclosures are Required By Law, or Business Associate obtains reasonable assurances from the person to whom the information is

disclosed that it will remain confidential and used or further disclosed only as Required By Law or for the purpose for which it was disclosed to the person, and the person notifies the Business Associate of any instances of which it is aware in which the confidentiality of the information has been breached.

(3) Business Associate may use Protected Health Information to report violations of law to appropriate Federal and State authorities, consistent with 45 CFR 164.502(j)(1).

(4) Business Associate may not aggregate or compile Agency's Protected Health Information with the Protected Health Information of other Covered Entities unless the Agreement permits Business Associate to perform Data Aggregation services. If the Agreement permits Business Associate to provide Data Aggregation services, Business Associate may use Protected Health Information to provide the Data Aggregation services requested by Agency as permitted by 45 CFR 164.504(e)(2)(i)(B), subject to any limitations contained in this Rider. If Data Aggregation services are requested by Agency, Business Associate is authorized to aggregate Agency's Protected Health Information with Protected Heath Information of other Covered Entities that the Business Associate has in its possession through its capacity as a Business Associate to such other Covered Entities provided that the purpose of such aggregation is to provide Agency with data analysis relating to the Health Care Operations of Agency. Under no circumstances may Business Associate disclose Protected Health Information of Agency to another Covered Entity absent the express authorization of Agency.

4. OBLIGATIONS OF AGENCY.

(a) Agency shall notify Business Associate of any limitation(s) in its notice of privacy practices of Agency in accordance with 45 CFR 164.520, to the extent that such limitation may affect Business Associate's use or disclosure of Protected Health Information. Agency may satisfy this obligation by providing Business Associate with Agency's most current Notice of Privacy Practices.

(b) Agency shall notify Business Associate of any changes in, or revocation of, permission by Individual to use or disclose Protected Health Information, to the extent that such changes may affect Business Associate's use or disclosure of Protected Health Information.

(c) Agency shall notify Business Associate of any restriction to the use or disclosure of Protected Health Information that Agency has agreed to in accordance with

45 CFR 164.522, to the extent that such restriction may affect Business Associate's use or disclosure of Protected Health Information.

5. PERMISSIBLE REQUESTS BY AGENCY.

Agency shall not request Business Associate to use or disclose Protected Health Information in any manner that would not be permissible under the Privacy Rule if done by Agency, except as permitted by Section 3(b) above.

6. TERM AND TERMINATION.

Effective Date; Term. This Rider shall be effective on the later of (i) the date on which all parties have executed it and all necessary approvals have been granted, or (ii) April 14, 2003. This Rider shall terminate on the earlier of (i) the date of termination of the Agreement, or (ii) the date on which termination of the Rider is effective under Section 6(b).

Termination for Cause. In addition to any other rights or remedies provided to Agency in the Agreement, upon Agency's knowledge of a material breach by Business Associate of Business Associate's obligations under this Rider, Agency shall either:

(1) Notify Business Associate of the breach and specify a reasonable opportunity in the Notice for Business Associate to cure the breach or end the violation, and terminate the Agreement and this Rider if Business Associate does not cure the breach of the terms of this Rider or end the violation within the time specified by Agency;

(2) Immediately terminate the Agreement and this Rider if Business Associate has breached a material term of this Rider and cure is not possible in Agency's reasonable judgment; or

(3) If neither termination nor cure is feasible, Agency shall report the violation to the Secretary.

(4) The rights and remedies provided in this Rider are in addition to any rights and remedies provided in the Agreement.

Effect of Termination.

(1) Except as provided in paragraph (2) of this Section, upon termination of the Agreement and this Rider, for any reason, Business Associate shall, at Agency's option, return or destroy all Protected Health Information received from Agency, or created or received by Business Associate on behalf of Agency. This provision shall

apply to Protected Health Information that is in the possession of subcontractors or agents of Business Associate. Business Associate shall retain no copies of the Protected Health Information.

(2) In the event that Business Associate determines that returning or destroying the Protected Health Information is infeasible, Business Associate shall provide to Agency notification of the conditions that make return or destruction infeasible. Upon Agency's written acknowledgement that return or destruction of Protected Health Information is infeasible, Business Associate shall extend the protections of this Rider to such Protected Health Information and limit further uses and disclosures of such Protected Health Information to those purposes that make the return or destruction infeasible, for so long as Business Associate maintains such Protected Health Information.

7. MISCELLANEOUS.

(a) **Regulatory References.** A reference in this Rider to a section in the Privacy Rule means the section as in effect or as amended.

(b) **Amendment; Waiver.** The Parties agree to take such action as is necessary to amend the Agreement and this Rider from time to time as is necessary for Agency to comply with the requirements of the Privacy Rule and HIPAA. No provision hereof shall be deemed waived unless in writing, duly signed by authorized representatives of the parties. A waiver with respect to one event shall not be construed as continuing, or as a bar to or waiver of any other right or remedy under this Rider.

(c) **Survival.** The respective rights and obligations of Business Associate under Section 6(c), this Section 7(c), Section 7(e) and Section 7(f) of this Rider shall survive the termination of the Agreement and this Rider.

(d) **Interpretation; Order of Precedence.** Any ambiguity in this Rider or the Agreement shall be resolved to permit Agency to comply with the Privacy Rule. The terms of this Rider amend and supplement the terms of the Agreement, and whenever possible, all terms and conditions in this Rider and the Agreement are to be harmonized. In the event of a conflict between the terms of this Rider and the terms of the Agreement, the terms of this Rider shall control; provided, however, that this Rider shall not supercede any other federal or state law or regulation governing the legal relationship of the parties, or the confidentiality of records or information, except to the extent that HIPAA preempts those laws or regulations. In the event of any conflict between the provisions of the Agreement (as amended by this Rider) and the Privacy Rule, the Privacy Rule shall control.

(e) **Indemnity.** In addition to any other indemnification obligations imposed on Business Associate in the Agreement, Business Associate shall defend, save, hold harmless, and indemnify the Organization and their officers, employees and agents from and against all claims, suits, actions, losses, damages, liabilities, costs and expenses of any nature whatsoever resulting from, arising out of, or relating to the activities of Business Associate or its officers, employees, subcontractors, or agents under this Rider. Business Associate shall have control of the defense and settlement of the claim, but neither Business Associate nor any attorney engaged by Business Associate shall defend the claim in the name of the State or Agency, nor purport to act as legal representative of the Organization, without the prior written consent of the Organization's Legal Counsel. The Organization may, at its election and expense, assume its own defense and settlement in the event that it determines that Business Associate is prohibited from defending the Organization, Business Associate is not adequately defending the Organization's interests, an important governmental principle is at issue or it is in the best interests of the Organization to do so.

(f) **No Third-Party Beneficiaries.** Agency and Business Associate are the only parties to this Rider and are the only parties entitled to enforce its terms. Nothing in this Rider gives, is intended to give, or shall be construed to give or provide any benefit or right, whether directly, indirectly, or otherwise, to third persons unless such third persons are individually identified by name herein and expressly described as intended beneficiaries of the terms of this Rider.

(g) **Time is of the Essence.** Agency agrees that time is of the essence under this Rider.

(h) **Successors and Assigns.** The provisions of this Rider and the Agreement shall be binding upon and shall inure to the benefit of the parties hereto and their respective successors and permitted assigns, if any.

(i) **Compliance With Applicable Law.** Business Associate shall comply with all federal, state, and local laws, regulations, executive orders and ordinances applicable to Agreement. Without limiting the generality of the foregoing, Business Associate expressly agrees to comply with the following laws, regulations, and executive orders, as they may be amended from time to time during the term of this Rider and the Agreement, to the extent they are applicable to this Rider and the Agreement:

(i) Titles VI and VII of the Civil Rights Act of 1964, as amended; (ii) Sections 503 and 504 of the Rehabilitation Act of 1973, as amended; (iii) the Americans with Disabilities Act of 1990, as amended; (iv) Executive Order 11246, as amended; (v) The Age Discrimination in Employment Act of 1967, as amended, and the Age Discrimination Act of 1975, as amended; (vi) The Vietnam Era Veterans' Readjustment Assistance Act of 1974, as amended; (vii) Title II, Subtitle F of the Health Insurance Portability and Accountability Act of 1996; (viii) ORS Chapter 659, as amended; (ix) all regulations and administrative rules established pursuant to the foregoing laws; and (x) all other applicable requirements of federal and state civil rights and rehabilitation statutes, rules and regulations. These laws, regulations, and executive orders are incorporated by reference herein to the extent that they are applicable to this Rider and the Agreement and required by law to be so incorporated. Agency's performance under this Rider and the Agreement is conditioned upon Business Associate's compliance with the provisions of ORS 279.312, 279.314, 279.316 and 279.320 which are incorporated by reference herein.

(j) **Independent Contractor.** Business Associate will function as an independent contractor and shall not be considered an employee of Agency for any purpose. Nothing in this Rider shall be interpreted as authorizing Business Associate or its agent and/or employees to act as an agent or representative for or on behalf of Agency.

(k) **Notices.** Any notices between the parties or notices to be given under this Rider shall be given in writing by personal or overnight courier delivery, or by mailing by certified mail with return receipt requested, to Business Associate or to Agency, to the addresses given for each below or to the address either party hereafter gives to the other. Any notice so addressed and mailed shall be deemed given five (5) days after mailing. Any notice delivered by personal or overnight courier delivery shall be deemed given upon receipt.

If to Business Associate, to: If to Agency, to:

_____   _____

_____   _____

_____   _____

Attention: _____   Attention: _____

Fax: _____   Fax: _____

Each party may change its address and fax number by giving notice thereof in the manner provided in this Rider.

(l) **Counterparts.** This Rider may be executed in any number of counterparts, each of which shall be deemed an original. Facsimile copies hereof shall be deemed to be originals.

(m) **Tax Compliance.** The individual signing below on behalf of Business Associate hereby certifies and swears under penalty of perjury that s/he is authorized to act on behalf of Business Associate, s/he has authority and knowledge regarding Business Associate's payment of taxes, and to the best of her/his knowledge, Business Associate is not in violation of any State tax laws.

(n) **Except As Amended.** Except as amended by this Rider, all terms and conditions of the Agreement shall remain in full force and effect.

8. SIGNATURES.

By signing this Rider, the parties certify that they have read and understood this Rider, that they agree to be bound by the terms of this Rider and the Agreement, as amended, and that they have the authority to sign this Rider.

AGENCY:

_____

By: _____

Title: _____

Date: _____

BUSINESS ASSOCIATE:

_____

By: _____

Title: _____

Date: _____

Physician's/Dentist's Office Scenario

Health care transactions performed by a physician or dentist's office include eligibility request/response and claim submission. This scenario describes some key steps for a small physician's office or a dentist's office to comply with HIPAA's Privacy Rule requirements.

There are five key steps involved for a physician's/dentist's office to comply with the Privacy Rule. Each is discussed in detail in the following sections:

1. Site assessment
2. Gap analysis
3. Remediation
4. Policies and procedures
5. Certification
6. Computer requirements
7. Fax requirements

Site Assessment

The objective of the site assessment step is to gather detailed information about the physician's facilities and operations practices. Information collected includes

- Total square footage
- Number of patient rooms
- Sites where diagnostics are performed
- Number of computer systems
- Types of software and applications installed

This process is repeated for each facility, then an inspection and audit needs to be done of the following areas:

- Records storage
- Record transmission
- Records disposition
- Computer systems and their usage and applications

- Policies and procedures
- Forms and paperwork
- Labs and diagnostic facilities
- Patient privacy
- Reception areas

Gap Analysis

The information determined from the site assessment step is now analyzed and interpreted. The analysis process may take one to three weeks depending on the size and scale of operations at the physician's office. The information collected from the physician's office is mapped and compared to the rules defined in HIPAA regulations. The result is a gap analysis report that is prioritized and details all gaps identified. Thus, it is possible to see the gaps graded based on priority for compliance.

The gap analysis report is then typically discussed, with the Physician and the Office Manager being involved in the process. Compliance issues are determined and remedial actions identified as the next steps in the compliance process.

Remediation

Remediation is the process of bringing gaps, which have been identified, into compliance. Remediation may take several weeks to several months depending on the tasks and complexities involved.

Policies and Procedures

The Policy and Procedures Manual is a critical element of any HIPAA Compliance Program. HIPAA Regulations require a Policies, Procedures, and Related Forms Manual in every HIPAA-regulated practice. The key documents that HHS's Office for Civil Rights HIPAA Agents are looking for if there is an audit are the Policies and Procedures Manual and the Notice of Privacy Policies for Patients. The Physician's practice needs to develop the Policy and Procedures Manual so that this can serve as an internal reference, as well in case there is an audit.

Certification

Once all gaps have been remediated there needs to be final assessment of the privacy policies and procedures to make sure that the practice is in compliance. All gaps identified in the gap analysis report are inspected and examined. If all gaps have been closed and recommendations in the report implemented, then the site can be confident that it has met the requirements for HIPAA's Privacy Rule.

After performing site assessment and inventory, your team will compare the existing conditions with the HIPAA mandates—a gap analysis. Shortly after starting gap analysis, the team will likely identify gaps in the existing policies and procedures. Waiting for the end of gap analysis usually only wastes valuable time. Using a little judgment, one or more team members should be able to begin creating policies, procedures, and related forms and manuals required to fill identified gaps.

After gap analysis is nearly complete, it is time to begin prioritizing remediation targets. Not everything will be of the same priority. Some problems involve high potential liability, or maybe there are a few relatively gross violations of HIPAA privacy mandates that need to be addressed as a high priority. Identify resources to work through these issues first. Also start on the quick hits; these can be anything that your organization is confident will require little resource and will demonstrate progress toward your goals.

After addressing the highest priority and easiest issues, schedule resources to address the longer-term remediation targets. Invest in the higher-priority issues before those that pose less risk.

Computer Requirements

There is no requirement that physicians or dentists must use computers. However, more physicians/dentists might want to use computers for submitting and receiving transactions (such as health care claims and remittances/payments) electronically, once the standard way of doing things goes into effect.

The Administrative Simplification provisions of HIPAA were passed with the support of the health care industry. The industry believed standards would lower the cost and administrative burdens of health care, but they needed government's help to get to one uniform way of doing things. In the past, individual providers (physicians and others) have had to submit transactions in whatever form each health plan required. Health plans could not agree on a standard without giving their competitors a market advantage, at least in the short-run.

HIPAA, which requires standards to be followed for electronic transmission of health care transactions, levels the playing field. It does not require providers to submit transactions electronically. It does require that all transactions submitted electronically comply with the standards.

Providers, even those without computers, may want to adopt these standard electronic transactions so that they can benefit directly from the reductions in cost and burden. This is possible because the law allows providers (and health plans too, for that matter) to contract with clearinghouses to conduct the standard electronic transactions for them.

Fax Requirements

PHI can be exchanged via faxes sent to business associates, covered entities, and others. Here are some recommendations for safeguarding information that might be sent or received via a fax machine:

- ◆ **Fax cover page.** State clearly on the fax cover page that the fax contains confidential and protected health information. Also, include language below this headline that clearly states that such information is to be safeguarded and protected and must not be shared or disclosed without the appropriate authorizations from the patient.

  The bottom of the fax cover page should state clearly that if the fax is received by an unintended person or organization, they must immediately inform your organization and subsequently destroy the fax.

- ◆ **Location of fax machine.** Keep the fax machine in an area that is not accessible by individuals who are not authorized to view PHI.

- ◆ **Faxes with PHI.** Faxes that your office may receive with PHI information must be promptly stored in a protected/secured area and must not, for example, be left in an in-box that may be easily accessible by unauthorized individuals.

- ◆ **Fax numbers.** To avoid sending faxes to unintended recipients, always confirm the accuracy of fax numbers. If the fax includes PHI, strongly consider defining processes for confirming that the recipient has received the fax. If the fax was sent to the wrong number, document that the fax was misrouted and take appropriate steps to minimize such occurrences in the future. Document all steps taken.

◆ **Confirmation.** Program the fax machine to print a confirmation for all faxes sent. Staple the confirmation to each PHI fax sent.

◆ **Fax storage.** Define processes and systems to document and maintain information on PHI that has been faxed.

◆ **Business Associates.** Require your business associates to keep their fax machines and the faxes received in protected areas.

◆ **Training.** Train all employees to understand the importance of safeguarding PHI data sent or received via fax. Develop a written fax policy and include this information as part of what is covered in the training session.

Privacy Compliance Documents

HIPAA Privacy Rule compliance will result in a covered entity developing the following documents:

◆ Notice of Privacy Practices

◆ Authorization form

Let us review some sample templates for Notice and Authorization documents.

Sample: Notice of Privacy Practices

This sample form from the American Medical Association provides the basis for HIPAA Notice of Privacy Practices. This form does not constitute legal advice and is for educational purposes only. This form is based on current federal law and subject to change based on changes in federal law or subsequent interpretative guidance. It must be modified to reflect state law where that state law is more stringent than the federal law or other state law exceptions apply. Here is a sample HIPAA Notice of Privacy Practices document for a hospital.

[NAME OF HOSPITAL]

Notice of Privacy Practices

This notice describes how medical information about you may be used and disclosed and how you can get access to this information. Please review it carefully.

If you have any questions about this Notice please contact: our Privacy Contact who is [NAME OF PRIVACY CONTACT].

This Notice of Privacy Practices describes how we may use and disclose your protected health information to carry out treatment, payment, or health care operations and for other purposes that are permitted or required by law. It also describes your rights to access and control your protected health information. "Protected health information" is information about you, including demographic information, that may identify you and that relates to your past, present, or future physical or mental health or condition and related health care services.

We are required to abide by the terms of this Notice of Privacy Practices. We may change the terms of our notice, at any time. The new notice is effective for all protected health information that we maintain at that time. Upon your request, we will provide you with any revised Notice of Privacy Practices by accessing our Web site **[WEB ADDRESS]**, calling the office and requesting that a revised copy be sent to you in the mail, or asking for one at the time of your next appointment.

1. Uses and Disclosures of Protected Health Information

Uses and Disclosures of Protected Health Information Based Upon Your Written Consent

You will be asked by your physician to sign a consent form. Once you have consented to use and disclosure of your protected health information for treatment, payment, and health care operations by signing the consent form, your physician will use or disclose your protected health information as described in this section (1). Your protected health information may be used and disclosed by your physician, our office staff, and others outside of our office who are involved in your care and treatment for the purpose of providing health care services to you. Your protected health information may also be used and disclosed to pay your health care bills and to support the operation of the physician's practice.

Following are examples of the types of uses and disclosures of your protected health care information that the physician's office is permitted to make once you have signed our consent form. These examples are not meant to be exhaustive, but to describe the types of uses and disclosures that may be made by our office once you have provided consent.

<u>Treatment</u>: We will use and disclose your protected health information to provide, coordinate, or manage your health care and any related services. This includes the coordination or management of your health care with a third party that has already obtained your permission to have access to your protected health information. For example, we would disclose your protected health information, as necessary, to a home health agency that provides care to you. We will also disclose protected health information to other physicians who may be treating you when we have the necessary permission from you to disclose your protected health information. For example, your protected health information may be provided to a physician to whom you have been referred to ensure that the physician has the necessary information to diagnose or treat you.

In addition, we may disclose your protected health information from time-to-time to another physician or health care provider (e.g., a specialist or laboratory) who, at the request of your physician, becomes involved in your care by providing assistance with your health care diagnosis or treatment to your physician.

<u>Payment</u>: Your protected health information will be used, as needed, to obtain payment for your health care services. This may include certain activities that your health insurance plan may undertake before it approves or pays for the health care services we recommend for you such as making a determination of eligibility or coverage for insurance benefits, reviewing services provided to you for medical necessity, and undertaking utilization review activities. For example, obtaining approval for a hospital stay may require that your relevant protected health information be disclosed to the health plan to obtain approval for the hospital admission.

<u>Health Care Operations</u>: We may use or disclose, as-needed, your protected health information to support the business activities of your physician's practice. These activities include, but are not limited to, quality assessment activities, employee review activities, training of medical students, licensing, marketing, and fund-raising activities, and conducting or arranging for other business activities.

For example, we may disclose your protected health information to medical school students that see patients at our office. In addition, we may use a sign-in sheet at the registration desk where you will be asked to sign your name and indicate your physician. We also may call you by name in the waiting room when your physician is ready to see you. We may use or disclose your protected health information, as necessary, to contact you to remind you of your appointment.

We will share your protected health information with third-party "business associates" that perform various activities (for example., billing, transcription services) for the practice. Whenever an arrangement between our office and a business associate involves the use or disclosure of your protected health information, we will have a written contract that contains terms that will protect the privacy of your protected health information.

We may use or disclose your protected health information, as necessary, to provide you with information about treatment alternatives or other health-related benefits and services that may be of interest to you. We also may use and disclose your protected health information for other marketing activities. For example, your name and address may be used to send you a newsletter about our practice and the services we offer. We also may send you information about products or services that we believe may be beneficial to you. You may contact our Privacy Contact to request that these materials not be sent to you.

We may use or disclose your demographic information and the dates that you received treatment from your physician, as necessary, to contact you for fund-raising activities supported by our office. If you do not want to receive these materials, please contact our Privacy Contact and request that these fundraising materials not be sent to you.

**Uses and Disclosures of Protected Health Information
Based upon Your Written Authorization**

Other uses and disclosures of your protected health information will be made only with your written authorization, unless otherwise permitted or required by law as described below. You may revoke this authorization, at any time, in writing, except to the extent that your physician or the physician's practice has taken an action in reliance on the use or disclosure indicated in the authorization.

Other Permitted and Required Uses and Disclosures That May Be Made with Your Consent, Authorization, or Opportunity to Object

We may use and disclose your protected health information in the following instances. You have the opportunity to agree or object to the use or disclosure of all or part of your protected health information. If you are not present or able to agree or object to the use or disclosure of the protected health information, then your physician may, using professional judgment, determine whether the disclosure is in your best interest. In this case, only the protected health information that is relevant to your health care will be disclosed.

<u>Facility Directories</u>: Unless you object, we will use and disclose in our facility directory your name, the location at which you are receiving care, your condition (in general terms), and your religious affiliation. All of this information, except religious affiliation, will be disclosed to people that ask for you by name. Members of the clergy will be told your religious affiliation. *[Please note that this section is only applicable to larger practices or those practices that operate facilities.]*

<u>Others Involved in Your Health Care</u>: Unless you object, we may disclose to a member of your family, a relative, a close friend, or any other person you identify, your protected health information that directly relates to that person's involvement in your health care. If you are unable to agree or object to such a disclosure, we may disclose such information as necessary if we determine that it is in your best interest based on our professional judgment. We may use or disclose protected health information to notify or assist in notifying a family member, personal representative, or any other person who is responsible for your care of your location, general condition, or death. Finally, we may use or disclose your protected health information to an authorized public or private entity to assist in disaster relief efforts and to coordinate uses and disclosures to family or other individuals involved in your health care.

<u>Emergencies</u>: We may use or disclose your protected health information in an emergency treatment situation. If this happens, your physician shall try to obtain your consent as soon as reasonably practicable after the delivery of treatment. If your physician or another physician in the practice is required by law to treat you and the physician has attempted to obtain your consent but is unable to obtain your consent, he or she may still use or disclose your protected health information to treat you.

Communication Barriers: We may use and disclose your protected health information if your physician or another physician in the practice attempts to obtain consent from you but is unable to do so due to substantial communication barriers and the physician determines, using professional judgment, that you intend to consent to use or disclosure under the circumstances.

Other Permitted and Required Uses and Disclosures That May Be Made without Your Consent, Authorization, or Opportunity to Object

We may use or disclose your protected health information in the following situations without your consent or authorization. These situations include

Required By Law: We may use or disclose your protected health information to the extent that the use or disclosure is required by law. The use or disclosure will be made in compliance with the law and will be limited to the relevant requirements of the law. You will be notified, as required by law, of any such uses or disclosures.

Public Health: We may disclose your protected health information for public health activities and purposes to a public health authority that is permitted by law to collect or receive the information. The disclosure will be made for the purpose of controlling disease, injury, or disability. We may also disclose your protected health information, if directed by the public health authority, to a foreign government agency that is collaborating with the public health authority.

Communicable Diseases: We may disclose your protected health information, if authorized by law, to a person who may have been exposed to a communicable disease or may otherwise be at risk of contracting or spreading the disease or condition.

Health Oversight: We may disclose protected health information to a health oversight agency for activities authorized by law, such as audits, investigations, and inspections. Oversight agencies seeking this information include government agencies that oversee the health care system, government benefit programs, other government regulatory programs, and civil rights laws.

Abuse or Neglect: We may disclose your protected health information to a public health authority that is authorized by law to receive reports of child abuse or neglect. In addition, we may disclose your protected health information if we believe that you have been a victim of abuse, neglect, or domestic violence to the governmental entity or agency authorized to receive such information. In this case, the disclosure will be made consistent with the requirements of applicable federal and state laws.

Food and Drug Administration: We may disclose your protected health information to a person or company required by the Food and Drug Administration to report adverse events, product defects or problems, biologic product deviations to track products, to enable product recalls, to make repairs or replacements, or to conduct post marketing surveillance, as required.

Legal Proceedings: We may disclose protected health information in the course of any judicial or administrative proceeding, in response to an order of a court or administrative tribunal (to the extent such disclosure is expressly authorized), in certain conditions in response to a subpoena, discovery request, or other lawful process.

Law Enforcement: We may also disclose protected health information, so long as applicable legal requirements are met, for law enforcement purposes. These law enforcement purposes include (1) legal processes and otherwise required by law, (2) limited information requests for identification and location purposes, (3) pertaining to victims of a crime, (4) suspicion that death has occurred as a result of criminal conduct, (5) in the event that a crime occurs on the premises of the practice, and (6) medical emergency (not on the Practice's premises) with which it is likely that a crime has occurred.

Coroners, Funeral Directors, and Organ Donation: We may disclose protected health information to a coroner or medical examiner for identification purposes, determining cause of death or for the coroner or medical examiner to perform other duties authorized by law. We also may disclose protected health information to a funeral director, as authorized by law, to permit the funeral director to carry out their duties. We may disclose such information in reasonable anticipation of death. Protected health information may be used and disclosed for cadaveric organ, eye, or tissue donation purposes.

Research: We may disclose your protected health information to researchers when their research has been approved by an institutional review board that has reviewed the research proposal and established protocols to ensure the privacy of your protected health information.

Criminal Activity: Consistent with applicable federal and state laws, we may disclose your protected health information, if we believe that the use or disclosure is necessary to prevent or lessen a serious and imminent threat to the health or safety of a person or the public. We also may disclose protected health information if it is necessary for law enforcement authorities to identify or apprehend an individual.

Military Activity and National Security: When the appropriate conditions apply, we may use or disclose protected health information of individuals who are Armed Forces personnel (1) for activities deemed necessary by appropriate military command authorities, (2) for the purpose of a determination by the Department of Veterans Affairs of your eligibility for benefits, or (3) to foreign military authority if you are a member of that foreign military services. We also may disclose your protected health information to authorized federal officials for conducting national security and intelligence activities, including for the provision of protective services to the President or others legally authorized.

Workers' Compensation: Your protected health information may be disclosed by us as authorized to comply with workers' compensation laws and other similar legally established programs.

Inmates: We may use or disclose your protected health information if you are an inmate of a correctional facility and your physician created or received your protected health information in the course of providing care to you.

Required Uses and Disclosures: Under the law, we must make disclosures to you and when required by the Secretary of the Department of Health and Human Services, to investigate or determine our compliance with the requirements of Section 164.500 et. seq.

2. Your Rights

Following is a statement of your rights with respect to your protected health information and a brief description of how you may exercise these rights.

You have the right to inspect and copy your protected health information. This means you may inspect and obtain a copy of protected health information about you that is contained in a designated record set for as long as we maintain the protected health information. A "designated record set" contains medical and billing records and any other records that your physician and the practice uses for making decisions about you.

Under federal law, however, you may not inspect or copy the following records: psychotherapy notes; information compiled in reasonable anticipation of, or use in, a civil, criminal, or administrative action or proceeding; and protected health information that is subject to law that prohibits access to protected health information. Depending on the circumstances, a decision to deny access may be reviewable. Please contact our Privacy Contact if you have questions about access to your medical record.

<u>**You have the right to request a restriction of your protected health information**</u>. This means you may ask us not to use or disclose any part of your protected health information for the purposes of treatment, payment, or health care operations. You may also request that any part of your protected health information not be disclosed to family members or friends who may be involved in your care or for notification purposes as described in this Notice of Privacy Practices. Your request must state the specific restriction requested and to whom you want the restriction to apply.

Your physician is not required to agree to a restriction that you may request. If a physician believes it is in your best interest to permit use and disclosure of your protected health information, your protected health information will not be restricted. If your physician does agree to the requested restriction, we may not use or disclose your protected health information in violation of that restriction unless it is needed to provide emergency treatment. With this in mind, please discuss any restriction you wish to request with your physician. You may request a restriction by contacting your physician and documenting the specific restrictions that the physician and you agree to.

<u>**You have the right to request to receive confidential communications from us by alternative means or at an alternative location**</u>. We will accommodate reasonable requests. We also may condition this accommodation by asking you for information as to how payment will be handled or specification of an alternative address or other method of contact. We will not request an explanation from you as to the basis for the request. Please make this request in writing to our Privacy Contact.

<u>**You may have the right to have your physician amend your protected health information**</u>. This means you may request an amendment of protected health information about you in a designated record set for as long as we maintain this information. In certain cases, we may deny your request for an amendment. If we deny your request for amendment, you have the right to file a statement of disagreement with us, and we may prepare a rebuttal to your statement and will provide you with a copy of any such rebuttal. Please contact our Privacy Contact to determine if you have questions about amending your medical record.

<u>You have the right to receive an accounting of certain disclosures we have made, if any, of your protected health information</u>. This right applies to disclosures for purposes other than treatment, payment, or health care operations as described in this Notice of Privacy Practices. It excludes disclosures we may have made to you, for a facility directory, to family members or friends involved in your care, or for notification purposes. You have the right to receive specific information regarding these disclosures that occurred after April 14, 2003. You may request a shorter time frame. The right to receive this information is subject to certain exceptions, restrictions, and limitations.

<u>You have the right to obtain a paper copy of this notice from us</u>, upon request, even if you have agreed to accept this notice electronically.

3. Complaints

You may complain to us or to the Secretary of Health and Human Services if you believe your privacy rights have been violated by us. You may file a complaint with us by notifying our privacy contact of your complaint. We will not retaliate against you for filing a complaint.

You may contact our Privacy Contact, [<u>NAME OF PRIVACY CONTACT</u>] at [PHONE NUMBER] or [<u>EMAIL ADDRESS OF PRIVACY CONTACT</u>] for further information about the complaint process.

This notice was published and becomes effective on <u>April 14, 2003</u>.

Sample: Notice of Privacy Practices

Source: State of Oregon's Department of Human Services (DHS)

In this section we review the Notice of Privacy Practices that was developed by the state's Department of Human Services. The Notice document communicates to the client/patient uses and disclosures of information, client rights, as well as contact information for complaints.

STATE DEPARTMENT OF HUMAN SERVICES
NOTICE OF PRIVACY PRACTICES

Effective Date: March 31, 2003

THIS NOTICE DESCRIBES HOW MEDICAL INFORMATION ABOUT YOU MAY BE USED AND DISCLOSED AND HOW YOU CAN GET ACCESS TO THIS INFORMATION. PLEASE REVIEW IT CAREFULLY.

This letter is available in other languages and alternate formats that meet the guidelines for the Americans with Disabilities Act (ADA). Contact DHS at: Phone 503-945-7021, TTY 503-947-5330 or fax 503-373-7690.

The Department of Human Services (DHS) provides many types of services, such as health and social services. DHS staff must collect information about you to provide these services. DHS knows that information we collect about you and your health is private. DHS is required to protect this information by Federal and State law. We call this information *protected health information* (PHI).

The Notice of Privacy Practices will tell you how DHS may use or disclose information about you. Not all situations will be described. DHS is required to give you a notice of our privacy practices for the information we collect and keep about you. DHS is required to follow the terms of the notice currently in effect.

DHS May Use and Disclose Information Without Your Authorization

- **For treatment.** DHS may use or disclose information with health care providers who are involved in your health care. For example, information may be shared to create and carry out a plan for your treatment.

- **For payment.** DHS may use or disclose information to get payment or to pay for the health care services you receive. For example, DHS may provide PHI to bill your heath plan for health care provided to you.

- **For health care operations.** DHS may use or disclose information to manage its programs and activities. For example, DHS may use PHI to review the quality of services you receive.

- **Appointments and other health information.** DHS may send you reminders for medical care or checkups. DHS may send you information about health services that may be of interest to you.

- **For public health activities.** DHS is the public health agency that keeps and updates vital records, such as births and deaths, and tracks some diseases.

- **For health oversight activities.** DHS may use or disclose information to inspect or investigate health care providers.

- **As required by law and for law enforcement.** DHS will use and disclose information when required or permitted by federal or state law or by a court order.

- **For abuse reports and investigations.** DHS is required by law to receive and investigate reports of abuse.

- **For government programs.** DHS may use and disclose information for public benefits under other government programs. For example, DHS may disclose information for the determination of Supplemental Security Income (SSI) benefits.

- **To avoid harm.** DHS may disclose PHI to law enforcement to avoid a serious threat to the health and safety of a person or the public.

- **For research.** DHS uses information for studies and to develop reports. These reports do not identify specific people.

- **Disclosures to family, friends, and others.** DHS may disclose information to your family or other persons who are involved in your medical care. You have the right to object to the sharing of this information.

- **Other uses and disclosures require your written authorization.** For other situations, DHS will ask for your written authorization before using or disclosing information. You may cancel this authorization at any time in writing. DHS cannot take back any uses or disclosures already made with your authorization.

- **Other laws protect PHI.** Many DHS programs have other laws for the use and disclosure of information about you. For example, you must give your written authorization for DHS to use and disclose your mental health and chemical dependency treatment records.

Your PHI Privacy Rights

When information is maintained by DHS as a public health agency, the public health records are governed by other state and federal laws and is not subject to the rights described below.

- **Right to see and get copies of your records.** In most cases, you have the right to look at or get copies of your records. You must make the request in writing. You may be charged a fee for the cost of copying your records.

- **Right to request to correct or update your records.** You may ask DHS to change or add missing information to your records if you think there is a mistake. You must make the request in writing and provide a reason for your request.

- **Right to get a list of disclosures.** You have the right to ask DHS for a list of disclosures made after April 14, 2003. You must make the request in writing. This list will not include the times that information was disclosed for treatment, payment, or health care operations. The list will not include information provided directly to you or your family, or information that was sent with your authorization.

- **Right to request limits on uses or disclosures of PHI.** You have the right to ask that DHS limit how your information is used or disclosed. You must make the request in writing and tell DHS what information you want to limit and to whom you want the limits to apply. DHS is not required to agree to the restriction. You can request that the restrictions be terminated in writing or verbally.

- **Right to revoke permission.** If you are asked to sign an authorization to use or disclose information, you can cancel that authorization at any time. You must make the request in writing. This will not affect information that has already been shared.

- **Right to choose how we communicate with you.** You have the right to ask that DHS share information with you in a certain way or in a certain place. For example, you may ask DHS to send information to your work address instead of your home address. You must make this request in writing. You do not have to explain the basis for your request.

- **Right to file a complaint.** You have the right to file a complaint if you do not agree with how DHS has used or disclosed information about you.

- **Right to get a paper copy of this Notice.** You have the right to ask for a paper copy of this Notice at any time.

How to contact DHS to Review, Correct, or Limit Your Protected Health Information (PHI)

You can contact your local DHS office or the DHS Privacy Officer at the address listed at the end of this Notice to

- Ask to look at or copy your records
- Ask to correct or change your records
- Ask to limit how information about you is used or disclosed
- Ask for a list of the times DHS used or disclosed information about you
- Ask to cancel your authorization

DHS can deny your request to look at, copy, or change your records. If DHS denies your request, DHS will send you a letter that tells you why your request is being denied and how you can ask for a review of the denial. You also will receive information about how to file a complaint with DHS or with the U.S. Department of Health and Human Services, Office for Civil Rights.

How to File a Complaint or Report a Problem

You can contact any of the people listed below if you want to file a complaint or to report a problem with how DHS has used or disclosed information about you. Your benefits will not be affected by any complaints you make. DHS cannot retaliate against you for filing a complaint, cooperating in an investigation, or refusing to agree to something that you believe to be unlawful.

State Department of Human Services
Governor's Advocacy Office
500 Summer St. NE, E17
Salem, Oregon 97301-1097
Phone:
Email:

Office for Civil Rights
Medical Privacy, Complaint Division
U.S. Department of Health and Human Services
200 Independence Avenue, SW, HHH Building, Room 509H
Washington, D.C. 20201
Phone: 866-627-7748 TTY: 886-788-4989
Web: www.hhs.gov/ocr

For More Information

If you have any questions about this Notice or need more information, please contact the DHS Privacy Officer.

State Department of Human Services
Privacy Officer
500 Summer Street NE
Salem, Oregon 97301
Phone:
Web: **For More Information**

In the future, DHS can change its Notice of Privacy Practices. Any changes will apply to information DHS already has, as well as any information DHS receives in the future. A copy of the new Notice will be posted at each DHS site and facility and provided as required by law. You may ask for a copy of the current Notice anytime you visit a DHS facility, or get it online at http://222.hr.state.or.us/hippa.

Model Authorization

Authorization to use or disclose protected health information must be obtained when a consent form does not apply or another exception otherwise permitting use or disclosure of protected health information does not apply. It is important to distinguish various authorization forms for different purposes. There is a difference between an Authorization that is sought for a use or disclosure by the physician's practice and an Authorization requested by the physician's practice for the purpose of obtaining information from another covered entity.

An Authorization must be valid to permit disclosure or use of protected health information. The following steps will help you guard against defective authorizations that do not allow the physician's practice to use or disclose protected health information.

- Check to make sure that the expiration date has not passed or an event that triggers an expiration has not occurred.
- Ensure that the patient has completed all sections of the Authorization.
- Confirm that the patient has not revoked the Authorization.
- Use the correct Authorization form for the appropriate purpose. For example, if the covered entity is requesting the use or disclosure to a third party on his or her own behalf, then use the Privacy Authorization Form.
- Do not combine the Authorizations in a manner prohibited by federal law.
- Ensure that all information included in the Authorization is not known by the physician's practice to be false.

Practices must also comply with requirements surrounding compound authorizations. An Authorization cannot be combined with any other document, except in the following instances:

- An Authorization for the use or disclosure of protected health information created for research that includes treatment of the individual.
- An Authorization can be combined with a consent to use or disclose for treatment, payment, and health care operations or a Notice of Privacy Practices.
- Authorizations for the use or disclosure of psychotherapy notes can only be combined with another Authorization for the use or disclosure of psychotherapy notes.

◆ An Authorization can be combined with another Authorization (except an authorization for psychotherapy notes) unless you are conditioning treatment upon obtaining one of the authorizations for research purposes.

The physician cannot condition the provision of treatment on the patient's signing an Authorization form except in the following circumstances:

◆ If the treatment is for research purposes.

◆ If the provision of health care services is solely for the purpose of creating protected health information for disclosure to a third party, then the covered entity might require the patient to sign an Authorization for disclosure to the intended third party.

A patient can revoke an Authorization to use or disclose protected health information, at any time; the revocation must be in writing. A revocation has no force and effect to the extent the physician's practice has taken an action relying on that Authorization.

In the case of an Authorization sought on behalf of the physician's practice, a copy of the signed Authorization must be provided to the patient.

Documentation requirements under federal, or state law as applicable, must be followed. Federal regulations require that

◆ Written policies and procedures for obtaining and retaining authorizations be maintained in written or electronic form.

◆ A paper or electronic copy of the signed Authorization be retained.

Authorization forms must be kept for six years from the date of creation or the date when it last was in effect, whichever is later.

The following form is an example of an Authorization Form—the purpose is to authorize the disclosure of information.

Sample Privacy Authorization Form—
Physician's Office and Patient

Authorization for Use or Disclosure of Information for Purposes Requested by Physician's Office

I, _____, hereby authorize **[Name of Practice]** to (check those that apply):

__ use the following protected health information, and/or

__ disclose the following protected health information to **[Name of entity to receive information]**:

[Specifically describe the information to be used or disclosed, including, but not limited to, meaningful descriptors such as date of service, type of service provided, level of detail to be released, origin of information, and so on.]

This protected health information is being used or disclosed for the following purposes:

[List specific purposes here.]

This authorization shall be in force and effect until **[specify (1) date or (2) event that relates to the patient or the purpose of the use or disclosure]** at which time this authorization to use or disclose this protected health information expires.

I understand that I have the right to revoke this authorization, in writing, at any time by sending such written notification to [Name of Privacy Contact] at [office address or e-mail address]. I understand that a revocation is not effective to the extent that [Name of Practice] has relied on the use or disclosure of the protected health information.

I understand that information used or disclosed pursuant to this authorization may be subject to redisclosure by the recipient and may no longer be protected by federal or state law.

[Name of Practice] will not condition my treatment, payment, enrollment in a health plan, or eligibility for benefits (if applicable) on whether I provide authorization for the requested use or disclosure.

I understand that I have the right to

- Inspect or copy the protected health information to be used or disclosed as permitted under federal law (or state law to the extent the state law provides greater access rights).
- Refuse to sign this authorization.

[The use or disclosure requested under this authorization will result in direct or indirect remuneration to the [Name of Practice] from a third party.] [If applicable.]

_____

Signature of Patient or Personal Representative

_____

Date

_____

Name of Patient or Personal Representative

_____

Description of Personal Representative's Authority

Sample Form: Request for Access to Patient's Health Information

This form may be used by a patient to request information about themselves that a provider may have in its records.

As a patient of [PRACTICE NAME], you are entitled under federal law to access your personal protected health information maintained in a "designated record set." In order to process your request for access to this information, please complete this form and submit it to the Privacy Officer. When received by the Privacy Officer, he or she will use the information to verify your identity and process your request. If you have any questions or concerns, please contact the Privacy Officer, [PO NAME] at [PO PHONE NUMBER].

Patient Information

Patient Name: _____ Birth date: _____

Patient Identifier: _____ Date of access request: _____

Access Method

You have the right to view your protected health information, obtain a copy of the information, or both. Please indicate below whether you wish to view the information only, obtain a copy, or both. If you select "copy," please indicate your method of delivery.

[ ] I would like to **view** my protected health information. I have/will schedule(d) an appointment with [PRACTICE NAME] to view my health information on _____. I understand [PRACTICE NAME] may have a staff member sit down with me as I review my health information.

[ ] I would like a **copy** of my protected health information. I understand that [PRACTICE NAME] may charge me a fee for the copies as set forth in the following schedule: $ _____ for research and retrieval, $ ____ per page for the first ____ pages, and $ ____ per page for each additional page. I also understand that I may be

required to pay the fee in full before I can obtain the copy. I have selected my delivery method below (if none is selected, I will pick up the copy at the practice):

[ ] I will return to [PRACTICE NAME] and pick up the copy when it is ready.

[ ] I would like [PRACTICE NAME] to send the copy via U.S. mail to the following address:

_____

_____

I understand that [PRACTICE NAME] may charge me all applicable postage fees.

[ ] I would like [PRACTICE NAME] to send the copy via facsimile to the following number: _____. I understand that [PRACTICE NAME] may charge me a fee of $ _____ per faxed page.

[ ] If possible, I would like a copy sent to me using the following format:

_____

Summary (Check if desired)

[ ] I would like [PRACTICE NAME] to provide to me an explanation or summary of the information provided. I understand that [PRACTICE NAME] may charge me a fee of $ _____ for the explanation or summary, and I may be required to pay the fee in full before I can obtain the explanation or summary.

I understand that [PRACTICE NAME] is given thirty days to process my request for access if my information is maintained on-site, sixty days if the information is maintained off-site, and that [PRACTICE NAME] may extend the deadline by an additional thirty days if I am notified in writing of the extension. I further understand that my rights are limited to any information in my "designated record set" as defined in Section 164.501 of the Code of Federal Regulations.

By signing below, I acknowledge and agree to the above conditions.

_____

Signature of Patient   Date

_____   _____

FOR INTERNAL OFFICE USE ONLY

Access request received on _____ by _____.

Access Request Reviewed by: _____

Request has been:

[ ] Accepted in full

[ ] Accepted in part

[ ] Denied

_____   _____

Signature of Reviewer   Date

Letter indicating decision mailed to patient on _____.

If patient was given access in full, complete the information below:

The record was:

[ ] Viewed by patient on _____. Staff member who assisted the patient in viewing his or her information was _____.

[ ] Copied on _____. Total cost for copies: $ _____.

[ ] Picked up by patient on _____.

[ ] Mailed via U.S. mail on _____.

[ ] Sent to patient via _____ on _____.

[ ] Faxed to patient at fax number on _____.

     Cost for postage/shipping: $ _____.

The fees were received in full by _____ on _____.

If decision was accepted in part, complete the information below:

If accepted in part, indicate which part(s) have been denied and the reason(s) why below:

_____

_____

_____

Has patient asked for a review of the decision?

[ ] Yes, letter asking for review received on _____.

Decision reviewed on _____ by _____.

Reviewing official's decision:

[ ] Affirm decision [ ] Overturn decision (complete the disclosure information above).

Patient notified of reviewing official's decision in letter/fax sent on _____.

If <u>denied</u>, complete the information below:

If denied, indicate why the request has been denied (be specific):

_____

_____

Has patient asked for a review of the decision?

[ ] Yes, letter asking for review received on _____.

Decision reviewed on _____.

Reviewing official: _____

Reviewing official's decision:

[ ] Affirm decision

[ ] Overturn decision (if overturned, complete the disclosure information above).

Patient notified of reviewing official's decision in letter/fax sent on
_____.

Comments of Health Care Practitioner or Reviewer:

_____

_____

_____

_____

_____

_____

Reviewing Official's Signature

_____

Date

Sample: Request for Amendment of Health Information

This form may be completed by a client/patient to request an amendment to their health information.

You have the right to request an amendment to your protected health information. If you would like to request an amendment to your protected health information, please complete the form below and hand it to the Privacy Officer.

Patient Name: _____ Birth date:_____

Patient Identifier: _____

Patient Address: _____

_____

_____

Date of amendment request: _____

Please explain how the entry is incorrect or incomplete. What should the entry say to be more accurate or complete?

_____

_____

_____

_____

_____

_____

_____

_____

_____

_____

_____

Would you like this amendment sent to anyone to whom we may have disclosed the information in the past? If so, please specify the name and address of the organization(s) or individual(s).

Name/Address: Name/Address:

_____   _____

_____   _____

_____   _____

Name/Address: Name/Address:

_____   _____

_____   _____

_____   _____

Note: If you have additional names, please attach an additional sheet to this page.

I understand that by listing the name(s) and address(es) of other organizations on this Amendment form, I am asking [PRACTICE NAME] to disclose the requested amendment to these organizations. I therefore give specific permission to [PRACTICE NAME] to disclose the amendment to these organizations, and I understand that [PRACTICE NAME] will take reasonable steps to send the requested amendment to these organizations.

In addition, I understand [PRACTICE NAME] may be required to send this amendment to Business Associates or other organizations that [PRACTICE NAME] identifies as needing the amendment. I therefore give specific permission to [PRACTICE NAME] to send the requested amendment to these organizations identified by [PRACTICE NAME] as needing the amendment.

I further understand that it is my responsibility to identify any originator(s) of my protected health information who may be no longer available to act on this amendment request, and present to [PRACTICE NAME] evidence that I have attempted to contact the originator(s). If I cannot present evidence of my attempts, [PRACTICE NAME] may deny the amendment request.

By signing below, I fully acknowledge and agree to the above terms.

_____

Signature of Patient

_____

Date

FOR INTERNAL OFFICE USE ONLY

Date Amendment Received: _____

Amendment Reviewed by: _____

Amendment has been: [ ] Accepted   [ ] Accepted in part [ ] Denied

If denied or accepted in part, check reason(s) for denial:

[ ] PHI was not created by this organization.

[ ] PHI is not part of patient's designated record set.

[ ] The patient's record is accurate to the standard of reasonable accuracy as defined by Section 164.516 of the federal regulations.

[ ] Other:

_____

_____

_____

Comments of Health Care Practitioner or Reviewer:

_____

_____

_____

_____

_____   _____

Signature of Reviewer   Date

Has patient asked for a review of the decision?

[ ] Yes, letter asking for review received on _____.

Decision reviewed on _____ by _____.

Reviewing official's decision:

[ ] Affirm decision [ ] Overturn decision (complete the disclosure information above).

Patient notified of reviewing official's decision in letter/fax sent on _____.

_____

Reviewing Official's Signature

_____

Date

Sample Privacy Policies

The source of content for this section is from the State of Oregon's Department of Human Services (DHS). The author had an opportunity to deliver HIPAA Privacy training sessions for DHS and was most impressed with the quality of Privacy Policy documents developed by the Privacy Program Office team. Note that the policies are in draft form and specific to the requirements for the Department of Oregon, State of Oregon.

A Policies, Procedures, and Related Forms Manual is required in every HIPAA-regulated practice. Key audit documents that HHS's Office for Civil Rights HIPAA Agents look for include the following:

- ◆ Policies and Procedures Manual
- ◆ Notice of Privacy Practices

For example, the State of Oregon's Department of Human Services (DHS) has developed the following HIPAA privacy policy documents:

- General Privacy Policy
- Patient (or Client) Rights Policy
- Uses and Disclosures of Patient (or Client or Participant) Information Policy
- Minimum Necessary Policy
- Administrative, Technical, and Physical Safeguards Policy
- Uses and Disclosures for Research Purposes and Waivers Policy
- Deidentification and Use of Limited Data Sets Policy
- Business Associates Policy
- Enforcement, Sanctions, and Penalties for Violation of Individual Privacy

Each of these policies is discussed in detail in the following sections.

General Privacy Policy

A General Privacy Policy outlines general guidelines and expectations for collection, use, and disclosure of confidential information and briefly summarizes each detailed policy. It differentiates expectations for clients, participants, licensees, and providers. The policy provides direction when requirements seem to be in conflict. Finally, it outlines the Notice of Privacy Practices.

Client Rights Policy

A Client Rights Policy outlines the client's right to access their own information, by alternative means if warranted, with some exceptions. This policy also describes a client's right to request restrictions or amendments to their information. The policy identifies the actions that DHS can take in response to those requests and the recourse that the individual has in light of those decisions. The policy describes the method for filing a complaint. The policy also explains the necessity of and the accounting procedure for disclosures of protected information.

Uses and Disclosures of Client or Participant Information Policy

The Uses and Disclosures of Client or Participant Information Policy specifies that clients or participants information can't be used or disclosed without their prior written authorization. There are a number of circumstances that are exceptions to the general rule outlined in this policy. Some examples of exceptions are: when DHS is acting as a public health authority; for treatment, payment, and health care operations; when required by law or statute (cases of abuse or neglect, law enforcement; judicial or administrative proceedings), and activities of health oversight. The policy further outlines restrictions on re-disclosure of information and an individual's right to revoke authorizations.

Minimum Necessary Policy

The Minimum Necessary Policy is designed to improve the privacy of confidential information by ensuring access to the minimum amount of information necessary to provide services and benefits to clients. Reasonable efforts must be taken to limit disclosing only the amount of information necessary to accomplish the purpose for which the disclosure is sought. The same standard holds true when making requests for information from a third party. Role-based access to information, which means access to enough information for DHS staff to carry out their duties, is also described in this policy.

Administrative, Technical, and Physical Safeguards Policy

The Administrative, Technical, and Physical Safeguards Policy describes reasonable steps to take in order to safeguard confidential information from any intentional or unintentional use or disclosure. Information to be safeguarded may be in any medium, including paper, electronic transmittal, oral conversation, and visual representation. This policy also provides tangible means for administrative safeguards to be implemented.

Use and Disclosures for Research Purposes and Waivers Policy

The Use and Disclosures for Research Purposes and Waivers Policy outlines the specific requirements for using and disclosing client or participant information with and without their written authorization. This policy also outlines the approval process required by Institutional Review Boards or privacy boards, including documentation. The policy identifies some allowable uses and disclosures of information when DHS is acting as a public health authority. Finally, the policy identifies studies and data analysis requirements as part of health care operations that allows DHS to conduct quality assurance activities and comply with reporting requirements.

Deidentification of Client Information and Use of Limited Data Sets Policy

The Deidentification of Client Information and Use of Limited Data Sets Policy describes the requirements for deidentification of client information so that the remaining information cannot reasonably be used to identify a particular person. This policy outlines the methods to be used and the information to be removed to ensure deidentification. The policy also describes the authority figure who will determine if the information has been rendered unidentifiable.

Business Associates Policy

The Business Associates Policy allows DHS to disclose protected information to business partners with whom there is a written contract or memorandum of understanding, so that this partner (or "business associate") can carry out or assist in a function on behalf of DHS. In doing that, DHS will impose certain security and reporting requirements on their associates. This policy involves Protected Health Information (PHI) only.

Enforcement, Sanctions, and Penalties for Violation of Individual Privacy Policy

The Enforcement, Sanctions, and Penalties for Violation of Individual Privacy Policy outlines the responsibilities of DHS to enforce privacy safeguards, of supervisors to ensure employees are informed of privacy policies, and of employees to safeguard the privacy of clients and individuals. The policy outlines penalties for policy violations as well as "knowing and willful" violations. The policy further outlines prohibition against coercion or retaliation, and describes protections for DHS employees or business associates who are whistle blowers and/or workforce crime victims.

Let us now examine sample policy documents.

General Privacy Policy

The intent of this policy is to outline DHS general guidelines and expectations for the necessary collection, use, and disclosure of confidential information about individuals to provide services and benefits to individuals, while maintaining reasonable safeguards to protect the privacy of their information.

1. General—DHS will safeguard confidential information about individuals.

  A. DHS may collect, maintain, use, transmit, share, and/or disclose information about individuals to the extent needed to administer DHS programs, services, and activities.

  B. DHS will safeguard all confidential information about individuals, inform individuals about DHS' privacy practices, and respect individual privacy rights, to the full extent required under this policy.

  C. This policy identifies three types of individuals from whom DHS is most likely to obtain, collect, or maintain individual information.

  I.DHS clients

  II.Participants

  III. Licensees or providers

D. DHS shall provide training to all employees on DHS' privacy policies, and shall require every employee to sign a DHS2091, "Privacy Program Statement of Understanding" outlining their role and responsibilities relating to protecting the privacy of DHS clients and participants.

2. Safeguarding information about clients.

A. A *client* is an individual who requests or receives services from DHS.

B DHS, its employees, and business associates will respect and protect the privacy of records and information about clients who request or receive services from DHS. This includes, but is not limited to

I. Applicants or recipients of public assistance

II. Minors and adults receiving protective services from DHS

III. Persons who apply for or who are admitted to a state training center, a state-operated group home, a state hospital, or who are committed to the custody of DHS

IV. Children in the custody of DHS either on a voluntary or committed basis

C. All information on DHS clients is confidential and must be safeguarded in accordance with DHS privacy policies and procedures.

D. DHS shall not use or disclose information unless either

I. The client has authorized the use or disclosure in accordance with DHS Policy AS-100-03, "Use and Disclosures of Client or Participant Information"

II. The use or disclosure is specifically permitted under DHS Policy AS-100-03, "Use and Disclosures of Client or Participant Information"

E. DHS program offices shall adopt procedures to reasonably safeguard client information.

3. Safeguarding information about participants.

Participants are individuals participating in DHS population-based services, programs, and activities that serve the general population, but who do not receive program benefits or direct services that are received by a client.

A. When DHS or its business associates obtain individually identifiable information about participants, DHS may use and disclose such information consistent with federal or state rules and regulations or DHS policies and procedures.

    B. DHS will safeguard all confidential information about Participants consistent with federal or state rules and regulations or DHS policies and procedures.

4. Safeguarding information about licensees and providers.

A *licensee* is a person or entity that applies for or receives a license, certificate, registration, or similar authority from DHS to perform or conduct a service, activity, or function. A *provider* is a person or entity who may seek reimbursement from DHS as a provider of services to DHS clients.

    A. When DHS obtains information about licensees or providers, DHS may use and disclose such information consistent with federal and state law and regulation. Information regarding the qualifications of licensees and providers are public records.

        I. DHS will safeguard confidential information about licensees and providers consistent with federal and state rules and regulations and DHS policies and procedures.

        II. When DHS obtains information about individuals that relates to determining payment responsibility when a provider submits a claim or other request for payment to DHS, DHS will safeguard such information consistent with federal and state law and regulations and DHS policies and procedures.

        III. DHS is also authorized to review the performance of licensees and providers in the conduct of their health oversight activities.

        IV. DHS will safeguard confidential information about individuals obtained during health oversight activities consistent with federal and state law and regulations and DHS policies and procedures.

5. Conflict with other requirements regarding privacy and safeguarding.

    A. DHS has adopted reasonable policies and procedures for administration of its programs, services, and activities. If any state or federal law or regulation, or order of a court having appropriate jurisdiction, imposes a stricter requirement upon any DHS policy regarding the privacy or safeguarding of information, DHS shall act in accordance with that stricter standard.

B. DHS staff shall act in accordance with established DHS policy and proce-dures regarding the safeguarding and confidentiality of individual informa-tion, whether health-related or not, in all DHS programs, services, and activities.

C. In the event that more than one policy applies but compliance with all such policies cannot reasonably be achieved, the DHS employee will seek guidance from supervisors according to established DHS policy and proce-dures. DHS staff should consult with their privacy coordinator or the DHS privacy program in appropriate circumstances.

6. DHS Notice of Privacy Practices.

A. DHS will make available a copy of the DHS 2090, "DHS Notice of Privacy Practices," to any client applying for or receiving services from DHS.

B. The DHS Notice of Privacy Practices shall contain all information required under federal regulations regarding the notice of privacy practices for protected health information under HIPAA.

C. Where DHS is a provider, DHS will seek to acquire a signed acknowl-edgement, DHS 2092, "Notice of Privacy Practices, Acknowledgement of Receipt," from each client.

7. Client Privacy Rights.

DHS policies and procedures, as well as other federal and state laws and regulations, outline the client's right to access his own information, with some exception. This policy also describes specific actions that a client can take to request restrictions or amendments to their information, and the method for filing complaints. These spe-cific actions are outlined in DHS Policy AS-100-02, "Client Privacy Rights."

8. Use and Disclosures of Client or Participant Information.

DHS shall not use or disclose any information about a client or participant of DHS programs or services without a signed authorization for release of that information from the individual, or the individual's personal representative, unless authorized by this policy, or as otherwise allowed or required by state or federal law, as outlined in DHS Policy AS-100-03, "Uses and Disclosures of Client or Participant Information."

9. Minimum Necessary Information.

A. DHS will use or disclose only the minimum amount of information necessary to provide services and benefits to clients, and only to the extent provided in DHS policies and procedures

B. This policy does not apply to

   I. Disclosures to or requests by a health care provider for treatment

   II. Uses or disclosures made to the individual

   III. Uses or disclosures authorized by the individual

   IV. Disclosures made to the Secretary of the United States Department of Health and Human Services in accordance with federal HIPAA regulations at 45 CFR 160, Subpart C

   V. Uses or disclosures that are required by law

   VI. Uses or disclosures that are required for compliance with federal HIPAA regulations at 45 CFR, Parts 160 and 164

C. When using or disclosing an individual's information, or when requesting an individual's information from a provider or health plan, DHS employees must make reasonable efforts to limit the amount of information to the minimum necessary needed to accomplish the intended purpose of the use, disclosure, or request, as outlined in DHS Policy AS-100-04, "Minimum Necessary Information"

10. Administrative, Technical, and Physical Safeguards.

DHS staff must take reasonable steps to safeguard confidential information from any intentional or unintentional use or disclosure, as outlined in DHS Policy AS-100-05, "Administrative, Technical, and Physical Safeguards."

11. Use and Disclosures for Research Purposes and Waivers.

DHS may use or disclose an individual's information for research purposes as outlined in DHS Policy AS-100-06, "Uses and Disclosures for Research Purposes and Waivers." This policy specifies requirements for using or disclosing information with and without an individual's authorization, and identifies some allowable uses and disclosure of information when DHS is acting as a Public Health Authority.

12. Deidentification of Client Information and Use of Limited Data Sets.

DHS staff will follow standards under which client information can be used and disclosed if information that can identify a person has been removed or restricted to a limited data set. Unless otherwise restricted or prohibited by other federal or state law, DHS can use and share information as appropriate for the work of DHS, without further restriction, if DHS or another entity has taken steps to deidentify the information as outlined in DHS Policy AS-100-07, "De-identification of Client Information and Use of Limited Data Sets."

13. Business Associate Relationships.

DHS may disclose protected health information to business associates with whom there is a written contract or memorandum of understanding as outlined in DHS Policy AS-100-08, "DHS Business Associate Relationships."

14. Enforcement, Sanctions, and Penalties for Violations of Individual Privacy.

All employees, volunteers, interns, and members of the DHS workforce must guard against improper uses or disclosures of DHS client or participant's information as outlined in DHS Policy AS-100-09, "Enforcement, Sanctions, and Penalties for Violations of Individual Privacy."

Client Privacy Rights Policy

The intent of this policy is to establish the privacy rights that DHS clients have regarding the use and disclosure of their protected information that is held by DHS, and to describe the process for filing a complaint should clients feel those rights have been violated.

This document contains guidance for developing procedures to implement this policy.

General

DHS clients have the right to, and DHS may not deny, the following.

- Access to their own information, consistent with certain limitations.
- Receive an accounting of disclosures DHS has made of their protected health information (PHI) for up to six years prior to the date of requesting such accounting. Information may not be available prior to the effective

date of this policy (April 13, 03) and certain limitations do apply as outlined in this policy, section 6.

- Submit complaints if they believe or suspect that information about them has been improperly used or disclosed, or if they have concerns about the privacy policies of DHS.

Clients may ask DHS to take specific actions regarding the use and disclosure of their information, and DHS may either approve or deny the request. Specifically, clients have the right to request the following:

- That DHS restrict uses and disclosures of their individual information while carrying out treatment, payment activities, or health care operations.
- To receive information from DHS by alternative means, such as mail, e-mail, fax or telephone, or at alternative locations.
- That DHS amend their information that is held by DHS.

Relationship to Notice of Privacy Practices.

- DHS will use the DHS 2090, "DHS Notice of Privacy Practices," to inform clients about how DHS may use and/or disclose their information. The Notice of Privacy Practices also describes the actions clients may take, or request DHS to take, with regard to the use and/or disclosure of their information.
- The policies related to the "Notice of Privacy Practices" and the distribution of the Notice are addressed in DHS Policy AS-100-01, "General Privacy."
- Nothing in this policy, or the policy related to the DHS 2090, "DHS Notice of Privacy Practices," shall prevent DHS from changing its policies or the Notice at any time, provided that the changes in the policies or Notice comply with state or federal law.

Decision-making authority within DHS.

- Prior to any decision, based on a client's request for DHS to amend a health or medical record, the program's medical director or a licensed health care professional designated by the program administrator shall review the request and any related documentation.
- The licensed health care professional may be a DHS staff person involved in the client's case.

- Prior to any decision to amend any other information that is not a health or medical record, a DHS staff person, designated by the program administrator, shall review the request and any related documentation.

- DHS may deny a client access to their own health information on the grounds that access may result in risk or harm to the client or to another person. However, prior to any decision to deny such access, the program's medical director or a licensed health care professional, designated by the program administrator, shall review the request and any related documentation. The licensed health care professional may be a DHS staff person involved in the client's case.

- Decisions related to any other requests made to DHS under this policy shall be handled in a manner consistent with federal and state rules and regulations and/or DHS policies and procedures applicable to the program, service, or activity.

Rights of Clients to Request Privacy Protection of Their Information

Clients have the right to request restrictions on the use and/or disclosure of their information.

- DHS applies confidentiality laws applicable to specific programs or activities to protect the privacy of client information. Even if those laws would permit DHS to make a use or disclosure of information, a DHS client has the right to request a restriction on a use or disclosure of that information.

- All requests will be submitted by completing a **DHS 2095**, "Restriction of Use and Disclosures Request Form."

- DHS is not obligated to agree to a restriction and may deny the request or may agree to a restriction more limited than what the client requested.

  Exception: Certain programs can only use information that is authorized by the client, such as alcohol and drug programs or vocational rehabilitation participants. For those program participants, DHS will honor their requests for restriction by making sure that the authorization clearly identifies the authorized recipients of the information.

Rights of clients to request to receive information from DHS by alternative means or at alternative locations.

A. DHS must accommodate reasonable requests by clients to receive communications by alternative means, such as by mail, e-mail, fax, or telephone.

B. DHS must accommodate reasonable requests by clients to receive communications at an alternative location.

C. In some cases, sensitive health information or health services must be handled with strict confidentiality under state law. For example, information about substance abuse treatment, mental health treatment, and certain sexually transmitted diseases may be subject to specific handling. DHS will comply with the more restrictive requirements.

Rights of Clients to Access Their Information

• Clients have the right to access, inspect, and obtain a copy of information on their own cases in DHS files or records, consistent with federal law and the State Public Records Law.

• All requests for access will be made having the client complete a DHS 2093, "Access to Records Request Form."

• Clients may request access to their own information that is kept by DHS by using a personal identifier (such as the client's name or DHS case number).

A. If DHS maintains information about the client in a record that includes information about other people, the client is only authorized to see information about him or herself, except as provided below:

I. If a person identified in the file is a minor child of the client, and the client is authorized under state law to have access to the minor's information or to act on behalf of the minor for making decisions about the minor's care, the client may also obtain information about the minor.

II. If the person requesting information is recognized under state law as a guardian or legal custodian of the client and is authorized by state law to have access to the client's information or to act on behalf of the client for making decisions about the client's services or care, DHS will release information to the requestor.

III. Under these special circumstances: the system in ORS 192.517 (1), to protect and advocate the rights of individuals with developmental disabilities under part C of the Developmental Disabilities Assistance and Bill of Rights Act (42 U.S.C. 6041 et seq.) and the rights of individuals with mental illness under the Protection and Advocacy for Individuals with Mental Illness Act (42 U.S.C. 10801 et seq.), shall have access to all records, as defined in ORS 192.515, as provided in ORS 192.517.

- DHS may deny clients access to their own health information if federal law prohibits the disclosure. Under federal law, clients have the right to access, inspect, and obtain a copy of health information on their own cases in DHS files or records except for

- Psychotherapy notes

- Information compiled for use in civil, criminal, or administrative proceedings

- Information that is subject to the federal Clinical Labs Improvement Amendments of 1988, or exempt pursuant to 42 CFR 493.3(a)(2)

- Information that, in good faith, DHS believes can cause harm to the client, participant, or to any other person

- Documents protected by attorney work-product privilege

- Information where release is prohibited by state or federal laws

Before DHS denies a client access to their information because there is a good faith belief that its disclosure could cause harm to the client or to another person, the DHS decision to deny must be made by a licensed health care professional or other designated staff, and DHS must make a review of this denial available to the client. If the client wishes to have this denial reviewed, the review must be done by a licensed health care professional who was not involved in the original decision.

Rights of Clients to Request Amendments to Their Information.

- Clients have the right to request that DHS amend their information held in DHS files by DHS.

- All requests for amendments will be made by having the client complete a DHS 2094, "Amendment of Health Record Request Form."

- DHS is not obligated to agree to an amendment and may deny the requests or limit its agreement to restrict.

Rights of Clients to an Accounting of Non-Routine Disclosures of Protected Health Information.

- Clients have the right to receive an accounting of non-routine disclosures of protected health information (PHI) that DHS has made for any period of time, not to exceed six years preceding the date of requesting the accounting.

- The accounting will only include health information NOT previously authorized by the client for use or disclosure, and will not include information collected, used, or disclosed for treatment, payment, or health care operations for that client (routine disclosures).

- All requests for amendments will be made by having the client complete a DHS 2096, "Accounting of Disclosures Request Form."

- This right does not apply to disclosures made prior to the effective date of this policy, which is April 13, 2003.

Rights of Clients to File Complaints Regarding Disclosure of Information

- Clients have a right to submit a complaint if they believe that DHS has improperly used or disclosed their protected information, or if they have concerns about the privacy policies of DHS or concerns about DHS compliance with such policies.

- Complaints may be filed with any of the following:
  - The State Department of Human Services, Governor's Advocacy Office

- The U.S. Department of Health and Human Services, Office for Civil Rights

Guidance for Procedure Development

The following guidelines should be used in developing procedures to implement this policy:

1. General Policy

There are no accompanying procedures.

2. Requesting Restrictions of Uses and Disclosures

A. Individual Clients may request that DHS restrict use and/or disclosure of their information for

  I. Carrying out treatment, payment, or health care operations

  II. Disclosure of health information to a relative or other person who is involved in the individual client's care

B. All requests for access will be made by having the client complete a DHS 2903, "Access to Records Request Form."

C. DHS is not required to agree to a restriction requested by the individual client.

D. DHS will not agree to restrict uses or disclosures of information if the restriction would adversely affect the quality of the individual client's care or services.

E. DHS cannot agree to a restriction that would limit or prevent DHS from making or obtaining payment for services.

F. Emergency treatment should be provided even with an agreed upon restriction (see "exception" under (e.1)(i.), below, of this Procedure).

  Exception: For Alcohol and Drug or Vocational Rehabilitation participants, Federal regulations (42 CFR Part 2 and 34 CFR) prohibit DHS from denying client requests for restrictions on uses and disclosures of their information regarding treatment or rehabilitation.

G. DHS will document the client's request, and the reasons for granting, denying, or not agreeing to comply, in the request in the client's hard-copy or electronic DHS case record file.

H. Prior to any use of disclosure of client information, DHS staff must confirm that such use or disclosure has not been granted a restriction by reviewing the client's case file.

I. If DHS agrees to an client's request for restriction, DHS will not use or disclose information that violates the restriction.

Exception: If the client needs emergency treatment and the restricted information is needed to provide emergency treatment, DHS may use or disclose such information to the extent needed to provide the emergency treatment. However, once the emergency situation subsides, DHS must ask the provider not to redisclose the information.

J. DHS may terminate its agreement to a restriction if

    I. The client agrees to or requests termination of the restriction in writing.

    II. The client orally agrees to, or requests termination of, the restriction. DHS will document the oral agreement or request in the client's DHS case record file.

    III. DHS informs the client in writing that DHS is terminating its agreement to the restriction. Information created or received while the restriction was in effect shall remain subject to the restriction.

3. Requesting Alternative Means or Locations

A. The client must specify the preferred alternative means or location.

B. Requests for alternative means or alternative locations for information may be made orally or in writing.

C. If a client makes a request orally, DHS will document the request and ask for the client's signature.

D. If a client makes a request by telephone or electronically, DHS will document the request and verify the identity of the requestor.

E. Prior to any information being sent to the client, DHS staff must confirm if the client has requested an alternate location or by alternate means, and if DHS has granted that request, by reviewing the client's case file.

F DHS may terminate its agreement to an alternative location or method of communication if

I. The client agrees to or requests termination of the alternative location or method of communication in writing or orally. DHS will document the oral agreement or request in the client's DHS case record file.

II. DHS informs the client that DHS is terminating its agreement to the alternative location or method of communication because the alternative location or method of communication is not effective. DHS may terminate its agreement to communicate at the alternate location or by the alternative means if

a. DHS is unable to contact the client at the location or in the manner requested.

b. If the client fails to respond to payment requests if applicable.

4. Requesting Access to Information

A. DHS will assure that clients may access their information that DHS uses in whole or part to make decisions about them, subject to certain limitations as outlined in Section (4.) of this policy.

B. Clients may request to access, inspect, and obtain information about themselves, subject to certain limitations as outlined in Section (4.) of this policy.

I. All requests for access will be made by having the client complete a DHS 2093, "Access to Records Request Form."

C. DHS may deny a client access to their information if the information

I. Is excepted under this policy.

II. Was obtained from someone other than a health care provider under a promise of confidentiality, and access would reveal the source of the information.

D. DHS may deny an client access to their information, provided that DHS gives the client a right to have the denial reviewed, in the following circumstances:

    I. A licensed health care professional or other designated staff has determined, in the exercise of professional judgment, that the information requested may endanger the life or physical safety of the client or another person.

    II. The protected information makes reference to another person, and a licensed health care professional or other designated staff has determined, in the exercise of professional judgment, that the information requested may cause substantial harm to the client or another person.

    III. The request for access is made by the client's personal representative, and a licensed health care professional or other designated staff has determined, in the exercise of professional judgment, that allowing the personal representative to access the information may cause substantial harm to the client or to another person.

E. If DHS denies access under Section (4.)(d.) of this Procedure, the client has the right to have the decision reviewed by a licensed health care professional or other designated staff not directly involved in making the original denial decision. DHS will then proceed based on the decision from this review.

    I. DHS must promptly refer a request for review to the designated reviewer. (See Section (4.)(f.) of this Procedure for timelines for these procedures).

    II. The reviewer must determine, within a reasonable time, whether or not to approve or deny the client's request for access, in accordance with this policy.

    III. DHS must then

        a. Promptly notify the client in writing of the reviewer's determination.

        b. Take action to carry out the reviewer's determination.

F. DHS must act on an client's request for access no later than 30 days after receiving the request, except in the case of written accounts under ORS 179.505 which must be disclosed within five (5) days.

    I. In cases where the information is not maintained or accessible to DHS on-site, and does not fall under ORS 179.505, DHS must act on the client's request no later than 60 days after receiving the request.

II. If DHS is unable to act within these 30-day or 60-day limits, DHS may extend this limitation by up to an additional 30 days, subject to the following:

    a. DHS must notify the client in writing of the reasons for the delay and the date by which DHS will act on the request.

    b. DHS will use only one such 30-day extension to act on a request for access.

G. If DHS grants the client's request, in whole or in part, DHS must inform the client of the access decision and provide the requested access.

    I. If DHS maintains the same information in more than one format (such as electronically and in a hard-copy file) or at more than one location, DHS need only provide the requested protected information once.

    II. DHS must provide the requested information in a form or format requested by the client, if readily producible in that form or format. If not readily producible, DHS will provide the information in a readable hard-copy format or such other format as agreed to by DHS and the client.

    III. If DHS does not maintain, in whole or in part, the requested information that is the subject of a request for access, and knows where the information is maintained, DHS will inform the client of where to direct the request for access.

    IV. DHS may provide the client with a summary of the requested information, in lieu of providing access, or may provide an explanation of the information if access had been provided, if

        a. The client agrees in advance, and

        b. The client agrees in advance to any fees DHS may impose.

    V. DHS must arrange with the client for providing the requested access in a time and place convenient for the client and DHS. This may include mailing the information to the client if the client so requests or agrees.

    VI. Fees: A client (or legal guardian or custodian) may request a copy of their information at no cost once every 12 months. If the client requests a copy of the information, or a written summary or explanation, more frequently than once every 12 months, then DHS may impose a reasonable, cost-based fee, limited to covering the following:

    a. Copying the requested information, including the costs of supplies and of the labor of copying.

    b. Postage, when the client has requested or agreed to having the information mailed.

    c. Preparing an explanation or summary of the requested information, if agreed to in advance by the client, per Subsection (4.)(g.)(iv.) of this Procedure, above.

H. If DHS denies access, in whole or in part, to the requested information, DHS must

    I. Give the client access to any other requested client information, after excluding the information to which access is denied.

    II. Provide the client with a timely written denial. The denial must

        a. Be sent or provided within the time limits specified in Section (4.) of this Procedure.

        b. State the basis for the denial, in plain language.

        c. If the reason for the denial is due to danger to the client or another, explain the individual client's review rights, including an explanation of how the individual client may exercise these rights.

        d. Provide a description of how the client may file a complaint with DHS, and if the information denied is protected health information, or with the Secretary of the United States Department of Health and Human Services (DHHS) Office or the Office for Civil Rights of DHHS.

I. If DHS does not maintain the requested protected information, and knows where such information is maintained (such as by a medical provider, insurer, other public agency, private business, or other non-DHS entity), DHS must inform the client of where to direct the request for access.

5. Requesting Amendments of Information

A. All requests for amendments will be made by having the client complete a DHS 2094, "Amendment of Health Record Request Form."

B. DHS will honor requests for alternative methods of making this request if reasonable accommodations are needed.

C. DHS must act on the client's request no later than 60 days of receiving the request. If DHS is unable to act on the request within 60 days, DHS may extend this time limit by up to an additional 30 days, subject to the following.

    I. DHS must notify the client in writing of the reasons for the delay and the date by which DHS will act on the receipt.

    II. DHS will use only one such 30-day extension.

D. Prior to any decision to amend a health or medical record, the request and any related documentation shall be reviewed by the program's medical director, a licensed health care professional designated by the program administrator, or a DHS staff person involved in the client's case.

E. Prior to any decision to amend any other information that is not a health or medical record, a DHS staff person designated by the program administrator shall review the request and any related documentation.

F. If DHS grants the request, in whole or in part, DHS must

    I. Make the appropriate amendment to the protected information or records, and document the amendment in the client's file or record.

    II. Provide timely notice to the client that the amendment has been accepted, pursuant to the time limitations.

    III. Seek the client's agreement to notify other relevant persons or entities, with whom DHS has shared or needs to share the amended information, of the amendment.

    IV. Make reasonable efforts to inform, and to provide the amendment within a reasonable time to

        a. Persons identified by the client as having received protected information and who thus need the amendment.

      b. Persons, including business associates of DHS, that DHS knows have the protected information that is the subject of the amendment and that may have relied, or could foreseeably rely, on the information to the client's detriment.

G. DHS may deny the client's request for amendment if

    I. DHS finds the information to be accurate and complete.

    II. The information was not created by DHS, unless the client provides a reasonable basis to believe that the originator of such information is no longer available to act on the requested amendment.

    III. The information is not part of DHS records.

    IV. It would not be available for inspection or access by the individual client.

H. If DHS denies the requested amendment, in whole or in part, DHS must provide the client with a timely written denial. The denial must

    I. Be sent or provided within the time limits specified in Section (4.)(f.)db. of this Procedure, above.

    II. State the basis for the denial, in plain language.

    III. Explain the client's right to submit a written statement of disagreement. The client may ask that if DHS makes any future disclosures of the relevant information. DHS will also include a copy of the client's original request for amendment and a copy of the DHS written denial.

    IV. Explain the client's right to submit a written statement disagreeing with the denial and how to file such a statement. If the client does so

      a. DHS will enter the written statement into the client's DHS case file.

      b. DHS may also enter a DHS written rebuttal of the client's written statement into the client's DHS case record. DHS will send or provide a copy of any such written rebuttal to the client.

      c. DHS will include a copy of that statement, and of the written rebuttal by DHS if any, with any future disclosures of the relevant information.

      d. Explain that if the client does not submit a written statement of disagreement, the client may ask that if DHS makes any future disclosures of the relevant information, DHS will also include a copy of the client's original request for amendment and a copy of the DHS written denial.

e. Provide information on how the client may file a complaint with DHS, or with the United States Department of Health and Human Services (DHHS), Office for Civil Rights of DHHS, subject to Section (7.) of this Procedure, below.

6. Requesting an Accounting of Disclosures

A. When a client requests an accounting of disclosures that DHS has made of their protected health information, DHS must provide the client with a written accounting of all non-routine health information disclosures made during the six-year period (or lesser time period if specified by the requesting client) preceding the date of the client's request, *except* for those disclosures.

B. All requests for an accounting of disclosures will be made by having the client complete a DHS 2096, "Accounting of Disclosures Request."

C. Examples of disclosures of protected health information (PHI) that are required to be listed in an accounting (assuming that the disclosure is permitted by other confidentiality laws applicable to the individual's information and the purpose for which it was collected or maintained) include

   I. **Abuse Report.** PHI about an individual provided by DHS staff (other than protective services staff who respond to such reports) pursuant to mandatory abuse reporting laws to an entity authorized by law to receive the abuse report.

   II. **Audit Review.** PHI provided by DHS staff from an individual's record in relation to an audit or review (whether financial, quality of care, or other audit or review) of a provider or contractor.

   III. **Health and Safety.** PHI about an individual provided by DHS staff to avert a serious threat to health or safety of a person.

   IV. **Licensee/Provider.** PHI provided by DHS from an individual's records in relation to licensing or regulation or certification of a provider, licensee, or entity involved in the care or services of the individual.

V. **Legal Proceeding.** PHI about an individual who is ordered to be disclosed pursuant to a court order in a court case or other legal proceeding—include a copy of the court order with the accounting.

VI. **Law Enforcement Official/Court Order.** PHI about an individual provided to a law enforcement official pursuant to a court order—include a copy of the court order with the accounting.

VII. **Law Enforcement Official/Deceased.** PHI provided to law enforcement officials or medical examiner about a person who has died for the purpose of identifying the deceased person, determining cause of death, or as otherwise authorized by law.

VIII. **Law Enforcement Official/Warrant.** PHI provided to a law enforcement official in relation to a fleeing felon or for whom a warrant for their arrest has been issued and the law enforcement official has made proper request for the information, to the extent otherwise permitted by law.

IX. **Media.** PHI provided to the media (TV, newspaper, etc.) that is not within the scope of an authorization by the individual.

X. **Public Health Official.** PHI about an individual provided by DHS staff (other than staff employed for public health functions) to a public health official, such as the reporting of disease, injury, or the conduct of a public health study or investigation.

XI. **Public Record.** PHI about an individual that is disclosed pursuant to a Public Record request without the individual's authorization.

XII. Research. PHI about an individual provided by DHS staff for purposes of research conducted without authorization, using a waiver of authorization approved by an IRB—a copy of the research protocol should be kept with the accounting, along with the other information required under the HIPAA privacy rule, 45 CFR § 164.528(b)(4).

D. Disclosures that are not required to be tracked and accounted for are those that are

I. Authorized by the client.

II. Made prior to the original effective date of this policy, which is April 13, 2003.

III. Made to carry out treatment, payment, and health care operations.

IV. Made to the client.

V. Made to persons involved in the client's health care.

VI. Made as part of a limited data set in accordance with the DHS Policy AS-100-07, "De-identification of Client Information and Use of Limited Data Sets."

VII. For national security or intelligence purposes.

VIII. Made to correctional institutions or law enforcement officials having lawful custody of an inmate.

E. The accounting must include for each disclosure

I. The date of the disclosure.

II. The name, and address if known, of the person or entity who received the disclosed information.

III. A brief description of the information disclosed.

IV. A brief statement of the purpose of the disclosure that reasonably informs the client of the basis for the disclosure, or, in lieu of such statement and if applicable, a copy of the client's written request for a disclosure, if any.

F. If, during the time period covered by the accounting, DHS has made multiple disclosures to the same person or entity for the same purpose, or as a result of a single written authorization by the client, DHS may provide the information related to the first disclosure, the last disclosure, and the total number of all such disclosures made to the same person or entity.

I. Although DHS must provide a written accounting for disclosures made over a six year period, only the first disclosure made during the time period is necessary (DHS need not list the same identical information for each subsequent disclosure to the same person or entity) if DHS adds

a. The frequency or number of disclosures made to the same person or entity.

b. The last date of the disclosure made during the requested time period.

G. DHS must act on the client's request for an accounting no later than 60 days after receiving the request, subject to the following:

   I. If unable to provide the accounting within 60 days after receiving the request, DHS may extend this requirement by another 30 days. DHS must provide the client with a written statement of the reasons for the delay within the original 60-day limit, and inform the client of the date by which DHS will provide the accounting.

   II. DHS will use only one such 30-day extension.

H. Fees: DHS must provide the first requested accounting in any 12-month period without charge. DHS may impose the client a reasonable cost-based fee upon the individual for each additional accounting requested by the client within the 12-month period following the first request, provided that DHS

   I. Informs the client of the fee before proceeding with any such additional request.

   II. Allows the client an opportunity to withdraw or modify the request in order to avoid or reduce the fee.

I. DHS must document, and retain in the client's DHS case record file, the information required to be included in an accounting of disclosures, as listed under Section (6.)(e.), of this Procedure, and send a copy of the written accounting provided to the client.

J. DHS will temporarily suspend a client's right to receive an accounting of disclosures that DHS has made to a health oversight agency or to a law enforcement official, for a length of time specified by such agency or official, if

   I. The agency or official provides a written statement to DHS that such an accounting would be reasonably likely to impede its activities.

   II. However, if such agency or official makes an oral request, DHS will

      a. Document the oral request, including the identity of the agency or official making the request.

      b. Temporarily suspend the client's right to an accounting of disclosures pursuant to the request.

      c. Limit the temporary suspension to no longer than 30 days from the date of the oral request, unless the agency or official submits a written request specifying a longer time period.

7. Filing a Complaint

  A. Clients may file complaints with either DHS, or with the Secretary of the United States Department of Health and Human Services (DHHS) or— the Office for Civil Rights of DHHS. DHS must give clients the specific person or office and address of where to submit complaints:

State Department of Human Services
Privacy Officer
Governor's Advocacy Office
P.O. Box 550 Summer Street, NE, E17
Salem, Oregon 97301-1097
Phone:
Fax:
E-mail:

U.S. Department of Health and Human Services, Officer for Civil Rights
Medical Privacy, Complaint Division
200 Independence Avenue, SW
Washington, D.C. 20201
Toll Free Phone: 877-696-6775
Phone: 866-627-7748
TTY: 886-788-4989
E-mail: http://222.hhs.gov/ocr

  B. DHS will not intimidate, threaten, coerce, discriminate against, or take any other form of retaliatory action against any person filing a complaint or inquiring about how to file a complaint.

  C. DHS may not require clients to waive their rights to file a complaint as a condition of providing of treatment, payment, enrollment in a health plan, or eligibility for benefits.

  D. DHS will designate staff to review and determine action on complaints filed with DHS. These designated staff will also perform these functions when DHS is contacted about complaints filed with the Secretary of the United States U.S. Department of Health and Human Services or the Office for Civil Rights.

E. DHS will document, in the client's DHS case file or record, all complaints, the findings from reviewing each complaint, and DHS actions resulting from the complaint. This documentation shall include a description of corrective actions that DHS has taken, if any are necessary, or of why corrective actions are not needed, for each specific complaint.

Use and Disclosures of Client or Participant Information Policy

The intent of this policy is to specify that client or participant information cannot be used or disclosed without the individual's prior authorization, and to identify those exceptions that could be applicable.

This document contains guidance for developing procedures to implement this policy.

1. General—Individual Authorization

DHS shall not use or disclose any information about a client or participant of DHS programs or services without a signed authorization for release of that information from the individual, or the individual's personal representative, unless authorized by this policy, or as otherwise required by state or federal law.

2. Public Health

For the purpose of carrying out duties in its role as a public health authority, DHS does not need to obtain an individual's authorization to lawfully receive, use, disclose or exchange protected information (see definitions of public health activities).

3. Exceptions where limited uses or disclosures are allowed without authorization, to the extent not prohibited or otherwise limited by federal or state requirements applicable to the program or activity.

A. DHS may use or disclose information without an individual's authorization if the law requires such use or disclosure, and the use or disclosure complies with, and is limited to, the relevant requirements of such law.

B. Internal communication within DHS is permitted without individual authorization, in compliance with the DHS Policy AS-100-04, "Minimum Necessary Information."

    I. Alcohol and drug, mental health, and vocational rehabilitation records' disclosure may be limited to particular program areas named on the authorization form. If such a limitation is noted on the authorization form, disclosure is limited to the parties named.

C. DHS clients or participants may access their own information, with certain limitations (see DHS Policy AS-100-02, "Client Privacy Rights").

D. DHS may use or disclose psychotherapy notes in the following circumstances:

    I. In training programs where students, trainees, or practitioners in mental health learn under supervision to practice or improve their skills in group, joint, family, or individual counseling.

    II. When a health oversight agency uses or discloses in connection with oversight of the originator of the psychotherapy notes.

    III. To the extent authorized under state law to defend DHS in a legal action or other proceeding brought by the individual.

E. DHS may disclose information for purposes of payment, treatment, and health care operations.

F. If DHS has reasonable cause to believe that a child is a victim of abuse or neglect, DHS may disclose protected information to appropriate governmental authorities authorized by law to receive reports of child abuse or neglect (including reporting to DHS protective services staff, if appropriate). If DHS receives information as the child protective services agency, DHS is authorized to use and disclose the information consistent with its legal authority.

G. If DHS has reasonable cause to believe that an adult is a victim of abuse or neglect, DHS may disclose protected information, as required by law, to a government authority, including but not limited to social service or protective services agencies (which may include DHS) authorized by law to receive such reports.

H. DHS may disclose individual information without authorization for health oversight activities authorized by law, including audits; civil, criminal, or administrative investigations, prosecutions, or actions; licensing or disciplinary actions; Medicaid fraud; or other activities necessary for oversight.

I. Unless prohibited, or otherwise limited, by federal or state law applicable to the program or activity requirements, DHS may disclose individual information without authorization for judicial or administrative proceedings, in response to an order of a court, a subpoena, a discovery request, or other lawful process.

J. For limited law enforcement purposes, to the extent authorized by applicable federal or state law, DHS may report certain injuries or wounds; provide information to identify or locate a suspect, victim, or witness; alert law enforcement of a death as a result of criminal conduct; and provide information that constitutes evidence of criminal conduct on DHS premises.

K. DHS may disclose to a coroner or medical examiner, for the purpose of identifying a deceased person, determining a cause of death, or other duties authorized by law. If DHS personnel are performing the duty or function of a coroner or medical examiner, they may use an individual's information for such purposes.

L. DHS may disclose individual information without authorization to funeral directors, consistent with applicable law, as needed to carry out their duties regarding the decedent. DHS may also disclose such information prior to, and in reasonable anticipation of, the death.

M. DHS may disclose individual information without authorization to organ procurement organizations or other entities engaged in procuring; banking; or transplantation of cadaver organs, eyes, or tissue, for the purpose of facilitating transplantation.

N. DHS may disclose individual information without authorization for research purposes, as specified in DHS Policy AS-100-06, "Uses and Disclosures for Research Purposes and Waivers."

O. To avert a serious threat to health or safety, DHS may disclose individual information without authorization if

    I. DHS believes in good faith that the information is necessary to prevent or lessen a serious and imminent threat to the health or safety of a person or the public.

    II. The report is to a person or persons reasonably able to prevent or lessen the threat, including the target of the threat.

P. DHS may disclose individual information without authorization for other specialized government functions, including authorized federal officials for the conduct of lawful intelligence, counterintelligence, and other national security activities that federal law authorizes.

Q. DHS may disclose limited information without authorization to a correctional institution or a law enforcement official having lawful custody of an inmate, for the purpose of providing health care or ensuring the health and safety of individuals or other inmates.

R. In case of an emergency, DHS may disclose individual information without authorization to the extent needed to provide emergency treatment.

S. The Family Educational Rights and Privacy Act (FERPA) and state law applicable to student records governs DHS access to, use, and disclosure of student records.

4. Client or participant's authorization that is not required if they are informed in advance and given a chance to object.

A. In limited circumstance, DHS may use or disclose an individual's information without authorization if

    I. DHS informs the individual in advance and the person has been given an opportunity to object.

    II. Unless otherwise protected by law, DHS may orally inform the individual and obtain and document the individual's oral agreement.

B. Disclosures are limited to disclosure of health information to a family member, other relative, close personal friend of the individual, or any other person named by the individual.

    I. For individuals receiving alcohol and drug, mental health, or vocational rehabilitation services, oral permission is not sufficient and written authorization is required.

C. Oral permission to use or disclose information for the purposes described in subsections (A) of this section is not sufficient when the individual is referred to or receiving substance abuse treatment services or mental health treatment services, where written authorization for the treatment program to make such disclosures is required.

5. **Re-disclosure of an individual's information.**

   A. Unless prohibited by state and federal laws, information held by DHS and authorized by the individual for disclosure may be subject to re-disclosure and no longer protected by DHS policy. Whether or not the information remains protected depends on whether the recipient is subject to federal or state privacy laws, court protective orders, or other lawful process.

   B. Vocational Rehabilitation and Alcohol and Drug Rehabilitation information: Federal regulations (42 CFR part 2 and 34 CFR 361.38) prohibit DHS from making further disclosure of vocational rehabilitation and alcohol and drug rehabilitation information without the specific written authorization of the individual to whom it pertains.

   C. State law and administrative rule (ORS 433.045 and OAR 333-12-270, and) prohibits further disclosure of HIV information.

   D. State law and administrative rule (ORS 659.700—659-720 and OAR 333-24-0500—0560) prohibits further disclosure of genetics information without the specific written consent of the person to whom it pertains, or as otherwise permitted by such regulations. A general authorization for the release of medical information is not sufficient for this purpose.

   E. State law (ORS 179.505) places restrictions on re-disclosure of information regarding clients of publicly funded mental health or developmental disability providers.

6. **Revocation of authorization.**

   A. An individual can revoke an authorization at any time.

   B. Any revocation must be in writing and signed by the individual.

      I. Exception: alcohol and drug treatment participants may orally revoke authorization to disclose information obtained from alcohol and drug treatment programs.

C. No such revocation shall apply to information already released while the authorization was valid and in effect.

7. Verification of individuals requesting information.

A. Information about an individual may not be disclosed without verifying the identity of the person requesting the information, if the DHS staff member fulfilling the request does not know that person.

8. Denial of requests for information.

A. Unless an individual has signed an Authorization, or the information about the individual can be disclosed pursuant to this Policy, DHS shall deny any request for individual information.

Guidance for Procedure Development

The following guidelines should be used in developing procedures to implement this policy:

1. When an authorization is required.

A. Except as otherwise permitted or required by law and consistent with these policies, DHS shall obtain a completed and signed authorization for release of information from the individual, or the individual's personal representative, before obtaining or using information about an individual from a third party or disclosing any information about the individual to a third party.

   I. A signed authorization is required in the following situations:

      a. Prior to an individual's enrollment in a DHS administered health plan, if necessary for determining eligibility or enrollment.

      b. For the use and disclosure of psychotherapy notes (for exception see subsection 3.C. of these procedures).

      c. For disclosures to an employer for use in employment-related determinations.

      d. For research purposes unrelated to the individual's treatment.

      e. For any purpose in which state or federal law requires a signed authorization.

B. DHS may obtain, use, or disclose information only if the written authorization includes all the required elements of a valid authorization. The required elements are described in subsection 1.G. of this procedure.

C. Uses and disclosures must be consistent with what the individual has authorized on a signed authorization form.

D. An authorization must be voluntary. DHS may not require the individual to sign an authorization as a condition of providing treatment services, payment for health care services, enrollment in a health plan, or eligibility for health plan benefits, except

  I. Before providing research-related treatment, a DHS health care provider may condition the individual to sign an authorization for the use or disclosure of health information for such research.

  II. Before enrolling the individual in a DHS health plan, DHS can condition the individual to sign an authorization if needed to help determine the applicant's eligibility for enrollment and the authorization is not for a use or disclosure of psychotherapy notes.

  III. DHS and its contracted health care providers can require the individual to sign an authorization before providing health care that is solely for the purpose of creating protected health information for disclosure to a third party. For example, in a juvenile court proceeding where a parent is required to obtain a psychological evaluation by DHS, the evaluator may, as a condition of conducting the evaluation, require the parent to sign an authorization to release the evaluation report (but not the underlying psychotherapy notes) to DHS.

E. An authorization that is required for enrollment in a health plan or to determine eligibility for benefits of the health plan cannot be combined with a voluntary authorization. A required authorization and a voluntary authorization must be separate documents, signed separately.

F. Each authorization for use or disclosure of an individual's information must be fully completed jointly by the staff member and the individual, whenever possible, with the staff worker taking reasonable steps to ensure that the individual understands why the information is to be used or released.

G. DHS staff will use the approved DHS authorization forms (DHS 2098, "Authorization for Release of Non-Health Information," and DHS 2099, "Authorization to Release Health Information").

  I. A valid authorization must contain the following information:

  a. A description of the information to be used or disclosed that identifies the purpose of the information in a specific and meaningful fashion.

  b. The name or other specific information about the person(s), classification of persons, or entity (for example, DHS or specified DHS program) authorized to make the specific use or disclosure.

  c. The name or other specific identification of the person(s), classification of persons, or entity to whom DHS may make the requested use or disclosure.

  d. "DHS authorization for release of information" forms allow for multiple releases on one form. The individual has the right to request that only one release be requested per form. DHS will always honor this request.

  e. An expiration date, or an expiration event that relates to the individual or to the purpose of the use or disclosure.

  f. Signature of the individual, or of the individual's personal representative, and the date of signature.

  g. If the individual's personal representative signs the authorization form instead of the individual, a description or explanation of the representative's authority to act for the individual, including a copy of the legal court document (if any) appointing the personal representative, must also be provided.

  II. DHS must document and retain each signed authorization form for a minimum of six years.

2. **Procedures for activities as a public health authority.**

  A. This policy does not prohibit DHS from receiving, using, or disclosing an individual's protected information in its role as a governmental public health authority; nor does it prohibit disclosure of such information to other governmental public health authorities.

B. Information about individuals received or held by DHS as a governmental public health authority shall be safeguarded against loss, interception, or misuse.

C. DHS does not need to obtain an individual's authorization to lawfully receive, use, or disclose an individual's protected information in its role as a governmental public health authority; nor does DHS need authorization with respect to exchanges of such information with other governmental public health authorities, or as otherwise required or permitted by law.

D. Allowable uses and disclosures for public health activities consist of the following:

   I. DHS may disclose an individual's protected information for governmental public health activities and purposes to

   a. A governmental public health authority that is authorized by law to collect or receive such information for the purpose of preventing or controlling disease, injury, or disability. This includes but is not limited to reporting disease, injury, vital events such as birth or death, and the conducting of public health surveillance, investigations, and interventions.

   b. An official of a foreign government agency that is acting in collaboration with a lawful governmental public health authority.

   c. A governmental public health authority, or other appropriate government authority, that is authorized by law to receive reports of child abuse or neglect.

   d. A person subject to the jurisdiction of the federal Food and Drug Administration (FDA), regarding an FDA-regulated product or activity for which that person is responsible, for activities related to the quality, safety, or effectiveness of such FDA-related product or activity. Such purposes include the following:

      i. To collect or report adverse events, product defects or problems (including product labeling problems), or biological product deviations.

      ii. To track FDA-related products.

        iii. To enable product recalls, repairs, or replacement, or look back.

        iv. To conduct post market surveillance.

E. A person who may have been exposed to a communicable disease, or may be at risk of contracting or spreading a disease or condition.

    I. As a public health authority, DHS is authorized to use and disclose an individual's protected information in all cases in which DHS is permitted to disclose such information for the public health activities listed above.

    II. Public health research will be conducted consistent with the DHS Policy AS-100-06, "Uses and Disclosures for Research Purposes & Waivers."

    III. Where state or federal law prohibits or restricts uses and disclosure of information obtained or maintained for public health purposes, such use and disclosure shall be denied or restricted.

F. Operation of the public health laboratory.

    I. State law establishes that for the "protection of the public health," a public health laboratory is created within DHS to conduct tests and examinations at the request of any state, county, or city institution or officer, and at the request of any licensed physician.

    II. Laboratories are health care providers with an "indirect treatment relationship" as defined in federal regulations 45 CFR 164.501 and in accordance with 45 CFR 164.506 (a)(2)(i).

    III. DHS is authorized to use and disclose information for purposes of the operation of the public health laboratory consistent with HIPAA and applicable law.

G. Verifying the authority of a public health officer.

    I. Health care providers and health care payers may request DHS to verify the authority of a DHS employee or contractor to conduct a public health activity. DHS employees or contractors must be prepared to explain and provide documentation to the provider or payer regarding their legal authority to collect or obtain information and be prepared to identify themselves.

3. Exceptions allowing limited disclosures without authorizations.

To the extent not otherwise prohibited or limited by federal or state requirements applicable to the DHS program or activity, DHS may use or disclose protected information without the written authorization of the individual in the following circumstances:

A. DHS may disclose information without authorization to individuals who have requested disclosure of their information to themselves.

B. DHS may disclose information without authorization for its own treatment, payment, or health care operations.

C. DHS may disclose information without authorization to another covered entity or a health care provider for the payment activities or the entity that receives the information.

D. DHS may disclose information without authorization to another entity covered by federal HIPAA law and rules for the health care activities of that entity, if

I. Both that entity and DHS has or has had a relationship with the individual who is the subject of the information.

II. The information pertains to such relationship.

III. The disclosure is for the purpose of

a. Conducting quality assessment and improvement activities, including outcome evaluation and development of clinical guidelines, provided that obtaining generalized knowledge is not the primary purpose of any studies resulting from such activities; population-based activities relating to improving health or reducing health care costs; protocol development; case management and care coordination; contacting health care providers and patients with information about treatment alternatives; and related functions that do not include treatment; or

b. Reviewing the competence or qualifications of health care professionals; evaluating practitioner and provider performance; conducting training programs in which students, trainees, or practitioners in areas of health care learn under supervision to practice or improve their skills as health care providers; training of non-health care professionals; accreditation, certification, licensing, or credentialing activities; or

c. Detecting health care fraud and abuse or for compliance purposes.

E. DHS may use or disclose psychotherapy notes without written authorization of the individual only for

I. Use by the originator of the psychotherapy notes, for treatment purposes.

II. Use or disclosures by DHS in training programs where students, trainees, or practitioners in mental health learn under supervision to practice or improve their skills in group, joint, family, or individual counseling.

III. When being used or disclosed by a health oversight agency in connection with oversight of the originator of the psychotherapy notes.

IV. To the extent authorized under state law to defend DHS in a legal action or other proceeding brought by the individual.

F. DHS may use or disclose information without the written authorization of the individual if DHS has reasonable cause to believe that a child is a victim of abuse or neglect, in which case DHS may disclose information to appropriate governmental authorities authorized by law to receive reports of child abuse or neglect (including reporting to DHS protective services staff, if appropriate).

I. Reports and records compiled under the provisions of ORS 419B.010 to 419B.050 are confidential and are not accessible for public inspection. However, if DHS receives the information, DHS will

a. Use and disclose the information consistent with its legal authority as a child protective services agency.

b. Subject to applicable law, DHS may make available records and reports to

i. Any law enforcement agency or a child abuse registry in any other state for the purposes of additional investigations of child abuse.

ii. Any physician, at the request of the physician, regarding any child brought to the physician or coming before the physician for examination, care, or treatment.

iii. Attorneys of records for the child or child's parent or guardian in any juvenile court proceeding.

iv. Citizen review boards established by the Judicial Department for the purpose of periodically reviewing the status of children, youths, and youth offenders under the jurisdiction of the juvenile court under ORS 419B.100 and 410C.005. Citizen review boards may make such records available to participants in case review.

v. A court-appointed special advocate (CASA) in any juvenile court proceeding in which it is alleged that a child has been abused or neglected.

vi. The Child Care Division for certifying, registering, or otherwise regulating child-care facilities.

II. Consistent with applicable law, DHS may make reports and records available to any person, administrative hearings officer, court, agency, organization, or other entity when the department determines that such disclosure is necessary to

a. Administer its child welfare services and is in the best interests of the affected child.

b. The disclosure is necessary to investigate, prevent, or treat child abuse and neglect.

c. Protect children from abuse and neglect.

d. Research when the assistant director gives prior written approval.

III. DHS may not disclose the name, address, or other identifying information about the person who made the report.

G. DHS may use or disclose information without the written authorization of the individual if DHS has reasonable cause to believe that an adult is a victim of abuse or neglect (elder abuse, nursing home abuse, or abuse of the mentally ill or developmentally disabled), DHS may disclose protected information to a government authority, including a social service or protective services agency, authorized by law to receive reports of such abuse or neglect:

I. If the disclosure is required by law and the disclosure complies with and is limited to the relevant requirements of such law.

II. If the individual agrees to the disclosure, either orally or in writing.

III. When DHS staff, in the exercise of professional judgment and in consultation with appropriate DHS supervisor, believes the disclosure is necessary to prevent serious harm to the individual or other potential victims.

IV. When the individual is unable to agree because of incapacity, a law enforcement agency, or other public official authorized to receive the report represents that

  a. The protected information being sought is not intended to be used against the individual, and

  b. An immediate law enforcement activity would be materially and adversely affected by waiting until the individual is able to agree to the disclosure.

V. When DHS staff make a disclosure permitted above, DHS must promptly inform the individual that such a report has been or will be made, except if

  a. DHS staff, in the exercise of professional judgment and in consultation with appropriate DHS supervisor, believes informing the individual would place the individual or another individual at risk of serious harm.

  b. DHS staff would be informing a personal representative and DHS staff reasonably believes the personal representative is responsible for the abuse, neglect, or other injury, and that informing such person would not be in the best interests of the individual, as determined by DHS staff, in the exercise of professional judgment and in consultation with appropriate DHS supervisor.

H. DHS may use or disclose information without the written authorization of the individual when DHS is acting as the governmental authority authorized by law to receive reports of abuse, neglect, or domestic violence. In those instances DHS is authorized to use and disclose the information consistent with its legal authority.

I. DHS may use or disclose information without the written authorization of the individual for the purpose of carrying out duties in its role as a health oversight agency. DHS does not need to obtain an individual's authorization to lawfully receive, use, or disclose individual information for oversight activities authorized by law.

    I. DHS may disclose information to a health oversight agency to the extent the disclosure is not prohibited by state or federal law for its oversight activities of

        a. The health care system.

        b. Government benefit programs for which the information is relevant to eligibility.

        c. Entities subject to government regulatory programs for which the information is necessary for determining compliance with program standards.

        d. Entities subject to civil rights laws for which the information is necessary for determining compliance.

    II. Exception: A health oversight activity for which information may be disclosed does not include an investigation or other activity of which the individual is the subject unless the investigation or other activity is directly related to

        a. The receipt of health care.

        b. A claim to recover public benefits related to health.

        c. Qualifying for or receiving public benefits or services based on the health of the individual.

    III. If a health oversight activity or investigation is conducted in conjunction with an oversight activity or investigation relating to a claim for public benefits not related to health, the joint activity is considered a health oversight activity for purposes of this section.

    IV. When DHS is acting as a health oversight agency, DHS may use information for health oversight activities as permitted under this section.

J. DHS may use or disclose information without the written authorization of the individual when DHS discloses information in a judicial or administrative proceeding subject to the following:

    I. DHS must follow any procedures for responding to subpoenas, discovery requests, or other requests for documents that DHS may have regarding an individual; DHS must not ignore any subpoena or other legal document.

        a. In general, DHS will respond by appearing before the court to explain that the information is confidential, or by filing a legal response through the Department of Justice. DHS will not disclose any confidential information in a court proceeding in which DHS is not a party except as required by law or by a court order.

        b. An administrative hearings officer or administrative law judge lacks legal authority, under State law, to require or authorize DHS to disclose information about an individual that is confidential under federal or state law. DHS staff should work with hearing officers to ensure that protective orders are used when appropriate in contested case hearings to prevent authorized uses and disclosures of information.

        c. DHS staff will refer any questions or concerns regarding what is required by law, or by a court order, to the DHS Privacy Officer, who may then consult with the Department of Justice to resolve the question.

        d. Exception: DHS may disclose information regarding mental health, alcohol or drug treatment, and vocational rehabilitation services only if required by a court order (ORS 179.505). For civil commitment proceedings, previous mental health histories may not be released.

    II. DHS may use or request information to investigate a grievance or appeal made to DHS about an individual's eligibility or right to benefits or services.

        a. Pursuant to applicable laws and rules, DHS may use or disclose information that DHS has compiled on its own or has received from external sources.

b. That information may be reviewed by DHS staff and legal counsel, the providers or health plan involved in the service or action, and may be provided to a hearing officer, to assist DHS in making a decision about the appeal or grievance.

III. If DHS is sued or if a suit is filed on behalf of DHS, the Department of Justice will address or respond to legal issues related to the use and disclosure of information. DHS will identify confidentiality issues for discussion with the assigned legal counsel, in consultation with the DHS Privacy Officer.

IV. If a court orders DHS to conduct a mental examination (such as in accordance with state law at ORS 161.315, 161.365, 161.370, ORS 419B.352), or orders DHS to provide any other report or evaluation to the court, such examination, report, or evaluation shall be deemed to be "required by law" for purposes of HIPAA, and DHS staff will comply with the court order.

V. If DHS has obtained information in performing its duties as a health oversight agency, public health authority, protective service entity, or public benefit program, nothing in this section supersedes DHS policies that otherwise permit or restrict uses or disclosures. For example, if DHS has obtained individual patient information as a result of an oversight action against a provider, DHS may lawfully use that patient information in a hearing consistent with the other confidentiality requirements applicable to that program, service, or activity.

VI. In any case in which federal or state law prohibits or restricts the use or disclosure of information in an administrative or judicial proceeding, DHS shall assert the confidentiality of such confidential information, consistent with DHS policies applicable to the program, service, or activity, to the presiding officer at the proceeding. A HIPAA-authorized protective order may not be sufficient to authorize disclosure if it does not address other applicable confidentiality laws.

K. DHS may use or disclose information without the written authorization of the individual for law enforcement purposes unless federal or state law prohibits such disclosure.

I. DHS may disclose information when reporting certain types of wounds or other physical injuries.

II. DHS may disclose information in compliance with, and limited to the relevant specific requirements of

   a. A court order or warrant, summons, or subpoena issued by a judicial officer.

   b. A grand jury subpoena.

   c. An administrative request, including administrative subpoena or summons, a civil or authorized investigative demand, or similar lawful process, provided that the information is relevant, material, and limited to a legitimate law enforcement inquiry.

     i. Follow DHS procedures for responding to subpoenas, discovery requests, or other requests for documents that DHS may have regarding an individual—do not ignore any subpoena or other legal document. See section 3(j)(i) of this policy's procedures.

III. Exception: Information regarding mental health, alcohol or drug treatment, and vocational rehabilitation services can be disclosed only on the basis of a court order (ORS 179.505, 42CFR Part 2).

IV. DHS may disclose limited protected information upon request of a law enforcement official without authorization for the purpose of identifying or locating a suspect, fugitive, material witness, or missing person, provided that

   a. The information DHS may thus disclose is limited to

     i. Name and address.

     ii. Date and place of birth.

     iii. Social Security Number.

     iv. ABO blood type and rh factor.

     v. Type of injury.

     vi. Date and time of treatment.

     vii. Date and time of death if applicable.

     viii. A description of distinguishing physical characteristics, including height, weight, gender, race, hair and eye color, presence or absence of beard or mustache, scars, and tattoos. In cases of criminal court commitments, a photograph may be provided.

ix. Exception: DHS may not disclose, for purposes of identification or location, protected health information related to the subject's DNA or DNA analysis, dental records, or typing, samples, or analysis of bodily fluids or tissues, unless ordered to do so by a court or a court approved search warrant.

V. DHS may disclose protected information upon request to a law enforcement official about an individual who is or is suspected to be the victim of a crime, if

a. DHS is otherwise authorized by law to disclose that information for purposes of an abuse reporting law or for public health or heath oversight purposes; or

b. The individual agrees to the disclosure, either orally or in writing; or

c. DHS is unable to obtain the individual's agreement due to incapacity or emergency circumstance, if

   i. The law enforcement official represents that such information is needed to determine whether a violation of law by someone other than the victim has occurred and such information is not intended for use against the victim.

   ii. The law enforcement official represents that immediate law enforcement activity would be materially and adversely affected by waiting until the individual is able to agree to the disclosure.

   iii. DHS determines that the disclosure is in the best interests of the individual.

VI. DHS may disclose protected information to a law enforcement official about an individual who has died, for the purpose of alerting law enforcement of the death, if DHS suspects that death may have resulted from criminal conduct.

VII. DHS may disclose protected information to a law enforcement official if DHS believes in good faith that the information constitutes evidence of criminal conduct on DHS premises.

VIII. Necessary for law enforcement authorities to identify or apprehend an individual:

  a. Because of a statement by a person admitting participation in a violent crime that DHS reasonably believes may have caused serious harm to the victim.

  b. Where it appears from all the circumstances that the individual has escaped from a correctional institution or from lawful custody.

L. DHS may disclose an individual's information without authorization for the following specialized government functions without individual authorization unless such disclosure is prohibited by federal or state law:

  I. For individuals who are Armed Forces personnel, as deemed necessary by appropriate military command authorities to ensure the proper execution of the military mission.

  II. To authorized federal officials for conducting lawful intelligence, counterintelligence, and other national security activities, as authorized by the federal National Security Act (50 U.S.C 401, et seq.) and implementing authority.

  III. To authorized federal officials for the protection of the President or of other persons authorized by applicable federal law.

M. DHS may use or disclose information without the written authorization of the individual consistent with applicable law to a correctional institution or a law enforcement official having lawful custody of an inmate or other person, if the institution or official represents that the information is necessary for

  I. Providing health care to the person.

  II. The health or safety of the person or of other inmates.

N. DHS may use or disclose protected information without the written authorization of the individual in the case of an emergency.

  I. Medical emergency information is restricted to information needed by the health care provider to deal with the emergency, and must be the minimum amount necessary to satisfy the request. Once the emergency situation subsides, DHS should obtain assurance that the information released will not be re-disclosed.

II. Any disclosure of Protected Health Information must be recorded in the DHS 2097, "Disclosures of Protected Information," as outlined in DHS Policy AS-100-02, "Client Privacy Rights."

4. Procedures when client or participant authorization is not required if they are informed in advance and given a chance to object.

A. In some limited circumstances, DHS may use or disclose an individual's information without authorization, but only if the individual has been informed in advance and has been given the opportunity to either agree or to refuse or restrict the use or disclosure. These circumstances are

   I. For disclosure of health care information to a family member, other relative, close personal friend of the individual, or any other person named by the individual, subject to the following limitations:

   a. DHS may reveal only the protected information that directly relates to such person's involvement with the individual's care or payment for such care.

   b. DHS may use or disclose protected information for notifying (including identifying or locating) a family member, personal representative, or other person responsible for care of the individual, regarding the individual's location, general condition, or death.

   c. If the individual is present for, or available prior to, such a use or disclosure, DHS may disclose the protected information if it

   i. Obtains the individual's agreement.

   ii. Provides the individual an opportunity to object to the disclosure, and the individual does not express an objection.

   iii. Reasonably infers from the circumstances that the individual does not object to the disclosure.

B. If the individual is not present, or the opportunity to object to the use or disclosure cannot practicably be provided due to the individual's incapacity or an emergency situation, DHS may determine, using professional judgment, that the use or disclosure is in the individual's best interests.

   I. Any agreement, objection, refusal, or restriction by the individual may be oral or in writing. DHS will document any such oral communication in the client's case file.

II. DHS will also document in the case file the outcome of any opportunity provided to object, the individual's decision not to object, or the inability of the individual to object.

C. **Note:** Oral permission to use or disclose information for purposes described in subsection (A) of this section is not sufficient when the individual is referred to or receiving substance abuse treatment, mental health services, or vocational rehabilitation services. A written Authorization is required under those circumstances.

5. Re-disclosure of an individual's information.

There are no accompanying procedures.

6. Revocation of an Authorization.

A. When an individual revokes a written Authorization to disclose information, DHS must boldly mark the Authorization form "revoked" and include the date and signature of the requesting individual.

B. When an individual revokes only one record holder on the Authorization form, DHS will boldly mark only that section "revoked" and include the date and the individual's signature.

C. Revoked forms must be maintained in the file.

7. Verification of individuals requesting information.

A. Protected Health Information may not be disclosed without verifying the identity of the person requesting the information if the person is not known to the DHS staff member fulfilling the request.

B. If the requestor is a provider, they need to supply their provider identification number and/or telephone number for call back.

C. For all other requestors, reasonable evidence should be supplied in the form of the following:

I. Identification badge.

II. Driver's license.

III. Written statement of identity on agency letterhead.

IV. Similar proof.

8. Denial of requests for information.

There are no accompanying procedures.

Minimum Necessary Information Policy

The intention of the DHS Minimum Necessary Information Policy is to

- Improve the privacy of confidential information that is used or disclosed by DHS employees in the course of their work.
- Ensure that DHS employees have access to the information they require to accomplish DHS's mission, goals, and objectives.

This document contains guidance for developing procedures to implement this policy.

1. General.

A. DHS will use or disclose only the minimum amount of information necessary to provide services and benefits to clients, and only to the extent provided in DHS policies and procedures.

B. This policy does not apply to

    I. Disclosures to or requests by a health care provider for treatment.

    II. Disclosures made to the individual about his or her own protected information.

    III. Uses or disclosures authorized by the individual that are within the scope of the authorization.

    IV. Disclosures made to the Department of Health and Human Services (HHS), Office for Civil Rights, in accordance with subpart C of part 160 of the HIPAA Privacy Rule.

    V. Uses or disclosures that are required by law.

    VI. Uses or disclosures that are required for compliance with the HIPAA Transaction Rule. The minimum necessary standard does not apply to the required or situational data elements specified in the implementation guides under the Transaction Rule.

2. Minimum necessary information.

A. When DHS policy permits use or disclosure of an individual's information to another entity, or when DHS requests an individual's information from another entity, DHS employees must make reasonable efforts to limit the amount of information to the minimum necessary needed to accomplish the intended purpose of the use, disclosure, or request.

B. If DHS policy permits making a particular disclosure to another entity, DHS employees may rely on a requested disclosure as being the minimum necessary for the stated purpose when

I. Making disclosures to public officials that are permitted under 45 CFR 164.512, and as stated in DHS policy AS-100-03, "Uses and Disclosures of Client or Participant Information," if the public official represents the information requested is the minimum necessary for the stated purpose(s). A "public official" is any employee of a government agency who is authorized to act on behalf of that agency in performing the lawful duties and responsibilities of that agency.

II. The information is requested by another entity that is a "covered entity" under the HIPAA Privacy rules. A "covered entity" is a health plan, a health care provider who conducts electronic transactions, or a health care clearinghouse.

III. The information is requested by a professional who is a member of the workforce of a covered entity or is a business associate of the covered entity for the purpose of providing professional services to the covered entity, if the professional represents that the information requested is the minimum necessary for the stated purpose(s).

IV. Documentation or representations that comply with the applicable requirements of DHS Policy AS-100-06, "Uses and Disclosures for Research Purposes and Waivers" have been provided by a person requesting the information for research purposes.

3. Access and uses of information.

A. DHS will establish role-based categories that identify types of information necessary for employees to do their jobs. DHS program areas will identify the category of information needed for persons, or classes of persons, in their respective workforces to carry out their duties, and will further identify any conditions appropriate to such access. Categories will include all information, such as information accessible by computer, kept in files, or other forms of information consistent with DHS Policy AS-100-05, "Administrative, Technical and Physical Safeguards."

4. Routine and recurring disclosure of an individual's information.

A. For the purposes of this policy, *routine and recurring* means the disclosure of records outside DHS, without the authorization of the individual, for a purpose that is compatible with the purpose for which the information was collected. The following section of this document identifies several examples of uses and disclosures that DHS has determined to be compatible with the purposes for which information is collected.

    I. DHS will not disclose an individual's entire medical record unless the request specifically justifies why the entire medical record is needed.

    II. Routine and recurring uses include disclosures required by law. For example, a mandatory child abuse report by a DHS employee would be a routine use.

    III. If DHS deems it desirable or necessary, DHS may disclose information as a routine and recurring use to the State Department of Justice for the purpose of obtaining its advice and legal services.

    IV. When federal or state agencies—such as the DHHS Office for Civil Rights, the DHHS Office of Inspector General, the State Medicaid Fraud Unit, or the Secretary of State—have the legal authority to require DHS to produce records necessary to carry out audit or oversight of DHS programs or activities, DHS will make such records available as a routine and recurring use.

    V. When the appropriate DHS official determines that records are subject to disclosure under the State Public Records Law, DHS may make the disclosure as a routine and recurring use.

5. Non-routine disclosure of an individual's information.

A. For the purpose of this policy, "non-routine disclosure" means the disclosure of records outside DHS that is not for a purpose for which it was collected.

B. DHS will not disclose an individual's entire medical record unless the request specifically justifies why the entire medical record is needed, and applicable laws and policy permit the disclosure of all the information in the medical record to the requestor.

C. Requests for non-routine disclosures must be reviewed on an individual basis in accordance with the criteria set forth in the procedure section.

D. For non-routine disclosures, DHS program areas will

 I. Implement procedures to limit the information disclosed to only the minimum amount of information necessary to accomplish the purpose for which the disclosure is sought.

 II. Review requests for non-routine disclosures on an individual basis in accordance with such procedures.

6. DHS's request for an individual's information from another entity.

When requesting information about an individual from another entity, DHS employees must limit requests to those that are reasonably necessary to accomplish the purpose for which the request is made.

A. DHS will not request an individual's entire medical record unless DHS can specifically justify why the entire medical record is needed.

Guidance for Procedure Development

The following guidelines should be used in developing procedures to implement this policy:

1. Disclosures of an individual's information on a routine or recurring basis.

For routine and recurring disclosures, DHS program areas will

A. Determine who is requesting the information and the purpose for the request.

 I. If the request is not compatible with the purpose for which it was collected, refer to and apply the "non-routine use" procedures in the following section.

B. Confirm that the applicable DHS policies and program rules apply to the requested use (disclosure is consistent with the program purposes), and that the nature or type of the use recurs (occurs on a periodic basis) within the program or activity.

C. Identify the kind and amount of information that is necessary to respond to the request.

    D. If the disclosure is one that must be included in the DHS accounting of disclosures, include required documentation in the accounting log.

2. Disclosures of an individual's information on a non-routine basis.

For non-routine disclosures, DHS clusters and program areas will

    A. Determine who is requesting the information and the purpose for the request.

        I. If the request is compatible with the purpose for which it was collected, apply the "routine and recurring use" procedures in the previous section.

    B. Determine which information of the individual is within the scope of the request, and what DHS policies and program rules apply to the requested use.

    C. If the information requested can be disclosed under the applicable program and HIPAA policies and limit the amount of information to the minimum amount necessary to respond to the request.

    D. Document the disclosure in the accounting log.

Administrative, Technical, and Physical Safeguards Policy

The intent of this policy is to establish criteria for safeguarding confidential information and to minimize the risk of unauthorized access, use, or disclosure.

This document contains guidance for developing procedures to implement this policy.

1. General.

DHS must take reasonable steps to safeguard information from any intentional or unintentional use or disclosure that is in violation of the privacy policies. Information to be safeguarded may be in any medium, including paper, electronic, oral, and visual representations of confidential information.

2. Safeguarding confidential information—DHS workplace practices.

  A. Paper.

      I. Each DHS workplace will store files and documents in locked rooms or storage systems.

     II. In workplaces where lockable storage is not available, DHS staff must take reasonable efforts to ensure the safeguarding of confidential information.

   III. Each DHS workplace will ensure that files and documents awaiting disposal or destruction in desk-site containers, storage rooms, or centralized waste/shred bins are appropriately labeled, are disposed of on a regular basis, and that all reasonable measures are taken to minimize access.

   IV. Each DHS workplace will ensure that shredding of files and documents is performed on a timely basis, consistent with record retention requirements.

  B. Oral.

      I. DHS staff must take reasonable steps to protect the privacy of all verbal exchanges or discussions of confidential information, regardless of where the discussion occurs.

     II. Each DHS workplace shall make enclosed offices and/or interview rooms available for the verbal exchange of confidential information.

   III. Exception: In work environments structured with few offices or closed rooms, such as in the State Hospital, State Operated Group Homes, or open office environments, uses or disclosures that are incidental to an otherwise permitted use or disclosure could occur. Such incidental uses or disclosures are not considered a violation provided that DHS has met the reasonable safeguards and minimum necessary requirements.

   IV. Each DHS workplace must foster employee awareness of the potential for inadvertent verbal disclosure of confidential information.

  C. Visual.

      I. DHS staff must ensure that observable confidential information on computer screens and paper documents is adequately shielded from unauthorized disclosure.

a. Computer screens: Each DHS workplace must make every effort to ensure that confidential information on computer screens is not visible to unauthorized persons.

b. Paper documents: DHS staff must be aware of the risks regarding how paper documents are used and handled, and must take all necessary precautions to safeguard confidential information.

3. Safeguarding confidential information—DHS administrative safeguards

A. Implementation of role-based access and the minimum necessary policy will promote administrative safeguards.

I. Role Based Access (RBA) is a form of security allowing access to data based on job function in accordance with DHS security procedures. Employees shall be assigned to an RBA group that give members access only to the minimum necessary information to fulfill their job functions.

B. Conducting internal reviews periodically permits DHS to evaluate the effectiveness of safeguards.

I. DHS managers and supervisors will use the DHS Safeguards Assessment Tool to conduct annual reviews in order to evaluate and improve the effectiveness of their current safeguards.

C. Development and implementation of department-wide security policies enhances administrative safeguards.

I. DHS staff will be required to sign a document that constitutes a formal commitment to adhere to the department-wide security policies.

Guidance for Procedure Development

The following guidelines should be used in developing procedures to implement this policy.

1. General.

There are no accompanying procedures.

2. Safeguarding confidential information—DHS workplace practices.

A. Paper

I. Files and documents being stored:

a. Lockable desks, file rooms, and open area storage systems must be locked.

b. Where DHS has desks, file rooms, or open area storage systems that are not lockable, reasonable efforts to safeguard confidential information must be implemented.

II. Files and documents awaiting disposal/destruction.

a. **Desk-site containers.** The DHS workplace will ensure that confidential information awaiting disposal is stored in containers that are appropriately labeled and are properly disposed of on a regular basis.

b. **Storage rooms containing confidential information awaiting disposal.** Each DHS workplace will ensure that storage rooms are locked after business hours or when authorized staff are not present.

c. **Centralized waste/shred bins.** Each DHS workplace will ensure that all centralized bins or containers for disposed confidential information are clearly labeled "confidential," sealed, and placed in a lockable storage room.

d. Each DHS workplace that does not have lockable storage rooms or centralized waste/shred bins must implement reasonable procedures to minimize access to confidential information.

III. Shredding of files and authorized documents consistent with record retention requirements follow:

a. DHS staff must ensure that shredding is done in a timely manner, preferably on a daily basis.

b. DHS must ensure that such outside contractors are under a written contract that requires safeguarding of confidential information throughout the destruction process.

B. Oral.

    I. DHS staff must take reasonable steps to protect the privacy of all verbal exchanges or discussions of confidential information, regardless of where the discussion occurs, and should be aware of risk levels.

        a. Locations of verbal exchange with various risk levels:

            i. **Low risk.** Interview rooms, enclosed offices, and conference rooms.

            ii. **Medium risk.** Employee only areas, telephone, and individual cubicles.

            iii. **High risk.** Public areas, reception areas, and shared cubicles housing multiple staff where clients are routinely present.

C. Visual.

    I. DHS staff must ensure that observable confidential information is adequately shielded from unauthorized disclosure.

    II. DHS offices must ensure that confidential information on computer screens is not visible to unauthorized persons. Suggested means for ensuring this protection include

        a. Use of polarized screens or other computer screen overlay devices that shield information on the screen from persons who are not the authorized user.

        b. Placement of computers out of the visual range of persons other than the authorized user.

        c. Clearing information from the screen when not actually being used.

        d. Locking-down computer workstations when not in use.

        e. Other effective means as available.

    III. DHS staff must be aware of the risks regarding how paper documents are used and handled, and must take all necessary precautions to safeguard confidential information.

    IV. DHS staff must take special care to ensure the protection and safeguarding of, and the minimum necessary access to, paper documents containing confidential information that are located on

        a. Desks.

b. Fax machines.

c. Photocopy machines.

d. Portable electronic devices (for example, laptop computers, palm pilots, and so on).

e. Computer printers.

f. Common areas (for example, break rooms, cafeterias, rest rooms, elevators, and so on).

3. **Safeguarding confidential information—DHS administrative safeguards.**

A. Role Based Access (RBA): Roles will be created and defined based on the information DHS owns, where it is located, how it is used, and why. A determination of who should have access to the specific data will be established.

  I. DHS managers and supervisors will decide the role of each of their staff and request exceptions based on the needs of their office.

  II. Managers are responsible for allowing access to enough information for their staff to do their jobs while holding to the minimum necessary standard.

B. DHS managers and supervisors will

  I. Follow the instructions given in the Guidance for DHS Managers and Supervisors to safeguard confidential information.

  II. Conduct a thorough assessment by using the DHS Safeguards Assessment Tool.

  III. Foster a more secure atmosphere and enhance the belief that confidential information is important and that protecting privacy is key to achieving DHS goals.

  IV. Managers will update the safeguards in place each year, seeking to achieve reasonable administrative, technical, and physical safeguards.

C. Utilize the security policies to augment safeguard procedures.

Use and Disclosure for Research Purposes and Waivers Policy

The intent of this policy is to specify when DHS may use or disclose information about individuals for research purposes.

1. General.

When DHS uses or discloses an individual's information for research purposes, they must consider the following:

    A. DHS may use or disclose an individual's information for research purposes as specified in this policy. Research means "a systematic investigation, including research development, testing, and evaluation, designed to develop or contribute to generalizable knowledge."

    B. All such research disclosures are subject to applicable requirements of state and federal laws and regulations and to the specific requirements of this policy.

Note: This policy is intended to supplement existing research requirements of the Common Rule, 45 CFR Part 46. The Common Rule is the rule for the protection of human subjects in research promulgated by the U.S. Department of Health and Human Services, and adopted by other federal governmental agencies, including the National Institutes for Health, for research funded by those agencies. In addition, some agencies have requirements that supplement the Common Rule that are applicable to a particular research contract or grant.

    C. Deidentified information may be used or disclosed for purposes of research, consistent with DHS Policy AS-100-07, "Deidentification of Client Information and Use of Limited Data Sets."

    D. A limited data set may be used or disclosed for purposes of research, consistent with the policies related to Limited Data Sets in DHS Policy AS-100-07, "De-identification of Client Information and Use of Limited Data Sets."

    E. DHS may also conduct public health studies, studies that are required by law, and studies or analysis related to its health care operations. Such studies will be discussed in Sections (4.) and (5.) of this Policy.

2. Institutional Review Board (IRB) or Privacy Board established by DHS.

DHS may use an IRB established in accordance with 45 CFR Part 46 or a Privacy Board that has been established by DHS pursuant to this Policy, to perform the duties and functions specified in this policy regarding a research project being conducted, in whole or in part, by DHS or by a DHS office or program.

3. Uses and disclosures for research purposes—specific requirements.

A. DHS may use or disclose client or participant information for research purposes with the client's specific written authorization.

I. Such authorization must meet all the requirements described in DHS Policy AS-100-03, "Uses and Disclosures of Client or Participant Information," and may indicate as an expiration date such terms as "end of research study," or similar language.

II. An authorization for use and disclosure for a research study may be combined with any other type of written permission for the same research study.

III. If research includes treatment, the researcher may condition the provision of research related treatment on the provision of an authorization for use and disclosure for such research.

B. DHS may use or disclose client or participant information for research purposes without the client's or participant's written authorization provided that:

I. DHS obtains documentation that a waiver of an individual's authorization for release of information requirements has been approved by either:

a. An Institutional Review Board (IRB); or

b. A Privacy Board that

i. Has members with varying backgrounds and appropriate professional competency as needed to review the effect of the research protocol on the individual's privacy rights and related concerns.

ii. Includes at least one member who is not affiliated with DHS, not affiliated with any entity conducting or sponsoring the research, and not related to any person who is affiliated with any such entity.

      iii. Does not have any member participating in a review of any project in which the member has a conflict of interest.

II. Documentation required of IRB or privacy board when granting approval of a waiver of an individual's authorization for release of information must include

  a. A statement identifying the IRB or privacy board that approved the waiver of an individual's authorization, and the date of such approval.

  b. A statement that the IRB or privacy board has determined that the waiver of authorization, in whole or in part, satisfies that the use or disclosure of an individual's protected information involves no more than minimal risk to the privacy of an individual, based on at least the following elements:

      i. An adequate plan to protect an individual's identifying information from improper use or disclosure.

      ii. An adequate plan to destroy an individual's identifying information at the earliest opportunity consistent with the conduct of the research, unless there is a health or research justification for retaining the identifiers or such retention is otherwise required by law.

      iii. Adequate written assurances that the protected health information will not be reused or disclosed to any other person or entity, except as required by law, for authorized oversight of the research study, or for other research for which the use or disclosure of the protected information would be permitted under this policy.

      iv. The research could not practicably be conducted without the waiver.

      v. The research could not practicably be conducted without access to and use of the individual's protected information.

III. Adequate written assurances that the protected health information will not be reused or disclosed to any other person or entity, except as required by law, for authorized oversight of the research study, or for other research for which the use or disclosure of the protected information would be permitted under this policy.

IV.The research could not practicably be conducted without the waiver.

V.The research could not practicably be conducted without access to and use of the individual's protected information.

C. A brief description of the protected health information for which use or disclosure has been determined to be necessary by the IRB or privacy board.

D. A statement that the waiver of an individual's authorization has been reviewed and approved under either normal or expedited review procedures, by either an IRB or a privacy board, pursuant to federal regulations at 45 CFR 164.512(2).

E. The Privacy Board chair must sign documentation of the waiver of an individual's authorization, or other member as designated by the chair of the IRB or the orivacy board, as applicable.

I. In some cases, a researcher may request access to individual information maintained by DHS in preparation for research or to facilitate the development of a research protocol in anticipation of research. Before agreeing to provide such access to individual information, DHS should determine whether federal or state law otherwise permits such use or disclosure without individual authorization or use of an IRB. If there is any doubt whether the use and disclosure of the information by the researcher falls within this HIPAA exception, review by an IRB or privacy board and formal waiver of authorization is required. If such access falls within this HIPAA exception to authorization and is otherwise permitted by other federal or state law, DHS will only provide such access if DHS obtains, from the researcher, written representations that

a. Use or disclosure is sought solely to review an individual's protected information needed to prepare a research protocol or for similar purposes to prepare for the research project.

b. No client information will be removed from DHS by the researcher in the course of the review; the client information for which use or access is sought is necessary for the research purposes.

c. Researcher and his or her agents agree not to use or further disclose the information other than as provided in the written agreement, and to use appropriate safeguards to prevent the use or disclosure of the information other than is provided for by the written agreement.

d. Researcher and his or her agents agree not to publicly identify the information or contact the individual whose data is being disclosed.

e. Applicable federal or state law may require such other terms or conditions.

II. In some cases, a researcher may request access to individual information maintained by DHS about individuals who are deceased. DHS should determine whether federal or state law otherwise permits such use or disclosure of information about decedents without individual authorization or use of an IRB. There may be instances where it would be inappropriate to disclose information, even where the individual subject of the information is dead—for example, individuals who died of AIDS may not have wanted such information to be disclosed after their deaths. If there is any doubt whether the use and disclosure of the information by the researcher falls within this HIPAA exception, review by an IRB or privacy board and formal waiver of authorization is required. If such access falls within this HIPAA exception to authorization and is otherwise permitted by other federal or state law, DHS will only provide such access if DHS obtains the following written representations from the researcher:

a. Representation that the use or disclosure is sought solely for research on the protected information of deceased persons;

b. Documentation, if DHS so requests, of the death of such persons;

c. Representation that the individual's protected information for which use or disclosure is sought is necessary for the research purposes.

d. Researcher and his or her agents agree not to use or further disclose the information other than as provided in the written agreement, and to use appropriate safeguards to prevent the use or disclosure of the information other than is provided for by the written agreement;

e. Researcher and his or her agents agree not to publicly identify the information or contact the personal representative or family members of the decedent; and

f. Applicable federal or state law may require such other terms or conditions.

4. DHS public health studies and studies required by law.

When DHS is operating as a public health authority, DHS is authorized to obtain and use individual information without authorization for the purpose of preventing injury or controlling disease and for the conduct of public health surveillance, investigations, and interventions. In addition to these responsibilities, DHS may collect, use, or disclose information, without individual authorization, to the extent that such collection, use, or disclosure is required by law. When DHS uses information to conduct studies pursuant to such authority, no additional individual authorization is required nor does this policy require IRB or privacy board waiver of authorization based on the HIPAA Privacy rules. Other applicable laws and protocols continue to apply to such studies.

5. DHS studies related to health care operations.

Studies and data analyses conducted for DHS's own quality assurance purposes and to comply with reporting requirements applicable to federal or state funding requirements fall within the uses and disclosures that may be made without individual authorization as DHS health care operations. Neither individual authorization nor IRB or privacy board waiver of authorization is required for studies or data analyses conducted by or on behalf of DHS for purposes of health care operations, including any studies or analyses conducted to comply with reporting requirements applicable to federal or state funding requirements. Health care operations, as defined in 45 CFR 164.512 include

A. Conducting quality assessment and improvement activities, including outcome evaluation and development of clinical guidelines, provided that the obtaining of generalizable knowledge is not the primary purpose of any studies resulting from such activities.

B. Conducting population-based activities relating to improving health care or reducing health care costs, protocol development, case management, care coordination, contacting health care providers and patients with information about treatment alternatives, and related functions that do not include treatment.

C. Reviewing the competence or qualifications of health care professionals; evaluating practitioner and provider performance and health plan performance; and conducting training programs and accreditation, certification, licensing, or credentialing activities.

D. Underwriting, premium rating, and other activities related to the creation, renewal, or replacement of a contract of health insurance or health benefits.

E. Conducting or arranging for medical review, legal services, and auditing functions, including fraud and abuse detection and compliance programs.

F. Business planning and development, such as conducting cost-management analysis and planning related analyses related to managing and operating DHS, including improvement of administration and development or improvement of methods of payment or coverage policies.

G. Business management and general administrative activities of DHS, including management activities related to HIPAA implementation and compliance; customer services, including the provision of data analyses for policy holders, plan sponsors, or other customers; resolution of internal grievances.

H. Creating deidentified information or a limited data set consistent with the DHS Policy AS-100-07, "De-identification of Client Information and Use of Limited Data Sets."

Exception: HIV-AIDS information may not be disclosed to anyone without the specific written authorization of the individual. Re-disclosure of HIV test information is prohibited, except in compliance with law or with written permission from the individual.

Deidentification of Client Information and Limited Data Sets Policy

The intent of this policy is to prescribe standards under which client information can be used and disclosed if information that can identify a person has been removed or restricted to a limited data set.

1. General

A. Deidentified information is client information from which DHS or another entity has deleted, redacted, or blocked identifiers, so that the remaining information cannot reasonably be used to identify a person.

B. Unless otherwise restricted or prohibited by other federal or state law, DHS can use and share information as appropriate for the work of DHS, without further restriction, if DHS or another entity has taken steps to deidentify the information consistent with the requirements and restrictions of this policy in Section (2.)

C. DHS may use or disclose a limited data set that meets the requirements of Section (4.) of this Policy, if DHS enters into a data use agreement with the limited data set recipient (or with the data source, if DHS will be the recipient of the limited data set) in accordance with the requirements of Section (5.) of this Policy.

D. DHS may disclose a limited data set only for the purposes of research, or non-governmental public health purposes. However, unless DHS has obtained a limited data set that is subject to a data use agreement, DHS is not restricted to using a limited data set for its own activities or operations.

E. If DHS knows of a pattern, activity, or practice of the limited data set recipient that constitutes a material breach or violation of a data set agreement, DHS will take reasonable steps to cure the breach or end the violation and, if such steps are unsuccessful, DHS will discontinue disclosure of information to the recipient and report the problem to the Secretary of the United States Department of Health and Human Services (HHS).

2. Requirements for deidentification of client information.

A. DHS may determine that client information is sufficiently deidentified, and cannot be used to identify an individual, only if **either** (I.) or (II.) below have occurred:

   I. A statistician or other person with appropriate knowledge of, and experience with, generally accepted statistical and scientific principles and methods for rendering information not individually identifiable

   a. Has applied such principles and methods, and determined that the risk is minimal and that the information could be used, alone or in combination with other reasonably available information, by a recipient of the information to identify the person whose information is being used.

   b. Has documented the methods and results of the analysis that justify such a determination, **or**

   II. DHS has ensured that

   a. The following identifiers of the individual or of relatives, employers, and household members of the individual are removed:

      i. Names.

      ii. All geographic subdivisions smaller than a state, including street address, city, county, precinct, zip code, and their equivalent geocodes. However, the initial three digits of a zip code may remain on the information if, according to current publicly available data from the Bureau of the Census, the geographic unit formed by combining all zip codes with the same three initial digits contains more than 20,000 people, and the initial three digits for all such geographic units containing 20,000 or fewer people is changed to 000.

      iii. All elements of dates (except year) for dates directly relating to an individual, including birth date, dates of admission and discharge from a health care facility, and date of death. For persons age 90 and older, all elements of dates (including year) that would indicate such age must be removed, except that such ages and elements may be aggregated into a single category of "age 90 or older."

    iv. Telephone numbers.

    v. Fax numbers.

    v. Electronic mail addresses.

    vi. Social Security Numbers.

    vii. Medical record numbers.

    viii. Health plan beneficiary numbers.

    ix. Account numbers.

    x. Certificate or license numbers.

    xi. Vehicle identifiers and serial numbers, including license plate numbers.

    xii. Device identifiers and serial numbers.

    xiii. Web Universal Resource Locators (URLs).

    xiv. Internet Protocol (IP) address numbers.

    xv. Biometric identifiers, including fingerprints and voice prints.

    xvi. Full face photographic images and any comparable images.

    xvii. Any other unique identifying number, characteristic, or codes, except as permitted under Section (3.), below, of this policy.

    xviii. DHS has no actual knowledge that the information could be used alone or in combination with other information to identify an individual who is the subject of the information.

B. The DHS Privacy Officer will designate the statistician or other person referred to in (2.)(a.)(i.), above, who may be either

    I. A DHS employee.

    II. An employee of another governmental agency.

    III. An outside contractor or consultant, subject to DHS contracting and personnel policy.

3. Re-identification of deidentified information.

A. DHS may assign a code or other means of record identification to allow information deidentified under this policy to be re-identified by DHS, except that

    I. The code or other means of record identification is not derived from or related to information about the individual and cannot otherwise be translated to identify the individual.

    II. DHS does not use or disclose the code or other means of record identification for any other purpose, and does not disclose the mechanism for re-identification.

4. Requirements for a limited data set.

    A. A *limited data set* is information that excludes the following direct identifiers of the individual, or of relatives, employers, or household members of the individual.

        I. Names.

        II. Postal address information, other than town or city, state, and zip code.

        III. Telephone numbers.

        IV. Fax numbers.

        V. Electronic mail addresses.

        VI. Social Security Numbers.

        VII. Medical record numbers.

        VIII. Health plan beneficiary numbers (such as Medicaid Prime Numbers).

        IX. Account numbers.

        X. Certificate/license numbers.

        XI. Vehicle identifiers and serial numbers, including license plate numbers.

        XII. Web Universal Resource Locators (URLs).

        XIII. Internet Protocol (IP) address numbers.

        XIV. Biometric identifiers, including fingerprints and voice prints.

        XV. Full face photographic images and any comparable images.

5. Contents of a data use agreement.

    A. DHS may disclose a limited data set only if the entity receiving the limited data set enters into a written agreement with DHS, in accordance with subsection (5.)(b.) immediately below, and that such entity will use or disclose the protected health information only as specified in the written agreement.

B. A data use agreement between DHS and the recipient of the limited data set must

    I. Specify the permitted uses and disclosures of such information by the limited data set recipient. DHS may not use the agreement to authorize the limited data set recipient to use or further disclose the information in a manner that would violate the requirements of this Policy if done by DHS.

    II. Specify who is permitted to use or receive the limited data set.

    III. Specify that the limited data set recipient will

        a. Not use or further disclose the information other than as specified in the data use agreement or as otherwise required by law.

        b. Use appropriate safeguards to prevent use or disclosure of the information other than as specified in the data use agreement.

        c. Report to DHS, if DHS is the source of the limited data set, if the recipient becomes aware of any use or disclosure of the information not specified in its data use agreement with DHS.

        d. Ensure that any agents, including a subcontractor, to whom it provides the limited data set agrees to the same restrictions and conditions that apply to the limited data set recipient with respect to such information.

        e. Not identify the information or contact the individuals whose data is being disclosed.

Business Associate Policy

The HIPAA Privacy rules identify a new category of business relationship, called a *business associate*. The purpose of this policy is to specify when DHS may disclose an individual's protected health information to a business associate of DHS, and to specify provisions that must be included in DHS contracts with business associates.

This document contains guidance for developing procedures to implement this policy.

1. General.

A. DHS has many contractual and business relationships, and DHS has policies related to its contracts and business relationships. However, not all contractors or business partners are business associates of DHS. This policy only applies to contractors or business partners that come within the definition of a business associate.

B. If a contractor or business partner is a business associate, those contracts that define the contractual relationship remain subject to all federal and state laws and policies governing the contractual relationship.

C. Business Associate means (per 45 CFR 160.103):

   I. With respect to DHS, a person who

   a. On behalf of DHS, but other than in the capacity of a DHS employee, performs or assists in the performance of

   i. A function or activity involving the use or disclosure of individually identifiable health information, including claims processing or administration, data analysis, processing or administration, utilization review, quality assurance, billing benefit management, practice management, and repricing or

   ii. Any other function or activity regulated by federal regulations at 45 CFR Subtitle A, Subchapter C.

   b. Provides, other than in the capacity of a DHS employee, legal, actuarial, accounting, consulting, data aggregation, management, administrative, accreditation, or financial services to or for DHS, or to or for an organized health care arrangement in which DHS participates, where the provision of the service involves the disclosure of individually identifiable health information from DHS, or from another business associate of DHS, to the person.

II. A covered entity participating in an organized health care arrangement that performs a function or activity as described in (I)(a) of this definition or that provides a service as described in (I)(b) of this definition to or for such organized health care arrangement, does not, simply through the performance of such function or activity or the provision of such service, become a business associate of other covered entities participating in such organized health care arrangement.

III. A covered entity may be a business associate of another covered entity.

D. A business associate relationship is formed only if protected health information is to be used, created, or disclosed in the relationship.

E. The following are not business associates or business associate relationships:

I. DHS employees, offices, and programs.

II. Medical providers providing treatment to individuals.

III. Enrollment or eligibility determinations, involving DHS clients, between government agencies.

IV. Payment relationships, such as when DHS is paying medical providers, child-care providers, OHP managed care organizations, or other entities for services to DHS clients or participants, when the entity is providing its own normal services that are not on behalf of DHS.

V. When an individual's protected health information is disclosed based solely on an individual's authorization.

VI. When an individual's protected health information is not being disclosed by DHS or created for DHS.

VII. When the only information being disclosed is information that is de-identified in accordance with DHS Policy AS-100-07, "De-identification of Client or Participant Information and Use of Limited Data Sets."

F. DHS may disclose an individual's protected health information to a business associate and may allow a business associate to create or receive an individual's protected health information on behalf of DHS, if

  I. DHS first enters into a written contract, or other written agreement or arrangement, with the business associate before disclosing an individual's protected health information to the business associate, in accordance with the requirements of Section 2, below, of this policy.

  II. The written contract or agreement provides satisfactory assurance that the business associate will appropriately safeguard the information.

2. Contract requirements applicable to business associates

A. A contract between DHS and a business associate must include terms and conditions (which may include reference to administrative rule) that

  I. Establish the permitted and required uses and disclosures of protected health information by the business associate. The contract may not authorize the business associate to further use or disclose health information obtained from DHS, except that the contract may permit the business associate to

    a. Use and disclose protected health information for the proper management and administration of the business associate.

    b. Collect data relating to DHS operations.

  II. Provide that the business associate will

    a. Not use or further disclose protected health information other than as permitted or required by the contract or as required by law.

    b. Use appropriate safeguards to prevent use or disclosure of the information other than as provided for by the contract.

    c. Report to DHS any use or disclosure not allowed by the contract of which the business associate becomes aware.

    d. Ensure that any agents or subcontractors to whom it provides protected health information agrees to the same restrictions and conditions that apply to the business associate under the contract.

e. Make protected health information available to the individual in accordance with DHS Policy AS-100-02, "Client Privacy Rights."

f. Make protected health information available for amendment and incorporate any amendments in accordance with DHS Policy AS-100-02, "Client Privacy Rights."

g. Make available the information required to provide an accounting of disclosures in accordance with DHS Policy AS-100-02, "Client Privacy Rights."

h. Makes its internal practices, books, and records relating to the use and disclosure of protected health information available to DHS and to the United States DHHS for the purpose of determining DHS compliance with federal requirements.

i. At termination of the contract, if reasonably feasible, return or destroy all protected health information that the business associate still maintains in any form, and keep no copies thereof. If not feasible, the business associate will continue to protect the information.

j. Authorize termination of the contract if DHS determines that the business associate has violated a material term of the contract.

B. If the business associate of DHS is another governmental entity,

I. DHS may enter into a memorandum of understanding, rather than a contract, with the business associate if the memorandum of understanding contains terms covering all of this policy.

II. The written contract, agreement, or memorandum does not need to contain specific provisions required in this document, if other laws or regulations contain requirements applicable to the business associate that accomplish the same objective.

a. If a business associate is required by law to perform a function or activity on behalf of DHS, or to provide a service to DHS, DHS may disclose protected health information to the business associate to the extent necessary to enable compliance with the legal requirement, without a written contract or agreement, if

i. DHS attempts in good faith to obtain satisfactory assurances from the business associate that the business associate will protect health information to the extent specified in this document.

    ii. If such attempt fails, DHS documents the attempt and the reasons that such assurances cannot be obtained.

C. The written contract or agreement between DHS and the business associate may permit the business associate to

    I. Use information it receives in its capacity as a business associate to DHS, if necessary.

      a. For proper management and administration of the business associate.

      b. To carry out the legal responsibilities of the business associate.

    II. Disclose information it receives in its capacity as a business associate if

      a. The disclosure is required by law.

      b. The business associate receives assurances from the person to whom the information is disclosed that

        i. It will be held or disclosed further only as required by law or for the purposes to which it was disclosed to such person; and

        ii. The person notifies the business associate of any known instances in which the confidentiality of the information has been breached.

3. Responsibilities of DHS in business associate relationships.

A. DHS responsibilities in business associate relationships include, but are not limited to, the following:

    I. Receiving and logging an individual's complaints regarding the uses and disclosures of protected health information by the business associate or the business associate relationship.

    II. Receiving and logging reports from the business associate of possible violations of the business associate contracts.

    III. Implementation of corrective actions plans, as needed.

       IV. Mitigation, if necessary, of known violations up to and including contract termination.

    B. DHS will provide business associates with applicable contract requirements, and may provide consultation to business associates as needed on how to comply with contract requirements regarding protected health information.

4. Business associate non-compliance.

    A. If DHS knows of a pattern of activity or practice of a business associate that constitutes a material breach or violation of the business associate's obligation under the contract or other arrangement, DHS must take reasonable steps to cure the breach or end the violation, as applicable, including working with and providing consultation to the business associate.

    B. If such steps are unsuccessful, DHS must

       I. Terminate the contract or arrangement, if feasible.

       II. If termination is not feasible, report the problem to the United States DHHS.

Guidance for Procedure Development

The following guidelines should be used in developing procedures to implement this Policy:

1. Tracking and identifying DHS' business associates.

    A. DHS will identify those business relationships that are also business associates. The DHS Office of Contracts and Procurement (OCP) will note that designation in the contract record in the CSTAT database.

    B. DHS will include legally appropriate business associate contract terms and conditions in such contracts, which may include incorporation by reference to administrative rule.

    C. OCP will input into CSTAT the HIPAA business relationship information provided to them by the contract requestor at the time the request is received.

I. Upon completion of the contract or amendment process, the appropriate OCP staff will input on the General tab of the contract record the current HIPAA status for that document.

II. This information will be available for contract administrators in DHS to access through a standard report that will be created on CSTAT and that they can generate at their convenience.

2. DHS' response to complaints about business associates inappropriate uses or disclosures.

A. DHS staff who receive a client complaint, or a report or complaint from any source, about inappropriate uses or disclosures of information by business associates, will

I. Provide information regarding that report or complaint to the DHS Privacy Officer, who will document such information in the business associate's contract record in the CSTAT database.

B. The DHS Privacy Officer will send a letter to the business associate, requesting that the business associate review the circumstances related to the alleged pattern or practice. DHS will require that the business associate respond, in writing, within 10 business days to the complaint.

C. The DHS Privacy Officer will coordinate with the business associate's DHS contract administrator to document the alleged violation.

I. If determined necessary and appropriate, DHS OCP will generate a "cure letter" outlining required remediation for the business associate to attain contract compliance.

D. In cases where contract compliance cannot be attained, DHS must terminate the contract, if feasible. If termination is not feasible, the DHS Privacy Officer will report the problem to the United States DHHS, Office for Civil Rights.

Enforcement, Sanctions, and Penalties for Violations of Individual Privacy Policy

The intent of this policy is to specify enforcement, sanction, penalty, and disciplinary actions that may result from violation of DHS policies regarding the privacy and protection of an individual's information and to offer guidelines on how to conform to the required standards.

This document contains guidance for developing procedures to implement this policy.

1. General.

    A. All employees, volunteers, interns, and members of the DHS workforce must guard against improper uses or disclosures of a DHS clients or participant's information.

        I. DHS employees, volunteers, interns, and members of the DHS workforce who are uncertain if a disclosure is permitted are advised to consult with a supervisor in the DHS workplace. The DHS Privacy Officer is a resource for any DHS workplace that cannot resolve a disclosure question, and may be consulted in accordance with the operational procedures of that DHS workplace.

    B. All employees are required to be aware of their responsibilities under DHS privacy policies.

        I. DHS employees will be expected to sign a DHS 2091, "Privacy Program Statement of Understanding," indicating that they have been informed of the business practices in DHS as it relates to privacy, and they understand their responsibilities to ensure the privacy of DHS clients and participants.

    C. Supervisors are responsible for assuring that employees who have access to confidential information, whether it be electronic, hard copy, or oral, are informed of their responsibilities.

D. DHS employees who violate DHS policies and procedures regarding the safeguarding of an individual's information are subject to disciplinary action by DHS up to and including immediate dismissal and legal action by the individual.

E. DHS employees who knowingly and willfully violate state or federal law for improper use or disclosure of an individual's information are subject to criminal investigation and prosecution or civil monetary penalties.

F. If DHS fails to enforce privacy safeguards, DHS as a state agency may be subject to administrative penalties by the Department of Health and Human Services (DHHS), including federal funding penalties.

2. Retaliation prohibited.

A. Neither DHS as an entity nor any DHS employee will intimidate, threaten, coerce, discriminate against, or take any other form of retaliatory action against:

 I. Any individual for exercising any right established under DHS policy, or for participating in any process established under DHS policy, including the filing of a complaint with DHS or with DHHS.

 II. Any individual or other person for

 a. Filing of a complaint with DHS or with DHHS as provided in DHS privacy policies.

 b. Testifying, assisting, or participating in an investigation, compliance review, proceeding, or hearing relating to DHS policy and procedures.

 c. Opposing any unlawful act or practice, provided that

 i. The individual or other person (including a DHS employee) has a good faith belief that the act or practice being opposed is unlawful.

 ii. The manner of such opposition is reasonable and does not involve a use or disclosure of an individual's protected information in violation of DHS policy.

3. Disclosures by whistle-blowers and workforce crime victims.

A. A DHS employee or business associate may disclose an individual's protected client information if

I. The DHS employee or business associate believes, in good faith, that DHS has engaged in conduct that is unlawful or that otherwise violates professional standards or DHS policy, or that the care, services, or conditions provided by DHS could endanger DHS staff, persons in DHS care, or the public.

II. The disclosure is to

a. An oversight agency or public authority authorized by law to investigate or otherwise oversee the relevant conduct or conditions of DHS.

b. An appropriate health care accreditation organization for the purpose of reporting the allegation of failure to meet professional standards or of misconduct by DHS.

c. An attorney retained by or on behalf of the DHS employee or business associate for the purpose of determining the legal options of the DHS employee or business associate with regard to this DHS policy.

B. A DHS employee may disclose limited protected information about an individual to a law enforcement official if the employee is the victim of a criminal act and the disclosure is

I. About only the suspected perpetrator of the criminal act.

II. Limited to the following information about the suspected perpetrator:

a. Name and address.

b. Date and place of birth.

c. Social Security Number.

d. Blood type and rh factor.

e. Type of any injury.

f. Date and time of any treatment.

g. Date and time of death, if applicable.

Guidance for Procedure Development

The following guidelines should be used in developing procedures to implement this policy:

1. General.

    A. DHS employees who violate DHS policies and procedures regarding the safeguarding of an individual's information are subject to

        I. Appropriate disciplinary action by DHS, up to and including immediate dismissal from employment.

        II. Legal action by the individual, who may want to pursue a tort claim against the state or a lawsuit against the state and the employee.

    B. DHS employees who knowing and willfully violate state or federal law for improper invasions of personal privacy may be subject to

        I. Criminal investigation and prosecution, both by the state and by the federal government, depending on the nature of the violation. Federal and state law provides substantial fines and prison sentences upon conviction, depending on the nature and severity of the violation.

        II. Civil monetary penalties that the federal Department of Health and Human Services (DHHS) may impose.

Summary

The emphasis the HIPAA Administrative Simplification legislation places on Protected Health Information (PHI) cannot be over emphasized. The penalties associated with the legislation for violations in this area further reinforce this point. HIPAA compliance starts with PHI but ends invariably by impacting business processes, communications, and systems. In short, it results in various e-business initiatives within your enterprise.

As organizations start to plan, prepare, and position their organizations for HIPAA compliance, they are required to pay careful attention to a number of areas, including evaluating all business associate relationships.

Any HIPAA privacy compliance initiative will require development of forms, creation of policies and procedures, and training of all members of the workforce. In this chapter we reviewed a number of different types of forms as well as policies so that your organization gains insight into information required to meet defined requirements.

A gap analysis between what HIPAA requires and what currently exists is key to identify initiatives that must be launched. This also helps identify documentation needed such as forms as well as procedures required so that all employees may be knowledgeable about changes in the workplace and in business processes and communication.

Lesson 7

In this chapter we focus on specific examples of implementation solutions related to the HIPAA Security Rule. After reading this chapter you will know about

- The impact of the Privacy Rule on HIPAA security implementation initiatives
- Key phases for any HIPAA security initiative
- Key steps for launching an assessment of vulnerabilities that a health care entity may be exposed to
- Phases associated with security project management for integrating merged or acquired health care organizations
- Security issues related to hardening an XP operating system environment

Privacy Requirements: Starting Point for Security Implementation

Privacy and security are addressed separately under HIPAA and, therefore, two distinct rules were established. In the context of HIPAA, privacy addresses what information needs to be protected and why. Security addresses how information is to be protected. Security in this context is the ability to control access and protect information from accidental or intentional disclosure to unauthorized persons and from alteration, destruction, or loss.

Achieving even a base level of this type of security can be harder that one might think. Software, argues John Pescatore, a Gartner Research Vice President, "can be made to do whatever any clever programmer wants it to do; however, it is more difficult to prevent software from doing what you don't want it do. Even worse, even if you succeed at that, it is nearly impossible to keep someone else from changing the software to do what you don't want it to do."

In a HIPAA-compliant environment where certainty, reliability, and carefully proscribed access to information is key, software's fluidity, relatively weak self-protection, and constant state of flux can make it an inappropriate foundation for protecting your highest-value information assets. Mr. Pescatore concluded that hardware provides "high levels of security by being more difficult to change than software." For systems that are relatively stable and must resist modification, he states, "hardware will be required to provide an appropriate level of security."[1]

Health Care Organizations (HCOs) and their business associates will be held accountable for inappropriate disclosures of patient information and are expected to implement administrative changes to protect information. The Privacy Rule covers the policies and procedures that must be in place to ensure that the patients' health information is protected and their rights are upheld.

The Security Rule is a companion to the Privacy Rule—to protect the information, HCOs are expected to put security safeguards in place. Complementing the Security Rule, the HIPAA Privacy Rule defines who is authorized to access patient-identifiable information. It also establishes the rights of individuals to keep information about themselves from being disclosed.

The provisions of the Privacy Rule likely will overlap with the Security Rule in some areas. For instance, the Security Rule also requires that health care organizations maintain audit controls for electronic PHI. Businesses need the assistance of skilled security professionals and architects for a successful implementation of HIPAA-related security assessment, policies, and technologies.

Secure Information Delivery

The HIPAA Administrative Simplification Title deals with securing information delivery between administrators, patients, and caregivers. It covers electronic capture, transformation, and delivery across health care industry entities. The health care industry has traditionally been impeded by

- Limited technology budgets
- Multiple proprietary systems
- Multiple legacy systems
- Paper-based processes

The mandated HIPAA regulations are the catalyst to improve processes and information flow throughout the health care industry.

As a direct consequence of health care transactions, it is becoming much more important to protect patient and medical information. This requires the health care organization to build a secure infrastructure.

Thus, the HIPAA-compliant health care organization is one that would use EDI for transactions, protect patient's medical information with a combination of notice and authorization, and secure all electronic medical records and transactions. This is e-business being implemented by the health care industry.

Security Implementation Considerations

According to the Gartner Group, "By 2004, 80% of enterprises will be using the Internet as an integral part of their business processes. Half will experience a financially significant loss due to Internet-borne incidents by that time. As such they are advised to invest in security strategies now."

HIPAA is highly likely to result in businesses investing in a trust framework for enterprise systems (Internet, intranet, and extranet) and security policies. Why is trust important? It is because a trusted infrastructure can make Internet medical transactions as secure as face-to-face transactions.

A trusted infrastructure deals with the reality that the inside and outside of an enterprise are becoming one. Building a trusted infrastructure is the next "infrastructure" challenge for all businesses. Trust is increasingly a core requirement for enterprise infrastructure. The HIPAA legislation will result in the establishment of a trusted infrastructure as a priority for businesses in the health care and insurance industries.

HIPAA's security requirements do not mandate a particular security technology. The rule describes the requirements, and it is up to each individual organization to determine how to best meet these requirements. HIPAA does have specific requirements in the areas of authentication, access control, data integrity, encryption, and non-repudiation.

Framework for Security Requirements

The Security Rule consists of the requirements that a health care entity must address to safeguard the following components of its electronic data:

- Confidentiality
- Integrity
- Availability

The recommendations from the Security Rule state that all organizations that handle patient-identifiable health care information—regardless of size—should adopt the set of technical and organizational policies, practices, and procedures described here to protect such information.

The Security Rule requires that each health care entity engaged in electronic maintenance or transmission of health information assess potential risks and vulnerabilities to the individual health data in its possession in electronic form, and develop, implement, and maintain appropriate security measures.

Most importantly, these measures must be documented and kept current. How individual security requirements are satisfied and which technology to use are business decisions that each organization must make.

HIPAA Security Project Phases

The HIPAA legislation emphasizes "what needs to get done." It does not describe "how to do it." This necessitates establishing a security compliance framework to coordinate activities and initiatives related to the identification and closing of gaps in the security infrastructure of the health care infrastructure.

A possible framework to consider is one that consists of

- Multiple phases
- Several tasks and initiatives associated with each phase
- One or more deliverables locked into each phase

E-security solutions require more than just perimeter defense strategies based on firewall systems and intrusion detection technologies. Today, health care enterprises require a layered security approach that delivers the core principals of confidentiality, integrity, and availability.

The core issue for an e-security framework for a health care enterprise is the protection of assets, resources, and transactions.

In this section we establish the key phases that any organization will need to step through to be in compliance with the Security Rule.

HIPAA Security Phases for Initiatives

There are five phases associated with any HIPAA Security Rule compliance-related project:

1. Phase I: Baseline assessment
2. Phase II: Gap analysis
3. Phase III: Remediation
4. Phase IV: Policies and procedures
5. Phase V: Evaluation

Phase I: Baseline Assessment

In Phase I, the organization must assess actual and potential risks to its information assets. It needs to review its current policies and procedures related to secure handling of PHI. Then it must examine how it interacts with external parties, like billing services, labs, and other entities. The key objective during a baseline assessment is to establish the current state of security of your enterprise network and systems.

Phase II: Gap Analysis

Next, the organization needs to compare where it stands with what HIPAA requires. Any shortfalls need to be added to the list of gaps. After the list is complete, an initial attempt should be made to identify costs and effort needed to close the gap. Some of the gaps are dependent on business associate solutions. The gaps identified then need to be prioritized.

Phase III: Remediation

Remediation is the process of bringing issues and gaps, which have been identified, into compliance. Remediation may take several weeks to several months depending on the tasks and complexities involved. A remediation project might consist of the following.

♦ Implementing physical access controls
♦ Supporting media controls and workstations
♦ Securing workstation location(s)
♦ Supporting technical security services requirements

- Satisfying emergency access
- Supporting data authentication
- Supporting unique user identification
- Internet and encryption

Example: Develop Contingency Plans

One example of a remediation project is the development of contingency plans as required as part of the HIPAA Security Rule. The organization must develop contingency plans to reduce or negate the damage resulting from processing anomalies. For example, the organization may

- Establish a routine process for maintaining backup floppy disks at a second location
- Obtain a PC maintenance contract
- Arrange for use of a backup PC should the need arise
- Identify an alternate billing service if the current service will not be compliant in time

The organization needs to periodically review its plan to determine whether it still meets the defined requirements.

Phase IV: Policies and Procedures

The next step is for the organization to develop security-related policies and procedures.

This includes an overall framework outlining information security activities and responsibilities, and repercussions for failure to meet those responsibilities.

Examples of policies and procedures to be developed need to include

- Personnel security policy and procedures document
- Personnel clearance procedures
- Security configuration management procedures
- Sanction policy
- Termination procedures
- Security awareness training

Additional requirements that would lend themselves to inclusion in an office procedures document developed by the organization include

◆ Contingency plans

◆ Formal records-processing procedures

◆ Information access controls (rules for granting access, actual establishment of access, and procedures for modifying such access)

◆ Security incident procedures (for example, who is to be notified if it appears that medical information has been accessed by an unauthorized party)

Finally, the organization should consider delivering a half-day security orientation/awareness session to all members of the workforce to address the Security Rule requirement for training.

Phase V: Evaluation

As each project is completed, the Security Officer needs to determine if the related gap is closed. Similarly, the policies and procedures need to be reviewed to determine that they meet HIPAA Security Rule compliance requirements.

Getting Started: Security Assessment

This section steps through a scenario to assess—establish a baseline of—vulnerabilities that a health care entity may be exposed to.

Objective

The objective of a security assessment is to analyze the enterprise infrastructure and identify all vulnerabilities and HIPAA compliance–related gaps. In this section, we develop specific recommendations to "close and lock" security gaps in a fictitious health care enterprise system and network infrastructure.

The purpose of the assessment is to

◆ Understand the business objectives of each business unit represented.

◆ Assess technology capabilities as they relate to business objectives.

◆ Determine technology limitations (gaps) as they exist today with the core focus driven by required HIPAA implementation features.

- ◆ Understand dissonance between business processes and systems and the IT systems and infrastructure.
- ◆ Identify business risks, security requirements, and possible vulnerabilities from the business unit's perspective.
- ◆ Identify technical risks, security requirements, and possible vulnerabilities from the Information Technology personnel's perspectives.

A security assessment is a critical step towards understanding the vulnerabilities that a health care organization may be susceptible to. It provides a baseline of where the organization is and positions the enterprise for gap analysis.

At a high level, there are a number of critical areas that need to be investigated during the process of security assessment. These areas include

- ◆ Summary of business scope and objectives
- ◆ Identification of business risks and vulnerabilities
- ◆ Inventory of infrastructure technology
- ◆ Assessment of technical skills, capabilities, and limitations

Scope

Security assessment assists in the following three areas:

- ◆ Predicting risk
- ◆ Quantifying risk
- ◆ Mitigating risk

The security assessment initiative needs to review the health care organization's IT security controls across management areas such as: policy, organization, personnel, physical controls, asset classification and control, system access control, network and computer management, business continuity, application development and maintenance, and compliance.

Security assessment addresses the following questions:

- ◆ What needs to be protected?
- ◆ What security measures are currently in place?
- ◆ Who and what are the threats and vulnerabilities?
- ◆ What are the implications if they were damaged or lost?

- ◆ What is the value to the organization?
- ◆ What can be done to minimize exposure to the loss or damage?

The outcome or objective of a security assessment is to provide recommendations that maximize the protection of confidentiality, integrity, and availability of patient information and health care systems while still providing functionality and usability.

A successful security assessment initiative is one that is collaborative between the health care entity and the consultant. Without the involvement of the various organizational levels within the organization, the assessment can lead to an ineffective security measure. Using outside consultants is typically a benefit because they do not have a vested interest in the organization and are free from personal and external constraints, which may impair an internal employee's independence.

The core areas in a security assessment service are

- ◆ Scope
- ◆ Data collection
- ◆ Analysis of current policies and procedures
- ◆ Correlation and assessment of risk acceptability

Security assessment provides the data and information required for the next essential steps of

- ◆ HIPAA gap analysis
- ◆ Threat analysis

The security assessment addresses questions such as

- ◆ Has there been a threat analysis?
- ◆ Does your organization have an overall view of how effectively the security plan is working?
- ◆ Are the right IT security controls in place to protect the information that is critical to the business?

Controls must cover all aspects of your business, including mechanisms used by hardware and software systems, networks, databases, and human resource systems.

The Security Assessment review will need to identify both strengths and weaknesses in your organization's compliance policy. When the business is aware of the business exposures resulting from inadequate security controls, it can begin to implement improved controls and also establish the processes that are required to ensure that the controls are effective.

Assessment Deliverables

The typical deliverables of an assessment include

- ◆ **Review.** To review existing policies and technology architectures from a HIPAA compliance perspective.

- ◆ **Interview.** To interview and communicate with all key personnel including executives, physicians, nurses, and system/network administrators.

- ◆ **Inventory.** To inventory and establish a list of all critical systems on the enterprise network infrastructure.

- ◆ **Executive Brief.** To deliver an executive brief at the end of the exercise to communicate findings, roles, responsibilities, policy requirements, and key next steps for enhancing HIPAA compliance at your organization.

- ◆ **Security Policy.** To develop recommendations for a corporate security policy that would provide the basis for enhancement based on HIPAA compliance requirements, vulnerabilities, and specific enterprise applications and initiatives.

- ◆ **Report.** A final report of the strengths and weaknesses found with business-oriented recommendations for actions that could improve the health care organization's compliance program and reduce risks to an acceptable level.

Case Study: Securing an Operating System: Windows XP

This section steps through operating system security issues. This is an example of understanding how to secure the end user operating system environment.

First, Windows XP security features and capabilities are identified. Windows XP represents an important step forward for Microsoft in its commitment to help secure an enterprise. The features and functionality included in XP ease the security burden for both administrators as well as end users. However, the implementation of security feature capabilities remains critical for a secure environment.

Core Capabilities

Windows XP includes several security and privacy features. These features enable the administrator to harden the operating system environment. They include

- ◆ **P3P.** XP supports the Platform for Privacy Preferences (P3P) user privacy settings in the browser. It ships at the medium setting, which denies cookies that don't have a compact P3P-compliant header.

- ◆ **Active directory.** Active directory is a hierarchical structure that stores information about objects on the network. Objects include shared resources such as servers, shared volumes, and printers; network user and computer accounts; domains, applications, services, security policies; and just about everything else in the network. In addition to providing a place to store data and services to make that data available, it also protects network objects from unauthorized access and replicates objects across a network so that data is not lost if one domain controller fails. The active directory also provides a baseline central repository of data for application development to extend and facilitate a unified database structure.

- ◆ **IPSec and Kerberos.** Security capabilities include IP Security (IPSec) and Kerberos. This enables health care entities to exchange confidential information in e-mail and engage in secure online conversations with clients. These extended capabilities help increase customer satisfaction while helping to reduce the interaction costs with clients. This can contribute to overall operational efficiency for the business.

- ◆ **Credential management.** Windows XP utilizes user credentials, including X.509 certificates, to assure greater interoperability. This permits a single and consistent sign-on facility for all roaming users.

- ◆ **Internet secure data storage.** Secure remote storage of encrypted files is supported by Windows XP. As the user decides to retrieve remotely stored files, Windows XP automatically decrypts the information when the local system presents the key.

- ◆ **Security dialog boxes.** Security warning dialog boxes pop up when the user attempts to enable a risky function such as file sharing.

- ◆ **Network monitor.** XP's Network Monitor detects and troubleshoots network device problems.

- ◆ **Security management.** Comprehensive security management features with support for
  - Computer lockdowns
  - Digital signatures
  - File and folder backups
  - File encryption
  - Password authentication
  - Smart cards

A smart card is the size of a credit card but includes a microprocessor and EEP-ROM memory. You can use it to store certificates and private keys and to perform public key cryptography operations, such as authentication, digital signing, and key exchange. A smart card enhances security as follows:

- ◆ It provides tamper-resistant storage for private keys and other forms of personal identification.

- ◆ It isolates critical security computations involving authentication, digital signatures, and key exchange from parts of the system that do not require this data.

- ◆ It enables moving credentials and other private information from one computer to another.

- ◆ Smart cards are used with Kerberos for secure two-factor authentication, with e-mail clients for signing and encrypting messages, when accessing an SSL-encrypted Web site, or even logging on to a dial-up or VPN server.

- ◆ Windows 2000/XP provides built-in support for smart cards and smart tokens through CryptoAPI, and tools to assist in their deployment.

- ◆ Smart tokens are similar to smart cards but smaller and have a USB interface.

- ◆ The ability to log on to a system with a smart card was introduced with Windows 2000. Now with Windows XP, this functionality is extended to terminal servers and administrators. Users with a smart card reader on their client machine can perform smart-card operations on the terminal server machine.

- XP also adds smart card support for running administrator tools and utilities. These applications can be very powerful and can easily compromise corporate security if they end up in the wrong hands. XP gives administrators the ability to control access to these tools, such as net.exe, by requiring smart cards to run them.

- Domain users can opt to use smart cards for authentication, which is a big improvement over passwords. Smart cards can often store your private key as well as any certificates, making them more secure than online storage.

 NOTE

Smart cards do have their weaknesses. For example, keystrokes can be monitored to record your PIN, but even then they still need the card.

Enterprise-level security needs to be flexible and robust so that administrators can configure rules to address possible security liability without hindering the free flow of needed information. Table 7.1 highlights Windows XP security features.

Each of the Windows XP security features have default settings that can be modified to suit a particular organization. Businesses also can make use of relevant tools to implement and modify access control. Many of these tools, such as the Microsoft Management Console snap-ins, are components of Windows XP Professional. Other tools are included with the Windows XP Professional Resource Kit.

Windows XP also provides built-in security to keep intruders out. It does this by limiting anyone trying to gain access to your computer from a network to guest-level privileges. If intruders attempt to break into your computer and gain unauthorized privileges by guessing passwords, they will be unsuccessful—or obtain only limited, guest-level access.

Policies and Templates

One of the features available in Windows XP Professional is the use of Group Policy Objects (GPO). GPOs enable system administrators to apply a single security profile to multiple computers and optionally use smart card technology to authenticate users by using information stored on a smart card.

Table 7.1 Windows XP Security Features

Feature	Description	Benefits
Security templates	Allows administrators to set various global and local security settings, including security-sensitive registry values, access controls on files and the registry, and security on system services.	Allows an administrator to define security configuration templates and then apply these templates to selected computers in one operation.
Kerberos authentication	The primary security protocol for access within or across Windows XP domains. Provides mutual authentication of clients and servers, and supports delegation and authorization through proxy mechanisms.	Speeds performance by reducing server loads while connections are being established. You can also use it to access other enterprise computing platforms that support the Kerberos protocol.
Public Key Infrastructure (PKI)	You can use integrated PKI for strong security in multiple Windows XP Internet and enterprise services, including extranet-based communications.	Using PKI, businesses can share information securely without having to create many individual Windows XP accounts. Also enables smart cards and secure e-mail.
Smart card infrastructure	Windows XP includes a standard model for connecting smart card readers and cards with computers and device-independent APIs to enable applications that are smart card–aware.	Windows XP smart card technologies can be used to enable security solutions throughout your intranet, extranet, and public Web site.
Internet Protocol Security (IPSec) management	IPSec supports network-level authentication, data integrity, and encryption to secure intranet, extranet, and Internet Web communications.	Transparently secures enterprise communications without user interaction. Existing applications can use IPSec for secure communications.
Windows media services	Consists of server and tool components for delivering audio, video, illustrated audio, and other types of multimedia over networks.	New opportunities in training, collaboration, and information-sharing improve productivity.
Removable storage	Allows an administrator to manage removable storage devices and functions. Administrators can create media pools that are owned and used by a particular application.	Allows an administrator to optimize network performance by controlling where data is stored. Also makes it possible for multiple applications to share the same storage media resources.

Group policy can be set at any level of the directory service, including sites, domains, and organizational units. Group policy also can be filtered based on security group memberships. Group policy also gives administrators control over which users have access to specific computers, features, data, and applications.

Security templates enable administrators to set various global and local security settings, including security-sensitive registry values, access controls on files and the registry, and security on system services. These templates provide policies and permission for basic, compatible, secure, and highly secure environments.

Windows Installer enables remote deployment and maintenance of applications by system administrators. This reduces the number of dynamic-link library (DLL) conflicts and enables self-repairing applications.

Remote Install eliminates the need to visit a computer to install the operating system. Remote OS Installation also provides a solution for propagating and maintaining a common desktop image throughout the enterprise.

XP Security Parameters

This section reviews key XP security parameters. Recommendations for high, medium, medium-lo, and low security are provided. Note that one of the most common security risks associated with the factors shown in Table 7.2 is the enabling of ActiveX controls, plug-ins, Java applets, scripts, and downloads.

Software Policies

To protect systems from malicious code execution, XP also includes support for software restriction policies. Administrators define rules in group policy that control when software is allowed to execute. These rules can be defined based on the file's extension, hash, path, signed certificate, or zone. For example, execution of Visual Basic Script (VBS) files can be denied unless digitally signed by a specified organization or group. Corporate administrators can now sleep well at night knowing their network is safe from users who continue to open suspect e-mail attachments.

Software restriction policies provide administrators with a policy-driven mechanism that identifies software running in their domain and controls the ability of that software to execute. Using a software restriction policy, an administrator can prevent unwanted applications from running; this includes viruses or other software that's known to cause conflicts when installed.

Table 7.2 Windows XP Security Risks

Security Parameters	High	Medium	Medium-Low	Low
Access Data Sources Across Domains	Disable	Disable	Prompt	Enable
Active Scripting	Disable	Enable	Enable	Enable
Allow Meta Refresh	Disable	Enable	Enable	Enable
Allow Paste Operations	Disable	Enable	Enable ·	Enable
Allow Paste Operations via Script	Disable	Enable	Enable	Enable
Display Mixed Content	Prompt	Prompt	Prompt	Prompt
Don't Prompt for Client Certificate	Disable	Disable	Enable	Enable
Download Signed ActiveX Controls	Disable	Prompt	Prompt	Enable
Download Unsigned ActiveX Controls	Disable	Disable	Disable	Prompt
Drag and Drop or Copy and Paste Files	Prompt	Enable	Enable	Enable
File Download	Disable	Enable	Enable	Enable
Font Download	Prompt	Enable	Enable	Enable
Initialize and Script ActiveX Controls Not Marked as Safe	Disable	Disable	Disable	Prompt
Installation of Desktop Items	Disable	Prompt	Prompt	Enable
Launching Programs or Files in an IFRAME	Disable	Prompt	Prompt	Enable
Navigate Sub Frames Across Different Domains	Disable	Enable	Enable	Enable
Run ActiveX Controls and Plug-ins	Disable	Enable	Enable	Enable
Scripting of Java Applets	Disable	Enable	Enable	Enable
Software Channel Permissions	High Safety	Medium Safety	Medium Safety	Low Safety
Submit Non-Encrypted Form Data	Prompt	Prompt	Enable	Enable
User Data Persistence	Disable	Enable	Enable	Enable

A software restriction policy is created through the Microsoft Management Console (MMC) Group Policy snap-in. A policy consists of a default rule about whether programs are allowed to run and exceptions to that rule.

There are two ways to use software restriction policies:

♦ If administrators identify all the software that is allowed to run, they can use a software restriction policy to limit execution to only that list of trusted applications.

♦ If administrators do not know about all the applications their users will run, they have to be reactive and restrict inappropriate applications as they're identified.

Software restriction policies isolate untrusted code that could potentially become harmful. Users can set the software policy to range from strictly managed to unmanaged. Untrusted code and scripts can be executed in segregated areas known as the sandbox. If the code or script proves to be nonharmful, then it can be used as designed. However, if the code is infected, then it will not spread beyond the sandbox. This feature also protects the user against URL/UNC links that can launch Internet Explorer or other browsers and download untrusted embedded script. Downloaded ActiveX controls also are monitored.

Internet Connection Firewall (ICF)

Microsoft has developed a wide variety of security features in Windows XP that proactively protect systems and make security a little easier for the enduser, including the addition of the Internet Connection Firewall (ICF) and automatic updates as well as advancements in the Encrypting File System (EFS), security templates, and smart card support.

ICF is activated by default when you use the networking wizard and blocks all inbound traffic to the system. The default setting is to deny all executables. You can easily tell if the firewall is active by looking at your network connections. Any network connection protected by ICF is red.

ICF provides basic packet filtering and custom settings for ActiveX controls and other executable files, but it does not have all the features and functionality of an enterprise solution. Its main purpose is to protect standalone systems with broadband Internet connections. ICF is ideal protection for telecommuters and corporate remote-access solutions.

ICF is either on or off; you cannot selectively protect specific ports or protocols. You do have the ability to allow a few protocols to pass, such as HTTP, FTP, and L2TP. You also have the ability to define additional ports. ICF also includes logging capabilities that allow you to record unsuccessful inbound traffic and successful outbound traffic. Recording all successful outbound traffic generates some large, unwieldy log files, but monitoring unsuccessful inbound attempts gives you a good picture of what attacks are being attempted against the system. The log files can be accessed by an administrator and copied to other administrators via the network, giving them the ability to determine if individual machines are under attack.

In an enterprise environment, system administrators want to limit the control individual users have over the ICF settings. Users should not have the ability to disable the firewall or open ports without proper authorization and approval. If they do have this ability, an administrator might be lulled into a false sense of security, thinking all users have systems protected from inbound connections when they really have disabled its functionality. To prevent this from happening, ICF settings for Windows XP Professional can be controlled through Group Policy settings. Group Policy can force users to enable the firewall when not connected to the corporate network, for example.

A Scenario: Securing a Small Physician's Office

The HIPAA security requirement includes a specific example of the steps that a small or rural provider may implement to secure their practice. For purposes of this example, a small or rural provider is a one to four physician office, with two to five additional employees. The office uses a PC-based practice management system, which is used to communicate intermittently with a clearinghouse for submission of electronic claims.

The number of providers is of less importance for this example than the relatively simple technology in use and the fact that there is insufficient volume and revenue to justify employment of a computer system administrator. There are numerous ways in which an entity could implement these requirements and features. This example does not necessarily represent the best way or the only way in which an entity can implement security.

It is anticipated that the small or rural provider office normally evaluates and self-certifies that the appropriate security is in place for its computer system and office procedures. This evaluation could be done by a knowledgeable person on the staff, or, more likely, by a consultant or by the vendor of the practice management system as a service to its customers.

The following are the key steps for securing a small physician's office:

1. **Assess risk.** The office should assess actual and potential risks to its information assets.

2. **Develop policies and procedures.** To establish appropriate security, the office develops policies and procedures to mitigate and manage those risks. These include an overall framework outlining information security activities and responsibilities, and repercussions for failure to meet those responsibilities.

3. **Develop contingency plans.** The office should develop contingency plans to reduce or negate the damage resulting from processing anomalies. (It should periodically review its plan to determine whether it still meets the office's needs.) For example, the practice may

   - Establish a routine process for maintaining backup floppy disks at a second location

   - Obtain a PC maintenance contract

   - Arrange for use of a backup PC should the need arise

4. **Create a personnel security policy and procedures document.** The office needs to create and document a personnel security policy and procedures to be followed. A key individual on the office staff should be charged with the responsibility for assuring the personnel security requirement is met. This responsibility includes seeing that the access authorization levels granted are documented and kept current. For example, records are kept of everyone who is permitted to use the PC and what files they may access, and training all personnel in security.

5. **Define personnel clearance procedures.** These procedures can be met in a small office with standard personal and professional reference checks, while a large organization may employ more formal, rigorous background investigations.

6. **Define security configuration management procedures.** This same individual can be responsible for security configuration management procedures. For the small provider, the security configuration management requirement is relatively easy to satisfy. The necessary features could be part of a purchased hardware/software package. For example, a new PC might be equipped with virus checking software, or virus checking software might be included as part of the support supplied with the purchase of equipment and software.

7. Specify termination procedures. Termination procedures incorporate specific security actions to be taken as a result of an employee's termination, such as obtaining all keys and changing combinations or passwords. A position description document describing this person's duties could specify the level of detail necessary. The small or rural provider office needs to ensure that the internal auditing capability of the software used to manage health data files is activated so that it tracks who has accessed the data.

8. Support administrative security requirements. A small or rural provider may document compliance with many of the foregoing administrative security requirements by including them in an office procedures type of document that should be required reading by new employees and always available for reference. Periodic security reminders should include visual aids, such as posters and screen savers, and oral reminders in recurring meetings. Requirements that lend themselves to inclusion in an office procedures document include

   • Contingency plans

   • Formal records processing procedures

   • Information access controls (rules for granting access, actual establishment of access, and procedures for modifying such access)

   • Security incident procedures (for example, who is to be notified if it appears that medical information has been accessed by an unauthorized party)

   • Training

9. Implement physical access controls. Physical access controls are relatively straightforward for a small or rural office—use locked rooms and/or closets to secure equipment and media from unauthorized access. The office procedures/policies manual should include directions for authorizing access and keeping records of authorized accesses.

10. Support media controls and secure workstations. Use policy instructions developed by the office must include additional instructions on such items as where to store backed-up data, how to dispose of data no longer needed, or logging off when leaving terminals unattended.

11. Deliver security awareness training. Safeguards for the security of workstation location(s) depend upon the physical surroundings in the small or rural office. The small or rural provider may meet the requirements by

locating equipment in areas that are generally populated by office staff and have some degree of physical separation from the public. Security awareness training should be part of the new employee orientation process and a periodic recurring discussion item in staff meetings.

12. Support technical security services requirements. The technical security services requirements for access control, entity authentication, and authorization control may be achieved simply by implementing a user-based data access model (assigning a username and password combination to each authorized employee). Other access models can be used, but would prove unwieldy for the small office. For example, the role-based access process groups users with similar data access needs, and context-based access is based upon the context of a transaction—not on the attributes of the initiator.

13. Satisfy emergency access. By assigning full access rights to a minimum of two key individuals in the office, implementation of the emergency access feature is satisfied. Audit control mechanisms, by necessity, are provided by software featuring that capability.

14. Support data authentication. By establishing and using a message authentication code, data authentication is achieved.

15. Support unique user identification. Use of the password system mentioned previously can satisfy the unique user identification requirement.

16. Implement chain of trust agreements. As the example provider contracts with a third party to handle claims processing, the claims-processing contract becomes the vehicle to provide for a chain of trust (requiring the contractor to implement the same security requirements and take responsibility for protecting the data it receives).

17. Define Internet and encryption usage procedures. If this provider chooses to use the Internet to transmit or receive health information, some form of encryption must be used. For example, the provider could procure and use commercial software to provide protection against unauthorized access to the data transmitted or received. This decision must take into account what encryption system the message recipient uses. On the other hand, health information when transmitted via other means such as VANs, private wires, or even dial-up connections may not require such absolute protection as is provided by encryption. This small or rural provider would likely not be part of a network configuration; therefore, only integrity controls and message authentication is required and can be

provided by currently available software products, most likely provided as part of their contract with their health care clearinghouse.

> **NOTE**
>
> Small providers may need guidance regarding the content of the documents required by the Security Rule, such as the specifics of a chain of trust partner agreement.

Security Policy

A health care enterprise's security policy document provides the framework for the deployment of security technology within the enterprise. It is a key responsibility of the security officer to align business and corporate objectives with security requirements in the development of the security policy document.

The security officer identifies what parts of the network and which systems are trusted and, thus, do not require any security services. The enterprise security team must clearly identify restricted network segments as well as the demilitarized zone (DMZ).

For example, to secure IP devices and data on an enterprise, businesses must strongly consider the following:

- Using encryption as much as possible to protect data
- Using strong authentication mechanisms including tokens, smart cards, and biometrics
- Using firewall(s) to secure critical segments
- Disabling all services that are not in use or those with uses of which you are uncertain
- Using wrappers around all services used to log usage as well as to restrict connectivity

The security officer identifies all security requirements for an enterprise. Careful planning and awareness of the types of threats that a system might experience are key to defining a security policy that leads to a secure environment.

An enterprise security document includes sections such as

- Introduction
- Risk management and security principles

- Security-related organizational roles and responsibilities
- Security planning processes and risk assessment
- Information classification
- Encryption
- Non-employee personnel and security
- Application communications
- Viruses and malicious code
- Physical security
- Incident reporting

Security Standard

The International Standards Organization (ISO) 17799 is a detailed security standard published in December 2000. The British Standard (BS) 7799 and the ISO 17799 are very similar—the ISO 17799 includes two non-action sections at the start of the document. The standards are organized into 10 major sections, each covering a different topic or area:

- **Security policy.** The objectives of this section are to provide management direction and support for information security. The information security policy document is a written policy that must be available to all employees responsible for information security.
- **Security organization.** There are two objectives for this section.
  - **Information security infrastructure.** To manage information security within the organization.
  - **Security of third-party access.** To maintain the security of organizational information-processing facilities and information assets accessed by third parties.
- **Asset classification and control.** There are two objectives of this section.
  - **Accountability of assets.** To maintain appropriate protection of corporate assets.
  - **Information classification.** To ensure that information assets receive an appropriate level of protection.

- **Personnel security.** There are three objectives of this section:
  - **Security in job definition and resourcing.** To reduce risk of human error, theft, fraud, or misuse of facilities.
  - **User training.** To ensure that users are aware of information security threats and concerns and are equipped to support the corporate security policy in the course of their normal work.
  - **Responding to incidents.** To minimize the damage caused by security incidents and malfunctions and to learn from such incidents.
- **Physical and environmental security.** There are two objectives of this section:
  - **Secure areas.** To prevent unauthorized access, damage, and interference to business premises and information.
  - **Equipment inventory.** To prevent loss, damage, or compromise of assets and interruption to business activities.
- **Computer and network management.** There are seven objectives of this section:
  - **Operational procedures and responsibilities.** To ensure the correct and secure operation of information processing facilities.
  - **System planning and acceptance.** To minimize the risk of systems failures.
  - **Protection from malicious software.** To protect the integrity of software and information.
  - **Housekeeping.** To maintain the integrity and availability of information processing and communication.
  - **Network management.** To ensure the safeguarding of information in networks and the protection of the supporting infrastructure.
  - **Media handling and security.** To prevent damage to assets and interruptions to business activities.
  - **Data and software exchange.** To prevent loss, modification, or misuse of information exchanged between organizations.
- **System access control.** There are seven objectives of this section:
  - **Business requirements for system access.** To control access to business information.
  - **User access management.** To prevent unauthorized access to information systems.

- **User responsibilities.** To prevent unauthorized user access.
- **Network access control.** To ensure the protection of networked services.
- **Computer access control.** To prevent unauthorized computer access.
- **Application access control.** To prevent unauthorized access to information held in computer systems.
- **Monitoring system access and use.** To detect unauthorized activities.

◆ **System Development and Maintenance.** There are four objectives of this section:

- **Security requirements of systems.** To ensure security is built into operational systems.
- **Security in application systems.** To prevent loss, modification, or misuse of user data in application systems.
- **Security of application system files.** To ensure IT projects and support activities are conducted in a secure manner.
- **Security in development and support environments.** To maintain the security of application system software and data.

◆ **Business Continuity Planning.** The objectives of this section are to counteract interruptions to business activities and to support critical business processes from the effects of major failures or disasters. This includes business continuity planning process, business continuity planning framework, testing business continuity plans, and updating business continuity plans.

◆ **Compliance.** There are three objectives in this section:

- **Compliance with legal requirements.** To avoid breaches of any criminal or civil law, statutory, regulatory, or contractual obligations; and any security requirements.
- **Security review of IT systems.** To ensure compliance of systems with organizational security policies and standards.
- **System audit considerations.** To maximize the effectiveness of and to minimize interference to/from the system audit process.

Example: Enterprise TCP/IP Security Policy

Every organization must develop its own customized TCP/IP security policy to describe corporate policy for each and every protocol and network device that communicates on the enterprise TCP/IP network. Each section of the TCP/IP security policy document must cover three areas: overview (of the protocol), recommendation (for use of the protocol on the enterprise network), and reasoning (justifying the recommendation).

An enterprise TCP/IP security policy includes the following core elements:

- Defining the security perimeter based on an organization's network topology and security requirements
- Developing a customized security policy based on business and application requirements
- Deploying firewall system(s) to implement the specifications of the organizations' security policy

Ask the following questions when creating the TCP/IP security policy:

- What is the objective or motivation for this document in your organization?
- Who is the intended audience for this document? Will all or some parts of this document be distributed?
- How frequently will this document be revised?
- Who is responsible for updating the document?
- Are there recommendations in the document that will be enforced?
- Identify the security philosophy that best reflects the belief of the organization.
- Which firewall systems are used to secure your connection to the Internet?
- What is the firewall system and network architecture?
- What is your policy for inbound access to systems? Which specific protocols will be allowed to access nodes on your internal network?
- What is your policy on outbound access to nodes on the Internet? Which specific protocols will be allowed to establish outbound connections to nodes on the Internet?
- Do you have remote offices or branches that connect to the home office? If yes, is the remote office directly connected to the Internet, or does it access the Internet through the home office?
- Are there external networks that are not trusted? Are there external networks that need access to your internal network via the Internet?

- Where are your key servers (Web server, DNS server, FTP server) located on the network?
- What is your policy on consultants and contractors who may have privileged access to systems and networks?
- What is your policy on employees who are no longer with the organization—how do you ascertain that they have no access, privileged or unprivileged, to system resources on the network?

Summary

In this lesson we first examined the HIPAA Security Rule from the perspective of implementation. We reviewed the five key phases for any HIPAA security initiative launched by a health care entity. These five phases are

- Phase I: Baseline assessment
- Phase II: Gap analysis
- Phase III: Remediation
- Phase IV: Policies and procedures
- Phase V: Evaluation

We then examined how to secure an XP operating system environment.

The steps identified and recommendations provided are useful as security professionals and architects launch projects to bring their health care entity into compliance with HIPAA security requirements.

Finally, each health care organization needs to define a security policy that is specific to its combination of systems, networks, and applications. A security policy defines the highest level of a security specification and states what is and what is not authorized in the general operation of a system or network element.

References

1. Pescatore, John. "Software Security Is Soft Security: Hardware Is Required." Gartner Group Note Number: COM-16-5309, http://www4.gartner.com/DisplayDocument?id=359830. June 2002.
2. Hunter, Richard. "Reuse: What to Do and Why To Do It." Garther Group, Symposium/Itxpo97, October 1997, Session Slides, p. 3.

Appendix A

AAHomecare. American Association for Homecare. An industry association for the homecare industry, including home medical services and manufacturers and home health providers.

Accredited Standards Committee (ASC). An organization that has been accredited by ANSI for the development of American National Standards.

ACG. Ambulatory Care Group.

ACH. Automated Clearinghouse.

ADA. American Dental Association.

ADG. Ambulatory Diagnostic Group.

Administrative Code Sets. A set of codes used to encode data elements that characterize a general business situation, rather than a medical condition or service.

Administrative Simplification (A/S). Title II, Subtitle F, Part C of HIPAA, which gives HHS the authority to mandate the use of standards for the electronic exchange of health care data; to specify what medical and administrative code sets should be used within those standards; to require the use of national identification systems for health care patients, providers, payers (or plans), and employers (or sponsors); and to specify the types of measures required to protect the security and privacy of personally identifiable health care information.

AFEHCT. The Association for Electronic Health Care Transactions.

AHA. American Hospital Association.

AHIMA. American Health Information Management Association.

AMA. American Medical Association.

American Dental Association (ADA). A professional organization for dentists. The ADA maintains the hardcopy dental claim form and the associated claim submission specifications, and also maintains the Current Dental Terminology (CDT) code set. The ADA has a formal consultative role under HIPAA, and hosts the Dental Content Committee.

American Health Information Management Association (AHIMA). An association of health information management professionals. AHIMA sponsors some HIPAA educational seminars.

American Hospital Association (AHA). A health care industry association that represents the concerns of institutional providers. The AHA hosts the NUBC, which has a formal consultative role under HIPAA.

American Medical Association (AMA). A professional organization for physicians. The AMA is the secretariat of the NUCC, which has a formal consultative role under HIPAA. The AMA also maintains the Current Procedural Terminology (CPT) code set.

American National Standards (ANS). Standards developed and approved by organizations accredited by ANSI.

American National Standards Institute (ANSI). An organization that accredits various standards-setting committees, and monitors their compliance with the open rule-making process that they must follow to qualify for ANSI accreditation.

American Society for Testing and Materials (ASTM). A standards group that has published general guidelines for the development of standards, including those for health care identifiers. ASTM Committee E31 on Health care Informatics develops standards on information used within health care.

ANS. American National Standards.

ANSI. The American National Standards Institute.

A/S, A.S., or AS. Administrative Simplification, as in HIPAA A/S.

ASC. Accredited Standards Committee, as in ANSI ASC X12.

ASO. Administrative Services Only.

Association for Electronic Health Care Transactions (AFEHCT). An organization that promotes the use of EDI in the health care industry.

ASTM. The American Society for Testing and Materials.

Automated Clearinghouse (ACH). Also referred to as Health Care Clearinghouse under HIPAA, this is an entity that processes or facilitates the processing of information received from another entity in a non-standard format or containing non-standard data content into standard data elements or a standard transaction, or it is an entity that receives a standard transaction from another entity and processes or facilitates the processing of that information into non-standard format or non-standard data content for a receiving entity.

BCBSA. The Blue Cross and Blue Shield Association.

Biometric Identifier. An identifier based on some physical characteristic, such as a fingerprint.

Blue Cross and Blue Shield Association (BCBSA). An association that represents the common interests of Blue Cross and Blue Shield health plans. The BCBSA serves as the administrator for both the Health Care Code Maintenance Committee and the Health Care Provider Taxonomy Committee.

BP. Business Partner.

Business Associate (BA). A person or organization that performs a function or activity on behalf of a covered entity, but is not part of the covered entity's workforce. A business associate can also be a covered entity in its own right.

Business Model. A model of a business organization or process.

Business Relationships. The term *agent* is often used to describe a person or organization that assumes some of the responsibilities of another one. This term has been avoided in the final rules so that a more HIPAA-specific meaning could be used for *business associate*. The term *business partner* (BP) was originally used for *business associate*.

A *Third Party Administrator* (TPA) is a *business associate* that performs claims administration and related business functions for a self-insured entity.

Under HIPAA, a *health care clearinghouse* is a *business associate* that translates data to or from a standard format in behalf of a *covered entity*.

The HIPAA Security NPRM used the term *Chain of Trust Agreement* to describe the type of contract that would be needed to extend the responsibility to protect health care data across a series of subcontractual relationships.

While a *business associate* is an entity that performs certain business functions for you, a *trading partner* is an external entity, such as a customer, that you do business with. This relationship can be formalized via a *trading partner agreement*. It is quite possible to be a *trading partner* of an entity for some purposes, and a *business associate* of that entity for other purposes.

Cabulance. A taxicab that also functions as an ambulance.

CDC. The Centers for Disease Control and Prevention.

CDT. Current Dental Terminology.

CE. Covered Entity.

Centers for Disease Control and Prevention (CDC). An organization that maintains several code sets included in the HIPAA standards, including the ICD-9-CM codes.

CFR. Code of Federal Regulations.

Chain of Trust (COT). A term used in the HIPAA Security NPRM for a pattern of agreements that extend protection of health care data by requiring that each *covered entity* that shares health care data with another entity require that that entity provide protections comparable to those provided by the *covered entity*, and that that entity, in turn, require that any other entities with which it shares the data satisfy the same requirements.

CHAMPUS. Civilian Health and Medical Programs of the Uniformed Services.

CHIP. Child Health Insurance Program.

Claim Adjustment Reason Codes. A national code set for indicating the reasons for any differences, or adjustments, between the original provider charge for a claim or service and the current payment for it. This code set is used in the X12 835 Claim Payment & Remittance Advice and the X12 837 Claim EDI transactions, and is maintained by the Health Care Code Maintenance Committee.

Claim Attachment. Any of a variety of hard-copy forms or electronic records needed to process a claim in addition to the claim itself.

Claim Medicare Remarks Codes. Medicare Remittance Advice Remark Codes.

Claim Status Category Codes. A national code set for indicating the general category of the status of health care claims. This code set is used in the X12 277 Claim Status Notification EDI transaction, and is maintained by the Health Care Code Maintenance Committee.

Claim Status Codes. A national code set for indicating the status of health care claims. This code set is used in the X12 277 Claim Status Notification EDI transaction, and is maintained by the

Health Care Code Maintenance Committee.

Clearinghouse (or Health Care Clearinghouse). For health care, an organization that translates health care data to or from a standard format.

CM. ICD.

COB. Coordination of Benefits, or crossover.

Code Set. Under HIPAA, this is any set of codes used to encode data elements, such as tables of terms, medical concepts, medical diagnostic codes, or medical procedure codes. This includes both the codes and their descriptions.

Comment. Commentary on the merits or appropriateness of proposed or potential regulations provided in response to an NOI, an NPRM, or other federal regulatory notice.

Computer-Based Patient Record Institute (CPRI). An industry organization that promotes the use of electronic health care records.

Confidentiality. Your right to talk with your health care provider without anyone else finding out what you have said.

Coordination of Benefits (COB). A process for determining the respective responsibilities of two or more health plans that have some financial responsibility for a medical claim. Also called crossover.

COT. Chain or Trust.

Covered Entity. Under HIPAA, this is a health plan, a health care clearinghouse, or a health care provider who transmits any health information in electronic form in connection with a HIPAA transaction.

CPRI. Computer-based Patient Record Institute.

CPT. Current Procedural Terminology.

Current Dental Terminology (CDT). A dental procedure code set maintained by the ADA that has been selected for use in the HIPAA transactions.

Current Procedural Terminology (CPT). A procedure code set maintained and copyrighted by the AMA that has been selected for use under HIPAA for non-institutional and non-dental professional transactions.

Data Content Committee. Designated Data Content Committee.

Data Council. A coordinating body within the HHS that has high-level responsibility for overseeing the implementation of the A/S provisions of HIPAA.

Data Dictionary (DD). A document or system that characterizes the data content of a system.

Data Element. Under HIPAA, this is the smallest named unit of information in a transaction.

Data Interchange Standards Association (DISA). A body that provides administrative services to X12 and several other standards-related groups.

Data Mapping. The process of matching one set of data elements or individual code values to their closest equivalents in another set of them.

Data Model. A conceptual model of the information needed to support a business function or process.

Data-Related Concepts. *Clinical* or *Medical Code Sets* identify medical conditions and the procedures, services, equipment, and supplies used to deal with them. *Non-clinical, non-medical,* or *administrative code sets* identify or characterize entities and events in a manner that facilitates an administrative process.

HIPAA defines a *data element* as the smallest unit of named information. In X12 language, that is a *simple data element.* But X12 also has *composite data elements,* which aren't really *data elements,* but are groups of closely related *data elements* that can repeat as a group. X12 also has *segments,* which also are groups of related *data elements* that tend to occur together, such as street address, city, and state. These *segments* can sometimes repeat, or one or more segments may be part of a *loop* that can repeat. For example, you might have a claim loop that occurs once for each claim, and a claim service loop that occurs once for each service included in a claim. An X12 *transaction* is a collection of such loops, segments, and so on. that supports a specific business process, while an X12 *transmission* is a communication session during which one or more X12 transactions is transmitted. *Data elements* and groups also may be combined into records that make up conventional files, or into the tables or segments used by database management systems, or DBMSs.

A *designated code set* is a *code set* that has been specified within the body of a rule.

These are usually *medical code sets.* Many other *code sets* are incorporated into the rules by reference to a separate document, such as an *implementation guide,* that identifies one or more such *code sets.* These are usually *administrative code sets.*

Electronic data is data that is recorded or transmitted electronically, while *non-electronic data* would be everything else. Special cases would be data transmitted by fax and audio systems, which is, in principle, transmitted electronically, but which lacks the underlying structure usually needed to support automated interpretation of its contents.

Encoded data is data represented by some identification or classification scheme, such as a provider identifier or a procedure code. *Non-encoded data* would be more nearly free-form, such as a name, a street address, or a description. Theoretically, of course, all data, including grunts and smiles, is encoded.

For HIPAA purposes, *internal data,* or *internal code sets,* are *data elements* that are fully specified within the HIPAA *implementation guides.* For X12 transactions, changes to the associated code values and descriptions must be approved via the normal standards development process, and can only be used in the revised version of the standards affected. X12 transactions also use many coding and identification schemes that are maintained by *external* organizations. For these *external code sets,* the associated values and descriptions can change at any time and still be usable in any version of the X12 transactions that uses the associated *code set.*

Individually identifiable data is data that can be readily associated with a specific individual. Examples would be a name, a personal identifier, or a full street address. If life was simple, everything else would be *non-identifiable* data. But even if you remove the obviously identifiable data from a record, other *data elements* present can also be used to *re-identify* it. For example, a birth date and a zip code might be sufficient to re-identify half the records in a file. The re-identifiability of data can be limited by omitting, aggregating, or altering such data to the extent that the risk of it being *re-identified* is acceptable.

A specific form of data representation, such as an X12 transaction, will generally include some *structural data* that is needed to identify and interpret the transaction itself, as well as the *business data content* that the transaction is designed to transmit. Under HIPAA, when an alternate form of data collection such as a browser is used, such *structural* or *format related data elements* can be ignored as long as the appropriate *business data content* is used.

Structured data is data the meaning of which can be inferred to at least some extent based on its absolute or relative location in a separately defined data structure. This structure could be the blocks on a form, the fields in a record, the relative positions of *data elements* in an X12 segment, and so on. *Unstructured data*, such as a memo or an image, would lack such clues.

DCC. Data Content Committee.

DD. Data Dictionary, as in HIPAA DD.

Dental Content Committee. An organization, hosted by the American Dental Association, that maintains the data element specifications for dental billing. The ADA has a formal consultative role under HIPAA for all transactions affecting dental health care services.

Department of Health and Human Services (HHS). The Federal Government Department that has overall responsibility for implementing HIPAA.

Designated Code Set. A medical or administrative code set, which HHS has designated for use in one or more of the HIPAA standards.

Designated Data Content Committee or Designated DCC. An organization that HHS has designated for oversight of the business data content of one or more of the HIPAA-mandated transaction standards.

Designated Standard. A standard that HHS has designated for use under the authority provided by HIPAA.

DHHS. See HHS.

DICOM. Digital Imaging and Communications in Medicine.

Digital Imaging and Communications in Medicine (DICOM). A standard for communicating images, such as Xrays, in a digitized form. It could be included in the claim attachments standards.

DISA. The Data Interchange Standards Association.

Disclosure. Release or divulgence of information by an entity to persons or organizations outside of that entity.

Disclosure History. Under HIPAA this is a list of any entities that have received personally identifiable health care information for uses unrelated to treatment and payment.

DME. Durable Medical Equipment.

DMEPOS. Durable Medical Equipment, Prosthetics, Orthotics, and Supplies.

DMERC. Medicare Durable Medical Equipment Regional Carrier.

Draft Standard for Trial Use (DSTU). An archaic term for any *X12 standard* that has been approved since the most recent release of X12 *American National Standards*. The current equivalent term is *X12 standard*.

DRG. Diagnosis Related Group.

EBFM. Electronic Business Flow Management. A form of procedural and control for deployment of HIPAA transactions.

EC. Electronic Commerce.

EDI. Electronic Data Interchange.

EDIFACT. Electronic Data Interchange for Administration, Commerce, and Transport.

EFT. Electronic Funds Transfer.

EHNAC. The Electronic Health care Network Accreditation Commission.

Electronic Commerce (EC). The exchange of business information by electronic means.

Electronic Data Interchange (EDI). This usually means X12 and similar variable-length formats for the electronic exchange of structured data. It is sometimes used more broadly to mean any electronic exchange of formatted data.

Electronic Data Interchange for Administration, Commerce, and Transport (EDIFACT). An international EDI format, sometimes referred to as UN/EDIFACT because the United Nations has a role in it. Interactive X12 transactions use the EDIFACT message syntax.

Electronic Health care Network Accreditation Commission (EHNAC). An organization that accredits health care clearinghouses.

Electronic Media Claims (EMC). This term usually refers to a flat file format used to transmit or transport claims, such as the 192-byte UB-92 Institutional EMC format and the 320-byte Professional EMC NSF.

Electronic Remittance Advice (ERA). Any of several electronic formats for explaining the payments of health care claims.

EMC. Electronic Media Claims.

EMR. Electronic Medical Record.

ERA. Electronic Remittance Advice.

FAQ(s). Frequently Asked Question(s).

FDA. Food and Drug Administration.

FERPA. Family Educational Rights and Privacy Act.

FFS. Fee-for-Service.

FI. Medicare Part A Fiscal Intermediary.

Flat File. This term usually refers to a file that consists of a series of fixed-length records that include some sort of record type code.

Format. Under HIPAA, those *data elements* that provide or control the enveloping or hierarchical structure, or assist in identifying data content of a transaction.

FR or F.R. Federal Register.

GAO. General Accounting Office.

GLBA. The Gramm-Leach-Bliley Act.

Group Health Plan. Under HIPAA this is an employee welfare benefit plan that provides for medical care and that either has 50 or more participants or is administered by another business entity.

HCFA. The Health Care Financing Administration.

HCFA-1450. HCFA's name for the institutional uniform claim form, or UB-92.

HCFA-1500. HCFA's name for the professional uniform claim form. Also known as the UCF-1500.

HCFA Common Procedural Coding System (HCPCS). A medical code set that identifies health care procedures, equipment, and supplies for claim submission purposes. It is maintained by HCFA, and has been selected for use in the HIPAA transactions.

HCPCS. HCFA Common Procedural Coding System.

Health Care Code Maintenance Committee. An organization administered by the BCBSA that is responsible for maintaining certain coding schemes used in the X12 transactions. These include the Claim Adjustment Group Codes, the Claim Adjustment Reason Codes, the Claim Status Category Codes, and the Claim Status Codes.

Health Care Financing Administration (HCFA). The HHS agency responsible for Medicare and parts of Medicaid. HCFA has historically maintained the UB-92 institutional EMC format specifications, the professional EMC NSF specifications, as well as specifications for various certifications and authorizations used by the Medicare and Medicaid programs. HCFA also maintains the HCPCS medical code set and the Medicare Remittance Advice Remark Codes.

Health Care Provider Taxonomy Committee. An organization administered by the BCBSA that is responsible for maintaining the Provider Taxonomy coding scheme used in the X12 transactions. The detailed code maintenance is done under the guidance of X12N/TG2/WG15.

Health Care Financial Management Association (HFMA). An organization for the improvement of the financial management of health care–related organizations. The HFMA sponsors some HIPAA educational seminars.

Health Industry Business Communications Council (HIBCC). A council of health care industry associations that has developed a number of technical standards used within the health care industry.

Health Informatics Standards Board (HISB). A standards group that has developed an inventory of candidate standards for consideration as possible HIPAA standards.

Health Insurance Association of America (HIAA). An industry association that represents the interests of commercial health care insurers. The HIAA participates in the maintenance of some code sets, including HCPCS Level II codes.

Health Insurance Portability and Accountability Act of 1996 (HIPAA). A Federal law that makes a number of changes that have the goal of allowing persons to qualify immediately for comparable health insurance coverage when they change their employment relationships. Title II, Subtitle F, of HIPAA gives HHS the authority to mandate the use of standards for the electronic exchange of health care data; to specify what medical and administrative code sets should be used within those standards; to require the use of national identification systems for health care patients, providers, payers (or plans), and employers (or sponsors); and to specify the types of measures required to protect the security and privacy of personally identifiable health care information. Also known as the Kennedy-Kassebaum Bill, the Kassebaum-Kennedy Bill, K2, or Public Law 104-191.

Health Level Seven (HL7). An ANSI-accredited group that defines standards for the cross-platform exchange of information within a health care organization. HL7 is responsible for specifying the Level Seven OSI standards for the health industry. Some HL7 standards will be encapsulated in the X12 standards used for transmitting claim attachments. The HL7 Claims Attachment SIG (CA-SIG) is responsible for the HL7 portion of this standard.

HFMA. The Health care Financial Management Association.

HHS. The U.S. Department of Health and Human Services. HHS administers many of the "social" programs at the Federal level dealing with the health and welfare of the citizens of the United States.

HIAA. The Health Insurance Association of America.

HIBCC. The Health Industry Business Communications Council.

HIPAA. The Health Insurance Portability and Accountability Act of 1996.

HIPAA Data Dictionary or HIPAA DD. A data dictionary that defines and cross-references the contents of all X12 transactions included in the HIPAA mandate. It is maintained by X12N/TG3.

HISB. The Health Informatics Standards Board.

HL7. Health Level Seven.

IAIABC. The International Association of Industrial Accident Boards and Commissions.

ICD & ICD-n-CM & ICD-n-PCS. International Classification of Diseases, with n = 9 for *Revision 9* (or 10 for *Revision 10*), with CM = *Clinical Modification*, and with PCS = *Procedure Coding System.*"

IG. Implementation Guide.

Implementation Guide (IG). A document explaining the proper use of a standard for a specific business purpose. The X12N HIPAA IG's are the primary reference documents used by those implementing the associated transactions, and are incorporated into the HIPAA regulations by reference.

Information Model. A conceptual model of the information needed to support a business function or process.

International Association of Industrial Accident Boards and Commissions (IAIABC). One of their standards is under consideration for use for the First Report of Injury standard under HIPAA.

International Classification of Diseases (ICD). A medical code set maintained by the World Health Organization (WHO). The primary purpose of this code set is to classify causes of death. A U.S. extension of this coding system, maintained by the NCHS within the CDC, is used to identify morbidity factors, or diagnoses. The ICD-9-CM codes have been selected for use in the HIPAA transactions.

International Standards Organization (ISO). An organization that coordinates the development and adoption of numerous international standards.

ISO. The International Standards Organization.

JCAHO. The Joint Commission on Accreditation of Health care Organizations.

Joint Commission on Accreditation of Health Care Organizations (JCAHO). An organization that accredits health care organizations. In the future, the JCAHO may play a role in certifying these organizations compliance with the HIPAA A/S requirements.

LTC. Long-Term Care.

Maximum Data Set. A framework envisioned under HIPAA whereby an entity creating a transaction is free to include whatever data any receiver might want or need. The recipient of a maximum data set is free to ignore any portion of the data not needed to conduct their part of the associated business transaction.

Medical Code Sets. Codes that characterize a medical condition or treatment. These code sets are usually maintained by professional societies and public health organizations.

Medicare Remittance Advice Remark Codes. A national code set for providing either claim-level or service-level Medicare-related messages that cannot be expressed with a Claim Adjustment Reason Code. This code set is used in the X12 835 Claim Payment & Remittance Advice EDI transaction, and is maintained by the HCFA.

Memorandum of Understanding (MOU). A document providing a general description of the kinds of responsibilities that are to be assumed by two or more parties in their pursuit of some goal(s). More specific information may be provided in an associated SOW.

Minimum Scope of Disclosure. The principle that, to the extent practical, individually identifiable health information should only be disclosed to the extent needed to support the purpose of the disclosure.

MOU. Memorandum of Understanding.

NAIC. The National Association of Insurance Commissioners.

NASMD. The National Association of State Medicaid Directors.

National Association of Insurance Commissioners (NAIC). An association of the insurance commissioners of the states and territories.

National Association of State Medicaid Directors (NASMD). An association of state Medicaid directors. NASMD is affiliated with the American Public Health Human Services Association (APHSA).

National Center for Health Statistics (NCHS). A federal organization within the CDC that collects, analyzes, and distributes health care statistics. The NCHS maintains the ICD-x-CM codes.

National Committee for Quality Assurance (NCQA). An organization that accredits managed care plans or Health Maintenance Organizations (HMOs). In the future, the NCQA may play a role in certifying these organizations' compliance with the HIPAA A/S requirements.

National Committee on Vital and Health Statistics (NCVHS). A Federal body within the HHS that has an important advisory role under HIPAA.

National Council for Prescription Drug Programs (NCPDP). An ANSI-accredited group that maintains a number of standard formats for use by the retail pharmacy industry, some of which are included in the HIPAA mandates.

National Drug Code (NDC). A medical code set that identifies prescription drugs and some over-the-counter products, and that has been selected for use in the HIPAA transactions.

National Employer ID. A system for uniquely identifying all sponsors of health care benefits.

National Health Information Infrastructure (NHHI). This is a health care–specific lane on the Information Superhighway, as described in the National Information Infrastructure (NII) initiative. Conceptually, this includes the HIPAA A/S initiatives.

National Patient ID. A system for uniquely identifying all recipients of health care services.

National Payer ID. A system for uniquely identifying all organizations that pay for health care services. Also known as Health Plan ID, or Plan ID.

National Provider ID. A system for uniquely identifying all providers of health care services, supplies, and equipment.

National Standard Format (NSF). Generically, this applies to any national standard format, but it is often used in a more limited way to designate the Professional EMC NSF, a 320-byte flat file record format used to submit professional claims.

National Uniform Billing Committee (NUBC). An organization, chaired and hosted by the American Hospital Association, that maintains the UB-92 hard-copy institutional billing form and the data element specifications for both the hard-copy form and the 192-byte UB-92 flat file EMC format. The NUBC has a formal consultative role under HIPAA for all transactions affecting institutional health care services.

National Uniform Claim Committee (NUCC). An organization, chaired and hosted by the American Medical Association that maintains the HCFA-1500 claim form and a set of data element specifications for professional claims submissions via the HCFA 1500 claim form, the Professional EMC NSF, and the X12 837. The NUCC has a formal consultative role under HIPAA for all transactions affecting non-dental, non-institutional professional health care services.

NCHS. The National Center for Health Statistics.

NCPDP. The National Council for Prescription Drug Programs.

NCPDP Batch Standard. An NCPDP standard designed for use by low-volume dispensers of pharmaceuticals, such as nursing homes. This is one of the proposed standards under HIPAA.

NCPDP Telecommunication Standards. An NCPDP standard designed for use by high-volume dispensers of pharmaceuticals, such as retail pharmacies. This is one of the proposed standards under HIPAA.

NCQA. The National Committee for Quality Assurance.

NCVHS. The National Committee on Vital and Health Statistics.

NDC. National Drug Code.

NDS. National Data Standards.

NHHI. National Health Information Infrastructure.

NOI. Notice of Intent.

Notice of Intent (NOI). A document that describes a subject area for which the federal government is considering developing regulations. It may describe what the government considers to be the relevant considerations and invite comments from interested parties. These comments can then be used in developing an NPRM or a final regulation.

Notice of Proposed Rulemaking (NPRM). A document that describes and explains regulations that the federal government proposes to adopt at some future date, and invites interested parties to submit comments related to them. These comments can then be used in developing a final regulation.

NPI. National Provider ID.

NPRM. Notice of Proposed Rulemaking.

NSF. National Standard Format.

NUBC. The National Uniform Billing Committee.

NUBC EDI TAG. The NUBC EDI Technical Advisory Group, which coordinates issues affecting both the NUBC and the X12 standards.

NUCC. The National Uniform Claim Committee.

Office of Management & Budget (OMB). A Federal Government agency that has a major role in reviewing proposed Federal regulations.

OIG. The Office of Inspector General.

OMB. The Office of Management and Budget.

Open System Interconnection (OSI). A multi-layer ISO data communications standard. Level seven of this standard is industry-specific, and HL7 is responsible for specifying the level seven OSI standards for the health industry.

OSI. Open System Interconnection.

PAG. Policy Advisory Group.

Payer. In health care, an entity that assumes the risk of paying for medical treatments. This can be an uninsured patient, a self-insured employer, or a health care plan or HMO.

PAYERID. HCFA's term for their pre-HIPAA National Payer ID initiative.

PCS. ICD.

PL or P. L. Public Law, as in PL 104-191 (HIPAA).

Policy Advisory Group (PAG). A generic name for many work groups at WEDI and elsewhere.

Provider Taxonomy Codes. A code set for identifying the provider type and area of specialization for all health care providers. A given provider can have several Provider Taxonomy Codes. This code set is used in the X12 278 Referrals and Authorization and the X12 837 Claim EDI transactions, and is maintained by the Health Care Provider Taxonomy Committee.

SC. Subcommittee.

SDO. Standards Development Organization.

SOW. Statement of Work.

Standard Transaction Format Compliance System (STFCS). An EHNAC-sponsored HIPAA certification service.

State Uniform Billing Committee (SUBC). A state-specific affiliate of the NUBC.

Statement of Work (SOW). A document describing the specific tasks and methodologies that will be followed to satisfy the requirements of an associated contract or MOU.

STFCS. The Standard Transaction Format Compliance System.

Structured Data. This term usually refers to data in which the meaning of a given part can be inferred by its location within an overall structure, such as a record layout.

SUBC. State Uniform Billing Committee.

TAG. Technical Advisory Group.

TG. Task Group.

Third Party Administrator (TPA). An entity that processes health care claims and performs related business functions for a *health plan.*

Transaction. Under HIPAA, this is the exchange of information between two parties to carry out financial or administrative activities related to health care.

Transaction Change Request System. A system established under HIPAA for accepting and tracking change requests for any of the HIPAA mandated transactions standards via a single web site: www.hipaa-dsmo.org.

UB. Uniform Bill, as in UB-82 or UB-92.

UB-82. A uniform institutional claim form developed by the NUBC that was in general use from 1983–1993.

UB-92. A uniform institutional claim form developed by the NUBC that has been in use since 1993.

UCF. Uniform Claim Form, as in UCF-1500.

UCTF. The Uniform Claim Task Force.

UN/EDIFACT. EDIFACT.

Uniform Claim Task Force (UCTF). An organization that developed the initial HCFA-1500 Professional Claim Form. The maintenance responsibilities were later assumed by the NUCC.

Unstructured Data. This term usually refers to data that is represented as free-form text, as an image, and so on, where it is not practical to predict exactly what data will appear where.

UPIN. Unique Physician Identification Number.

UR. Utilization Review.

USC or U.S.C. United States Code.

Value-Added Network (VAN). A vendor of EDI data communications and translation services.

Virtual Private Network (VPN). A technical strategy for creating secure connections, or tunnels, over the Internet.

Washington Publishing Company (WPC). A company that publishes the X12N HIPAA Implementation Guides and the X12N HIPAA Data Dictionary, and that also developed the X12 Data Dictionary.

WEDI. The Workgroup for Electronic Data Interchange.

WG. Work Group.

WHO. The World Health Organization.

Workgroup for Electronic Data Interchange (WEDI). A health care industry group that lobbied for HIPAA A/S, and that has a formal consultative role under the HIPAA legislation.

World Health Organization (WHO). An organization that maintains the International Classification of Diseases (ICD) code set.

WPC. The Washington Publishing Company.

X12. An ANSI-accredited group that defines EDI standards for many American industries, including health care insurance. Most of the electronic transaction standards proposed under HIPAA are X12 standards.

X12 148. X12's First Report of Injury, Illness, or Incident EDI transaction.

X12 270. X12's Health care Eligibility and Benefit Inquiry EDI transaction.

X12 271. X12's Health care Eligibility and Benefit Response EDI transaction.

X12 274. X12's Provider Information EDI transaction.

X12 275. X12's Patient Information EDI transaction.

X12 276. X12's Health care Claims Status Inquiry EDI transaction.

X12 277. X12's Health care Claim Status Response EDI transaction.

X12 278. X12's Referral Certification and Authorization EDI transaction.

X12 811. X12's Consolidated Service Invoice and Statement EDI transaction.

X12 820. X12's Payment Order and Remittance Advice EDI transaction.

X12 831. X12's Application Control Totals EDI transaction.

X12 834. X12's Benefit Enrollment and Maintenance EDI transaction.

X12 835. X12's Health care Claim Payment and Remittance Advice EDI transaction.

X12 837i. X12's Institutional Health care Claim or Encounter EDI transaction.

X12 837p. X12's Professional Health care Claim or Encounter EDI transaction.

X12 837d. X12's Dental Health care Claim or Encounter EDI transaction.

X12 997. X12's Functional Acknowledgement EDI transaction.

X12F. A subcommittee of X12 that defines EDI standards for the financial industry. This group maintains the X12 811

(generic) Invoice and the X12 820 (generic) Payment and Remittance Advice transactions, although X12N maintains the associated HIPAA Implementation Guides.

X12J. A subcommittee of X12 that reviews X12 work products for compliance with the X12 design rules.

X12N. A subcommittee of X12 that defines EDI standards for the insurance industry, including health care insurance.

X12N/SPTG4. The HIPAA Liaison Special Task Group of the Insurance Subcommittee (N) of X12. This group's responsibilities have been assumed by X12N/TG3/WG3.

X12N/TG1. The Property and Casualty Task Group (TG1) of the Insurance Subcommittee (N) of X12.

X12N/TG2. The Health care Task Group (TG2) of the Insurance Subcommittee (N) of X12.

X12N/TG2/WG1. The Health care Eligibility Work Group (WG1) of the Health care Task Group (TG2) of the Insurance Subcommittee (N) of X12. This group maintains the X12 270 Health care Eligibility and Benefit Inquiry and the X12 271 Health care Eligibility and Benefit Response EDI transactions.

X12N/TG2/WG2. The Healthdare Claims Work Group (WG2) of the Health care Task Group (TG2) of the Insurance Subcommittee (N) of X12. This group maintains the X12 837 Health care Claim or Encounter EDI transaction.

X12N/TG2/WG3. The Health care Claim Payments Work Group (WG3) of the Health care Task Group (TG2) of the Insurance Subcommittee (N) of X12. This group maintains the X12 835 Health care Claim Payment and Remittance Advice EDI transaction.

X12N/TG2/WG4. The Health care Enrollments Work Group (WG4) of the Health care Task Group (TG2) of the Insurance Subcommittee (N) of X12. This group maintains the X12 834 Benefit Enrollment and Maintenance EDI transaction.

X12N/TG2/WG5. The Health Claims Status Work Group (WG5) of the Health care Task Group (TG2) of the Insurance Subcommittee (N) of X12. This group maintains the X12 276 Health care Claims Status Inquiry and the X12 277 Health care Claim Status Response EDI transactions.

X12N/TG2/WG9. The Health care Patient Information Work Group (WG9) of the Health care Task Group (TG2) of the Insurance Subcommittee (N) of X12. This group maintains the X12 275 Patient Information EDI transaction.

X12N/TG2/WG10. The Health care Services Review Work Group (WG10) of the Health care Task Group (TG2) of the Insurance Subcommittee (N) of X12. This group maintains the X12 278 Referral Certification and Authorization EDI transaction.

X12N/TG2/WG12. The Interactive Health care Claims Work Group (WG12) of the Health care Task Group (TG2) of the

Insurance Subcommittee (N) of X12. This group maintains the IHCCLM EDI transaction.

X12N/TG2/WG15. The Health Care Provider Information Work Group (WG15) of the Health care Task Group (TG2) of the Insurance Subcommittee (N) of X12. This group maintains the X12 274 Provider Information EDI transaction.

X12N/TG2/WG19. The Health care Implementation Coordination Work Group (WG19) of the Health care Task Group (TG2) of the Insurance Subcommittee (N) of X12. This is now X12N/TG3/WG3.

X12N/TG3. The Business Transaction Coordination and Modeling Task Group (TG3) of the Insurance Subcommittee (N) of X12. TG3 maintains the X12N Business and Data Models and the HIPAA Data Dictionary.

X12N/TG3/WG1. The Property and Casualty Work Group of the Business Transaction Coordination and Modeling Task Group (TG3) of the Insurance Subcommittee (N) of X12.

X12N/TG3/WG2. The Health care Business and Information Modeling Work Group of the Business Transaction Coordination and Modeling Task Group (TG3) of the Insurance Subcommittee (N) of X12.

X12N/TG3/WG3. The HIPAA Implementation Coordination Work Group of the Business Transaction Coordination and Modeling Task Group (TG3) of the Insurance Subcommittee (N) of X12. This was formerly X12N/TG2/WG19 and X12N/SPTG4.

X12N/TG3/WG4. The Object-Oriented Modeling and XML Liaison Work Group of the Business Transaction Coordination and Modeling Task Group (TG3) of the Insurance Subcommittee (N) of X12.

X12N/TG4. The Implementation Guide Task Group of the Insurance Subcommittee (N) of X12. This group supports the development and maintenance of X12 Implementation Guides, including the HIPAA X12 IGs.

X12N/TG8. The Architecture Task Group of the Insurance Subcommittee (N) of X12.

X12/PRB. The X12 Procedures Review Board.

X12 Standard. The term currently used for any *X12 standard* that has been approved since the most recent release of X12 *American National Standards*. Because a full set of X12 *American National Standards* is only released about once every five years, it is the *X12 standard*s that are most likely to be in active use. These standards were previously called *Draft Standards for Trial Use.*

XML. Extensible Markup Language.

Appendix B

**HIPAA Frequently
Asked Questions
(FAQs)**

General Overview

What is HIPAA and what are its major components?

HIPAA stands for the Health Insurance Portability and Accountability Act, which was passed by Congress in 1996. Title I of the law addresses continuous group health insurance coverage for individual workers changing their place of employment. Title II includes an Administrative Simplification section that requires establishing standards to ensure the security, confidentiality, and integrity of health care transactions involving patient-identifiable information.

What organizations are affected by this new ruling under the provisions of HIPAA?

Any organization that accesses, stores, maintains, or transmits patient-identifiable information or health care records is affected. Typically, health care providers, hospitals, health plans and insurers, and health care clearing-houses are considered covered entities under HIPAA regulations.

How will HIPAA affect claims management?

HIPAA's requirements may cause significant changes in process, organization, and/or staffing in the area of claims management. HIPAA compliance requirements are meant to encourage health care organizations to move claims processing and management functions from manual to electronic systems to improve security, lower costs, and reduce error rates.

Where can I find a glossary of HIPAA terminology?

A comprehensive glossary of HIPAA terminology is available in the Notice of Proposed Rule Making for Security and Electronic Signature Standards. Go to http://aspe.os.dhhs.gov/admnsimp/nprm/seclist.htm and choose Addendum 2 from the list of sections.

Compliance and Planning

When must covered organizations comply with HIPAA requirements?

- Privacy Standards. April 14, 2003; April 14, 2004 for small health plans.
- Transactions and Code Sets. October 16, 2002 or October 16, 2003 if an extension was filed per the Administrative Simplification Compliance Act.
- Security Standard. April 21, 2005; April 21, 2006 for small health plans.
- Unique Employer Identification—Final Rule out on May 31, 2002; compliance date set for July 30, 2004.

Remember that a broader scope of the question is not *when* can we become compliant with HIPAA, but rather *how* can we change the way we do business to bring the very best in health care to the patients in a way that always protects the privacy of their health care information.

Does HIPAA compliance apply only to patient information sent via the Internet?

No, HIPAA compliance does not only apply to patient information sent via the Internet. For specific information, refer to the Privacy Final Rule and the Security Notice for Proposed Rule Making.

What steps should a health care organization take now to prepare for HIPAA compliance?

Be proactive. Obtain executive management commitment to an organization-wide HIPAA Compliance Program. Review the organization's strategic and financial plan; allocate resources for the upcoming years. Consider establishing a program management position similar to that established for Y2K. Initiate discussions with your IT partners on how to assess your organization's current performance relative to new HIPAA standards. Obtain subject training for key executives, information management professionals, and IT professionals on the subject.

What information would be useful to brief the organization's executives on the scope of HIPAA?

HIPAA compliance will be a multi-year, large cost, institution-wide effort required by Federal Laws and Regulations within the next two to four years.

How can I prepare Information Management systems for HIPAA?

Begin now to assess your readiness. Use the inventories of systems, networks, and devices to assess the ability to adopt the new transaction standards, code set identifiers, and security requirements. Continue to maintain these inventories as you upgrade systems.

Conduct a risk analysis and weigh various means of implementing security in light of your potential liability and your ability to mitigate that risk. Contact your application systems vendors, as well as the vendors of your hardware and software to determine what already exists and how some security can be hard-coded to address multiple applications. Assess your business partners' and affiliates' timelines for compliance with HIPAA to determine if it will be necessary to run parallel systems or use multiple identifiers for a period of time.

Isn't it just an IT issue to become HIPAA compliant?

HIPAA compliance is better focused as a business issue than as an IT issue, although IT will play a major role in implementing compliant systems. Implementing HIPAA will affect how health care organizations make adjustments to staffing requirements and revisions of policies, procedures, and processes to achieve and monitor compliance with patient privacy and confidentiality needs. Larger organizations will need executive sponsorship and dedicated resources to lead the HIPAA compliance effort.

What are the consequences or penalties for non-compliance with HIPAA?

HIPAA sets severe penalties for non-compliance. Penalties are substantial with monetary fines and, in some cases, imprisonment:

- ◆ **Civil penalties.** Up to $100 per person per violation and up to $25,000 per person per violation of a single standard per calendar year.
- ◆ **Federal criminal penalties.** Up to $50,000 and 1 year in prison for obtaining or disclosing protected health information; up to $100,000 and 5 years in prison for obtaining protected health information under

false pretenses; up to $250,000 and 10 years in prison for obtaining or disclosing health information with the intent to sell, transfer, or use it for commercial advantage, personal gain, or malicious harm.Penalties are higher for actions designed to generate monetary gain.

Privacy Standards

Has there ever been any sort of standard before to protect the privacy of patient records?

No. This is the first time ever on a national scale that a standard has been released to protect the privacy of personal health records, and it is the first time that non-compliance can be enforced on civic and federal levels.

Did the Department of Health and Human Services issue additional information about the privacy standards?

Yes. The Department of Health and Human Services (HHS) issued a fact sheet about the privacy standards as well as additional guidance information. This information can be found on the HHS Web site. Go to: http://aspe.hhs.gov/admnsimp/

Technology and Security Solutions

Are there any products out there that are HIPAA compliant?

No. There is no such thing as a HIPAA-compliant product per se. It is actually organizations, not technology, that must become HIPAA-compliant. Technology and security solutions are deployed to support an organization's efforts to become HIPAA compliant. Perform assessments to determine your strategy for HIPAA compliance and then look for products or consulting services that can help enforce and support your strategy.

You may be an organization that can use the security features of your current systems and applications instead of having to purchase new and/or additional third-party products.

Is biometrics technology the answer to HIPAA security requirements?

The key for HIPAA compliance is to build a secure infrastructure with strong authentication (for instance, accurate identification of users accessing information). The biometrics industry has matured significantly in the past few years and is primed for substantial growth in the very near future. Incorporating biometrics identity verification, as a core component of a health care organization's security, is critical for knowing that only authorized individuals have access to your most sensitive systems.

What is biometrics authentication?

Authentication verifies a user's identity. An individual can be identified and authenticated by what he knows (password), by what he owns (smart card), or by his human characteristics (biometrics). Unlike a password or Personal Identification Number (PIN), a biometric trait cannot be lost, stolen, or re-created. Examples of biometric technology options include

◆ Fingerprints
◆ Facial recognition
◆ Iris scanning
◆ Hand geometry
◆ Voice patterns

Appendix C

HIPAA

Source: Office for Civil Rights (OCR), December 3, 2002

If I believe that my privacy rights have been violated, when can I submit a complaint?

By law, health care providers (including doctors and hospitals) who engage in certain electronic transactions, health plans, and health care clearinghouses, (collectively, *covered entities*) have until April 14, 2003, to comply with the HIPAA Privacy Rule. (Small health plans have until April 14, 2004, to comply.) Activities occurring before April 14, 2003 are not subject to the Office for Civil Rights (OCR) enforcement actions. After that date, a person who believes a covered entity is not complying with a requirement of the Privacy Rule may file with OCR a written complaint, either on paper or electronically. This complaint must be filed within 180 days of when the complainant knew or should have known that the act had occurred. The Secretary may waive this 180-day time limit if good cause is shown. See 45 CFR 160.306 and 164.534. OCR will provide further information on its Web site about how to file a complaint (www.hhs.gov/ocr/hipaa/).

In addition, after these compliance dates, individuals have a right to file a complaint directly with the covered entity. Individuals should refer to the covered entity's notice of privacy practices for more information about how to file a complaint with the covered entity.

If patients request copies of their medical records as permitted by the Privacy Rule, are they required to pay for the copies?

The Privacy Rule permits the covered entity to impose reasonable, cost-based fees. The fee may include only the cost of copying (including supplies and labor) and postage, if the patient requests that the copy be mailed. If the patient has agreed to receive a summary or explanation of his or her protected health information, the covered entity may also charge a fee for preparation of the summary or explanation. The fee might not include costs associated with searching for and retrieving the requested information. See 45 CFR 164.524.

Does the HIPAA Privacy Rule protect genetic information?

Yes, genetic information is health information protected by the Privacy Rule. Like other health information, to be protected it must meet the definition of protected health information: it must be individually identifiable and maintained by a covered health care provider, health plan, or health care clearinghouse. See 45 C.F.R 160.103 and 164.501.

A provider might have a patient's medical record that contains older portions of a medical record that were created by another/previous provider. Will the HIPAA Privacy Rule permit a provider who is a covered entity to disclose a complete medical record even though portions of the record were created by other providers?

Yes, the Privacy Rule permits a provider who is a covered entity to disclose a complete medical record, including portions that were created by another provider, assuming that the disclosure is for a purpose permitted by the Privacy Rule, such as treatment.

Can a physician's office fax patient medical information to another physician's office?

The HIPAA Privacy Rule permits physicians to disclose protected health information to another health care provider for treatment purposes. This can be done by fax or by other means. Covered entities must have in place reasonable and appropriate administrative, technical, and physical safeguards to protect the privacy of protected health information that is disclosed using a fax machine. Examples of measures that could be reasonable and appropriate in such a situation include the sender confirming that the fax number to be used is in fact the correct one for the other physician's office, and placing the fax machine in a secure location to prevent unauthorized access to the information. See 45 CFR164.530(c).

Are hospitals able to inform the clergy about parishioners in the hospital?

Yes, the HIPAA Privacy Rule allows this communication to occur, as long as the patient has been informed of this use and disclosure, and does not object. The Privacy Rule provides that a hospital or other covered health care provider may maintain in a directory the following information about that individual: the individual's name, location in the facility, health condition expressed in general terms, and religious affiliation. The facility may disclose this directory information to members of the clergy. Thus, for example, a hospital may disclose the names of Methodist patients to a Methodist minister unless a patient has restricted such disclosure. Directory information, except for religious affiliation, may be disclosed only to other persons who ask for the individual by name. When, due to emergency circumstances or incapacity, the patient has not been provided an opportunity to agree or object to being included in the facility's directory, these disclosures may still occur, if such disclosure is consistent with any known prior expressed preference of the individual and the disclosure is in the individual's best interest as determined in the professional judgment of the provider. See 45 CFR 164.510(a).

Are state, county, or local health departments required to comply with the HIPAA Privacy Rule?

Yes, if a state, county, or local health department performs functions that make it a covered entity, or otherwise meets the definition of a covered entity. For example, a state Medicaid program is a covered entity as defined in the Privacy Rule. Some health departments operate health care clinics and thus are health care providers. If these health care providers transmit health information electronically in connection with a transaction covered in the HIPAA Transaction Rule, they are covered entities. For more information, see the definitions of covered entity, health care provider, health plan, and health care clearinghouse in 45 CFR 160.103. See also, the "Covered Entity Decision Tools" posted at http://www.cms.gov/hipaa/hipaa2/support/tools/decisionsupport/default.asp. These tools address the question of whether a person, business, or agency is a covered health care provider, health care clearinghouse, or health plan.

If the health department performs some covered functions (those activities that make it a provider that conducts certain transactions electronically—a health plan or a health care clearinghouse) and other non-covered functions, it may designate those components (or parts thereof) that perform covered functions as the health care component(s) of the organization and thereby become a type of covered entity known as a *hybrid entity*. Most of the requirements of the Privacy Rule apply only to the hybrid entity's health care component(s). If a health department elects to be a hybrid entity, there are restrictions on how its health care component(s) may disclose protected health information to other components of the health department. See 45 CFR 164.504 (a)—(c) for more information about hybrid entities.

Are the following types of insurance covered under HIPAA: Long/short term disability, workers compensation, automobile liability that includes coverage for medical payments?

No, the listed types of policies are not health plans. The HIPAA Administrative Simplification regulations specifically exclude from the definition of a health plan any policy, plan, or program to the extent that it provides, or pays for the cost of, excepted benefits, which are listed in section 2791(c)(1) of the Public Health Service Act, 42 U.S.C. 300gg-91(c)(1). See 45 CFR 160.103. As described in the statute, excepted benefits are one or more (or any combination thereof) of the following policies, plans, or programs:

◆ Coverage only for accident, disability income insurance, or any combination thereof

◆ Coverage issued as a supplement to liability insurance

◆ Liability insurance, including general liability insurance and automobile liability insurance

◆ Workers' compensation or similar insurance

◆ Automobile medical payment insurance

◆ Credit-only insurance

◆ Coverage for on-site medical clinics

◆ Other similar insurance coverage, specified in regulations, under which benefits for medical care are secondary or incidental to other insurance benefits

Is an entity that is acting as a third-party administrator to a group health plan a covered entity?

No, providing services to or acting on behalf of a health plan does not transform a third-party administrator (TPA) into a covered entity. Generally, a TPA of a group health plan would be acting as a business associate of the group health plan. Of course, the TPA may meet the definition of a covered entity based on its other activities (such as by providing group health insurance). See 45 CFR 160.103.

The Social Security Administration (SSA) collects medical records for the Social Security Income (SSI) disability program. Is SSA a covered entity (for instance, a health plan)?

The SSA is not a covered entity. The collection of individually identifiable health information is not a factor in determining whether an entity is a covered entity. Covered entities are defined in HIPAA. They are (1) health plans, (2) health care clearinghouses, and (3) health care providers that transmit any health information in electronic form in connection with a transaction covered in the HIPAA Transactions Rule. These terms are defined in detail at 45 CFR 160.103.

Is the Privacy Rule compliance date delayed by the Administrative Simplification Compliance Act (ASCA) that was enacted in December 2001?

No, the compliance date for the Privacy Rule is April 14, 2003, or, for small health plans, April 14, 2004. ASCA does not apply to the HIPAA Privacy Rule. Rather, ASCA delays compliance with the transaction and code set standards adopted by the HIPAA Transactions Rule for covered entities that file a compliance plan. More information about ASCA can be found on the Web site for the Centers for Medicare and Medicaid Services at http://cms.hhs.gov/hipaa/.

HIPAA allows *small health plans*, defined as health plans having annual receipts of $5 million or less, an additional year (in the case of the Privacy Rule, until April 14, 2004) to come into compliance. How should a health plan determine what receipts to use to decide whether it qualifies as a "small health plan?"

Health plans that file certain federal tax returns and report receipts on those returns should use the guidance provided by the Small Business Administration at 13 CFR 121.104 to calculate annual receipts. Health plans that do not report receipts to the IRS—for example, ERISA group health plans that are exempt from filing income tax returns—should use proxy measures to determine their annual receipts. Further information about the relevant provisions of 13 CFR 121.104 and these proxy measures, and additional information related to small health plans, may be found at http://cms.hhs.gov/hipaa/hipaa2/default.asp.

Does the HIPAA Privacy Rule require that covered entities provide patients with access to oral information?

No, the Privacy Rule requires covered entities to provide individuals with access to protected health information about themselves that is contained in their *designated record sets*. The term *record* in the term *designated record set* does not include oral information; rather, it connotes information that has been recorded in some manner.

The Rule does not require covered entities to tape or digitally record oral communications, nor retain digitally or tape recorded information after transcription. But if such records are maintained and used to make decisions about the individual, they may meet the definition of *designated record set*. For example, a health plan is not required to provide a member access to tapes of a telephone advice line interaction if the tape is maintained only for customer service review and not to make decisions about the member.

Does the HIPAA Privacy Rule require that covered entities document all oral communications?

No, the Privacy Rule does not require covered entities to document any information, including oral information that is used or disclosed for treatment, payment, or health care operations.

The Rule includes, however, documentation requirements for some information disclosures for other purposes. For example, some disclosures must be documented to meet the standard for providing a disclosure history to an individual upon request. Where a documentation requirement exists in the final Privacy Rule, it applies to all relevant communications, whether in oral or some other form. For example, if a covered physician discloses information about a case of tuberculosis to a public health authority as permitted by the final Privacy Rule at 45 CFR 164.512, then he or she must maintain a record of that disclosure regardless of whether the disclosure was made orally, by phone, or in writing.

Appendix D

The Platform for Privacy Preferences Project (P3P) defined by the World Wide Web Consortium (W3C) is an emerging industry standard that enables Web sites to express their privacy practices in a standardized format that can be automatically retrieved and interpreted by user agents. P3P is about increasing user trust and confidence in the Web.

About P3P

The Platform for Privacy Preferences Project (P3P) provides a technical mechanism for assisting users about privacy policies before they release personal information. *Privacy* is defined as the protection of the collection, storage, processing, dissemination, and destruction of personal information. Increasingly, consumers want to choose who does and does not have access to their information. Consumers are demanding heightened privacy protection, and the focus of P3P is on the disclosure of Web site privacy practices.

Privacy statements are an important component in establishing a "trusted relationship" with Web site visitors. P3P creates a common vocabulary and syntax for expressing Web site data management practices. The goal of P3P is to help users find the privacy practices of a particular site and how these practices compare to the user's preferences. P3P does not solve all privacy issues but is a part of a larger and more comprehensive set of technical and legal solutions.

The current version of P3P, P3Pv1.0, uses the standard HTTP 1.1 protocol for the exchange of policies. The matching of policies to user preferences takes place on the client-side. P3P-enabled Web sites cite their policy reference files to indicate the parts of their site to which each P3P policy applies. Administrators may create one policy for the entire site or may have multiple policies that each applies to different parts of the site.

P3P was developed by a large number of W3C member organizations, including America Online, AT&T, HP, IBM, Microsoft, NCR, NEC, Nokia, and many others.

P3P and Cookies

P3P is complimentary to cookie-blocking software and anonymity tools. Increasingly, vendors are building P3P into their products. P3P is useful for informing users about how their data will be used. This is not a function provided by cookie-blocking software or anonymity tools.

What P3P Is Not

P3P is not a mechanism for ensuring that sites act according to its policies. P3P does require all Web sites to indicate mechanisms by which enforcement can take place. Sites may describe remedies available to users who feel that their privacy has been violated.

P3P also does not include mechanisms for transferring or securing personal data. P3P can be built into tools designed to facilitate data transfer.

Also, an area where there has been some discussions and where there are differences is the Open Profiling Standard (OPS). The OPS proposal co-authored by Netscape, Firefly, and VeriSign is not relevant to the P3P specification. The OPS proposal specified a means for the exchange of user profile information—that is how to store and release, with the user's permission, data which is often requested or required by a Web site. Data transfer protocol is not a part of P3Pv1.0.

P3P and Other Languages

Web sites that use P3P encode their information in an XML format. The Resource Description Framework (RDF), an application of XML that is used for encoding metadata, is not used to encode privacy policy information. A P3P Preferences Exchange Language (APPEL) is a W3C working draft that specifies a language for describing sets of preferences about P3P policies. Using this language, a user can express preferences in a set of preference rules, called a *rule-set*, which can then be used by the user agent to make automated or semi-automated decisions regarding the exchange of data with P3P-enabled Web sites.

How P3P Works

P3P policies can be referenced in three different ways:

- ◆ Server administrators may deploy the policy reference file, p3p.xml, in the directory called /w3c. The user agent could request this file by using an HTTP GET request for the resource /w3c/p3p.xml.

- Servers may be configured to insert a P3P header into an HTTP response to indicate the location of a site's P3P policy.
- Servers may be configured to insert the information into HTML content as a LINK tag.

Getting Started with P3P

Your organization needs to start evaluating the deployment of P3P privacy policies on your Web site. For example, to successfully use cookies with Microsoft's Internet Explorer 6, the privacy features of the browser require Web services to deploy compact policies as defined by the Platform for Privacy Preferences (P3P) Project. The Internet Explorer 6 privacy features filter cookies based on these compact policies as well as the user's privacy settings.

For example, the following list summarizes the common steps to deployment of P3P privacy policies on your Web site:

- Name the policy-reference file, p3p.xml, and deploy it at /w3c/p3p.xml.
- Deploy full P3P policy files within the same directory, for example, /w3c/full_p3p_policy.xml.
- Set compact policies for all cookies in the HTTP header.

Organizations need to develop and deploy P3P privacy policies. Privacy is not just a risk or an operational issue. Privacy is about earning customer trust, and trust is ultimately a core requirement for an e-business infrastructure and can be the catalyst for enhanced trade.

Appendix E

Bibliography

Electronic Health Care Transactions and Code Sets Standards Model Compliance Plan. U.S. Department of Health and Human Services. Retrieved from http://cms.hhs.gov/hipaa/hipaa2/ASCAForm.pdf.

Final Rule Information on Electronic Transactions As It Relates to the Pharmacy Industry. National Council from Prescription Drug Programs. Retrieved from http://ncpdp.org/PDF/finalrule.pdf.

Health Insurance Portability and Accountability Act. American Medical Association. Retrieved from http://www.ama-assn.org/ama/pub/category/4234.html.

Health Insurance Portability and Accountability Act of 1996: Title I Statutory Text. Retrieved from http://cms.hhs.gov/hipaa/hipaa1/content/HIPAASTA.pdf.

Health Insurance Reform: Modifications to Transactions and Code Sets Standards for Electronic Transactions. U.S. Department of Health and Human Services. Office of the Secretary. 45 C.F.R. Part 162.

Health Insurance Reform: Standards for Electronic Transactions; National Standard Health Care Provider Identifier; Proposed Rules. U.S. Department of Health and Human Services. Health Care Financing Administration. 45 C.F.R. Part 142. Retrieved from http://aspe.hhs.gov/admnsimp/nprm/txnprm.pdf.

Health Insurance Reform: Standard Unique Employer Identifier. U.S. Department of Health and Human Services. Office of the Secretary. 45 C.F.R. Parts 160, 162. Retrieved from http://frwebgate.access.gpo.gov/cgi-bin/getdoc.cgi?dbname=2002_register&docid=02-13616-filed.pdf.

Health Insurance Reform: Standards for Electronic Transactions; Announcement of Designated Standard Maintenance Organization; Final Rule and Notice. U.S. Department of Health and Human Services. Office of the Secretary. 45 C.F.R. Parts 160, 162.

Retrieved from http://aspe.hhs.gov/admnsimp/final/txfinal.pdf.

HIPAA Administrative Simplification. Centers for Medicare and Medicaid Services. Retrieved from http://www.cms.hhs.gov/hipaa/hipaa2/default.asp.

HIPAA Administrative Simplification. U.S. Department of Health and Human Services. Retrieved from http://aspe.os.dhhs.gov/admnsimp/.

HIPAA Insurance Reform. Centers for Medicare and Medicaid Services. Retrieved from http://cms.hhs.gov/hipaa/hipaa1/default.asp.

Nondiscrimination in Health Coverage in the Group Market; Interim Final Rules and Proposed Rules. U.S. Department of Health and Human Services. 45 C.F.R. Part 146. Retrieved from http://cms.hhs.gov/hipaa/hipaa1/content/nondiscr.pdf.

Privacy of Health Records. Office for Civil Rights. Retrieved from http://www.hhs.gov/ocr/hipaa/finalreg.html.

Protecting Your Health Insurance Coverage. U.S. Department of Health and Human Services. Retrieved from http://cms.hhs.gov/hipaa/hipaa1/content/protect.pdf.

Security and Electronic Signature Standards; Proposed Rule. U.S. Department of Health and Human Services. Office of the Secretary. 45 C.F.R Part 142. Retrieved from http://aspe.hhs.gov/admnsimp/nprm/secnprm.pdf.

Standards for Privacy of Individually Identifiable Health Information; Final Rule. U.S. Department of Health and Human Services. 45 C.F.R. Parts 160, 164. Retrieved from http://www.hhs.gov/ocr/hipaa/dates.pdf.

Technical Corrections to the Standards for Privacy of Individually Identifiable Health Information. U.S. Department of Health and Human Services. Office of the Secretary. 45 C.F.R. Parts 160, 164. Retrieved from http://www.hhs.gov/ocr/pvcfix01.pdf.

Appendix F

MODIFICATIONS TO THE STANDARDS FOR PRIVACY OF INDIVIDUALLY IDENTIFIABLE HEALTH INFORMATION— FINAL RULE

The Department of Health and Human Services on August 14th will publish final modifications to the Privacy Rule to ensure that the final Privacy Rule provides strong privacy protection without hindering access to quality health care. President Bush and Secretary Thompson are committed to maintaining protections for the privacy of individually identifiable health information. Based on the comments received on the notice of proposed rule-making, the Department modified a number of provisions of the Privacy Rule.

The Standards for Privacy of Individually Identifiable Health Information (the Privacy Rule) took effect on April 14, 2001. The Privacy Rule creates national standards to protect individuals' personal health information and gives patients increased access to their medical records. As required by the Health Insurance Portability and Accountability Act of 1996 (HIPAA), the Privacy Rule covers health plans, health care clearinghouses, and those health care providers who conduct certain financial and administrative transactions electronically. Most covered entities must comply with the Privacy Rule by April 14, 2003. Small health plans have until April 14, 2004 to comply with the final Privacy Rule.

Final Modifications

◆ **Marketing.** The final Privacy Rule requires a covered entity to obtain an individual's prior written authorization to use his or her protected health information for marketing purposes except for a face-to-face encounter or a communication involving a promotional gift of nominal value. The Department of HHS defines marketing to distinguish between the types of communications that are and are not marketing, and makes clear that a covered entity is prohibited from selling lists of patients and enrollees to third parties or from disclosing protected health information to a third party for the marketing activities of the third party, without the individual's authorization. The final Privacy Rule clarifies that doctors and other covered entities communicating with patients about treatment options or the covered entity's own health-related products and services are not considered marketing. For example, health care plans can inform patients of additional health plan coverage and value-added items and services, such as discounts for prescription drugs or eyeglasses.

◆ **Consent and Notice.** The Department of HHS makes changes to protect privacy while eliminating barriers to treatment by strengthening the notice requirement and making consent for routine health care delivery purposes (known as treatment, payment, and health care operations) optional. The final Privacy Rule requires covered entities to provide patients with notice of the patient's privacy rights and the privacy practices of the covered entity. The strengthened notice requires direct treatment providers to make a good faith effort to obtain patient's written acknowledgement of the notice of privacy rights and practices.

The final Privacy Rule promotes access to care by removing mandatory consent requirements that would inhibit patient access to health care while providing covered entities with the option of developing a consent process that works for that entity. The final Privacy Rule also allows consent requirements already in place to continue.

◆ **Uses and Disclosures Regarding Food and Drug Administration (FDA)-Regulated Products and Activities.** The final Privacy Rule permits covered entities to disclose protected health information, without authorization, to a person subject to the jurisdiction of the FDA for public health purposes related to the quality, safety, or effectiveness of FDA-regulated products or activities, such as collecting or reporting adverse events, dangerous products, and defects or problems with FDA-regulated products. This assures that information will continue to be available to protect public health and safety, as it is today.

◆ **Incidental Use and Disclosure.** The final Privacy Rule acknowledges that uses or disclosures that are incidental to an otherwise permitted use or disclosure may occur. Such incidental uses or disclosures are not considered a violation of the final Privacy Rule provided that the covered entity has met the reasonable safeguards and minimum necessary requirements. For example, if these requirements are met, doctors' offices may use waiting room sign-in sheets, hospitals may keep patient charts at bedside, doctors can talk to patients in semi-private rooms, and doctors can confer at nurse's stations without fear of violating the rule if overheard by a passerby.

◆ **Authorization.** The final Privacy Rule clarifies the authorization requirements to the Privacy Rule to, among other things, eliminate separate authorization requirements for covered entities. Patients have to grant permission in advance for each type of non-routine use or disclosure, but providers do not have to use different types of forms. These modifications also consolidate and streamline core elements and notification requirements.

◆ **Minimum Necessary.** The final Privacy Rule exempts from the minimum necessary standards any uses or disclosures for which the covered entity has received an authorization. The Privacy Rule previously exempted only certain types of authorizations from the minimum necessary requirement, but because the rule has only one type of authorization, the exemption now applies to all authorizations. Minimum necessary requirements are still in effect to ensure an individual's privacy for most other uses and disclosures.

The Department of HHS clarifies in the preamble that the minimum necessary standard is not intended to impede disclosures necessary for workers' compensation programs. The Department of HHS will actively monitor to ensure that workers' compensation programs are not unduly affected by the final Privacy Rule.

◆ **Parents and Minors.** The final Privacy Rule clarifies that state law, or other applicable law, governs in the area of parents and minors. Generally, the Privacy Rule provides parents with new rights to control the health information about their minor children, with limited exceptions that are based on state or other applicable laws and professional practice. For example, where a state has explicitly addressed disclosure of a minor's health information to a parent, or access to a child's medical record by a parent, the final Privacy Rule clarifies that state law governs. In addition, the final Privacy Rule clarifies that, in the special cases in which the minor controls his or her own health information under such law and that law does not define the parents' ability to access the child's health information, a licensed health care provider continues to be able to exercise discretion to grant or deny such access as long as that decision is consistent with the state or other applicable law.

◆ **Business Associates.** The final Privacy Rule gives covered entities (except small health plans) up to an additional year to change existing written contracts to come into compliance with the business associate requirements. The additional time will ease the burden of covered entities renegotiating contracts all at once. The Department has also provided sample business associate contract provisions.

◆ **Research.** The final Privacy Rule facilitates researchers' use of a single combined form to obtain informed consent for the research and authorization to use or disclose protected health information for such research. The final Privacy Rule also clarifies the requirements relating to a researcher obtaining an IRB or Privacy Board waiver of authorization by streamlining the privacy waiver criteria to more closely follow the requirement of the Common Rule, which governs federally funded research. The transition provisions have been expanded to prevent needless interruption of ongoing research.

◆ **Limited Data Set.** The final Privacy Rule permits the creation and dissemination of a limited data set (that does not include directly identifiable information) for research, public health, and health care operations. In addition, to further protect privacy, the final Privacy Rule conditions disclosure of the limited data set on a covered entity and the recipient entering into a data use agreement, in which the recipient would agree to limit the use of the data set for the purposes for which it was given, and to ensure the security of the data, as well as not to identify the information or use it to contact any individual.

◆ **Other Provisions.**

• **Hybrid Entities.** The final Privacy Rule permits any entity that performs covered and non-covered functions to elect to use the hybrid entity provisions and provides the entity additional discretion in designating its health care components.

• **Health Care Operations: Changes in Legal Ownership.** The final Privacy Rule clarifies the definition of health care operations to allow a covered entity who sells or transfers assets to, or consolidates or merges with, an entity who is, or will be, a covered entity upon completion of transaction, to use and disclose protected health information in connection with such transaction, which include due diligence and transferring records containing protected health information as part of the transaction.

• **Group Health Plan Disclosures of Enrollment and Disenrollment Information.** The final Privacy Rule allows a group health plan, a health insurance issuer, or HMO acting for a group health plan to disclose to a plan sponsor, such as an employer, information on whether the individual is enrolled in or has dis-enrolled from a plan offered by the sponsor without amending the plan documents.

- **Accounting of Disclosures.** The final Privacy Rule exempts disclosures made pursuant to an authorization from the accounting requirements. The authorization process itself adequately protects individual privacy by assuring that the individual's permission is given both knowingly and voluntarily. The final Privacy Rule also exempts from the accounting requirements incidental disclosures, and disclosures that are part of a limited data set. The final Privacy Rule provides a simplified alternative approach for accounting for multiple research disclosures that includes providing a description of the research for which an individual's protected health information may have been disclosed and the researcher's contact information.

- **Disclosure for Treatment, Payment, or Health Care Operations of Another Entity.** The final Privacy Rule clarifies that covered entities can disclose protected health information for the treatment and payment activities of another covered entity or a health care provider, and for certain health care operations of another covered entity.

- **Protected Health Information: Exclusion for Employment Records.** The final Privacy Rule clarifies that employment records maintained by a covered entity in its capacity as an employer are excluded from the definition of protected health information. The modifications do not change the fact that individually identifiable health information created, received, or maintained by a covered entity in its health care capacity is protected health information.

The final Privacy Rule also includes technical corrections and additional clarifications related to various sections of the existing rule. The final Privacy Rule is designed to ensure that protections for patient privacy are implemented in a manner that maximizes privacy while not compromising either the availability or the quality of medical care.

On July 6, 2001, the Department of HHS issued its first guidance to answer common questions and clarify certain of the Privacy Rule's provisions. The Department of HHS is committed to assisting covered entities to come into compliance with the final Privacy Rule. Therefore, the Department of HHS will update the guidance to reflect the modifications adopted in this final Privacy Rule.

Appendix G

The HIPAA Academy is about developing and validating HIPAA knowledge. The training program is designed to deliver the skills required for Certified HIPAA Professionals, Security Specialists, and Administrators to be effective members of enterprise HIPAA implementation initiatives.

It is strongly recommended that members of the HIPAA implementation team have acquired the necessary skills to enable solutions required for meeting compliance requirements.

HIPAA Academy delivers solutions to assist organizations with their HIPAA initiatives in the areas of HIPAA Professional Services, HIPAA Assessment, Interim HIPAA Compliance Officer, HIPAA Project Managers, and HIPAA Training and Certification.

Access www.HIPAAAcademy.Net for more details about HIPAA Academy and additional resources such as HIPAA FAQs and white papers.

Certification Exams

The Certified HIPAA Administrator (CHA) exam validates knowledge and skills of end users that are responsible for delivery and support of health care services and administration.

The Certified HIPAA Professional (CHP) exam validates knowledge and skills in the core areas of HIPAA Administrative Simplification legislation, Transactions and Code Sets Requirements, Privacy Requirements, and Security Requirements.

The Certified HIPAA Administrator (CHA) exam validates knowledge and skills of end users that are responsible for delivery and support of health care services and administration.

The Certified HIPAA Professional (CHP) exam validates knowledge and skills in the core areas of HIPAA Administrative Simplification legislation, Transactions and Code Sets Requirements, Privacy Requirements, and Security Requirements.

The Certified HIPAA Security Specialist (CHSS) exam validates knowledge and skill sets in

- ◆ The core domain areas of the HIPAA Security Rule: Administrative Safeguards, Physical Safeguards, and Technical Safeguards (75 percent of exam).

◆ Security technology fundamentals, including firewall systems, Intrusion Detection Systems (IDS), authentication solutions, IPSec, VPN, digital signatures, digital certificates, PKI, PGP, and International standards such as the ISO 17799 (25 percent of exam).

Exam Grid

Exam	Exam Name	Number of Exam Questions	Allowed	Time Score	Passing Exam Format
HIPADM-1	HIO-101	40	60 Minutes	75%	Standard
HIPPROF-1	HIO-201	60	60 Minutes	75%	Standard
HIPSEC-1	HIO-301	60	60 Minutes	75%	Standard

Exam Fees

The Certified HIPAA Administrator exam fee is $40. The Certified HIPAA Professional exam fee is $150. The Certified HIPAA Security Specialist exam fee is $195. Exam fees are not included in training costs. All exams are delivered by Authorized Prometric Testing Centers.

Pricing

The HIPAA Academy delivers both end-user awareness training and certification courses on HIPAA. These include

◆ Privacy for Beginners (3 hours)

◆ Introduction to HIPAA Security (3 hours)

◆ HIPAA Awareness: An Overview (1 day)

◆ Certified HIPAA Administrator (1 day)— focus is only on Privacy Rule

◆ Certified HIPAA Professional (3 days)

◆ Certified HIPAA Security Specialist (2 days)

Contact HIPAA Academy at http//:www.HIPAAAcademy.Net for a complete list of Certified HIPAA Academy Training Partners and their course schedule.

Bring HIPAA Academy training, certification, and executive briefs to your site. HIPAA Academy will customize the session to meet your specific requirements and time frames. Ask HIPAA Academy for flat rate pricing for an on-site customized session.

Training Options

To bring HIPAA Academy training, certification, and executive briefs to your site, call HIPAA Academy at **1.877.899.9974, ext. 20** or **ext. 22**. HIPAA Academy will customize the session to meet your specific requirements and time frames.

◆ 2-hour HIPAA Executive Brief

◆ 1-day Certified HIPAA Administrator (CHS) program (focused on HIPAA Privacy Rule)

◆ 3-day Certified HIPAA Professional (CHP) program (focused on HIPAA's Administrative Simplification subtitle)

◆ Certified HIPAA Security Specialist (CHSS) program

◆ Several HIPAA e-learning solutions for HIPAA Awareness, Privacy, and Security

HIPAA Academy Faculty

Uday O. **Ali** Pabrai is a highly sought after HIPAA consultant and speaker. Ali has delivered keynote and other sessions at numerous conferences worldwide, including the National Council for Prescription Drug Programs (NCPDP), the National HIPAA Summit, COMDEX, COMNET, Internet World, and DCI's Internet Expo. Ali is an accomplished expert in the areas of HIPAA and enterprise security policy in a health care industry.

Mr. Pabrai has delivered HIPAA Executive Briefs, Certified HIPAA Professional (CHP), and the Certified HIPAA Security Specialist (CHSS) programs nationally, including Webinars for clients such as RSA Security, New Horizons,

Element K, and many others. His attendees have included hospital personnel, pharmacists, legal professionals, physicians, office administrators, clinicians, corporate executives, HIPAA compliance officers, as well as IT professionals that have CISSPs, SCNAs, and transactions and security experts. Ali's clients have included Blue Cross Blue Shield affiliates, the State of Oregon, Department of Human Services, State of Iowa, MediNotes, Wells Fargo, Marsh, and many others.

Ali created the industry-leading CIW program and is the co-creator of the highly successful Security Certified Program (SecurityCertified.Net). Ali is the author of numerous books and articles on HIPAA, privacy, e-business, and security and business threats. At ecfirst.com, Ali developed E-Accelerator—a HIPAA security-related implementation methodology for enterprise environments.

Mr. Pabrai earned his Master of Science in Electrical Engineering from the Illinois Institute of Technology and a Bachelors of Science in Computer Engineering from Clemson University. Ali is a Security Certified Network Architect (SCNA) and Vice Chairman for CompTIA's i-Net+ and Security+ certification programs.

AAPC CEU Credits for HIPAA Academy Program

The American Academy of Professional Coders (AAPC) has granted prior approval of 18.0 Continuing Education Units (CEUs) to individuals completing the three-Day HIPAA Awareness Boot Camp.

The AAPC grants prior approval for continuing education programs based on the relevance of the program content to the medical coding and reimbursement profession. To retain the credential of CPC or CPC-H, coding and reimbursement professionals are required to participate in the continuing education program for maintenance of certification. Participation with continuing education coding seminars, workshops, and publications are methods of obtaining continuing education credits and maintaining competence.

ACHE Grants Continuing Education Credits to HIPAA Academy Programs

The American College of Health Care Executives (www.ACHE.org) has granted prior approval of continuing education credits for members completing any of four HIPAA certification classes offered by the HIPAA Academy.

- ◆ HIPAA Executive Brief: 2 CE credits
- ◆ Certified HIPAA Administrator (CHA): 8 CE credits
- ◆ Certified HIPAA Professional (CHP): 18 CE credits
- ◆ Certified HIPAA Security Specialist (CHSS): 16 CE credits

National Accreditations and CE Credits

The following organizations have accredited the HIPAA Academy training courses. CE credits may be earned by attending the HIPAA Academy training courses. HIPAA Academy's training courses are offered across the United States. For a complete list of locations where HIPAA Academy courses are offered, visit http://www.HIPAAAcademy.net.

1. **State of Nebraska—Board of Public Accountancy**

    The Nebraska Board of Public accountancy is responsible for licensing and regulating Certified Public Accountants (CPA) and Public Accountants (PA) in Nebraska. Its mission is to protect the welfare of the citizens of the state by assuring the competency of licensed accountants and to serve the needs of the public accountancy membership by assisting them in complying with Nebraska law and Board-promulgated rules and regulations.

    - • Certified HIPAA Administrator (CHA)   8 CE credits
    - • Certified HIPAA Professional (CHP)   18 CE credits

2. **West Virginia Insurance Commission**

    The West Virginia Insurance commission is charged with regulating all insurance companies licensed in West Virginia; that currently includes over 1,500 companies. The commission is responsible for licensing all

West Virginia insurance agents and regulating the market in a fair manner to protect the insurance-buying public and insure solvency of the companies.

- HIPAA Executive Brief — 2 CE credits
- Certified HIPAA Administrator (CHA) — 8 CE credits
- Certified HIPAA Professional (CHP) — 12 CE credits

3. The American Health Information Management Association (AHIMA)

The American Health Information Management Association (AHIMA) is the dynamic professional association that represents more than 45,000 specially educated health information management professionals who work throughout the health care industry. Health information management professionals serve the health care industry and the public by managing, analyzing, and utilizing data vital for patient care—and by making that data accessible to health care providers when it is needed most.

- HIPAA Executive Brief — 2 CE credits
- Certified HIPAA Administrator (CHA — 8 CE credits
- Certified HIPAA Professional (CHP) — 18 CE credits

4. American Academy of Professional Coders (AAPC)

AAPC membership spans all 50 states and several foreign countries. It is supported by a National Advisory Board made up of certified members representing clinics, facilities, payers, and consulting firms. The AAPC National Advisory Board offers direct input into the certification programs, educational curricula, and membership services offered by the Academy. AAPC is also supported by a National Physician Advisory Board with physicians from many different specialties. The AAPC grants prior approval for continuing education programs based on the relevance of the program content to the medical coding and reimbursement profession.

- Certified HIPAA Professional — 18 CE Units

5. The American College of Healthcare Executives (ACHE)

The American College of Healthcare Executives is an international professional society of nearly 30,000 health care executives who lead our nation's hospitals, health care systems, and other health care organizations. ACHE is known for its prestigious credentialing and educational programs and its annual Congress on Healthcare Management, which draws more than 4,000 participants each year. ACHE is also known for its journal, the *Journal of Healthcare Management*, and magazine, *Healthcare Executive*, as well as ground-breaking research and career development and public policy programs. ACHE's publishing division, Health Administration Press, is one of the largest publishers of books and journals on all aspects of health services management as well as text books used in college and university courses. Through its efforts, ACHE works toward its goal of improving the health status of society by advancing health care leadership and management excellence.

- HIPAA Executive Brief   2 CE credits
- Certified HIPAA Administrator (CHA)   8 CE credits
- Certified HIPAA Professional (CHP)   18 CE credits
- Certified HIPAA Security Specialist (CHSS)   16 CE credits

6. American Nurses Credentialing Center (ANCC)

The American Nurses Association established the ANA Certification Program in 1973 to provide tangible recognition of professional achievement in a defined functional or clinical area of nursing. The American Nurses Credentialing Center (ANCC) became its own corporation, a subsidiary of ANA, in 1991. More than 150,000 nurses throughout the U.S. and its territories in 40 specialty and advanced practice areas of nursing carry ANCC certification. While the role for nurses continues to evolve, ANCC has responded positively by the re-conceptualization of certification and "Open Door 2000," a program that enables all qualified registered nurses, regardless of their educational preparation, to become certified in any of five specialty areas: Gerontology, Medical-Surgical, Pediatrics, Perinatal, and Psychiatric and Mental Health Nursing.

Because nearly every state nursing board in the country is accredited by the ANCC, nurses nationwide are able to use the Certified HIPAA Administrator (CHA).

- Certified HIPAA Administrator (CHA)   8 CE credits

Testimonials

"As a project manager for DHS Oklahoma, I found the training session held by Ali a very informative and productive use of my time. The session covered the key aspects of HIPAA and how it affects government and health care organizations along with the key high level tasks that need to be completed to be HIPAA compliant. Ali also shared his insights and experiences with the group and this was extremely beneficial to me. I would recommend that anybody that needs a decent overview of HIPAA must attend this session. It will help you get out of the starting block in a hurry."

> **Sarjoo Shah, HIPAA Project Manager**
> **Department of Health Services (DHS), State of Oklahoma**

"The instructor was very knowledgeable about HIPAA Compliance. This is the most information I've gotten about HIPAA. I've been to other HIPAA training and I have never gotten the wealth of information I received today."

> **Inez Wondeh, Peninsula Medical Group**

"The class was very well paced with information in all areas of the new requirements."

> **Kellien Duncan, County of Alameda, State of California**

"A fast paced, informative overview of the Administrative Simplification portion of the HIPAA legislation. Excellent reference tools and indicators to help administrators identify the 'next course of action.'"

> **Deborah Windish, Michigan Academy of Family Physicians (MAFP)**

"This is a good overview. Most of us that are involved with HIPAA often feel overwhelmed. I'm still overwhelmed but I can finally see the light at the end of the tunnel."

> **Deeann M. Biondi, SET SEG, Inc.**

"Excellent course to provide an overview of HIPAA in a short period of time. Excellent and very knowledgeable instructor who was able to cover key issues of HIPAA in an easy to understand manner and in a very short time (2 hours)."

> **Steve Trosty, AP Assurance**

"Ali's presentation was both highly informative and a basic building block for implementation of HIPAA regulations. This was a fundamental step toward a large training opportunity for New Horizons of Michigan."

Mark McManus, Sr, Chairman, New Horizons of Michigan

"Excellent overview of HIPAA regulations. I look forward to attending the advanced programs on the implementation."

Steven Shurts, Harris HeathTrends, Inc.

"Was very helpful, I would even call it vital. I will urge all my co-workers and associates to get trained. Everyone should attend the 3-Day Professional boot camp. I wish I'd done this last year."

Trish Chandler, Sharp, Inc.

"We covered an enormous amount of material in a short period of time. The Certified HIPAA Instructor made complex and hard to understand material easy to learn!"

Joe Flippin

"The Certified HIPAA Professional course has not only enlarged my knowledge and expertise, but also opened wider the door to professional and entrepreneurial opportunities."

Laurice Green, Child and Family

"I enjoyed the class. I initially thought that the health care portion would be hard to follow coming from a technical background. The course and the regulations related a lot to network technologies. I just passed the CISSP exam and combined with this credential, I feel this will help my consulting business tremendously."

Lisa Jones, Slipknot Technologies

"I have an EDI X12 background in distributing manufacturing and finance. I am familiar with mapping software and principles. This course explained many new terms and procedures in an easy to learn style and I would recommend it to people with or without a health care background."

Ernie Schum, Schum Consulting, Inc.

"The course by itself is outstanding! But Mark took it to the next level."

Moqueet Syed, Batuta, Inc.

"Well-organized information. A solid understanding of the topic was presented as well as insights into opportunities that will be available as a result of this initiative."

Terry Roberts, Business Systems Engineering

"I realize the professional importance of understanding this information. I really believe my professional life is dependent on acquiring this knowledge. It is a lot of information in a short time, but I have a reference book. I am accustomed to federal and state rules and regulations and this is just one more very important tool to do a better job. I have now been given the tools and opportunity to succeed. I will recommend this course to others without hesitation."

John Palmer, Shelby County Government
Oakville Healthcare Center

"The information in the course is clear and concise and will serve as a good HIPAA reference!"

Gina Winchester, Sharp, Inc.

"The class was extremely informative. I've learned many new things and also received confirmation that I understand certain aspects of HIPAA correctly."

Darcey Gartner, Vista Healthplan, Inc.

"I have learned a tremendous amount!"

Victoria Sunshine

"I'm amazed at how much I was able to learn in just three days. I feel very confident that the information I picked up, the practical exercises, and the class interactions provided me with what I need to help my customers through the HIPAA hoop! The instructors were knowledgeable and always willing to address specific questions. All in all, this was a great experience that will benefit me, my clients, and my company!"

Cathy Pitt, Hewlett-Packard

"This was by far the most in-depth HIPAA course I have attended. The instruction staff is very knowledgeable of the Administrative Simplification Title. They did a great job of operating a comfortable environment."

Kelly Gruber, Des Moines Orthopedic Surgeons

"I have been following HIPAA progression for two years and found this course the most comprehensive of all my studies, especially in the privacy section. The instructor seemed to take personal responsibility to assure the students understood that this section was important to all areas of the HIPAA legislation."

"Lorna is an excellent instructor, her examples of in-the-box and out-of-the-box were excellent."

Betty Aukee, ADP

"The task of bringing my client to HIPAA compliance was dumped in my lap. As a consultant more on the management side of the health care industry, I felt overwhelmed when given the responsibility. Being only slightly familiar with the medical transactions, codes, and procedure, I thought it impossible to even grasp HIPAA from a class. Boy was I wrong! I now am aware and feel competent in my knowledge of the scope of HIPAA, and I am convinced that it will be evident in my report/briefs to my clients. Thank you HIPAA Academy!"

Anita Herron, Primary Care Partners

"This class was very intense and extremely beneficial at breaking down the core components of Title II. I was already familiar with HIPAA and had attended previous courses; however, I feel this class brought it all together for me."

Tracie Martin, Baylor Health Care Systems

"I am excited to learn about the HIPAA Academy and its services."

Bill Bendall, SeniorCare, Inc.

"I would recommend this course to anyone in the medical field responsible for HIPAA compliance. I had very little knowledge of HIPAA and the medical industry as a whole. This course educated me in these areas. I feel that I came away with a good base to build on. I believe that many people will struggle with compliance without this help!"

Tom Agnitsch, ANE Technology Services

"One of the strengths of the course was the overview of upcoming changes to HIPAA legislation."

Karla Combs, Lipscomb & Pitts

"What an eye opener. Before the course I had only a vague idea of the implications and scope of HIPAA. Now I realize how much work is left to be done to get into compliance and how this is going to touch every aspect of the health care industry."

James Cerney, J.C. Solutions

"I would highly recommend the HIPAA Academy to anyone in health care that wants to obtain the knowledge that will be crucial to implement HIPAA legislation in their organization. I found the instructors and the course material to be first rate and the information taught will help health care professionals at all levels to navigate the risky waters of HIPAA."

Joel H. Snook, CPA, Chief Financial Officer, St. Petersburg, FL

"The Certified HIPAA Professional course is one of the best, if not the best, courses on the down and dirty of HIPAA. I highly recommend this course as a "Train the Trainer" for health care organizations looking to comply with current and pending requirements. This course is going to help me immensely in architecting solutions for organizations to comply with Title 2 requirements."

Bob Tahmaseb, CISSP, Systems Engineer, RSA Security Inc.

"The Size and scope of the HIPAA legislation was brought into perspective by the HIPAA Academy. I now have a far greater understanding of the impact on the entire health care industry. The importance of the Professional class can not be understated."

Allan Gilbreath, Network Edge

"Fast paced, well organized, data packed, lively and entertaining."

Sumner Buck, VP Open Road Technologies

"The HIPAA Academy training course is comprehensive and practical. I walked away from this course with a very clear understanding of the Administrative Simplification components of HIPAA. This course allowed me to get my arms around some very complicated requirements and helped me piece the requirements together. I was surprised at how helpful it was because I had a fairly comprehensive understanding of HIPAA prior to taking the course. I highly recommend it to anyone who will be involved with HIPAA compliance; in fact, anyone who is involved with HIPAA would be foolish for not taking this course."

Teri Ann Lawyer , HIPAA Attorney, Pingel & Templer, P.C.

"The strength of the course was the instructor's knowledge base beyond the scope of requirements for certification. This was a great learning experience and a non-intimidating atmosphere."

Francoise Ager, AT&T

"The Certified HIPAA Professional course is a great source of information. It really lets you get your hands around what HIPAA and the Administrative Simplification Title mean and how it will change business. Not only does the course show business requirements, but the business opportunities that will arise as well."

Chris Reynolds, ExecuTrain of Nebraska

"They are the only organization that could help me achieve my goal of certification. I would rate them very highly. They have a broad background of HIPAA knowledge."

Tom Eilers, HIPAA Consultant & Project Manager

"This is by far the most comprehensive course I have ever taken. The instructors' personality and knowledge of the course really moves things along without making you feel too overwhelmed. For anyone involved with HIPAA in any capacity, I wholeheartedly recommend attending this course."

Barbara Slocumb, Orlando, FL

"The Certified Professional Course is a great course packed with useful information."

Margie Pullock, Orlando, FL

"The instructor was great; his enthusiasm for the course material was only surpassed by his knowledge of the material."

Lori Lederman, Orlando, FL

"This class gave me an overview of the steps needed to become HIPAA compliant. The most impressive aspect of the course is the amount of information covered in such a short period of time. I had no idea how many areas needed this much attention. This has really given me the foundation to cover all the bases."

Lorna Waggoner, Owner of Sales for Hire

"The HIPAA Security Specialist training has been of the utmost importance to understanding and developing my organization's HIPAA security policy. Ali is an excellent trainer with vast knowledge of all areas of both HIPAA and security. His ability to bring current technology considerations to bear on HIPAA policy has been instrumental to how I will develop, implement, and maintain my organization's security policy. Course is a 10. Instructor is a 10. Instructor was extremely well prepared. Thank you Ali. Thank you HIPAA Academy."

Seth K. Misenar, MS. Division of Medicaid

"The enthusiasm of the instructor matches the course."

Ahmed Osmani

"This course was an excellent launching pad into HIPAA security and an invaluable resource for me as a consultant and trainer. Thanks Ali."

Michael Shannon, CISSP, Mindworks, Inc.

"This course helped pair my knowledge of security systems with the HIPAA privacy requirements. It provided great flow chart and design templates to help start the process."

Will T. Scott, Southern Methodist University

"I suggest anyone considering tackling the area of HIPAA security compliance to take the CHSS course. This course not only simplified the Security Rule, but gives solutions and templates for compliance. Ali created a phenomenal book that flows smoothly."

Jamie McDaniel, New Horizons

"This is a great class for an administrator or a manager who finds themselves having to consider ways to deal with HIPAA security. It is hard to talk to vendors and consultants without knowing their language. This class delivers that HIPAA security dictionary."

Mark Glowacki

"An excellent overview of how security is implemented for HIPAA. The concepts discussed are backed up with detailed examples of how to apply them in a wide variety of situations. Well done."

Jerry Moore, New Horizons

"First, Ali is an extremely engaging and energetic instructor. He makes learning fun! Also, his ability to break down complex technical concepts, issues, and technology into easily understandable ideas is a great skill. Though the class may appear intimidating to a technical audience, have no fear—you will be surprised how much of a good understanding of security (in general) you will take with you after only two days of training."

David Mader, Babbage-Simmel, Ohio

"The CHSS course contains a wealth of technical knowledge presented in such a way that an average entity would be better prepared to comply with the security and electronic signature area of HIPAA."

Heidi Cockerhan, New Horizons

"This course presents security topics in an easy to understand and digestable format. The application inside and outside of the HIPAA environment will be invaluable."

James M. Cerney, J. C. Solutions

"The pace was great. I really enjoyed breaking up the lessons with written questions and especially the group labs."

Ahren Sims, New Horizons

"This course provides an excellent overview of the HIPAA security requirements and recommendations. This course should be a requirement for anyone charged with bringing an organization's security practices in line with HIPAA regulations."

Shane Smith, Clark University

"Excellent course. Very good overview of security requirements with many aspects presented with solution options."

Charles Morgan, New Horizons

"I took great pleasure in having Ali as an instructor. His knowledge and real-world experience is invaluable in HIPAA security training to all students."

MJ Juarez

Pabrai Addresses the National Council for Prescription Drug Programs (NCPDP)

In the health care arena, pharmacy leads the way among electronic health care claims. Over 88 percent of pharmacy claims in 1999 were submitted electronically, according to Faulkner & Gray's 2000 Health Data Dictionary. It is through the diligent work of NCPDP members that our standards keep up with the ever-evolving marketplace. NCPDP is also known for its annual conference and other meetings. Because NCPDP is an ANSI-accredited Standards Development Organization, the attendees at NCPDP's meetings are leading the industry in both the business and technical arenas. No other organization brings together the diversity of industry leaders and decision makers that NCPDP does.

With cutting-edge educational conferences and technical work groups, NCPDP offers you an unmatched opportunity to learn what drives some of the hottest issues in health care. NCPDP members are responsible for developing many of today's key innovations in pharmacy and health care.

NCPDP's Educational Forums are designed to educate industry colleagues about important issues relating to the pharmacy services sector of the health care industry. These sessions are open to all interested parties, for a fee. On Tuesday, August 27, 2002 at the Renaissance Washington DC Hotel, NCPDP held an Educational Forum on HIPAA Privacy and Confidentiality.

Uday O. **Ali** Pabrai was invited by the NCPDP for the conference in Washington, DC. Ali delivered a session on "HIPAA Privacy and Security: Administrative Requirements."

Index

Numerics

270 standard (Eligibility, Coverage, or Benefit Inquiry), 41

270 standard (Health Care Eligibility Request), 68–70

271 standard (Eligibility, Coverage, or Benefit Information), 41, 71–72

276 standard (Health Care Claim Status Request), 41, 72–73, 310

277 standard (Health Care Claim Status Notification), 41, 74–75

278 standard (Health Care Services Review), 41, 76–77

820 standard (Payment Order/Remittance Advice), 41, 77–78

834 standard (Benefit Enrollment and Maintenance), 41, 79–81

835 standard (Health Care Claim Payment/Advice), 41, 81–82

837 Health Claim Form-Institutional, 67

837 Health Claim Form-Professional, 67

837 standard (Health Care Claim-Dental, Institutional, Professional), 41, 83–88

4050 Version, Implementation Guides, 45

A

A P3P Preferences Exchange Language (APPEL), 535

A/S (Administrative Simplification), 502

AAHomecare, 502

AAPC (American Academy of Professional Coders), 549

AAR (Association of American Railroads), 25

access
  authorization, 228
  defined, 212
  establishment and modification, 228
  portability and renewability, 4
  RBAC (role-based access control), 215
  unauthorized, 198
  user-based, 216

access control, 211
  defined, 209, 212
  facility, 236
  technical safeguards, 238–239
  validation procedures and, 236

access control lists, 212

accidental threats, 202

accountability, 212

Accredited Standards Committee (ASC), 24, 65, 288, 502

ACG (Ambulatory Care Group), 502

ACH (Automated Clearinghouse) system, 77–78, 502–503

Active Military Personnel health plan, 28

active threats, 202, 212

ADA (American Dental Association), 90, 502

ADG (Ambulatory Diagnostic Group), 502

Administration Simplification title, 9–10

Administrative, Technical, and Physical Safeguards Policy, 391, 443–448

Administrative Code Sets, 502

administrative requirements, Privacy Rule, 324–326

administrative safeguards, security, 216, 221–223

Administrative Services Only (ASO), 503

Administrative Simplification (A/S), 502

Administrative Simplification Compliance Act (ASCA), 18, 27, 50–51

AFEHACT (Association for Electronic Health Care Transactions), 502

AHA (American Hospital Association), 502

AHIMA (American Health Information Management Association), 502

AIAG (Automotive Industry Action Group), 25

AISI (American Iron and Steel Institute), 26

Aluminum Association, 26

AMA (American Medical Association), 67, 89, 363–371, 502

ambulance services, 25

Ambulatory Care Group (ACG), 502

Ambulatory Diagnostic Group (ADG), 502

American Academy of Professional Coders (AAPC), 549

American Dental Association (ADA), 90, 502

American Health Information Management Association (AHIMA), 502

American Hospital Association (AHA), 502

American Iron and Steel Institute (AISI), 26

American Medical Association (AMA), 67, 89, 363–371, 502

American National Standards (ANS), 502–503

American National Standards Institute (ANSI), 65, 289, 502

American Society for Testing and Materials (ASTM), 503

American Trucking Association (ATA), 25

ANS (American National Standards), 502–503

ANSI (American National Standards Institute), 65, 289, 502–503

APPEL (A P3P Preferences Exchange Language), 535

Application Center 2000, 282–283

applications and data criticality analysis, 233

archiving and auditing requirements, 319

AS (Autonomous System), 254

ASC (Accredited Standards Committee), 24, 65, 288, 502

ASC X12 standards, 65–66

ASCA (Administrative Simplification Compliance Act), 18, 27, 50–51

ASO (Administrative Services Only), 503

assessment
Privacy Rule, 161–162, 336–337
security, 480–483

assigned security responsibility, security, 225–226

Association for Electronic Health Care Transactions (AFEHACT), 502

Association of American Railroads (AAR), 25

ASTM (American Society for Testing and Materials), 503

at rest, 2

ATA (American Trucking Association), 25

attacks. *See also* threats
denial of service, 203, 213
examples of, 204
insider, 203
masquerade, 202–203, 214
outsider, 203
spoofing, 202–203
trapdoors, 203
Trojan horse, 203
types of, 198

audit controls, security, 240

audit trails, security, 211, 215

auditing
archiving requirements and, 319
processes, transactions, 275

authentication, 17, 211
authentication exchange, 212
defined, 209, 212
peer-entity, 214
person or entity, 241

Authorizations

access, 228

compound, 142

conditioning of, prohibition on, 141

data elements and required statements, 139–140

defective, 140–141

defined, 212

for disclosure and use, 141–142

express legal permission and, 142

final impact, 142–143

individual, 139

limits on medical record use and release, 146–147

overview, 138–139, 377–378

revocations, 142

sample forms

patient amendment information, 386–389

patient information requests, 381–385

physicians office and patient, 379–380

use and disclosure, 141–142

Automated Clearinghouse (ACH) system, 77–78, 502–503

automatic logoff, 240

Automotive Industry Action Group (AIAG), 25

Autonomous System (AS), 254

availability

defined, 213

loss of, 219

awareness and training, security, 229

B

backups, data, 232

BAS (Business Associate Contract), 154–155

baselines assessment security phase, 478

BCBSA (Blue Cross and Blue Shield Association), 503

Berg, T., 8

BGP (Border Gateway Protocol), 254

billing

claims acceptance and, 12

patient accounting systems, 8

BIND servers, 256

biometrics, 17, 264–265, 503

BISAC (Book Industry Systems Advisory Committee), 25

bits, 288

BizTalk Accelerator, 282

advantages of, 276–277

components of, 276

minimum requirements for, 277

overview, 275

BizTalk Editor, 296

BizTalk Server 2002, 279–282

Blue Cross and Blue Shield Association (BCBSA), 503

Book Industry Systems Advisory Committee (BISAC), 25

Border Gateway Protocol (BGP), 254

Business Associate Contract (BAC), 154–155

Business Associate Terms Rider, sample of, 349–357

business associates

covered entities, 27, 34

Privacy Rule

BAC (Business Associate Contract), 154–155

example scenario, 192–193

exemptions, 155–156

overview, 152–153

privacy violations, 154

security, 234, 242

Business Associates Policy, 392, 461–467

C

cabluance, 504

call/contact center system, 8

CDT (Code on Dental Procedures and Nomenclature), 89–90

Centers for Medicare and Medicaid Services (CMS), 23–24, 91

certification exams, 546–549

Certified HIPAA Administrator (CHA), 546

Certified HIPAA Professional (CHP), 546

Certified HIPAA Security Specialist (CHSS), 546

CEUs (Continuing Education Units), 549

CHA (Certified HIPAA Administrator), 546

Chain of Trust (COT), 504

CHAMPUS (Civilian Health and Medical Program of the Uniformed Services), 28

channels, 213

Chargen port, TCP/IP security, 253

Child Health Insurance Program (CHIP), 504

children

    rights of, Privacy Rule, 151

    state child health plans, 29

CHIP (Child Health Insurance Program), 504

CHP (Certified HIPAA Professional), 546

CHSS (Certified HIPAA Security Specialist), 546

ciphertext, 213

civil penalties, 20, 114–115

Civilian Health and Medical Program of the Uniformed Services (CHAMPUS), 28

claims clearinghouse, 8

claims submissions, insurance, 12

CLIA (Clinical Laboratory Improvements Amendments) of 1998, 184

Client Rights Policy, 390, 398–417

Clinical Laboratory Improvements Amendments (CLIA) of 1998, 184

clinical reports, HL7, 25

CMS (Centers for Medicare and Medicaid Services), 23–24, 91

Code on Dental Procedures and Nomenclature (CDT), 89–90

code sets, defined, 37

Common Criteria, 205

Common Rule, research, Privacy Rule impact, 183

communications, internal, 303. *See also* oral communications

compartmentalization, 158

complaints

    filing timelines, 21

    persons impacted by, 21–22

    who can file, 21

compliance

    dates, health plans, 35, 43–45

    extension forms, 51

    frequently asked questions, 521–523

    noncompliance, penalties for, 19–20

compound Authorizations, 142

Computer Crime and Security Survey, 200–201

confidentiality

    data, 209

    defined, 213

    loss of, 219

    traffic flow, 216

    violations, 19

Consent

    defined, 137

    revocation, 138

    state law, 138

contingency plans, 213, 231–233, 479

Continuing Education Units (CEUs), 549

conversations, Privacy Rule impact, 170–171

cookies, 534

COT (Chain of Trust), 504

covered entities

    business associates, 27, 34

    health plans, 27–29

payers, 27

providers, 27

CPT-4 (Current Procedural Terminology, fourth revision), 88–90

credentials, defined, 213

criminal penalties, 20, 114–115

cryptanalysis, 213

cryptography, 213

Current Procedural Terminology, fourth revision (CPT-4), 88–90

customer relationship management system, 8

D

data and applications criticality analysis, 233

data confidentiality, 209

data content, 36

Data Dictionary (DD), 505

data flow, 300, 304

data integrity, 209, 211, 213

Data Interchange Standards Association (DISA), 505

data mapping, 273

data recovery plans, 232

data segments, 285

data types, 294

data use agreement, 126

Davis, M. (Care Delivery Organization Financial and Administrative Study), 38

DD (Data Dictionary), 505

DDNS (Dynamic DNS), 257

Deidentification of Client Information and Use of Limited Data Sets Policy, 392, 456–460

de-militarized zone (DMZ), 249, 495

Dearborn, R., 8

decipherment, 213

decryption
    defined, 213

    encryption and, 240

defective authorization, 140–141

deidentification information (DII), 121–123

denial of service attacks, 198, 203, 213

dentist/physicians compliance scenario, Privacy Rule
    certifications, 360

    computer requirements, 360–361

    fax requirements, 361–362

    gap analysis, 359

    policies and procedures, 359

    site assessment, 358–359

Department of Human Services (DHS), 372–376

Depository Financial Institutions (DFIs), 82

designated record sets, 172

Designated Standards Maintenance Organizations (DMSOs), 24

device and media controls, security, 237–238

DFIs (Depository Financial Institutions), 82

DHS (Department of Human Services), 372–376

digital signatures, 210, 213, 216, 247–248

DII (deidentification information), 121–123

direct data entry processes, 46

DISA (Data Interchange Standards Association), 505

disclosures. *See also* use and disclosure
    accounting of, 146

    to federal and state agencies, 165

    mandatory, 131

    of medical record, 165–166

    non-routine, 127

    Privacy Rule, 159–160, 189–192

    routine, 126–127

    to third parties, 165

    use for healthcare operations and, 130–131

    use for payment and, 129–130

    use for treatment and, 129, 164

DLL (dynamic link library), 488
DME (durable medical equipment), 91
DMSOs (Designated Standards Maintenance Organizations), 24
DMZ (de-militarized zone), 249, 495
DNS, TCP/IP security, 256–257
doctors. *See* physicians
document imaging management system, 8
document mapping, transactions, 297–298
document tracking, transactions, 310–312
Document Tracking Activity (DTA), 310
documentation
  Notices, 137
  to oral communications, 172–173
  TCP/IP security policy, 248–249
documents, Privacy Rule, 327
DTA (Document Tracking Activity), 310
durable medical equipment (DME), 91
Dynamic DNS (DDNS), 257
dynamic link library (DLL), 488

E

e-security, 477
EB (Eligibility or Benefit), 71
EC Gateway, 318
ECHO port, TCP/IP security, 254
ECMap application program
  auditing and archiving requirements, 319
  data communication, 319
  EC Gateway, 318
  ECRTP engine, 315–316
  Enterprise application, 317–318
  mailbox services, 319
  overview, 314–315
  process scripting, 318
  reporting components, 320
  Scheduler application, 318
  standard and proprietary formats, 315
  support, 315
  trading partner management, 319
ECRTP Engine, 315–316
EDI (Electronic Data Interchange), 12, 25–26, 289
EFS (Encrypting File System), 490
EFT (Electronic Funds Transfer), 77
EIN (Employer Identification Number), 103–104
Electronic Data Interchange (EDI), 12, 25–26, 289
Electronic Funds Transfer (EFT), 77
electronic Notices, 136–137
Electronic Remittance Advice (ERA), 81
electronic signatures, security, 245–248
electronic transactions, standards, enhancements to, 48–49
Eligibility or Benefit (EB), 71
emergency access procedure, security, 240
emergency department systems, 8, 25
emergency mode operation plans, 232
emergency treatments, Privacy Rule, 116
Employer Identification Number (EIN), 103–104
encipherment
  defined, 210, 213
  end-to-end, 214
  link-by-link, 214
Encrypting File System (EFS), 490
encryption, 210
  decryption and, 240
  defined, 213
end-to-end encipherment, 214
Enterprise application, 317–318
enterprise resource planning systems, 8
enumerators, NPI, 97–98
EOB (Explanation Of Benefits), 81
ERA (Electronic Remittance Advice), 81
evaluations, security, 233, 480
execution and tracking, transactions, 307–310

exemptions, business associates, Privacy Rule, 155–156

Explanation of Benefits (EOB), 81

express legal permissions, Authorization and, 142

extensible Mark-up Language (XML), 289

F

facility access controls, 236

Fair Credit Reporting Act (FCRA), 128

fax requirements, physician/dentist compliance scenario, 361–362

FBI (Federal Bureau of Investigations), 199

FCRA (Fair Credit Reporting Act), 128

FDA (Food and Drug Administration), 178

Federal Bureau of Investigations (FBI), 199

Federal Employees Health Benefits Program, 28

Federal Trade Commission (FTC), 117

file transfer protocol (FTP), 252–253

Final Privacy rule, 6

Finger service, TCP/IP security, 257

firewalls, 264, 490–491

First Report of Injury transaction, 85

flow of PHI, tracking, 332–335

Flowchart Panel, 302

FOIA (Freedom of Information Act), 52

Food and Drug Administration (FDA), 178

Freedom of Information Act (FOIA), 52

frequently asked questions, 521–524

FTC (Federal Trade Commission), 117

FTP (file transfer protocol), 252–253

functional groups, 65

G

GAO (General Accounting Office), 11

gap analysis
    Privacy Rule, 338–339
    security phase, 478

Gartner Group researchers, 7

General Accounting Office (GAO), 11

general financial systems, 8

General Privacy Policy, 390, 393–398

GLB (Gramm-Leach-Bliley) Act, 117–118

government entities, Privacy Rule, 117
    government access to health information, 185–186
    government enforcement process, 186–187
    law enforcement agencies, 187–188
    medical records to government, 186
    Privacy Act of 1974, 188
    public health, 188

GPO (Group Policy Objects), 486

Gramm-Leach-Bliley (GLB) Act, 117–118

group health plans, 28, 243

Group Policy Objects (GPO), 486

H

HCDA-1500 (Health Insurance Claim Form), 67

HCFA (Health Care Financing Administration), 23

HCOs (Health Care Organizations), 16

HCPCS (Health Care Common Procedure Coding System), 89–90

Health and Human Services (HHS), 5–6, 22, 51, 108

health care clearinghouse, 29–30

Health Care Common Procedure Coding System (HCPCS), 89–90

Health Care Financing Administration (HCFA), 23

Health Care Organizations (HCOs), 16

Health Insurance Claim Form (HCFA-1500), 67

health insurance issuers, 28

Health Insurance Portability and Accountability Act. See HIPAA

Health Level Seven (HL7), 24–25

Health Maintenance Organization (HMO), 28
health plans
Active Military Personnel, 28
CHAMPUS (Civilian Health and Medical Program of the Uniformed Services), 28
compliance date, 35, 43–45
Federal Employees Health Benefits Program, 28
group, 28, 243
health insurance issuers, 28
HMO (Health Maintenance Organization), 28
Indian Health Service program, 28
long-term care policies, 29
Medicaid, 29
medical care, 35
Medicare, 29
Medicare + Choice program, 29
Medicare supplemental policy, 29
MEWAs (Multiple Employer Welfare Arrangements), 28
Notices, 135–136
participants, 35
private sector, 42
small, 35
state child health plans, 29
veterans health care program, 29
HHS (Health and Human Services), 5–6, 22, 51, 108
hierarchies, defined, 295
HIPAA Academy, 546–548
HIPAA (Health Insurance Portability and Accountability Act)
access, portability, renewability, 4
Kennedy-Kassebaum bill, 4
overview, 2–3
Privacy Rule, 16
Section 1177, 19
titles of, 5, 10

Transaction Implementation Guide, 14–15
Transactions and Code sets, 13–14
HL7 (Health Level Seven), 24–25
HMO (Health Maintenance Organization), 28
HTTP port, TCP/IP security, 257
hybrid covered entities, Privacy Rule, 156–157

I

IB (Integration Brokers), 30
ICD-9-CM (International Classification of Diseases, Clinical Modification), 88–89
ICF (Internet Connection Firewall), 490–491
ICMP (Internet Control Messages Protocol), 254
identifiers, defined, 11, 88
identity-based security, 214
IDS (Intrusion Detection Systems), 17, 264
IIHI (individually identifiable health information), 31–32, 120
IIS (Internet Information Software), 278
IMAP service, TCP/IP security, 259
implementation
NPIs, 103
Security Rule, 217–218, 476
Implementation Guides, 4050 Version, 45
Implementation Panel, 302
in transit, 2
incident procedures, security, 230
Indian Health Service program, 28
indirect treatment relationships, Privacy Rule, 149–150
individually indentifiable health information (IIHI), 31–32, 120
individuals
Authorization, 139
impacted by Privacy Rule, 143–147
national health identifiers, 105
NPI for, 95–96

information delivery, secure, 475–476

information system activity review, security, 225

Information system agreement, 25

information system management, security, 227–228

insider attacks, 203

instances, 306

instantiation, 306

Institutional Review Board (IRB), 160, 183

insurance

claims submissions, 12

eligibility verification, 12

health insurance issuers, 28

NAIC (National Association of Insurance Commissioners), 118

plan enrollment, 12

pre-certification and adjudication, 12

Integration Brokers (IB), 30

integrity, 240

data integrity, 209, 211, 213

loss of, 219

intentional threats, 202

internal communications, 303

International Classification of Diseases, Clinical Modification (ICD-9-CM), 88–89

International Standards Organization (ISO), 496

Internet Connection Firewall (ICF), 490–491

Internet Control Messages Protocol (ICMP), 254

Internet Information Software (IIS), 278

Internet transactions, 46

interviews, security, 483

intimidation acts, 329

Intrusion Detection Systems (IDS), 17, 264

inventory, security, 483

IPSec services, 264–265

IRB (Institutional Review Board), 160, 183

ISO (International Standards Organization), 496

K

Kennedy-Kassebaum bill, 4

Kerberos, TCP/IP security, 261–262

key management, security, 214

L

labels, security labels, 211, 215

law enforcement agencies, government entities, Privacy Rule, 187–188

LDAP service, TCP/IP security, 260–261

limited data sets, 124–125

link-by-link encipherment, 214

local codes, 92

log-in monitoring, 230

long-term care policies, 29, 37

loss of availability, 219

loss of confidentiality, 219

loss of integrity, 219

M

mailbox services, EC Gateway, 319

malicious software, protection from, 229

mandatory disclosures, 131

manipulation detection, 214

masquerade attacks, 202–203, 214

materials management systems, 8

media and device controls, security, 237–238

medial record use, limits on, Authorizations, 146–147

Medicaid, 29

medical care health plans, 35

medical charts, Privacy Rule provisions, 167–168

medical records, government entities, Privacy Rule, 186

Medicare, 29

Medicare + Choice program, 29

Medicare supplemental policy, 29

medications, HL7, 25

Message Queuing Services check box (Windows Components Wizard), 278

Messaging Manager, 308

MEWAs (Multiple Employer Welfare Arrangements), 28

Microsoft BizTalk Accelerator. *See* BizTalk Accelerator

Minimum Necessary Policy, 391, 439–443

minors and parents rights, 150–152

mitigation, Privacy Rule, 329

model compliance plan
  alternative submissions, 61
  how to file, 60
  implementation strategy phases, 63–64
  instructions: overview, 58–59
  paper submissions, 56–58
  section A: covered entity and contact information, 54, 61–62
  section B: reason for filing for this extension, 55, 62–63
  section C: implementation budget, 55, 63
  section D: implementation strategy, 56–58, 63
  when to file, 60
  who should file, 59–60

Model Compliance Plans, 53

monetary penalties, noncompliance, 47

Multiple Employer Welfare Arrangements (MEWAs), 28

N

NAIC (National Association of Insurance Commissioners), 118

NAPM (National Association of Purchasing Managers), 26

National Association of Insurance Commissioners (NAIC), 118

National Association of Purchasing Managers (NAPM), 26

National Committee on Vital and Health Statistics (NCVHS), 26–27, 52

National Council for Prescription Drug Programs (NCPDP), 24, 26, 65, 559–560

National Drug Code (NDC), 89–90

National Employer Identifiers (NEI), 42

National Health Plan Identifier (PlanID), 104–105

National Health Plan Identifiers (NHPI), 42

National Provider File (NPF), 97

National Provider Identifications (NPI), 42
  applying for, 99
  enumerators, 97–98
  implementation, 102
  for individuals, 95–96
  locations, multiple, 97
  for organizations, 96
  overview, 94–95
  requirements for, 100–103
  sizes of, 97
  uses of, 96

National Provider System (NPS), 98–99

National Uniform Billing Committee (NUBC), 24, 67

National Uniform Claim Committee (NUCC), 24

NCPDP (National Council for Prescription Drug Programs), 24, 26, 65, 559–560

NCVHS (National Committee on Vital and Health Statistics), 26–27, 52

NDC (National Drug Code), 89–90

NEI (National Employer Identifiers), 42

NETSTAT service, TCP/IP security, 255

network abuse attacks, 198

NHPI (National Health Plan Identifiers), 42

NNTP service, TCP/IP security, 259

non-repudiation, 209–210, 214

non-routine disclosures, 127

noncompliance
    monetary penalties, 47
    penalties for, 19–20
NOS (Not Otherwise Specified), 92
Not Otherwise Specified (NOS), 92
notarization, 211, 214
Notice of Privacy Practices, sample form
    for AMA, 363–371
    for DHS, 372–376
Notice of Proposed Rule Making (NPRM),
    97, 108
Notices
    activity in, 135
    changes to, 135
    documentation, 137
    electronic, 136–137
    element of, 134
    first interaction, 136
    health plans, 135–136
    providers with direct treatment relationship,
        135
NPF (National Provider File), 97
NPI (National Provider Identifications). *See*
    National Provider Identifications (NPI)
NPRM (Notice of Proposed Rule Making),
    97, 108
NPS (National Provider System), 98–99
NTP service, TCP/IP security, 259
NUBC (National Uniform Billing Committee),
    24, 67
NUCC (National Uniform Claim Committee),
    24
nurse triage systems, 8

O

OCR (Office for Civil Rights), 186
Office for Civil Rights (OCR), 186
office space design, Privacy Rule provisions, 167

OHCA (Organized Health Care Arrangements),
    157–158
Open Profiling Standard (OPS), 535
operating room systems, 8
operating system security, case study, 483–491
OPS (Open Profiling Standard), 535
oral communications, Privacy Rule impact
    business associates and marketing, 176
    conversations, 170–171
    documentation to, 172–173
    general requirements, 169–170
    health-related marketing, 173
    marketing, limitations on, 175
    office environment, 171–172
    patient access to oral information, 172
    PHI, selling or disclosing, 176
    telemarketing, 177
    that are not marketing, 174–175
Orchestration Designer, 299–301, 304–305
Orchestration Designer (BizTalk Server 2002),
    282
ordering, scheduling and, 12
Organization Health Care Arrangements
    (OHCA), 157–158
organizational requirements, security, 241–243
organizations, NPI for, 96
outsider attacks, 203

P

P3P (Privacy Preferences Project), 534–536
packets, defined, 309
paper submission, model compliance plan, 58
parents and minors rights, 150–152
parsed transactions, 292
participants, health plans, 35
passive threats, 202, 214
password management, 230
password security, 214

patient accounting/billing systems, 8

patient events, defined, 37

patient identifiable information (PII), 32, 120

patients

    Authorization forms, sample of, 379–389

    confidentiality violation, 19

    information, sharing between physicians, 12

payers, covered entities, 27

payment

    TPO (Treatment, Payment or Health care operation), 33

    use and disclosures, 127–128

peer-entity authentication, 214

penalties

    effective dates, 22

    monetary, 47

    noncompliance, 19–20

    Privacy Rule, 114–115

Pescatore, John, 15–16

petroleum industry data exchange, 25

PHI (Protected Health Information). *See* Protected Health Information (PHI)

physical security, 214, 216, 235–238

physicians

    Authorization forms, sample of, 379–380

    office security scenario, 491–495

    sharing of patient information between, 12

physicians/dentist compliance scenario, Privacy Rule

    certifications, 360

    computer requirements, 360–361

    fax requirements, 361–362

    gap analysis, 359

    policies and procedures, 359

    site assessment, 358–359

PII (patient identifiable information), 32, 120

PIN (Unique Physician Identification Number), 103

PK2 (Service Pack 2), 278

PKI (Public Key Infrastructure), 17, 265

PlanID (National Health Plan Identifier), 104–105

planning, frequently asked questions, 521–523

policies and procedures

    development of, 326

    privacy

        Administrative, Technical, and Physical Safeguards Policy, 391, 443–448

        Business Associates Policy, 392, 461–467

        Client Rights Policy, 390, 398–417

        Deidentification of Client Information and Use of Limited Data Sets Policy, 392, 456-460

        Enforcement, Sanctions, and Penalties of Violation of Individual Policy, 393, 468-471

        General Privacy Policy, 390, 393–398

        Minimum Necessary Policy, 391, 439–443

        overview, 389

        Use and Disclosures for Research Purposes and Waivers Policy, 392

        Use and Disclosures of Client or Participant Information, 391, 417–438

    Privacy Rule provisions, 168

    security phase, 479–480

    Security Rule standard, 244

POP service, TCP/IP security, 257–258

Portmapper service, TCP/IP security, 2 58–259

ports, 303

practice management systems, 8

Princeton Survey Research Associates, 6

privacy

    defined, 11, 215

    frequently asked questions, 525–531

Privacy Act of 1974, 188

Privacy Officers, responsibilities of, 326, 330–331

Privacy Policies

Administrative, Technical, and Physical Safeguards Policy, 391, 443–448

Business Associates Policy, 392, 461–467

Client Rights, 390, 398–417

Deidentification of Client Information and Use of Limited Data Sets Policy, 392, 456–460

Enforcement, Sanctions, and Penalties for Violation of Individual Privacy, 393, 468–471

General Privacy, 390, 393–398

Minimum Necessary Policy, 391, 439–443

overview, 389

Use and Disclosures for Research Purposes and Waivers Policy, 392, 449–455

Use and Disclosures of Client or Participant Information Policy, 391

Privacy Preferences Project (PAP), 534–536

Privacy regulations, HAS, 6

Privacy Rule

accounting of disclosures, 146

administrative requirements, 324–326

assessment, 336–337

background, 110

business associates impacted by

BAC (Business Associate Contract), 154–155

exemptions, 155–156

overview, 152–153

privacy violations, 154

data use agreement, 126

defined, 109

definitions (alternative approaches), 343–348

DII (deidentification information), 121–123

direct treatment relationships, 148–149

discussed, 16

documents, 327

emergency treatment situations, 116

example scenarios, 189–193

gap analysis, 338–339

government entities, 117

government access to health information, 185–186

government enforcement process, 186–187

law enforcement agencies, 187–188

medical records to government, 186

Privacy Act of 1974, 188

public health, 188

health care providers and payers, 147–148

hybrid covered entities, 156–157

IIHI (Individually Identifiable Health Information), 120

indirect treatment relationships, 149–150

individuals impacted by, 143–147

intimidation acts, 329

limitations, 115–116

limited data sets, 124–125

minimum necessary provisions

assessment tasks, 161–162

disclosure and use for treatment, 164

disclosure of medical records, 165–166

disclosure to federal and state agencies, 165

disclosures to third parties, 165

health care operations, 164

medical charts and X-ray light boards, 167–168

office space design, 167

overview, 158

PHI uses, disclosures, and requests, 159–160

policies and procedures, 168

reasonable effort, 160–161

reasonable reliance, 160

routine communication considerations, 162–164

transaction standards, 166–167

Privacy Rule *(continued)*

mitigation, 329

Notice of Privacy Practices, sample form

from AMA, 363–371

from DHS, 372–376

OHCA (Organized Health Care Arrangements), 157–158

oral communications

business associates and marketing, 176

conversations, 170–171

documentation to, 172–173

general requirements, 169–170

health-related marketing, 173

marketing, limitations on, 175

office environment, 171–172

patient access to oral information, 172

PHI, selling or disclosing, 176

telemarketing, 177

that are not marketing, 174–175

overview, 108–109

parents and minors, 150–152

penalties, 114–115

PHI (Protected Health Information), 121

physician's/dentist's office compliance scenario

certifications, 360

computer requirements, 360–361

fax requirements, 361–362

gap analysis, 359

policies and procedures, 359

site assessment, 358–359

PII (patient identifiable information), 120

policies and procedures, development of, 326

psychotherapy notes, special protection for, 117

purpose of, 111–113

request for amendment, 145–146

research

authorization and common rule informed consent, 184–185

CLIA (Clinical Laboratory Improvements Amendments), 184

common rule and, 183

database for research purposes, 182–183

IRBs and privacy boards, 183

overview, 178–179

patients right to inspect, 183–184

studies, conditions for enrollment in, 182

use/disclosure with authorization, 179–181

use/disclosure with individual authorization, 181–182

waiver criteria, 182

rights of access, exclusions from, 144–145

safe harbor application, 123–124

safeguards, 327

sanctions, 329

scope of coverage, 111

state laws, 117

timelines, 118–119

training, 327–328

use and disclosure, 126–133

waiver of rights, 329

who is impacted by, 110

private sector health plans, 42

process scripting, 318

prohibition, on conditioning of authorizations, 141

Protected Health Information (PHI), 2, 32, 109

flow of, tracking, 332–335

Privacy Rule uses, 159–160

releasing to third parties, example of, 335–336

selling or disclosing, 176

providers

covered entities, 27

with direct treatment relationship, 135

psychotherapy notes, special protection for, 116

public health, government entities, Privacy Rule, 188

Public Key Infrastructure (PKI), 17, 265

R

RBAC (role-based access control), 215
RDP (Remote Desktop Protocol), 263
record keeping, use and disclosures, 133
records, designated record sets, 172
recovery planning, data, 232
rehabilitation services, HL7, 25
remediation security phase, 478–479
Remote Desktop Protocol (RDP), 263
reporting, security, 483
reporting and response, security, 231
reporting components, 320
repudiation, 209–210, 214
request for amendment, Privacy Rule, 145–146
requesters, defined, 37
requests, Privacy rule, 159–160
research, Privacy Rule impact
    authorization and common rule informed
        consent, 184–185
    CLIA (Clinical Laboratory Improvements
        Amendments), 184
    common rule and, 183
    database for research purposes, 182–183
    IRBs and privacy boards, 183
    overview, 178–179
    patients right to inspect, 183–184
    studies, conditions for enrollment in, 182
    use/disclosure with authorization, 179–181
    use/disclosure with individual authorization,
        181–182
    waiver criteria, 182
response and reporting, security, 231
reviews, security, 483
revision and testing procedures, security, 232
revocations, Authorization, 142
REXEC services, TCP/IP security, 261
rights of access, Privacy Rule, exclusions from,
    144–145
risk analysis, security, 223

risk assessment, threats, 206–208
risk management, security, 224
RLOGIN/RSH services, TCP/IP security, 261
role-based access control (RBAC), 215
routine disclosures, 126–127
routing control, security, 215
RWHO services, TCP/IP security, 261

S

sabotage attacks, 198
safe harbor application, Privacy Rule, 123–124
safeguards, Privacy Rule, 327
sanction policy, security, 224–225
sanctions, Privacy Rule, 329
scans, for vulnerabilities, 264
Scheduler application, 318
scheduling, ordering and, 12
schemas, defined, 282
SCHIP (State Children's Health Insurance
    Program), 23
SDO (Standards Developing Organization), 25,
    65
Secretary of HHS, 22, 35
Section 1177, 19
Section 1178, 8
secure information delivery, 475–476
secure shell (SSH), 253–254
security
    assessment, 480–483
    biometrics, 17
    defined, 11
    firewalls, 17
    IDS (Intrusion Detection Systems), 17
    information delivery, 16–17
    PKI (Public Key Infrastructure), 17
    security labels, 211, 215
    security recovering, 211
    smart cards, 17
    VPNs (Virtual Private Networks), 17

Security Rule
access authorization, 228
access control, 209
access establishment and modification, 228
administrative safeguards, 216, 221–223
assessment, 480–483
assigned security responsibility, 225–226
attacks
examples of, 204
types of, 202–203
authentication, 209
awareness and training, 229
business associate contracts, 234
Common Criteria, 205
contingency plans, 231–233
data confidentiality, 209
data integrity, 209
device and media controls, 237–238
documentation standard, 244
electronic signatures, 245–248
emergency access procedure, 240
evaluations, 233
group health plans, 243
implementation guidelines, 476
implementations and specifications, 217–218
incident procedures, 230
information access management, 227–228
information system activity review, 225
initiative phases, 478–480
isolating health care clearinghouse function, 228
log-in monitoring, 230
malicious software, protection from, 229
mechanism, specific security, 210–211
operating system security, case study, 483–491
organizational requirements, 241–243
password management, 230

pervasive security mechanisms, 210–211
physical safeguards, 216, 235–238
policies and procedures standard, 244
principals, 219
repudiation, 209–210
requirements, 476–477
response and reporting, 231
risk analysis, 223
risk management, 224
sanction policy, 224–225
secure information delivery, 475–476
security mechanisms, 210–211
security reminders, 229
selection criteria, 220–221
standards, 196–198, 218–219
technical safeguards, 216, 238–241
termination procedures, 227
terminologies, list of, 212–216
threats
accidental, 202
active, 202
defined, 205
intentional, 202
overview, 198–199
passive, 202
risk assessment, 206–207
user identification, 239
vulnerability, 205
workforce security, 226
workstation security, 237
selection criteria, Security Rule, 220–221
sensitivity, security, 216
Serials Industry Systems Advisory Committee (SISAC), 25
Service Pack 2 (PK2), 278
service providers, 38
Simple Network Management Protocol (SNMP), 260

SISAC (Serials Industry Systems Advisory Committee), 25

small health plans, 35

smart cards, 17, 485–486

smart tokens, 485

SMTP, TCP/IP security, 255–256

SNMP (Simple Network Management Protocol), 260

Social Security Act, Title XIX, Section 1171(5)(E), 46

Social Security Administration (SSA), 165

specifications
  defined, 294
  Security Rule, 217–218

spoofing, 202–203

SQL Server 7.0, 279

SQL Server 2000, 278–279

SQL (Structured Query Language), 308

SSA (Social Security Administration), 165

SSH (secure shell), 253–254

standards
  ASC X12, 65–66
  frequently asked questions, 523
  Security Rule, 196–198, 218–219

Standards Developing Organization (SDO), 25, 65

state child health plans, 29

State Children's Health Insurance Program (SCHIP), 23

state laws
  Consent, 138
  Privacy Rule, 117
  Privacy Rule, parents and minors, 151

Structured Query Language (SQL), 308

Subtitle F, Title II, 10

SUID (super-user ID), 203

super-user ID (SUID), 203

Sybase HIPPA Studio
  ECMap application program
    auditing and archiving requirements, 319
    data communication, 319
    EC Gateway, 318
    ECRTP engine, 315–316
    Enterprise application, 317–318
    mailbox services, 319
    overview, 314–315
    process scripting, 318
    reporting components, 320
    Scheduler application, 318
    standard and proprietary formats, 315
    support, 315
    trading partner management, 319
  overview, 312–313

SYSTAT service, TCP/IP security, 255

T

TCP/IP security policy. *See also* Security Rule
  BGP (Border Gateway Protocol), 254
  Chargen, 253
  DDNS, 257
  DNS, 256–257
  documentation, 248–249
  ECHO port, 254
  executive summary, 250
  Finger service, 257
  FTP (file transfer protocol), 252–253
  HTTP port, 257
  ICMP (Internet Control Messages Protocol), 254
  IMAP service, 259
  Kerberos, 261–262
  LDAP service, 260–261
  NETSTAT service, 255

TCP/IP security policy *(continued)*
  network services, 250–251
  NNTP service, 259
  NTP service, 259
  POP, 257–258
  Portmapper, 258–259
  RDP (Remote Desktop Protocol), 263
  recommendations for enterprise, 252
  REXEC services, 261
  RLOGIN/RSH services, 261
  RWHO services, 261
  security perimeter, 249
  SMTP, 255–256
  SNMP service, 260
  SSH (secure shell), 253–254
  SYSTAT service, 255
  Telnet, 255
  TFTP service, 257
  transport layer, 251
  UUCP services, 261
  X Window System, 262–263
technical safeguards, security, 216, 238–241
technology-enabled marketing systems, 8
technology solutions, frequently asked questions, 523–524
telecommunications information forum, 25
telemarketing, Privacy Rule impacts, 177
Telnet, TCP/IP security, 255
termination procedures, security, 227
testimonials, 551–559
testing and revision procedures, security, 232
TFTP service, TCP/IP security, 257
theft attacks, 198
Third Party Administrators (TPAs), 46, 74
threats. *See also* attacks
  accidental, 202
  active, 202, 212
    Computer Crime and Security Survey, 200–201
    defined, 205
    intentional, 202
    overview, 198–199
    passive, 202, 214
    risk assessment, 206–208
timelines, Privacy Rule, 118–119
TIPS (transactions, identifiers, privacy, and security), 11
Title I (Health Care Insurance Access, Portability, and Renewability), 10
Title II (Preventing Health Care Fraud and Abuse, Administrative Simplification, Medical Liability), 10
Title III (Tax-related Health Provisions), 10
Title IV (Application and Enforcement of Group Health Insurance Requirements), 10
Title V (Revenue Offsets), 10
Title XIX, Section 1171(5)(E) of Social Security Act, 46
titles, defined, 4
tokens, security, 216, 485
TPAs (Third Party Administrators), 46, 74
TPO (Treatment, Payment or Health care operation), 33, 141
tracking and execution, transactions, 307–312
trading partner management, 319
traffic analysis, 216
traffic flow confidentiality, 216
traffic padding, 211
training and awareness, security, 229, 327–328
training options, certifications, 548
Transaction and Code Sets, 40, 44
Transaction Implementation Guides, 14–15
transactions
  analyzing processes, 273–274
  auditing processes, 275

components of, 12

data and documents, 288

defined, 11, 36, 268

document mapping, 297–298

document tracking, 310–312

electronic, standards for, 48–49

execution and tracking, 307–310

information exchanges, list of, 36

Internet, 46

orchestration, 298–303

parsed, 292

planning processes, 272–273

remediation process, 274–275

sets, list of, 284

standards, 36–37

transactions, identifiers, privacy, and security (TIPS), 11

Transactions and Code sets, 13–14

transmission security, 241

transport mechanisms, 300

trapdoors, 203

treatment

    direct treatment relationships, 148–149

    providers with direct treatment relationship, 135

Treatment, Payment or Health care operation (TPO), 33, 141

Trojan horse attacks, 203

trusted functionality, security mechanism, 211

U

ub-92 claim form, 47–48, 67

UM (Utilization Management Organization), 76

unauthorized access, 198

Unique Physician Identification Number (PIN), 103

UP services, TCP/IP security, 261

use and disclosure. *See also* disclosures

    Authorization, 132–133, 141–142

    Consent, 132–133

    Fair Debt Collection Practices Act, 128–129

    FARCE (Fair Credit Reporting Act), 128

    Notices, 132

    payment, 127–128

    PHI, without authorization, 179–181

    Privacy Rule example scenarios, 189–192

    record keeping, 133

Use and Disclosures for Research Purposes and Waivers Policy, 392, 449–455

Use and Disclosures of Client or Participant Information Policy, 391, 417–439

user-based access, 216

user identification, security, 239

Utilization Management Organization (UM), 76

V

validation, access control procedures and, 236

VBS (Visual Basic Script), 488

veterans health care program, 29

Virtual Private Networks (VPNs), 17

virus attacks, 198

Visual Basic Script (VBS), 488

VPNs (Virtual Private Networks), 17

vulnerabilities

    defined, 205

    scans for, 264

W

waiver criteria, 182

waiver of rights, 329

Washington Publishing Company (WPC), 14, 25–26

watershed legislation for health care information systems, 10

WEDI (Workgroup for Electronic Data Interchange), 24

Windows Components Wizard, Message Queuing Services check box, 278

Windows XP, operating system security case study, 483–491

workforce security, 226

workforces clearance procedure, 226

Workgroup for Electronic Data Interchange (WEDI), 24

workstation security, 237

WPC (Washington Publishing Company), 14, 25–26

X

X-ray light boards, Privacy Rule provisions, 167–168

X Window System, TCP/IP security, 262–263

XLANG schedule, 298–300, 305–306

XML (extensible Mark-up Language), 289

The Premier Press *Professional Projects* series offers intermediate to advanced programmers hands-on guides for accomplishing real-world, professional tasks. Each book includes several projects—each one focusing on a specific programming concept and based on a real-world situation. Use the skills developed throughout the book and modify the projects to fit your professional needs!

Palm OS Programming Professional Projects
1-931841-28-4

Dynamic Web Forms Professional Projects
1-931841-13-6

J2EE Professional Projects
1-931841-22-5

Microsoft ADO.NET Professional Projects
1-931841-54-3

Microsoft ASP.NET Professional Projects
1-931841-21-7

Microsoft C# Professional Projects
1-931841-30-6

Microsoft .NET Framework Professional Projects
1-931841-24-1

Microsoft VBA Professional Projects
1-931841-55-1

Microsoft Visual Basic .NET Professional Projects
1-931841-29-2

Microsoft Visual C++ .NET Professional Projects
1-931841-31-4

PHP Professional Projects
1-931841-53-5

XML Web Services Professional Projects
1-931841-36-5

STEP INTO THE 3D WORLD OF ANIMATION WITH THE PREMIER PRESS *INSPIRED* SERIES!

Inspired 3D Character Animation
1-931841-48-9

Inspired 3D Character Setup
1-931841-51-9

Inspired 3D Lighting and Compositing
1-931841-49-7

Inspired 3D Modeling and Texture Mapping
1-931841-50-0

Filled with tips, tricks, and techniques compiled by the animators of blockbuster films at Hollywood's biggest studios, these four-color books are a must-have for anyone interested in character creation.

Series Editor Michael Ford is a senior technical animator at Sony Pictures Imageworks. He is a certified Level 2 Softimage instructor whose film credits include *Stuart Little*, *Stuart Little 2*, *The Perfect Storm*, *The Mummy*, *Godzilla*, *Species II*, *Mortal Kombat II*, and *The Faculty*.

Series Editor Kyle Clark is a lead animator at Microsoft's Digital Anvil Studios. His film credits include *Star Wars Episode I—The Phantom Menace*, *Sleepy Hollow*, *Deep Blue Sea*, *The Adventures of Rocky and Bullwinkle*, *Harry Potter and the Sorcerer's Stone*, and *Brute Force* video game for the Xbox.

fast&easy web development

Less Time. Less Effort. More Development.

Don't spend your time leafing through lengthy manuals looking for the information you need. Spend it doing what you do best— Web development. The Premier Press *fast & easy* web development series leads the way with step-by-step instructions and real screen shots to help you grasp concepts and master skills quickly and easily.

Microsoft® ASP.NET
Fast & Easy®
Web Development
1-931841-46-2 ▪ Companion Web Site

Adobe® LiveMotion™
Fast & Easy®
Web Development
0-7615-3254-4 ▪ CD Included

ASP 3 *Fast & Easy®*
Web Development
0-7615-2854-7 ▪ CD Included

CGI *Fast & Easy®*
Web Development
0-7615-2938-1 ▪ CD Included

Java™ 2 *Fast & Easy®*
Web Development
0-7615-3056-8 ▪ CD Included

JavaServer Pages™
Fast & Easy®
Web Development
0-7615-3428-8 ▪ CD Included

Macromedia®
Director® 8 and Lingo™
Fast & Easy®
Web Development
0-7615-3049-5 ▪ CD Included

Macromedia®
Dreamweaver® MX
Fast & Easy®
Web Development
1-931841-88-8 ▪ Companion Web Site

Macromedia®
Dreamweaver® UltraDev™ 4
Fast & Easy®
Web Development
0-7615-3517-9 ▪ CD Included

Macromedia®
Fireworks® MX *Fast & Easy®*
Web Development
1-59200-031-2 ▪ Companion Web Site

Macromedia®
Flash™ 5 *Fast & Easy®*
Web Development
0-7615-2930-6 ▪ CD Included

Microsoft® C# *Fast & Easy®*
Web Development
1-931841-05-5 ▪ Companion Web Site

Perl *Fast & Easy®*
Web Development
1-931841-17-9 ▪ Companion Web Site

PHP *Fast & Easy®*
Web Development,
2nd Edition
1-931841-87-X ▪ Companion Web Site

Premier Press
A Division of Course Technology
www.premierpressbooks.com

Call now to order!
1.800.842.3636

for the absolute beginner™

the fun way
to learn programming

Let's face it.

C++, JavaScript, and Java can be a little intimidating. That's why Premier Press has developed the for the absolute beginner series—a fun, non-intimidating introduction to the world of programming. Each book in this series teaches a specific programming language using simple game programming as a teaching aid. If you are new to programming, want to learn, and want to have fun, then Premier Press's for the absolute beginner series is just what you've been waiting for!

 ASP Programming for the Absolute Beginner
ISBN 0-7615-3620-5

 C Programming for the Absolute Beginner
ISBN 1-931841-52-7

 C++® Programming for the Absolute Beginner
ISBN 0-7615-3523-3

 Excel VBA Programming for the Absolute Beginner
ISBN 1-931841-04-7

 Java™ Programming for the Absolute Beginner
ISBN 0-7615-3522-5

 JavaScript™ Programming for the Absolute Beginner
ISBN 0-7615-3410-5

 Microsoft® Access VBA Programming for the Absolute Beginner
ISBN 1-59200-039-8

 Microsoft® C# Programming for the Absolute Beginner
ISBN 1-931841-16-0

 Microsoft® Visual Basic® .NET Programming for the Absolute Beginner
ISBN 1-59200-002-9

 Palm™ Programming for the Absolute Beginner
ISBN 0-7615-3524-1

Premier Press
A Division of Course Technology
www.premierpressbooks.com

Call now to order
1.800.842.3636